TRANSPORTATION

AMERICA'S LIFELINE

ISSN 1536-5247

TRANSPORTATION

AMERICA'S LIFELINE

Linda Schmittroth

INFORMATION PLUS® REFERENCE SERIES
Formerly published by Information Plus, Wylie, Texas

Detroit • New York • San Diego • San Francisco • Cleveland • New Haven, Conn. • Waterville, Maine • London • Munich

Transportation: America's Lifeline
Linda Schmittroth

Project Editor
Ellice Engdahl

Editorial
Andrew Claps, Paula Cutcher-Jackson, Kathleen J. Edgar, Dana Ferguson, Debra Kirby, Prindle LaBarge, Elizabeth Manar, Sharon McGilvray, Charles B. Montney, Heather Price

Permissions
Peg Ashlevitz

Product Design
Cynthia Baldwin

Composition and Electronic Prepress
Evi Seoud

Manufacturing
Keith Helmling

For more information, contact
The Gale Group, Inc.
27500 Drake Rd.
Farmington Hills, MI 48331-3535
Or you can visit our Internet site at
http://www.gale.com

Permissions Department
The Gale Group, Inc.
27500 Drake Rd.
Farmington Hills, MI 48331-3535
Permissions Hotline: 248-699-8006 or 800-877-4253, ext. 8006
Fax: 248-699-8074 or 800-762-4058

LIBRARY OF CONGRESS CATALOGING-IN-PUBLICATION DATA

ISBN 0-7876-5103-6 (set)
ISBN 0-7876-7345-5
ISSN 1536-5247

Printed in the United States of America
10 9 8 7 6 5 4 3 2 1

TABLE OF CONTENTS

PREFACE

Transportation: America's Lifeline is one of the latest volumes in the Information Plus Reference Series. The purpose of each volume of the series is to present the latest facts on a topic of pressing concern in modern American life. These topics include today's most controversial and most studied social issues: abortion, capital punishment, care for the elderly, crime, health care, the environment, immigration, minorities, social welfare, women, youth, and many more. Although written especially for the high school and undergraduate student, this series is an excellent resource for anyone in need of factual information on current affairs.

By presenting the facts, it is Gale's intention to provide its readers with everything they need to reach an informed opinion on current issues. To that end, there is a particular emphasis in this series on the presentation of scientific studies, surveys, and statistics. These data are generally presented in the form of tables, charts, and other graphics placed within the text of each book. Every graphic is directly referred to and carefully explained in the text. The source of each graphic is presented within the graphic itself. The data used in these graphics are drawn from the most reputable and reliable sources, in particular from the various branches of the U.S. government and from major independent polling organizations. Every effort has been made to secure the most recent information available. The reader should bear in mind that many major studies take years to conduct, and that additional years often pass before the data from these studies are made available to the public. Therefore, in many cases the most recent information available in 2003 dated from 2000 or 2001. Older statistics are sometimes presented as well if they are of particular interest and no more recent information exists.

Although statistics are a major focus of the Information Plus Reference Series, they are by no means its only content. Each book also presents the widely held positions and important ideas that shape how the book's subject is discussed in the United States. These positions are explained in detail and, where possible, in the words of their proponents. Some of the other material to be found in these books includes: historical background; descriptions of major events related to the subject; relevant laws and court cases; and examples of how these issues play out in American life. Some books also feature primary documents or have pro and con debate sections giving the words and opinions of prominent Americans on both sides of a controversial topic. All material is presented in an even-handed and unbiased manner; the reader will never be encouraged to accept one view of an issue over another.

HOW TO USE THIS BOOK

Modern American society relies on a vast and complicated transportation network for its very existence. Aircraft, ships, railroads, and especially cars and trucks transport hundreds of millions of Americans around the country every day, as well as millions of tons of goods. Each type of transportation is explored in detail in this book. Their particular advantages and drawbacks are discussed and their importance to America is made clear.

Transportation: America's Lifeline consists of eight chapters and three appendices. Each of the chapters is devoted to a particular segment of the U.S. transportation system. For a summary of the information covered in each chapter, please see the synopses provided in the Table of Contents at the front of the book. Chapters generally begin with an overview of the basic facts and background information on the chapter's topic, then proceed to examine subtopics of particular interest. For example, Chapter 4: Automobiles begins by describing how automobiles came to dominate personal transportation in the United States during the mid-twentieth century, a trend that has continued to the present day. The chapter then provides detailed statistics on the number of automobiles built, sold, and used in the United States and in the rest of the world. The chapter moves on to examine a number of auto-related issues. Highlights include: the costs of purchasing, driving, and maintaining an automobile; the relative safety of different types of automobiles; the annual numbers and types of automobile accidents in America and their causes; alternative fuel automobiles; and much more. Readers can find their way through a chapter by looking for the section and sub-section headings, which are clearly set off from the text. They can also refer to the book's extensive index if they already know what they are looking for.

Statistical Information

The tables and figures featured throughout *Transportation: America's Lifeline* will be of particular use to the reader in learning about this issue. These tables and figures represent an extensive collection of the most recent and important statistics on transportation and related issues—for example, graphics in the book cover waterborne commerce; rail freight; highway systems; trucking; motor vehicle accidents; bicycle, motorcycle, and recreational vehicle sales and usage; airline travel; and trends in mass transit utilization. Gale believes that making this information available to the reader is the most important way in which we fulfill the goal of this book: to help readers to understand the issues and controversies surrounding transportation in the United States and to reach their own conclusions.

Each table or figure has a unique identifier appearing above it for ease of identification and reference. Titles for the tables and figures explain their purpose. At the end of each table or figure, the original source of the data is provided.

In order to help readers understand these often complicated statistics, all tables and figures are explained in the text. References in the text direct the reader to the relevant statistics. Furthermore, the contents of all tables and figures are fully indexed. Please see the opening section of the index at the back of this volume for a description of how to find tables and figures within it.

Appendices

In addition to the main body text and images, *Transportation: America's Lifeline* has three appendices. The first is the Important Names and Addresses directory. Here the reader will find contact information for a number of government and private organizations that can provide further information on the American transportation system. The second appendix is the Resources section, which can also assist the reader in conducting his or her own research. In this section, the author and editors of *Transportation: America's Lifeline* describe some of the sources that were most useful during the compilation of this book. The final appendix is the detailed Index, which facilitates reader access to specific topics in this book.

ADVISORY BOARD CONTRIBUTIONS

The staff of Information Plus would like to extend their heartfelt appreciation to the Information Plus Advisory Board. This dedicated group of media professionals provides feedback on the series on an ongoing basis. Their comments allow the editorial staff who work on the project to make the series better and more user-friendly. Our top priorities are to produce the highest-quality and most useful books possible, and the Advisory Board's contributions to this process are invaluable.

The members of the Information Plus Advisory Board are:

- Kathleen R. Bonn, Librarian, Newbury Park High School, Newbury Park, California
- Madelyn Garner, Librarian, San Jacinto College—North Campus, Houston, Texas
- Anne Oxenrider, Media Specialist, Dundee High School, Dundee, Michigan
- Charles R. Rodgers, Director of Libraries, Pasco-Hernando Community College, Dade City, Florida
- James N. Zitzelsberger, Library Media Department Chairman, Oshkosh West High School, Oshkosh, Wisconsin

COMMENTS AND SUGGESTIONS

The editors of the Information Plus Reference Series welcome your feedback on *Transportation: America's Lifeline*. Please direct all correspondence to:

Editors

Information Plus Reference Series

27500 Drake Rd.

Farmington Hills, MI 48331-3535

ACKNOWLEDGMENTS

The editors wish to thank the copyright holders of material included in this volume and the permissions managers of many book and magazine publishing companies for assisting us in securing reproduction rights. We are also grateful to the staffs of the Detroit Public Library, the Library of Congress, the University of Detroit Mercy Library, Wayne State University Purdy/Kresge Library Complex, and the University of Michigan Libraries for making their resources available to us.

Following is a list of the copyright holders who have granted us permission to reproduce material in Information Plus: Transportation. *Every effort has been made to trace copyright, but if omissions have been made, please let us know.*

For more detailed source citations, please see the sources listed under each individual table and figure.

Air Transport Association of America, Inc.: Table 7.1, Table 7.3, Table 7.4, Table 7.9, Table 7.10, Figure 7.2

Alternative Fuels Data Center: Table 4.6

American Public Transportation Association: Table 8.2, Table 8.4, Table 8.5, Figure 8.3

American Trucking Associations: Table 6.2, Figure 6.1, Figure 6.2, Figure 6.5

Association of American Railroads: Table 2.1, Table 2.2, Table 2.3, Table 2.4, Figure 2.1, Figure 2.2, Figure 2.3, Figure 2.4, Figure 2.5, Figure 2.6

ATW Research: Table 7.2

Bureau of Transportation Statistics: Table 1.3, Table 1.6, Table 3.6, Table 3.7, Table 3.8, Figure 1.4, Figure 2.10, Figure 5.1, Figure 5.3, Figure 7.1, Figure 8.4, Figure 8.10

Center for Transportation Analysis: Table 4.2, Figure 4.1

DuPont Performance Coatings: Figure 4.2

Energy Information Administration: Table 4.7, Figure 6.4

Eno Transportation Foundation: Figure 8.1, Figure 8.2

Federal Aviation Administration: Table 7.5, Table 7.6, Table 7.11, Figure 7.3, Figure 7.8

Federal Highway Administration: Table 3.1, Table 3.2, Table 3.3, Table 3.4, Table 3.5, Table 3.9, Table 4.8, Table 8.1, Figure 3.1, Figure 3.2, Figure 3.3, Figure 3.4, Figure 3.5, Figure 4.5, Figure 8.8, Figure 8.11

Federal Motor Carrier Safety Administration: Table 6.4, Table 6.5

Federal Transit Administration: Table 3.9, Figure 3.3, Figure 8.6, Figure 8.7

Foundation for Clean Air Progress: Table 6.7

General Aviation Manufacturers Association: Table 7.7, Table 7.8, Figure 7.4, Figure 7.6, Figure 7.7

Maritime Administration: Table 1.2, Table 1.3, Table 1.4, Table 1.6, Figure 1.7

Motorcycle Safety Foundation: Figure 5.6

National Association of Railroad Passengers: Figure 2.8

National Automobile Dealers Association: Figure 4.3

National Bicycle Dealers Association: Table 5.1, Table 5.2

National Center for Statistics & Analysis: Table 4.9

National Highway Traffic Safety Administration: Table 4.4, Table 4.5, Table 4.10, Table 5.3, Table 5.4, Table 5.6, Table 5.7, Table 6.3, Figure 3.6, Figure 4.6, Figure 5.1, Figure 5.4, Figure 5.5

National Safety Council: Table 4.11

Recreation Vehicle Industry Association: Table 5.8, Figure 5.7

Research and Special Programs Administration: Table 6.6

Shipbuilders Council of America: Table 1.7

Surface Transportation Policy Project: Figure 8.5

U.S. Army Corps of Engineers: Table 1.1, Table 1.5, Figure 1.1, Figure 1.2, Figure 1.5

U.S. Census Bureau: Table 8.3, Figure 5.2

U.S. Centers for Disease Control and Prevention: Table 5.5

U.S. Department of Energy: Figure 6.3

U.S. Department of Transportation: Figure 1.3, Figure 1.6

U.S. General Accounting Office: Figure 2.7, Figure 2.9, Figure 7.5

Volpe National Transportation Systems Center: Figure 8.9

Ward's Communications: Table 4.1, Table 4.3, Table 6.1, Figure 4.4

CHAPTER 1

SHIPS—TRAVELING THE WATERWAYS

Shipping played a major role in the early growth and development of the United States. The first European settlers made their way to the New World by boat. Slaves were packed into the holds of slave ships and brought over to work the fields of the growing colonies. The very existence of the colonies and later of the young republic depended on the flow of passengers and vital goods on both inland and oceanic waterways. For almost two hundred years after the arrival of those first settlers, ships were the country's primary mode of transporting both passengers and commercial cargo. From the mid-1800s through the early 1900s, ships brought millions of European and Asian immigrants to American shores.

All of this spawned the development of thousands of ocean, Great Lakes, and inland waterway (river) ports. Together, the waterways, lakes, oceans, harbors, and ports form the network of the national waterborne transportation system. The waterborne transportation system provides the link for the exchange of goods and passengers between land and water. It includes ships, piers and wharves, cargo handling equipment, storage facilities, and connections to other types of transportation. This system plays a vital role in the nation's trade and economy, providing jobs, income, tax revenues, and a magnet for other industries.

U.S. SHIPPING OVER THE YEARS

For thousands of years, the movement of ships depended on sails and oars. The first European settlers in what would become the United States all arrived on sailing ships. Without modern technology like radios and aircraft, or even good maps and roads, these early settlers depended on ships for trade and communication with the rest of the world. Population and development tended to concentrate near major ports and rivers.

A Revolutionary Technology

In 1787, the same year that the U.S. Constitution was drafted, John Fitch (1743–98), a surveyor and silversmith, launched the first fully operational steamboat. By 1790 one of his steamboats was regularly carrying passengers and freight between Philadelphia and Burlington, New Jersey. Fitch took out patents in the United States and France for his invention, but he could not capture the interest of the American public. He lost financial backing for his enterprise and died in 1798. A few years later, Robert Fulton was able to popularize the steamboat and begin a dramatic transformation of U.S. and world shipping. Fulton's steamship, the *Clermont,* cruised up the Hudson River in 1807 to instant success and a place in the history of navigation. The potential for steamships—unlike sailing ships—to move upstream or downstream, with or against the currents, independent of the direction of the wind or the strength of oars, was finally recognized. On May 22, 1819, the steam-powered *SS Savannah* crossed the Atlantic Ocean.

The steamboat is now perhaps most closely associated with the mighty Mississippi River. The well-dressed riverboat gambler, who traveled the river on paddlewheel steamboats, is as familiar a folk figure as the cowboy riding the range. More significantly, however, steam power made the process of navigating ships across oceans much more predictable and dependable, as they were not at the complete mercy of the weather and currents. As engines gradually became more powerful, steamships became faster and more efficient, capable of carrying large amounts of passengers or cargo at consistently high speeds. Steam powered many of the large ships that plied the oceans of the world throughout the nineteenth and twentieth centuries, gradually driving sailing ships out of commercial shipping. As the twentieth century dawned, however, both types of ships carried people, raw materials, and finished products across the oceans. They brought generations of immigrants to this country, carried agricultural products—

cotton, tobacco, wheat—to markets overseas, and hauled imported goods from Europe and Asia. Shipping, which required ports and harbors, stimulated the growth of cities adjacent to harbors. As the industrial age began, dependable shipping connected the world.

The Canal Age

At about the same time as steamships were first powering across oceans and up rivers, new cross-country shipping routes were being sought, from the East Coast to the largely unsettled West. People wanted economical ways to connect lakes and rivers in order to link large portions of the country. Settlers and merchants were eager to go westward. Yet travel by water remained by far the best way to move large quantities of goods and people.

In 1817 the New York State Legislature authorized the construction of a canal as a watercourse between the Hudson River at Albany and Lake Erie at Buffalo. During its construction, opponents derisively called it "Clinton's Big Ditch" (after Governor DeWitt Clinton), but the canal became a tremendous success once completed. Financed, built, and operated solely with state funds, the waterway returned its $8 million construction cost within seven years of its completion in 1825. By using the 338-mile canal rather than overland routes, the cost of hauling a ton of freight between Buffalo and New York City dropped from $100 to $10 and travel time was reduced from 26 to 6 days. As it became relatively easy to travel to Ohio, Michigan, Indiana, and the rest of the Midwest, the region became a destination for farmers seeking new land to cultivate, who needed efficient transportation to carry crops to the major marketplaces in the east.

While several canals had been constructed earlier, the success of the Erie Canal prompted other states with navigable waterways to make serious commitments to canal building. Unfortunately, many of the new canals were not as successful as the Erie. Lack of capital for construction and maintenance, mismanagement, corruption, and overbuilding created huge debts that many states were unable to pay off. Nevertheless, the canals filled an important transportation need.

Domestic Shipping Begins to Fade

Soon after the Civil War (1861–65), the railroads were connected across the country and trains rapidly became the dominant means of transporting people and goods from coast to coast and points in between. As railroad routes proliferated across the country at the turn of the twentieth century and the auto industry also rose to prominence, shipping declined somewhat. In addition, an economic depression and a five-month United Mine Workers strike in 1901 made the procurement of coal for steamships difficult.

Despite the shipping industry's slump and declining use of the Erie Canal and other waterways, shipping traffic on major rivers and in the Great Lakes continued to be essential to the transport of goods across the nation. In 1900 the Chicago Sanitary and Ship Canal opened, connecting Lake Michigan (and the other Great Lakes) with the Des Plaines River and ultimately with the Mississippi River and the Gulf of Mexico.

International shipping received another boost in 1901 when the U.S. Congress and President Theodore Roosevelt decided to proceed with construction of the Panama Canal. The canal would allow ships to travel from the Atlantic to the Pacific without the long and arduous trip around the southern tip of South America. That same year U.S. Steel executive Charles M. Schwab founded the United States Shipbuilding Company.

World War I (1914–18)

The American shipping industry was still strong if in decline as World War I drew near. The shipbuilding industry was in somewhat worse shape. As industrialization spread, the industry faced more and more foreign competitors, some of whom could produce ships at a lower price than U.S. shipyards. The onset of World War I generated federal government interest in the shipping industry when it became apparent that the country was practically without ships for transporting arms and troops to the fighting fronts in Europe. To correct the situation, Congress passed the Shipping Act of 1916. The new law authorized the creation of the Emergency Fleet Corporation, which built 2,318 vessels between 1918 and 1922. Most of these ships were delivered too late to serve in the war and were often so poorly designed and constructed that they could not be used for any other purpose.

To stimulate the shipping industry, Congress soon passed another significant piece of maritime legislation, the Merchant Marine Act of 1920 (PL 66-261), known as the Jones Act. Under the Jones Act, U.S. owners were not permitted to buy less expensive foreign-made ships. By law, all waterborne goods between ports throughout the United States and its territories had to be carried on ships built and registered in America and owned by U.S. citizens.

The Merchant Marine Act of 1936

The Great Depression of the 1930s created another slump in shipbuilding and transport. Congress responded by passing the Merchant Marine Act of 1936 (HR-8555), declaring it national policy to foster the creation of a merchant marine fleet capable of handling domestic and foreign commerce and of serving in time of war. The fleet was to be owned and operated "insofar as practicable" by private U.S. concerns. The federal government would provide subsidies to private companies to make up the

FIGURE 1.1

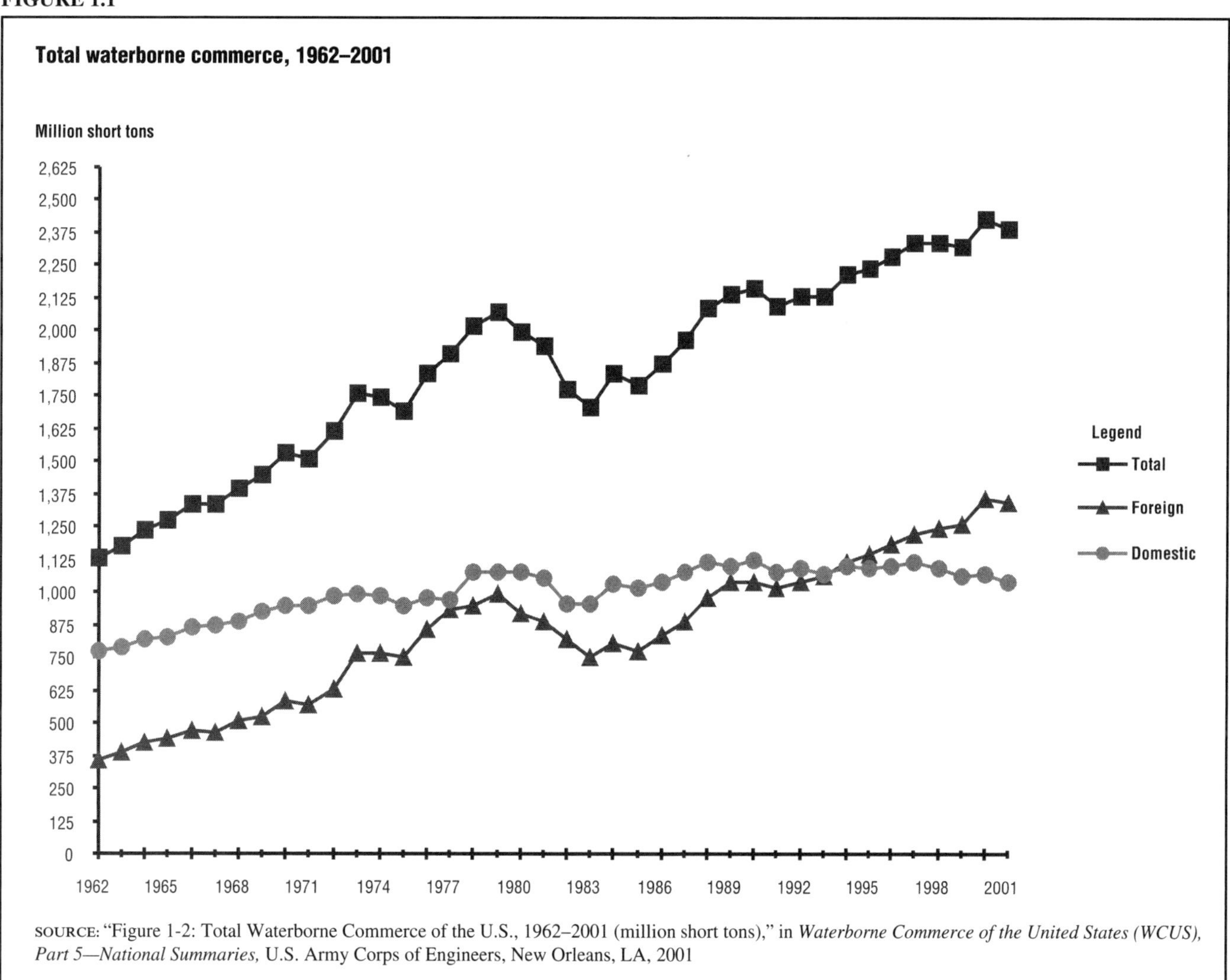

SOURCE: "Figure 1-2: Total Waterborne Commerce of the U.S., 1962–2001 (million short tons)," in *Waterborne Commerce of the United States (WCUS), Part 5—National Summaries,* U.S. Army Corps of Engineers, New Orleans, LA, 2001

difference between the cost of building and operating ships in the United States and the often much lower costs of these activities in foreign countries. Freight rates and trade routes were placed under federal jurisdiction. A Maritime Commission was formed to survey the state of the merchant marine fleet and develop a long-range program to meet future needs.

World War II (1941–45)

Within five years of the passage of the Merchant Marine Act of 1936, the United States was again at war. This time, however, the country's maritime fleet was in much better condition. Under the newly created War Shipping Administration, the federal government took full control of almost all shipping operations. Between 1942 and 1945, 5,592 merchant ships were built, half of which were the mass-produced, cheaply made Liberty ships, often derisively referred to as "tin cans." These new ships, along with those acquired from private owners, were instrumental in securing an Allied victory.

After the war ended, the War Shipping Administration was dissolved and merchant fleets returned to private control. The government sold off excess ships for a total of almost $2 billion while retaining some vessels in reserve fleets for emergency use. These reserve fleets were called into action in both the Korean (1950–53) and Vietnam (1961–75) wars.

The Maritime Administration (MARAD)

In 1950 the Maritime Commission was disbanded and replaced with the Federal Maritime Board and the Maritime Administration (MARAD) under the U.S. Department of Transportation. The Maritime Administration was assigned many functions that it continues to carry out. Most significantly, it maintains the National Defense Reserve Fleet, administers government subsidies to ship builders and operators, promotes and provides technical assistance for the development of port facilities and intermodal (transportation by more than one means of conveyance) systems, and operates the U.S. Merchant Marine Academy at Kings Point, New York, which

TABLE 1.1

Waterborne commerce, 1962–2001

(Short tons or 2000 pounds)

Year	Total	Foreign	Domestic
1962	1,129,404,375	358,599,030	770,805,345
1963	1,173,766,964	385,658,999	788,107,965
1964	1,238,093,573	421,925,133	816,168,440
1965	1,272,896,243	443,726,809	829,169,434
1966	1,334,116,078	471,391,083	862,724,995
1967	1,336,606,078	465,972,238	870,633,840
1968	1,395,839,450	507,950,002	887,889,448
1969	1,448,711,541	521,312,362	927,399,179
1970	1,531,696,507	580,969,133	950,727,374
1971	1,512,583,690	565,985,584	946,598,106
1972	1,616,792,605	629,980,844	986,811,761
1973	1,761,552,010	767,393,903	994,158,107
1974	1,746,788,544	764,088,905	982,699,639
1975	1,695,034,366	748,707,407	946,326,959
1976	1,835,006,819	855,963,909	979,042,910
1977	1,908,223,619	935,256,813	972,966,806
1978	2,021,349,754	946,057,889	1,075,291,865
1979	2,073,757,628	993,444,963	1,080,312,665
1980	1,998,887,402	921,404,000	1,077,483,402
1981	1,941,558,947	887,102,150	1,054,456,797
1982	1,776,740,579	819,730,983	957,009,596
1983	1,707,661,011	751,140,194	956,520,817
1984	1,836,020,619	803,338,133	1,032,682,486
1985	1,788,434,822	774,323,283	1,014,111,539
1986	1,874,416,280	837,223,503	1,037,192,777
1987	1,967,458,261	890,980,045	1,076,478,216
1988	2,087,993,484	976,220,985	1,111,772,499
1989	2,140,442,372	1,037,910,213	1,102,532,159
1990	2,163,854,373	1,041,555,740	1,122,298,633
1991	2,092,108,462	1,013,557,036	1,078,551,426
1992	2,132,095,154	1,037,466,130	1,094,629,024
1993	2,128,221,188	1,060,041,217	1,068,179,971
1994	2,214,754,086	1,115,742,828	1,099,011,258
1995	2,240,393,059	1,147,357,782	1,093,035,277
1996	2,284,065,249	1,183,386,621	[1] 1,100,678,628
1997	2,333,142,046	1,220,615,132	1,112,526,914
1998	2,339,500,081	1,245,388,049	1,094,112,032
1999	2,322,557,251	1,260,770,656	1,061,786,595
2000	2,424,588,877	1,354,790,984	1,069,804,693
2001	2,386,557,759	1,344,085,586	1,042,472,173

[1] Beginning in 1996, fish was excluded for internal and intraport domestic traffic.

SOURCE: "Table 1-1: Total Waterborne Commerce of the U.S., 1962–2001 (in short tons of 2000 pounds)," in *Waterborne Commerce of the United States (WCUS), Part 5—National Summaries,* U.S. Army Corps of Engineers, New Orleans, LA, 2001

graduates officers to serve the economic and defense interests of the United States.

The Post-War Era

It was not long after the end of World War II that the development of long-distance passenger air travel and a national network of highways made passenger travel by ship effectively obsolete. However, shipping remained the most practical method for moving large amounts of heavy goods from place to place, especially over long distances. Nevertheless, the U.S. merchant fleet declined greatly after World War II. The cause was the increasing number of ships registered in "flag of convenience" countries such as Panama or The Bahamas, where laws are favorable to shippers and labor relatively cheap. The shipbuilding industry suffered even more as it lost almost all of its business to foreign shipyards that could produce ships at low cost.

THE MODERN U.S. FLEET

In 1955 America's ports were handling about one billion tons (also called short tons) of freight. At the end of the 1970s, the ports handled just over two billion tons of cargo

FIGURE 1.2

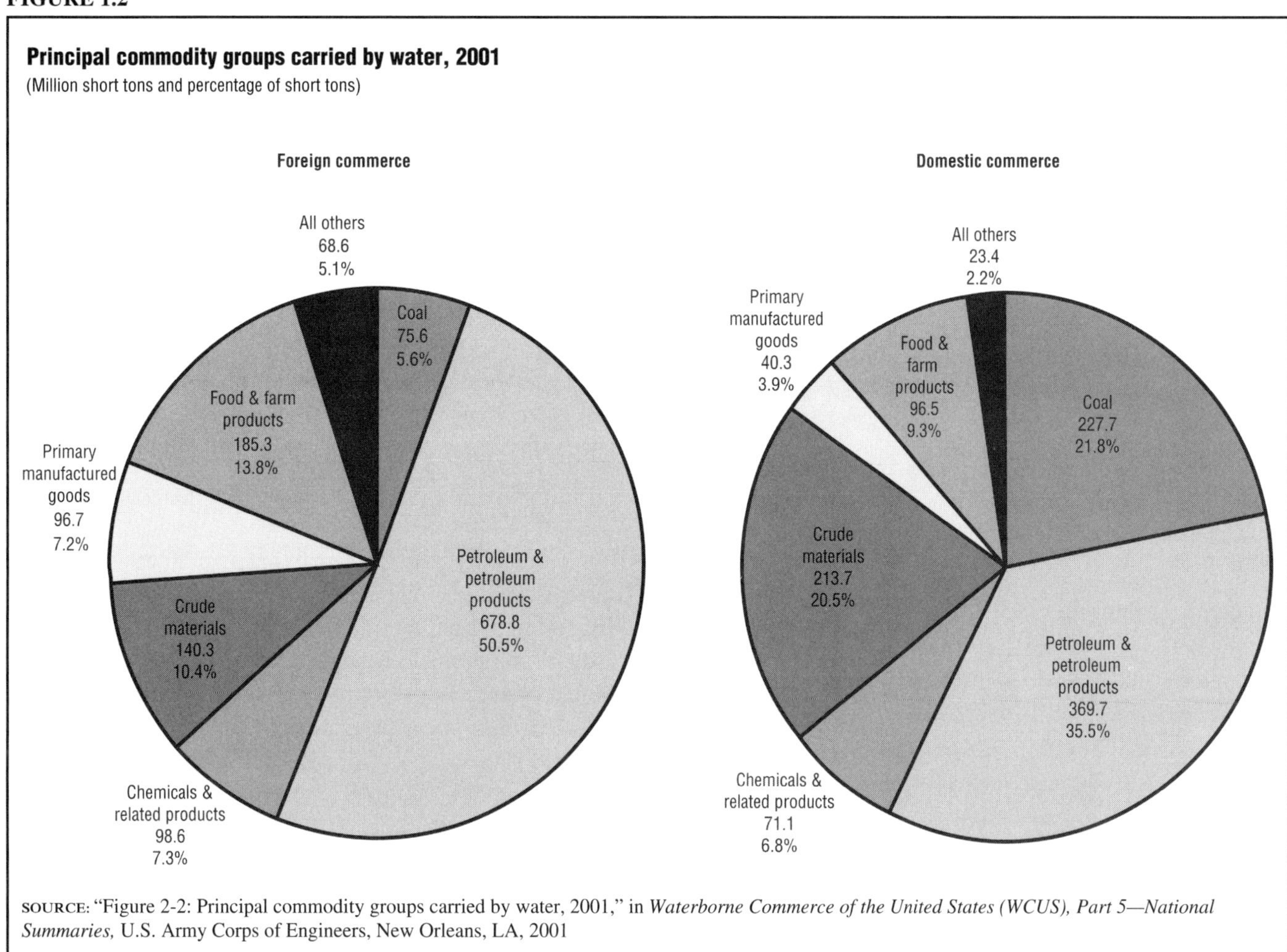

SOURCE: "Figure 2-2: Principal commodity groups carried by water, 2001," in *Waterborne Commerce of the United States (WCUS), Part 5—National Summaries,* U.S. Army Corps of Engineers, New Orleans, LA, 2001

each year, divided almost equally between foreign and domestic commerce. (See Figure 1.1 and Table 1.1.) In 1983, in the midst of a recession, total U.S. tonnage dropped to a low of 1.7 billion tons and then rose again in 1990 to 2.16 billion tons. By 1997 tonnage had risen to 2.3 billion tons, with the cargo fairly evenly divided between domestic and foreign traffic. It maintained this approximate level through 1999 then rose again, exceeding 2.4 billion tons in 2000 and coming close to 2.4 billion tons in 2001.

Domestic cargo moving through U.S. ports declined slightly after 1997 while foreign cargo increased. (See Figure 1.1). This reflects a trade imbalance that began in 1998 as falling foreign currency values made Asia's exports to the United States more affordable and demand for U.S. goods fell.

What Is Carried?

The advantage of shipping by water is that ships can move large amounts of heavy goods efficiently with relatively low energy consumption. It should not be surprising, then, that coal and oil account for over half of those commodities carried by water between U.S. ports and sources both domestic and foreign. Food and farm products also account for a significant percentage, as do crude raw materials (such as iron or copper ore). (See Figure 1.2.)

The Domestic Fleet

The U.S. domestic fleet (the Jones Act fleet of ships that primarily carries goods from one part of the United States to another) operates in three sectors: the inland waterways, the domestic deep-sea trade, and the Great Lakes. The majority of the 41,000-vessel fleet plies the Mississippi River system and the intracoastal and navigable internal waterways of the Atlantic, Gulf, and Pacific coasts. The dry cargo barge, which carries dry materials, is the main vessel in the fleet. Also included in the fleet are tank barges, which carry liquid bulk cargo. Towboats and tugboats, as their names imply, push and pull dumb (non-self-propelled) vessels and rafts. They are considered part of the fleet but do not carry cargo.

According to *MARAD 2001* (U.S. Department of Transportation, Bureau of Transportation Statistics, Washington, D.C., 2001), in January 2001 the inland waterway cargo-carrying fleet consisted of 3,112 tank barges, 22,425 dry bulk barges, and 2,827 other dry cargo barges, supported by a fleet of 5,392 towboats and tugboats.

FIGURE 1.3

U.S. oceanborne foreign trade routes

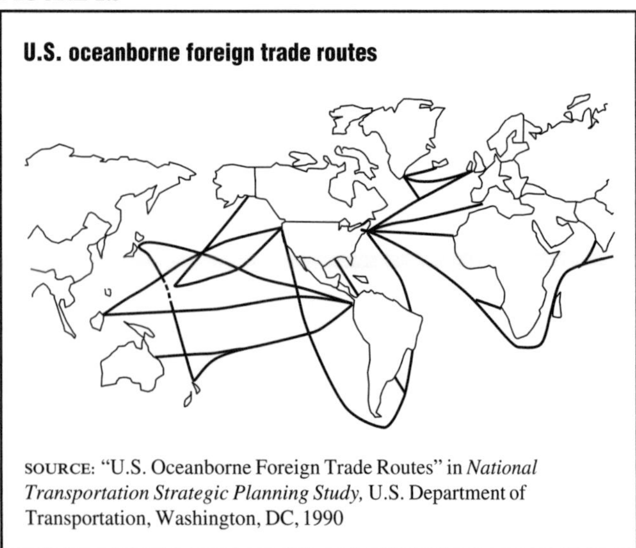

SOURCE: "U.S. Oceanborne Foreign Trade Routes" in *National Transportation Strategic Planning Study,* U.S. Department of Transportation, Washington, DC, 1990

The U.S. Oceangoing Fleet

The oceangoing fleet is involved in both domestic and foreign trade and travels along the nation's coasts and to Alaska and Hawaii, Puerto Rico, Guam, and Wake and Midway islands. The bulk of the domestic deep-sea fleet (which had 159 ships in 1999) is comprised of tankers carrying American petroleum products and coal. Less cargo is being hauled due to the decline in production and shipments of crude oil from the Alaska North Slope. The domestic ocean fleet moved 223.6 million tons in 2001—a 23 percent decline from 1999 tonnage, according to *Waterborne Commerce of the United States* (U.S. Army Corps of Engineers, New Orleans, LA, 2001).

The foreign trade fleet carries goods between U.S. and foreign ports and is in direct competition with all other international fleets. Figure 1.3 shows the primary foreign trade routes. In 2001 America's principal trading partners were Canada, Mexico, Japan, China, and the United Kingdom (*Statistical Abstract of the United States: 2002*, U.S. Census Bureau).

As of July 1, 2002, 431 oceangoing vessels with a total carrying capacity of about 14 million deadweight tons (DWT, weight of a vehicle without a load) were registered in the United States (counting both privately-owned and government-owned ships). (See Table 1.2.) Each of the oceangoing ships weighs 1,000 gross tons or more. (A gross ton is 2,240 pounds.). About 248 of these ships (57 percent) comprised the merchant marine (of which 220 were involved in commerce) and about 52 were foreign-owned ships registered in the United States as a flag of convenience (*The World Factbook 2002,* Central Intelligence Agency, Washington D.C., 2002). As of July 1, 2002, about 142 of the ships were primarily involved in domestic trade (Jones Act vessels) per MARAD. Nearly 100 federally owned vessels were either in storage or distributed around the globe in case they are needed during a national emergency (Robert Little, "Merchant Marine's Demise Endangers War Readiness," *Baltimore Sun*, August 5, 2001).

The U.S. fleet plays a very minor role in international shipping. In 2002 the world fleet of oceangoing ships weighing 1,000 tons or more consisted of 28,694 ships. (See Table 1.2.) The U.S. fleet made up less than 2 percent of this figure, down from 17 percent in 1960 and 8 percent in 1970. According to the U.S. Coast Guard, most of the ships that dock at American ports are foreign-owned. According to the U.S. Coast Guard's Web site in 2003, each year more than 8,000 vessels flying the flags of more than 100 countries carry more than 90 percent of the international commercial freight coming to or leaving the United States.

Compared to other nations' merchant fleets, the United States is at a distinct disadvantage for several reasons. Most international operators use lower-cost foreign shipyards for maintenance and repairs. They also save on fuel costs because they usually use more modern, efficient ships. Foreign operators can use smaller crews than are allowed by U.S. labor union contracts and safety requirements. Furthermore, they can employ low-priced labor from developing nations. Total employment expenditures per day on a foreign ship with a non-U.S. crew are far lower than the total cost for crew wages on an American ship of the same size and number of crew members. In fact, according to a report from the Australia-based International Commission on Shipping (*Ships, Slaves and Competition,* March 6, 2001), thousands of seamen in 10 to 15 percent of the world's ships work in slave conditions for little or no pay. Because of the relatively higher labor costs in the United States, many privately owned vessels belonging to U.S. citizens or corporations are registered in other countries. The practice of registering a ship in a country where the laws are less restrictive and costs cheaper is known as carrying a "flag of convenience."

TYPES OF SHIPS. The ocean transportation system is devoted almost entirely to freight shipping. There are three categories of service: general cargo, dry bulk, and liquid bulk. General cargo, primarily finished products, is usually carried on regularly scheduled ocean freighters, often in large boxes on container ships. Dry bulk cargoes, such as grain, coal, and fertilizer, are shipped in specialized vessels under contract. Liquid bulk cargoes, mainly petroleum products, are handled by tankers and tank barge fleets. Most of the oceangoing liquid bulk cargo ships are tankers.

Today's oil tankers are bigger than they have ever been. In 1945, the largest tanker held 16,500 tons of oil; today's supertankers carry more than 550,000 tons. Freight ships have also grown dramatically in size and so has their

TABLE 1.2

Top 20 merchant fleets of the world, self-propelled oceangoing vessels 1,000 gross tons and greater, as of July 1, 2002

(Tonnage in thousands)

	Total		Tanker		Dry bulk		Full container		Other**	
Flag of Registry	**Number**	**Deadweight**	**Number**	**Deadweight**	**Number**	**Deadweight**	**Number**	**Deadweight**	**Number**	**Deadweight**
Panama*	4,864	187,454	1,153	62,515	1,505	92,753	560	18,067	1,646	14,119
Liberia*	1,475	77,209	566	41,503	326	20,553	318	10,841	265	4,313
Greece	729	48,432	297	29,659	280	16,230	42	1,832	110	711
Bahamas*	1,012	46,120	252	29,080	160	9,310	78	2,245	522	5,484
Malta*	1,311	44,877	323	20,033	457	19,343	59	1,246	472	4,256
Cyprus*	1,208	36,151	164	7,172	449	21,364	125	2,899	470	4,717
Singapore*	850	32,792	407	17,285	129	9,210	166	4,169	148	2,128
Norway (NIS)*	637	28,622	318	17,455	86	7,565	6	101	227	3,501
Hong Kong*	465	23,688	55	3,097	275	16,638	73	2,665	62	1,287
China	1,445	22,606	269	3,798	325	11,094	102	1,762	749	5,951
Marshall Islands	293	20,656	121	13,493	86	5,062	59	1,561	27	539
United States	431	13,923	123	6,661	18	797	90	3,198	200	3,267
Japan	599	13,652	250	7,393	150	4,742	19	594	180	923
India	290	10,147	100	5,237	110	4,398	7	143	73	369
St. Vincent & Grenadines	741	9,958	85	1,157	136	5,191	30	235	490	3,376
Italy	431	9,642	219	4,139	42	3,086	28	982	142	1,435
Isle of Man	212	9,276	95	6,535	24	1,678	22	480	71	582
Korea (South)	482	8,910	142	1,872	100	5,207	48	834	192	998
Turkey	532	8,794	96	1,616	143	5,394	28	311	265	1,472
Denmark (DIS)	288	8,472	77	3,364	6	357	75	4,261	130	490
All other flags	10,399	146,878	2,089	51,285	1,009	38,959	897	21,891	6,404	34,743
Grand total	28,694	808,260	7,201	334,349	5,816	298,930	2,832	80,319	12,845	94,662

* Open registries.
**Roll-on/Roll-off, passenger, breakbulk ships, partial containerships, refrigerated cargo, barge carriers, and specialized cargo ships.
(NIS) = Norway International Shipping Registry
(DIS) = Denmark International Shipping Registry

SOURCE: "Top 20 Merchant Fleets of the World Self-Propelled Oceangoing Vessels 1,000 Gross Tons and Greater As of July 1, 2002," in *Maritime Statistics,* U.S. Department of Transportation, Maritime Administration, Washington, DC, October 11, 2002 [Online] http://www.marad.dot.gov/Marad_Statistics/mfw_top20.htm [accessed March 24, 2003]

FIGURE 1.4

The largest container vessels, 1980–2000

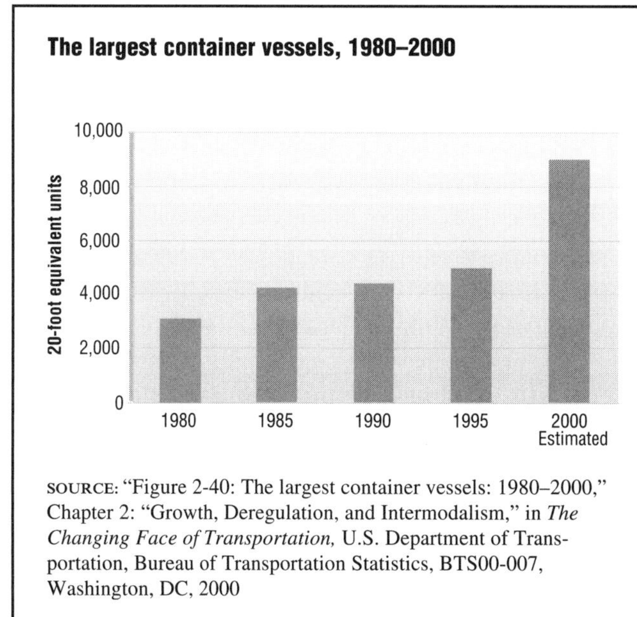

SOURCE: "Figure 2-40: The largest container vessels: 1980–2000," Chapter 2: "Growth, Deregulation, and Intermodalism," in *The Changing Face of Transportation,* U.S. Department of Transportation, Bureau of Transportation Statistics, BTS00-007, Washington, DC, 2000

carrying capacity. Figure 1.4 illustrates the growth in the size of the world's oceangoing container ships since 1980, when their capacity was below 4,000, 20-foot equivalent units (TEUs; one TEU is the length of a container divided by 20). In 1997 Germany introduced the world's first mega-container ship; it had a capacity of 8,000 TEUs. By 2000 the world's largest container ships were already approaching a capacity of 10,000 TEUs. The age and vessel sizes of all oceangoing fleets vary considerably by vessel type, but all the newer ships are larger and more fuel-efficient and have smaller crews. The U.S. fleet is mature. According to the U.S. Army Corps of Engineers, as of December 31, 2001, one-half (50 percent) of the U.S. fleet was more than 20 years old. To remain competitive, the American fleet will have to be rebuilt or replaced.

WHERE THE LAND AND SEA MEET

Ports and Harbors

The U.S. port system consists of two basic components: harbor works and port facilities. By definition, harbors

TABLE 1.3

U.S. ocean port terminals by type and region,[1] 1998

Berth Type	North Atlantic	South Atlantic	Gulf	South Pacific	North Pacific	Great Lakes	Total
General cargo	**264**	**204**	**264**	**208**	**149**	**96**	**1,185**
General cargo	135	78	193	63	56	35	560
Container	46	19	12	66	20	0	163
Lash/Seabee	0	1	2	0	0	0	3
Ro-Ro	6	19	3	4	3	0	35
Auto Carrier	17	4	0	9	2	0	32
General cargo/container	16	12	2	1	10	1	42
General cargo/Ro-Ro	13	9	14	6	6	4	52
General cargo/passenger	0	11	4	0	6	0	21
General cargo/dry bulk	19	15	20	26	24	51	155
General cargo/liquid bulk	2	27	11	22	11	4	77
Container/Ro-Ro	9	8	2	11	11	0	41
Container/dry bulk	1	1	1	0	0	0	4
Dry bulk	**96**	**48**	**163**	**51**	**74**	**260**	**692**
Coal	11	2	12	0	2	23	50
Grain	9	1	28	5	10	34	87
Ores	7	3	6	0	5	37	58
Logs	0	0	0	1	13	0	14
Wood chips	0	0	0	1	11	0	12
Cement	10	5	7	2	4	18	46
Chemicals	9	6	47	3	4	7	76
Other dry bulk	39	23	46	23	16	133	280
Dry/liquid bulk	11	8	17	16	9	8	69
Liquid bulk	**188**	**51**	**182**	**73**	**71**	**45**	**610**
Crude petroleum	8	0	37	10	5	0	60
Petroleum products	109	28	37	31	41	33	279
Crude & products	29	15	64	28	20	5	161
Liquid propane gas	1	1	5	0	0	0	7
Liquid natural gas	3	0	1	0	1	0	5
Other liquid bulk	38	7	38	4	4	7	98
Passenger	**19**	**24**	**10**	**18**	**10**	**6**	**87**
Passenger	13	24	10	18	0	1	66
Ferry	6	0	0	0	10	5	21
Other berths	**194**	**22**	**167**	**64**	**61**	**76**	**584**
Barge	126	11	133	33	36	15	354
Mooring	39	7	19	9	20	30	124
Inactive	29	4	13	14	5	31	96
Other	0	0	2	8	0	0	10
Total	**761**	**349**	**786**	**414**	**365**	**483**	**3,158**

[1] Includes those commercial cargo handling facilities with a minimum alongside depth of 25 feet for coastal ports and 18 feet for Great Lakes ports.

SOURCE: "Table 1-22: U.S. ocean port terminals by type and region," in *Maritime Trade & Transportation 99,* U.S. Bureau of Transportation Statistics, Maritime Administration, BTS99-02, Washington, DC, 1999

provide ships and boats shelter from wind, high waves, and storms. In 2002 the U.S. Army Corps of Engineers maintained 926 coastal and inland harbors nationwide in a system that encompassed 4,690 deep-draft and 4,619 shallow-draft commercial facilities. Most of the harbors are located on the nation's four major shorelines—Atlantic, Gulf, Pacific, and Great Lakes ("Complete Statement of Colonel Randall J. Butler, District Engineer, Portland District, Before the Surface Transportation and Merchant Marine Subcommittee of the Committee on Commerce, United States Senate, on Oregon's Maritime Commerce: Protecting Trade and Securing Ports", July 2, 2002).

Ports, on the other hand, allow the loading and unloading of both freight and passengers. Not all harbors have port facilities. While Congress has declared that every town and city located on federally improved harbors and waterways should have at least one public port terminal for shipping, port development has traditionally relied on local and private initiative.

The United States has the world's largest port system. According to MARAD, there are 4,970 port berths and other ship facilities (3,158 major U.S. seaport berths plus 1,812 river port berths located in 21 states on the U.S. inland waterway system. (See Table 1.3 and Table 1.4.) The East Coast (North and South Atlantic) maintains 1,110 (35 percent) of the U.S. seaport berths, followed by the Gulf Coast with 786 (25 percent) and the West Coast with 779 (25) percent. The Great Lakes have 483 (15 percent) of the berths. The Mississippi River system has by far the largest number of river port terminals (1,748). (See Table

TABLE 1.4

Inland and riverport shipping terminal facilities by state, 1997

State	Number of terminals	Number and type of facilities									
		General cargo	Dry bulk cargo				Liquid bulk cargo			Multi-purpose
			Grain	Coal	Ore	Other	Petrol	LPG	Other	
Alabama	137	8	16	21	–	41	21	–	15	15
Arkansas	84	2	26	–	–	24	7	–	6	19
Illinois	267	6	64	18	1	70	37	–	42	29
Indiana	60	2	8	14	1	16	9	–	2	8
Iowa	75	–	16	9	–	17	8	–	11	14
Kansas	8	–	4	–	–	1	–	–	2	1
Kentucky	175	3	13	48	–	49	32	1	15	14
Louisiana	66	1	8	2	–	12	19	1	14	9
Minnesota	55	1	10	–	–	20	8	–	7	9
Mississippi	69	1	16	–	–	13	16	1	6	16
Missouri	133	2	22	6	–	59	14	–	18	12
Nebraska	17	1	7	–	–	4	–	–	4	1
Ohio	132	6	7	21	2	43	23	–	19	11
Oklahoma	27	3	5	–	–	9	4	–	2	4
Pennsylvania	145	9	–	41	2	49	18	–	18	8
Tennessee	129	6	21	7	1	47	23	–	12	12
West Virginia	149	9	–	47	1	52	21	1	15	3
Wisconsin	20	1	1	4	–	7	3	–	2	2
Mississippi System sub-total	**1,748**	**61**	**244**	**238**	**8**	**533**	**263**	**4**	**210**	**187**
Idaho	4	1	2	–	–	1	–	–	–	–
Oregon	24	3	7	–	–	12	–	–	1	1
Washington	36	5	18	–	–	5	2	–	4	2
Columbia/Snake sub-total	**64**	**9**	**27**	**–**	**–**	**18**	**2**	**–**	**5**	**3**
Total	**1,812**	**70**	**271**	**238**	**8**	**551**	**265**	**4**	**215**	**190**

SOURCE: "Table 18: U.S. Inland/Riverport Terminal Facilities by State," in *A Report to Congress on the Status of the Public Ports of the United States 1996–1997,* U.S. Department of Transportation, Maritime Administration, Washington, DC, 1997

1.4.) Figure 1.5 illustrates the distribution of both river and seaports in the United States.

Naturally, the states involved to the greatest degree in waterborne commerce are those located on major waterways. Table 1.5 shows the waterborne commerce of 41 states and several territories. Nine western states do not have waterborne commerce. Louisiana and Texas led the 50 states in the amount of waterborne commerce, followed by California, Ohio, Florida, Illinois, Pennsylvania, Washington, and New York. There are significant regional differences in waterborne foreign trade, according to the Bureau of Transportation Statistics (*Maritime Trade & Transportation 2002,* Bureau of Transportation Statistics, Washington, D.C., 2002):

- California, Oregon, and Washington rank first in container traffic because of the heavy use of containers in trade with Asia.
- Texas ranks first for tanker traffic because of the use of tankers in trade with Latin America.
- Alabama, Florida, Georgia, Louisiana, Mississippi, North Carolina, South Carolina, and Virginia rank first for dry-bulk traffic because of heavy trade with Asia, Europe, the Mediterranean, and Latin America.

THE INTERMODAL PROCESS. The United States developed intermodal shipping systems, which plan and execute the movement of goods from point of departure to final destination, using containerized vessels, port terminals, computerized technology, and inland delivery systems, including trucking and rail. (See Figure 1.6.) This process not only reduces transportation and inventory costs, but reduces damage and theft as well.

According to the MARAD "Glossary of Shipping Terms," a container is a "truck trailer body that can be detached from the chassis for loading into a vessel, a rail car or stacked in a container depot." Container ships make loading and unloading faster and easier and enable more efficient transportation of cargo to and from the port area. One example of the container ship is the Roll-on/Roll-off ship, or Ro-Ro. Vehicles such as trucks and trailers that carry cargo can drive directly on and off a Ro-Ro ship. Most experts expect intermodal ships to continue to grow in size and DWT capacity.

LARGER U.S. SEAPORTS. Global trade expanded greatly in the 1990s. (See Figure 1.1.) Because most U.S. ports could not handle the modern megaships, the U.S. port industry invested billions of dollars on port improvements such as dredging for deep-draft ships, construction of

FIGURE 1.5

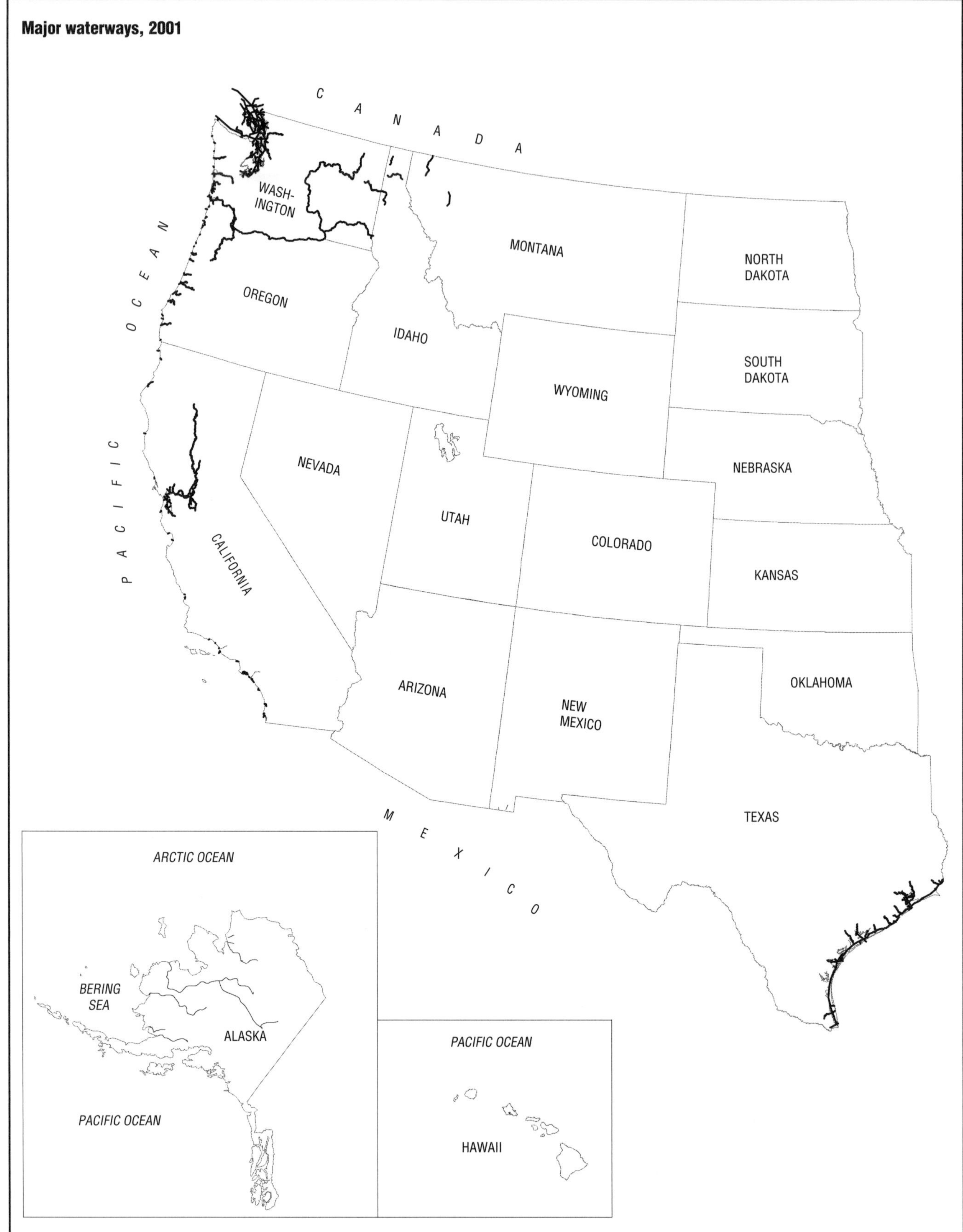

SOURCE: "Figure 1-1: Major waterways of the United States," in *Waterborne Commerce of the United States (WCUS), Part 5—National Summaries,* U.S. Army Corps of Engineers, New Orleans, LA, 2001

FIGURE 1.5

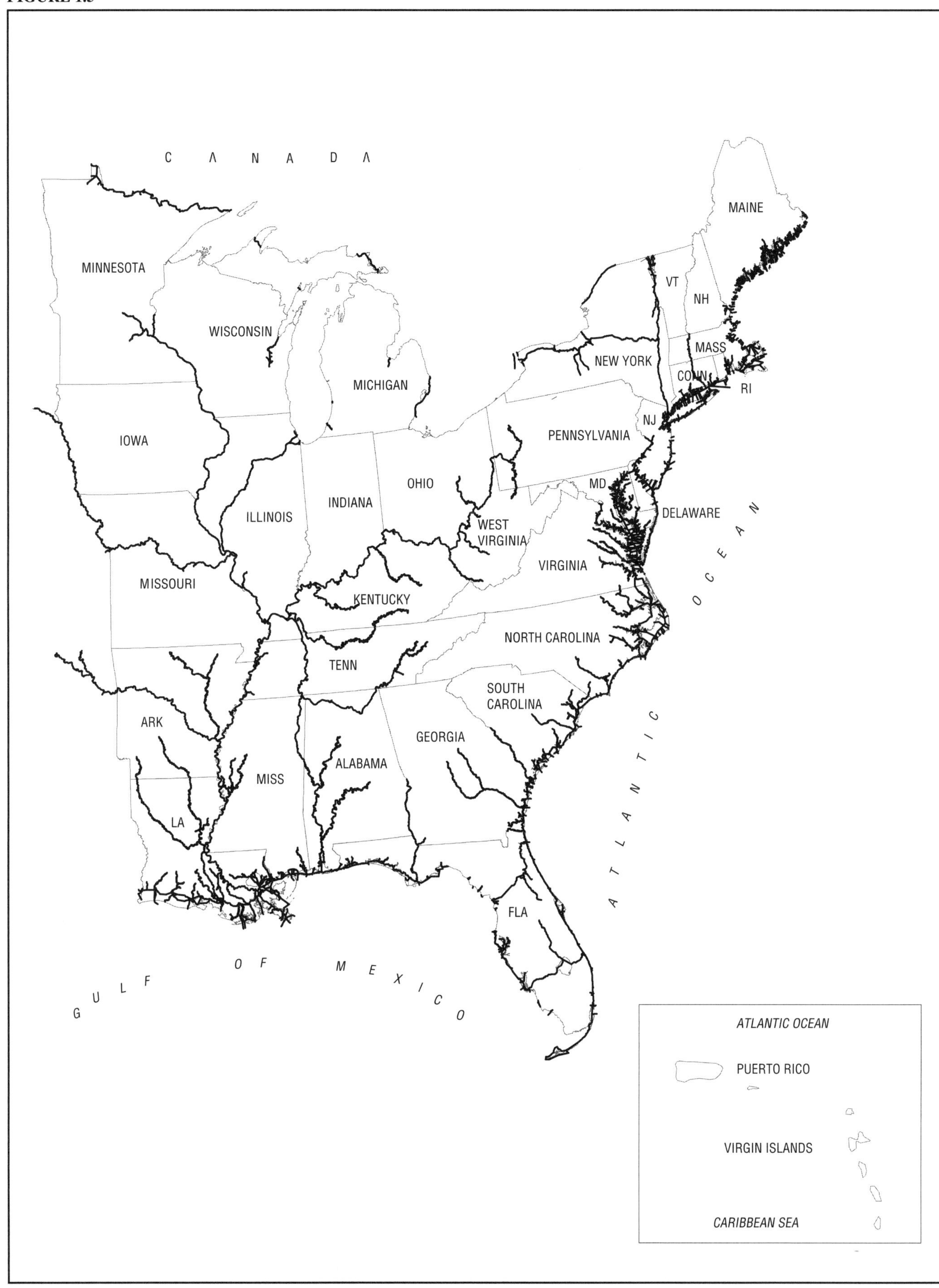

C A N A D A
MINNESOTA
WISCONSIN
MICHIGAN
IOWA
ILLINOIS
INDIANA
OHIO
MISSOURI
KENTUCKY
WEST VIRGINIA
VIRGINIA
PENNSYLVANIA
NEW YORK
VT
NH
MAINE
MASS
CONN
RI
NJ
MD
DELAWARE
NORTH CAROLINA
TENN
SOUTH CAROLINA
GEORGIA
ALABAMA
MISS
ARK
LA
FLA
ATLANTIC OCEAN
GULF OF MEXICO
ATLANTIC OCEAN
PUERTO RICO
VIRGIN ISLANDS
CARIBBEAN SEA

TABLE 1.5

Waterborne commerce by state, 2001

In thousands of short tons

State	Total[1]	Shipping Domestic	Shipping Foreign	Receiving Domestic	Receiving Foreign	Intrastate
Total	**2,386,558**	**734,049**	**399,011**	**734,049**	**945,075**	**308,423**
Alabama	68,244	10,459	10,263	17,026	17,723	12,774
Alaska	67,238	52,361	7,802	2,561	587	3,926
Arkansas	11,639	4,385	–	4,801	–	2,453
California	186,480	5,584	41,345	29,962	100,647	8,941
Connecticut	18,267	872	37	11,653	4,397	1,308
Delaware	37,192	13,729	689	2,028	18,735	2,011
District of Columbia	663	–	-	663	–	–
Florida	121,765	8,937	17,767	57,031	34,353	3,677
Georgia	22,023	808	8,402	1,739	10,888	185
Guam	369	46	–	323	–	–
Hawaii	23,113	1,067	746	5,631	6,893	8,776
Idaho	1,335	1,004	–	9	–	322
Illinois	122,739	89,859	568	19,939	2,078	10,295
Indiana	71,013	14,142	556	49,743	2,442	4,130
Iowa	14,347	9,624	–	4,115	–	607
Kansas	2,339	196	–	1,828	–	315
Kentucky	101,101	53,356	–	33,258	–	14,487
Louisiana	496,218	105,096	105,591	127,507	117,579	40,445
Maine	30,586	98	415	2,674	27,242	157
Maryland	49,903	6,926	7,670	11,594	19,010	4,702
Massachusetts	26,446	950	655	9,506	13,398	1,937
Michigan	76,617	25,135	5,758	20,795	8,517	16,411
Minnesota	44,031	28,342	6,423	6,340	708	2,217
Mississippi	46,261	13,778	4,252	10,825	16,529	877
Missouri	34,705	17,665	–	8,523	–	8,517
Nebraska	178	102	–	76	–	–
New Hampshire	4,447	17	81	556	3,792	–
New Jersey	93,834	29,472	4,560	20,370	34,574	4,859
New York	103,253	16,566	4,205	21,026	44,851	16,605
North Carolina	10,667	154	2,167	2,627	3,889	1,830
Ohio	119,539	18,751	20,568	62,314	5,314	12,593
Oklahoma	4,133	1,958	–	2,168	–	7
Oregon	35,830	3,436	14,165	10,036	4,312	3,879
Other	64,076	5,334	–	8,093	50,637	12
Pacific Islands	26	2	–	24	–	–
Pennsylvania	125,090	18,548	715	36,323	47,078	22,427
Puerto Rico	23,306	1,280	863	7,251	11,785	2,126
Rhode Island	9,170	330	412	5,436	2,957	36
South Carolina	24,668	432	6,158	3,628	12,353	2,096
Tennessee	46,733	7,997	–	33,942	–	4,794
Texas	454,765		62,622	20,684	270,805	56,873
Trans-Shipment[2]	280		–	72	–	–
Vermont	–	–	–	–	–	–
Virgin Islands	42,277	18,626	937	–	22,231	483
Virginia	61,840	13,171	25,096	5,892	11,209	6,471
Washington	104,975	14,855	30,927	30,116	15,732	13,345
West Virginia	79,450	53,175	–	15,889	–	10,386
Wisconsin	37,438	21,432	6,595	7,452	1,829	131

[1] Excludes duplication.

[2] Ports and offshore anchorages where cargo is moved from one vessel to another. These are St. Lucia, Virgin Islands Heald Bank off LA-TX coast, Cherique Grande, Panama, Puerto Amuelles, Panama and Hondo Platform-Pacific Ocean.

– Data not available.

SOURCE: "Table 4-1: Waterborne commerce by state: 2001," in *Waterborne Commerce of the United States (WCUS), Part 5—National Summaries,* U.S. Army Corps of Engineers, New Orleans, LA, 2001

FIGURE 1.6

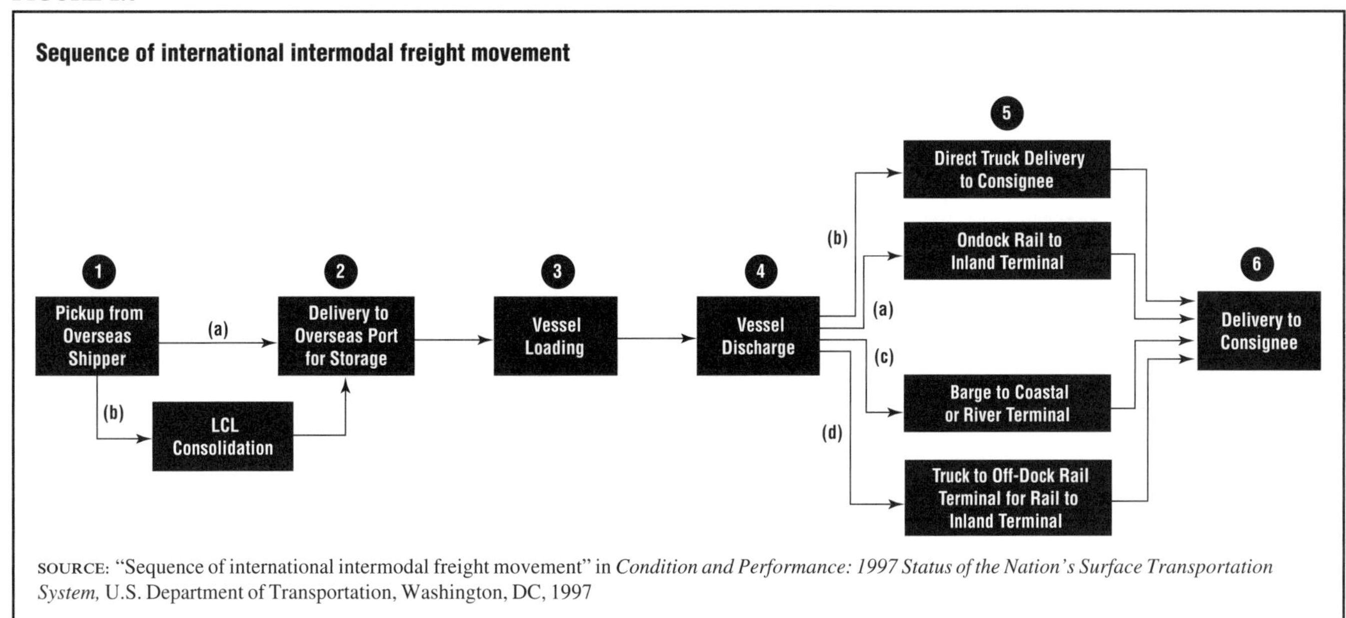

SOURCE: "Sequence of international intermodal freight movement" in *Condition and Performance: 1997 Status of the Nation's Surface Transportation System,* U.S. Department of Transportation, Washington, DC, 1997

FIGURE 1.7

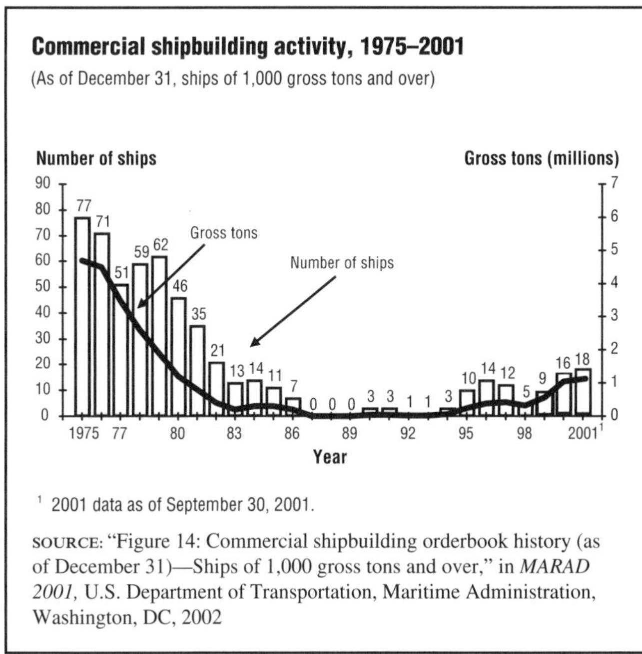

[1] 2001 data as of September 30, 2001.

SOURCE: "Figure 14: Commercial shipbuilding orderbook history (as of December 31)—Ships of 1,000 gross tons and over," in *MARAD 2001,* U.S. Department of Transportation, Maritime Administration, Washington, DC, 2002

modern berths, huge cranes, rail lines, and roads to handle interface with the huge post-Panamax vessels—1,000-foot cargo ships that require harbors at least 50 feet deep. (They are called post-Panamax vessels because they are too large to pass through the Panama Canal.) The American Association of Port Authorities reported that at least $7.7 billion was spent by the port industry on improvements between 1998 and 2002. Some of the port cities with major projects include:

- Savannah, Georgia—A $70 million container berth with two enormous cranes was completed in 1998.
- New York and New Jersey—The Port of New York and New Jersey, the largest port in the eastern United States, committed $1.8 billion to port redevelopment projects during the period 2001–06, including deepening major channels to 50 feet from their current 40 feet.
- Houston, Texas—A $1.2 billion, 720-acre Bayport intermodal container complex is planned to expand the port facilities. In 2003 the project was being assessed by the Transportation Security Administration (formed in November 2001) to determine security risks in the aftermath of the terrorist attacks of September 11, 2001.
- Long Beach, California—The Port of Long Beach, the largest container port in the United States, is in the process of building a mega-terminal that will offer 5,000 linear feet of wharf, 50-foot water depths, a dockside rail yard, and as many as 16 huge cranes capable of unloading post-Panamax size ships. The second phase of this terminal is expected to be completed in 2004.

The billions of dollars invested in port modernization are not enough, according to a September 2002 report from the U.S. General Accounting Office (GAO) (*Marine Transportation: Federal Financing and an Infrastructure Investment Framework,* GAO-02-1090T, Washington, D.C.). International freight tonnage transported by water is expected to increase 27 percent (to 1.5 billion tons) between 1998 and 2010. Maritime industry analysts believe that substantial new investments must be made to address an aging infrastructure, changes in the shipping industry, and concerns about security.

TABLE 1.6

World commercial shipbuilding orderbook as of September 30, 2001

Country of build	Ship rank	Number of ships	Gross tons	Gross rank
Korea (South)	1	507	31,299	1
Japan	2	455	19,153	2
China (People's Republic)	3	307	5,433	3
Poland	5	132	2,806	4
Germany	7	100	2,253	5
Italy	10	65	2,221	6
Croatia	14	50	1,554	7
United States	15	46	1,038	8
China (Republic of Taiwan)	17	32	961	9
Finland	22	13	871	10
Romania	6	103	871	11
Spain	8	92	691	12
France	19	23	668	13
Netherlands	4	196	578	14
Denmark	23	13	529	15
Ukraine	18	30	436	16
Russia	9	79	356	17
Philippines	24	11	338	18
Singapore	11	54	328	19
Turkey	12	54	273	20
Total top 20 country of build		**2,362**	**72,667**	
Percent of total world orderbook		**89.1**	**98.7**	
Total world orderbook		**2,648**	**73,581**	

SOURCE: "Table 2-1. World commercial shipbuilding orderbook, gross tonnage 1,000 and above as of September 30, 2001 (thousands)," in *Maritime Trade & Transportation 2002,* Bureau of Transportation Statistics, Maritime Administration, Washington, DC, 2002

Inland Waterways

The United States has a total of 11,703 miles of commercially navigable inland waterways. More than half are on the Mississippi River system and its tributaries (6,651 miles), with most of the rest running along the coasts of the Gulf of Mexico and the Atlantic ocean. The fleet of barges and tugboats that navigate these waters consists of more than 33,000 vessels. (See Figure 1.5 for an illustration of the nation's major waterways.)

THE MODERN U.S. SHIPBUILDING INDUSTRY—NEW HOPE

In the twentieth century, the U.S. fleet experienced significant growth only during the two world wars. After World War II, new shipbuilding decreased sharply as naval ship orders declined and U.S. commercial shipping experienced little growth. In the 1980s the Reagan administration earmarked $100 billion to double the size of the U.S. Navy to 600 ships but simultaneously ended federal subsidies for commercial shipbuilding (by the time President Ronald Reagan left office in 1988, the navy had nearly 600 ships). After the Cold War ended in 1989, orders for U.S. warships declined 60 percent over a 10-year period. By 1990 the U.S. shipbuilding industry's commercial orderbook for merchant vessels fell to zero. This was the lowest activity level for the industry since before World War II. (See Figure 1.7.)

A global economic recession during the 1980s and an excess inventory of ships, particularly oil tankers, contributed to a continuing decline of the shipbuilding industry worldwide. Major shipbuilders in Europe and Japan also faced serious drops in demand, but unlike U.S. shipbuilders were able to turn to their governments for support. As a result, Japan and South Korea are now the leading merchant ship builders, with a combined 69 percent share on September 30, 2001, based on gross tonnage. (See Table 1.6.) The United States ranked eighth in terms of its shipbuilding orderbook (a 1.4 percent share).

In the booming economy of the 1990s U.S. shipbuilders experienced an increase in orders for offshore supply vessels (used in the exploration and production of oil and natural gas). Some aging vessels were replaced and new federal assistance programs were initiated. As of December 31, 2001, there were 18 commercial oceangoing vessels on order from U.S. shipyards. According to *Maritime Trade & Transportation 2002,* gross commercial tonnage on order was 37 percent higher on September 30, 2001, than it had been a year earlier. The same publication reported that about 70 percent of the revenue from shipbuilding and repair comes from U.S. Navy procurements. There were 31 military ships under construction as of October 2001.

According to a report from the Shipbuilders Council of America (*The Economic Contribution of the U.S. Shipbuilding Industry,* Washington, D.C., April 2002), the U.S. commercial shipbuilding industry grew at an average annual rate of 6.8 percent between 1992 and 2001, compared with an average annual rate of only 3.4 percent for the economy as a whole. (See Table 1.7.)

National Shipbuilding and Shipyard Conversion Act

The increase in U.S. shipbuilding orders closely followed the 1993 passage of the National Shipbuilding and Shipyard Conversion Act (PL 103-160). The act includes a five-point revitalization plan:

- Extension of government guarantees to finance vessels purchased in U.S. shipyards by foreign owners through the existing domestic loan guarantee program (Title XI)
- Efforts to ensure fair international competition
- Improvement of commercial competitiveness
- Elimination of unnecessary government regulation
- Assistance in international marketing

The act also funded research and development projects under MARITECH (short for "maritime technology"), which focuses on market penetration and longer-term technology development. The original MARITECH program ended in 1999 and MARITECH ASE (advanced shipbuilding enterprise) took its place.

TABLE 1.7

Commercial shipbuilding industry compared to the national economy, 1992–2001

	Commercial shipbuilding		National economy	
	Value of shipments (billions 2001 dollars)	Average annual growth	GDP (billions 2001 dollars)	Average annual growth
1992	$2.130		$7,524.0	
1997	$2.983	7.0%	$8,923.0	3.5%
2001 Estimate	$3.895	6.9%	$10,205.8	3.4%
	Value added (billions 2001 dollars)	**Average annual growth**		
1992	$1.138			
1997	$1.587	6.9%		
2001 Estimate	$2.065	6.8%		
	Inputs from others (billions 2001 dollars)	**Average annual growth**		
1992	$0.992			
1997	$1.396	7.1%		
2001	$1.829	7.0%		
	Employees	**Average annual growth**	**Nonfarm employment (thousands)**	**Average annual growth**
1992	18,200		108,601	
1997	24,907	6.5%	122,690	2.5%
2001	31,283	5.9%	132,212	1.9%

Notes:
Real GDP for 2001 is the preliminary estimate from U.S. Bureau of Economic Analysis.
Nonfarm employment for 2001 is a preliminary estimate from the U.S. Bureau of Labor Statistics.
Value of shipments for commercial shipbuilding growth from 1997 to 2001 is based on growth of the number of commercial shipbuilding contracts from Marinelog.
Estimated 2001 commercial shipbuilding employees is estimated based on growth rate of value of shipments and the historical re lationship between productivity (ratio of employment to value added) in the shipbuilding industry and in the national economy.
Estimated 2001 commercial shipbuilding value added is estimated based on value of shipments and the historical relationship of value added and value of shipments.
Estimated 2001 commercial shipbuilding inputs from other is estimated based on the value of shipments and the historical relationship of inputs from others.

SOURCE: "Table 2: A comparison of the U.S. commercial shipbuilding industry and the national economy: 1992 to 2001," in *The Economic Contribution of the U.S. Commercial Shipbuilding Industry,* Prepared for Shipbuilders Council of America by LECG, LLC, Washington, DC, April 2002

The Title XI loan guarantee program allows MARAD to guarantee private sector debt financing for up to 87.5 percent of the cost of the vessel. Under the terms of a Title XI loan all construction or reconstruction work must be done in U.S. shipyards and this applies to both U.S.- and foreign-flag vessels. This program extends to U.S. shipyard modernization and improvement projects as well as new vessel construction and older vessel maintenance.

A Dilemma

For many years the merchant marine had faced a dilemma related to shipbuilding. Under Section 27 of the Jones Act, U.S. owners were not permitted to buy less expensive foreign-made ships. Since 1920, the law had required all waterborne shipping between ports throughout the United States and its territories to be carried on ships built and registered in this country and owned by U.S. citizens. This put U.S. shippers at a disadvantage in the competitive shipping industry abroad.

Realizing the extent of the financial problem facing the merchant marine, Congress passed and President Bill Clinton signed the Maritime Security Act of 1996 (PL 104-239) ordering an annual appropriation of $100 million to maintain a U.S.-flag presence in international trade and a U.S. shipbuilding capability. The program gives limited assistance to the U.S. merchant marine involved in U.S.-foreign commerce in an effort to help that industry become more competitive internationally.

In return, participating carriers would be required to enroll in an Emergency Preparedness Program to provide intermodal sealift support (a system for transporting persons or cargo by ship) in time of war or national crisis. Vessel owners would be required to provide ships, intermodal equipment, terminal facilities, and management services. This partnership would provide the government with cost-effective sealift capability, using commercial vessels to complement U.S. Department of Defense sealift programs. (The utility of this partnership was demonstrated in

February 2003 when the Military Sealift Command requested that the Jones Act trailership *SS Northern Lights* load military hardware in San Diego for delivery to Southwest Asia in support of Operation Enduring Freedom [the war against terrorism]).

In May 2001 the U.S. Department of Commerce, Bureau of Export Administration (BXA) completed an assessment of the U.S. shipbuilding industry (*U.S. Shipbuilding and Repair: National Security Assessment of the U.S. Shipbuilding and Repair Industry,* 003-009-00719-4). The BXA reported that in general the U.S. commercial shipbuilding industry is not internationally competitive in the construction of vessels over 1,000 gross tons but there is a limited market for such vessels. The United States does have a significant world market share in certain niches: offshore oil platforms, yachts, fast patrol boats, and recreational vessels. The report noted that shipbuilding and repair are important to the national security of the United States.

SECURING THE NATION'S BORDERS

Legislation

In the aftermath of the September 11, 2001, terrorist attacks, ensuring the security of America's borders, including its ports, became an urgent issue. Foreign-flag ships are a ubiquitous presence in U.S. ports. Container shipments are seen as a potential delivery system of weapons of mass destruction because cargo can be quickly transferred from ships and transported to anywhere in the country. On November 25, 2002, President George W. Bush signed into law the Maritime Transportation Security Act (S 1214), a bill aimed at improving security at U.S. seaports and preventing terrorists from using the maritime transportation system to launch attacks on the United States. The law will strengthen security through the development of security plans for ports and an improved identification and screening system of port personnel. On March 31, 2003, the Anti-Terrorism and Port Security Act of 2003 (S 746), a bill to prevent and respond to terrorism and crime at or through U.S. ports, was introduced in the U.S. Senate.

CHAPTER 2
RAILROADS

While the ship was a major factor in the birth of the United States, the railroad played a dominant role in its growth and development. It contributed to westward expansion and allowed access to the land's vast resources. California was bound to the Union as a result of the physical and commercial ties provided by the railroad, which opened the continent from ocean to ocean.

Railways offered some distinct advantages over canals, which had previously provided the major routes for inland transportation. They were cheaper to construct, offered faster service, and did not freeze in winter. By no means were railroads problem-free: timetables reflected more wishful thinking than actual times of arrivals and departures, breakdowns were frequent, and the lack of standard-gauge tracks (gauge is the distance between the rails of a track) could mean numerous transfers from line to line. Moreover, trains were dangerous. Soft roadbeds, broken rails, collapsed bridges, and almost nonexistent brakes led to frequent and often serious wrecks. Nonetheless, the technology was well suited to the pioneering spirit and economic needs of a young and growing nation.

UNITING THE COUNTRY

In 1830 only 23 miles of railroad track existed in the United States. The advantages of rail transport were becoming obvious, however, and the industry experienced rapid growth. Congress designated the nation's railways as postal routes in 1838 and the postmaster general ordered them to be used for all reasonable transportation of the mail. Track mileage increased to 30,000 miles by 1860, and Chicago was the terminal for 11 major railroads.

Railroads exacerbated the strained relationship between the northern and southern states before the Civil War (1861–65). Most lines ran east-west, connecting the major cities and the seacoasts to the Mississippi River. Virtually all southern railroads served southern river port cities, with almost no ties to the North. Different size track gauges, a problem throughout a nation that still had 12 different track sizes in 1860, were most apparent in the South. The inability to run southern trains on northern tracks (and vice-versa) further separated the two segments of the country. The superior railroads of the North contributed to the Union victory during the Civil War, providing the North with a formidable means of transporting millions of men, arms, and supplies to strategic locations.

Go West

Even during the Civil War, the federal government was looking toward California and the western territories. The government wanted to make sure that this rich land remained a part of the Union, even though an entire continent separated it from the centers of government and commerce. The solution was to connect west to east with thousands of miles of railroad tracks. This not only created a physical link to the West but also provided a means of exploiting its vast commercial potential. As an incentive to build railroads in the largely unsettled and sometimes hostile expanse between the Mississippi River and California, the government offered financial support as well as land grants to those who would build the railroads.

In 1862 Congress passed legislation to promote a transcontinental railway. The legislation granted the Central Pacific and the Union Pacific Railroads direct subsidies of:

- $16,000 for each mile of track laid on smooth ground
- $32,000 per mile through uneven regions
- $48,000 per mile through mountainous regions
- A substantial right-of-way on lands on either side of the tracks.

A virtual explosion of railroad building followed the Civil War. The dream of uniting the country by rail was realized on May 10, 1869, when the tracks laid by the Union Pacific, building from the east, and the Central Pacific, building from the west, met at Promontory Point, Utah. The momentous occasion was celebrated by driving the Gold Spike uniting the two tracks. For their efforts, the two companies received between 10 and 20 square miles of public land for every mile of track.

The 1880s saw 166,000 miles of track completed and by 1893, five transcontinental railroads were transporting huge quantities of agricultural, forestry, and mining products, along with settlers, adventurers, and businessmen. The railroad companies owned 12 percent of all the land west of the Mississippi—130 million acres—received in land grants from state and federal governments.

Time Zones

With the development of improved tracks and equipment, timetables began to reflect reality. This led to service complications, for the railways had to contend with almost 100 local times observed in different parts of the country. In order to provide scheduling uniformity, on November 18, 1883, the railroad companies established the four time zones that are still used today—Eastern, Central, Mountain, and Pacific. While these time standards quickly came into general use, it was not until the Standard Time Act of 1918 that they became national law.

STEAM TO DIESEL—BUT NOT ELECTRICITY

In 1895 the nation's first electrified train service began on the Nantasket Branch of the New York, New Haven, and Hartford Railroad. The first mainline electrification was through the 3.6-mile Baltimore Tunnel of the Baltimore and Ohio Railroad in 1895. However, despite early inroads, electric locomotives were largely replaced by steam locomotives. This was due in part to the extremely high start-up and maintenance costs for electric railroads, especially with long distances to cover. In addition, coal for fuel was abundant in the United States at the time of the rapid growth of railroads. In Europe, where distances are shorter and coal harder to get, most railroads are electrified.

While steam remained the major source of locomotive power for many years, diesel slowly began making inroads. In 1925 a diesel switch locomotive went into service for the Central Railroad of New Jersey. In 1934 the Chicago, Burlington, and Quincy Railroad put the first diesel locomotive into mainline service, and in 1940 the Santa Fe Railroad began using diesels in regular freight service. Gradually, the industry turned to diesel locomotives and the last steam locomotive was retired in the 1950s.

GOVERNMENT REGULATION

As the railroad industry flourished, so did its abuses. Excessive rates, internal price wars, fraudulent investment schemes, and scandalous behavior became so widespread that eventually the government and the public reacted. In response to public pressure, many states formed commissions to control rates. But while states were granted the right to regulate businesses within their own state boundaries, the Supreme Court ruled that they could not control rates on interstate commerce. This set the stage for controls at the federal level. In 1887 Congress passed the Act to Regulate Commerce, which resulted in the formation of the Interstate Commerce Commission (ICC). The Elkins Act (1903) and the Hepburn Act (1906) gave the ICC further authority to regulate rates. On January 1, 1996, the Surface Transportation Board superseded the ICC.

FADING GLORY

Like the shipping industry, railroads could not maintain their monopoly on moving the people and products of an entire nation when they were themselves faced with new competitive forms of transportation: the car, the truck, and the airplane. Several factors contributed to the decline of the railroads. As is often the case, success led to excess. In 1916, 254,000 miles of railway line crisscrossed the nation. The supply of tracks and equipment had outstripped the demand for their use. Multiple lines served the same routes, reducing the market share for each operator and making it difficult for any of them to turn a profit.

It was under these conditions that the railroads faced dramatic changes in the U.S. transportation market. Railroads recorded almost 34 billion revenue passenger-miles (one paid passenger traveling one mile) in 1929, as three out of four Americans traveling the United States took the train. For the vast majority of people, railroads were the only way to travel long distances over land. After that peak, however, passenger miles and revenue began to drop off as automobiles became more affordable and popular with Americans. After World War II (1941–45) Americans were richer than ever before and automobile ownership surged. The building of a nationwide network of interstate highways in the 1950s meant that one could now drive almost anywhere in the United States. Perhaps even worse for railroads was the development of passenger air travel. As early as 1939, airplanes accounted for 2 percent of all revenue passenger-miles in the United States and air travel developed rapidly. Long-distance travel by air was faster than by train and only slightly more expensive, making it almost impossible for railroads to compete.

During this same period, railroads faced a changing freight market. The U.S. economy was shifting from manufacturing toward services and technology, reducing the requirement for large quantities of bulk commodities, the mainstay of the railroad's freight business. Industrial centers sprang up all across the South, Southwest, and West, so that the need for long-haul transport of commodities from the Northeast to the rest of the country was diminished. Industry and population were also moving from the central cities into the suburbs. This made many older railroad routes obsolete, but financing for new tracks was often unavailable. Trucks saw dramatic increases in size and power, allowing them to haul goods that could only have been transported by train or by ship in the past.

CRISIS IN THE INDUSTRY

By the 1970s the railroad industry was in serious trouble. Forced to maintain passenger operations but unable to compete effectively with aircraft and automobiles, and burdened by price regulations, their profits had disappeared or greatly diminished. Tracks, equipment, and facilities deteriorated. Many lines went bankrupt, including the Penn-Central Transportation Company. The bankruptcy of this, the nation's largest railroad, shook the financial world and brought the poor condition of the nation's rail system to the public's attention. Congress decided to intervene. Its goals were to shore up the freight industry, which still served a vital role in transporting bulk goods and employed tens of thousands of people, as well as to reestablish a national passenger rail network.

Conrail

Congress established the United States Railroad Association (USRA) under the Regional Rail Reorganization Act of 1973 (PL 93-236) to plan and finance the restructuring of the Penn-Central and seven smaller bankrupt railways in the northeastern United States. The 3R Act, as amended by the Railroad Revitalization and Regulatory Reform (4R) Act of 1976 (PL 94-210), also created the Consolidated Rail Corporation, known as Conrail, which was to eventually become a "for profit" railroad. Conrail carried only freight, not passengers.

Conrail began operating on April 1, 1976, with a $2.1 billion congressional authorization to repair, upgrade, and replace track, equipment, and facilities. Later legislation added more monies for a total of $3.3 billion in federal operating subsidies. Conrail slashed staff, phased out unprofitable routes, rebuilt many of the deteriorating roadbeds and tracks, and used modern technology to help run the railroad more efficiently. By the time the company was sold to the public in 1987, it was profitable. In 1993 Conrail had 11,831 miles of track, 64,834 rail cars, and 24,728 employees. Many other freight railroads followed Conrail's example and with government assistance were able to remain in business and return to profitability. (Conrail was sold to CSX Corporation and Norfolk Southern Corporation in 1997.)

Amtrak

To fill the gap left by the decline in available passenger service, Congress passed the Railroad Passenger Service Act of 1970 (PL 91-518), creating the National Railroad Passenger Corporation, better known as Amtrak, a private/public corporation to operate on a "for-profit basis." Amtrak was given three mandates from Congress: first, to provide modern, efficient intercity rail passenger service; second, to help alleviate the overcrowding of airports, airways, and highways; and third, to give Americans an alternative to private automobiles and airplanes to meet their transportation needs.

Amtrak's beginnings could be described as shaky at best. Amtrak began managing a national transportation system in May 1971 with a motley assortment of 20-year-old railway passenger cars from a variety of railroads. Ticketing and reservations were mostly handwritten. These limitations, coupled with poor on-time performance and lack of on-board amenities (no food service), did nothing to lure customers away from other forms of transportation and the corporation steadily lost money. (It should be noted that even the extensive, modern passenger systems in other countries, notably the high-speed lines in Germany, France, and Japan, do not return a profit.)

Realizing that Amtrak would probably not make a profit and would require government subsidy, Congress eventually ordered it to operate on an "as-for-profit" (rather than "for-profit") basis. The passage of the Regional Rail Reorganization Act in 1973 and the Railroad Revitalization and Regulatory Reform (4R) Act of 1976 gave Amtrak the authority to take over 621 miles of rail from the bankrupt Penn-Central Railroad, which included the vital Northeast Corridor (NEC) between Washington and Boston. The Amtrak Reorganization Act of 1979 (PL 95-73) required that the company cover 50 percent of its annual costs by 1985.

DEREGULATION AND MODERNIZATION

In 1980, at the same time that deregulation was taking place in the airline and trucking industries, Congress passed the Staggers Rail Act (PL 96-448). After decades of close supervision by the ICC, this legislation permitted the railroads greater freedom in setting their rates, although in many cases they were required to justify rate hikes. The railways were also allowed to contract with other shippers to offer special services at special rates, a practice previously prohibited.

Rail deregulation, however, was not as comprehensive as air or trucking deregulation and the Federal Railroad Administration (FRA) still plays a significant role in monitoring the railroads. It approves mergers and abandonment of rail lines, establishes standards for evaluating the financial condition of railroads, performs evaluations of a railroad's financial condition, and resolves rate and service disputes between railroads and shippers.

With the help of deregulation, freight railroads were able to increase their revenues and secure stronger financial backing in the 1980s. In many cases they used this money to modernize their systems. Older rail lines and trains were sold off or shut down, to be replaced with new equipment. New control centers featuring high levels of computerization were also developed. This increasing efficiency strengthened freight railroads financially and made the U.S. freight railroad system one of the most modern in the world.

At the same time that the freight industry was being deregulated, Amtrak came under attack. In 1981 the incoming administration of President Ronald Reagan listed Amtrak among the government agencies that it wanted to severely cut back, if not eliminate. The administration felt that Amtrak should be forced to sustain itself through its own revenues or be allowed to fail. In virtually every budget proposal, the administration tried to either sharply cut or completely eliminate Amtrak but ran into resistance from members of Congress representing the Northeast Corridor, where Amtrak was most successful and popular. The program continued to receive public funds but also continued to be criticized as a waste of public money.

A GLOBAL PASSENGER RAIL REVIVAL?

Some analysts believe that rail is poised to make a comeback in much of the world. Indeed, in many places rail never faltered as it did in the United States. The United States is unusual in that trains play such a small role in transporting passengers. Airlines in Europe successfully lobbied for more rail service to free overloaded terminals of short-trip passengers—by 2003 the high-speed French TGV (*Train à Grande Vitesse*) had captured 90 percent of former air passengers on the Paris-Lyon route. In Japan the bullet train has almost eliminated air travel between Nagoya and Tokyo.

Trains offer a vital alternative to people who cannot afford a car or airline ticket or are physically unable to drive or fly. According to author John Ryan of Northwest Environment Watch (*Seven Wonders*, September 1999), only an estimated 10 percent of the world's people can afford a car. Rail offers many advantages over highway or air transport, according to Worldwatch Institute, an environmental activist group, including:

- Greater energy efficiency
- Less dependence on oil
- Reduced air pollution
- Lower emissions of greenhouse gases
- Less air and road congestion
- Fewer injuries and deaths
- Less paved land area
- Local economic development
- Sustainable land use patterns
- Greater social equity

Despite these advantages, Americans began to use rail less as automobile use grew. Western European countries, however, never abandoned their passenger rail systems when the automobile became popular—intercity trains, metros, and new light rail systems have been an established part of the landscape and lifestyle and formed an integral part of their transportation system. The national railways, the largest employers in several countries, represent some of the most comprehensive rail networks in the world. Japan is notable for maintaining high train ridership even as cars have become widespread. All of this demonstrates that railroads play an important passenger transportation role in much of the world and presumably could do the same in the United States. However, it would not come without a substantial cost. Even the most successful rail systems in other countries require government subsidies, just as Amtrak does in the United States.

Adequate funding is hard to find for all infrastructure—rail included—and critics of federal and state subsidies for rail ask where the money will come from. Supporters of rail contend that funding problems exist because national policymakers channeled billions of dollars into other transport modes, particularly highways. Contrary to popular belief, car and truck drivers do not pay their own way through user fees but are heavily subsidized. The American Public Transit Association (APTA) noted in its *1999 Transit Fact Book* (Washington, D.C.) that the public pays $2 to $3 trillion annually for highways and motor vehicle use but only 53 percent to 68 percent of that amount is paid by users. The costs for building, maintaining, and operating highways are mostly paid by all citizens through taxes not directly related to use of an automobile.

TRANSPORTATION EQUITY ACT FOR THE 21ST CENTURY

In 1998 President Bill Clinton signed the Transportation Equity Act for the 21st Century (TEA-21; PL 105-178), a $218 billion infrastructure enhancement program for America's transit systems, highways, and bridges that included several programs for the rail industry. Among them was a $60 million appropriation for fiscal years (FYs) 1999–2003 to fund projects to determine whether transportation systems using magnetic levitation (Maglev) are both possible and safe. Of this amount, $15 million was to be used for research and development of low-speed superconductivity Maglev technology in urban areas. If Maglev was found to be feasible, up to $950 million would be

TABLE 2.1

Freight railroad industry totals by type of railroad, 2001

Railroad	Number	Miles Operated*	Employees	Freight Revenue ($ billions)
Class 1*	8	97,631	162,155	$33.53
Regional	34	17,439	10,302	1.58
Local Linehaul	314	20,881	5,023	0.88
S&T	215	6,682	6,889	0.59
Canadian**	2	728	n/a	n/a
Total	573	143,361	184,369	$36.58

* Excludes trackage rights.
** Includes CN and CP operators that are not part of a Class 1, regional or local carrier.

SOURCE: "The U.S. Freight Railroad Industry: 2001," in "Overview of U.S. Freight Railways," Association of American Railroads, Washington, DC, January 2003 [Online] http://www.aar.org/PubCommon/Documents/AboutTheIndustry/Overview.pdf [accessed April 21, 2003]

FIGURE 2.1

Freight revenue per ton-mile, 1964–2001

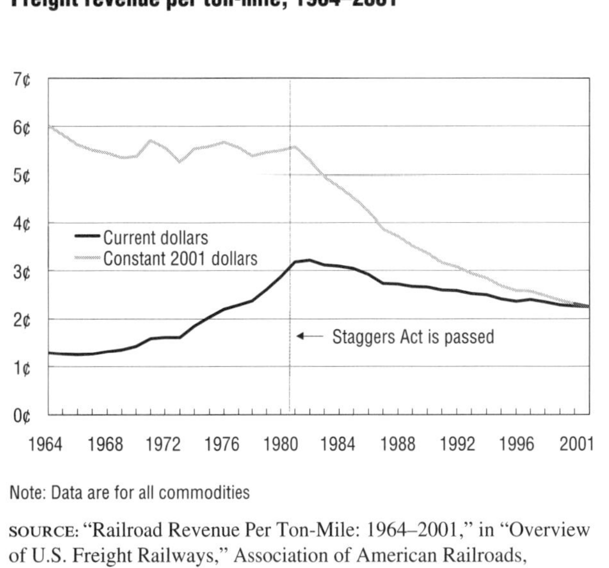

Note: Data are for all commodities

SOURCE: "Railroad Revenue Per Ton-Mile: 1964–2001," in "Overview of U.S. Freight Railways," Association of American Railroads, Washington, DC, January 2003 [Online] http://www.aar.org/PubCommon/Documents/AboutTheIndustry/Overview.pdf [accessed April 21, 2003]

FIGURE 2.2

Revenue ton-miles, 1930–2000

(Billions)

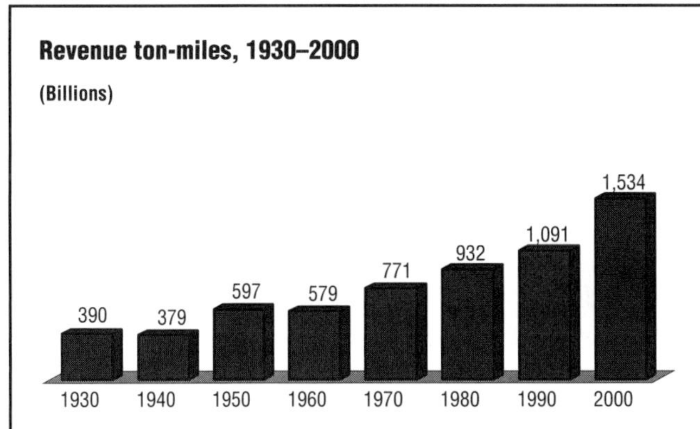

SOURCE: "U.S. Railroad Ton-Miles," in "Class I Railroad Statistics," Association of American Railroads, Washington, DC, January 2003 [Online] http://www.aar.org/PubCommon/Documents/AboutTheIndustry/Statistics.pdf [accessed April 21, 2003]

appropriated in 2003 for development. Other funds were appropriated for corridor planning, technology improvements, light-density rail line pilot projects, and rehabilitation and improvement of the Alaska Railroad.

The U.S. Department of Transportation (DOT) reported on the effects of the investment in transportation infrastructure undertaken since the enactment of the TEA-21 in its *Status of the Nation's Highways, Bridges, and Transit: 2002 Conditions and Performance Report.* With reference to rail transit, the report stated that

> Over the past few years, funding levels have been sufficient to Maintain Performance for bus modes of public transport, but may not have been sufficient for rail modes, as evidenced by a slight decline in the average speed and slight increase in vehicle utilization rates of rail transit services. . . . In 2000, the average rail speed was 24.9 miles per hour—its lowest rate since 1990 (average rail speeds were slightly lower between 1987 and 1989)—and rail vehicle utilization rates (an indicator of potential crowding) reached new highs in 2000, well above the utilization rates that existed in any of the previous years back to 1987.

The report noted that the need for investment in transit infrastructure will continue to grow as the nation's population becomes more urban-centered. TEA-21 expires on September 30, 2003, unless renewed by Congress as urged by the Federal Transit Administration.

TODAY'S FREIGHT SYSTEM

America's freight railroads are classified into five groups (see Table 2.1):

- Class I
- Regional
- Local linehaul
- Switching and terminal (S&T, railroads whose primary responsibility is to facilitate the flow of traffic from one railroad to another)
- Canadian (the Canadian National Railway and Canadian Pacific Railway, because they have extensive operations in the United States)

The eight railroads classified as Class I in 2001 had operating revenue in excess of $266.7 million each: The Burlington Northern and Santa Fe Railway, CSX Transportation, Grand Trunk Western Railroad, Illinois Central Railroad, Kansas City Southern Railway, Norfolk Southern Combined Railroad Subsidiaries, Soo Line Railroad, and Union Pacific Railroad. Only Class

FIGURE 2.3

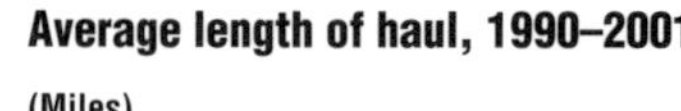

(Miles)

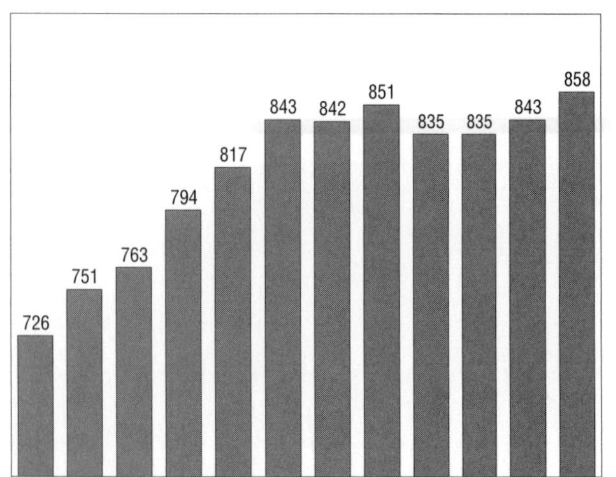

SOURCE: Data for 1990–99 from "Average Length of Haul," in *Railroad Facts 2000 Edition,* Association of American Railroads, Washington, DC, 2000. Data for 2000–01 from "Class I Railroad Statistics," Association of American Railroads, January 10, 2003 [Online] http://www.aar.org/PubCommon/Documents/AboutTheIndustry/Statistics.pdf [accessed April 22, 2003]

TABLE 2.2

Type of freight carried and revenue by commodity, 2001

	Tons originated		Gross revenue	
Commodity group	(000)	% of Total	(millions)	% of Total
Coal	801,013	46.0%	$8,181	22.7%
Chemicals & allied prod.	151,141	8.7	4,548	12.6
Farm products	137,026	7.9	2,741	7.6
Non-metallic minerals	122,739	7.0	945	2.6
Food & kindred products	97,945	5.6	2,579	7.2
Misc. mixed shipments*	91,963	5.3	4,581	12.7
Metals & products	54,257	3.1	1,358	3.8
Stone, clay & glass products	46,485	2.7	1,090	3.0
Lumber & wood products	45,729	2.6	1,519	4.2
Petroleum & coke	40,744	2.3	971	2.7
Waste & scrap materials	37,484	2.2	685	1.9
Motor vehicles & equipment	34,533	2.0	3,471	9.6
Pulp, paper & allied products	33,549	1.9	1,457	4.0
Metallic ores	24,829	1.4	288	0.8
All other commodities	22,531	1.3	1,651	4.6
Total	**1,741,967**	**100.0%**	**36,063**	**100.0%**

* Miscellaneous mixed shipments (STCC 46) is mostly intermodal traffic. Some intermodal traffic is also included in commodity-specific categories.

SOURCE: "Type of Freight Carried for Year 2001," in "Class I Railroad Statistics," Association of American Railroads, Washington, DC, January 2003 [Online] http://www.aar.org/PubCommon/Documents/AboutTheIndustry/Statistics.pdf [accessed April 21, 2003]

FIGURE 2.4

Type of freight carried, 2001

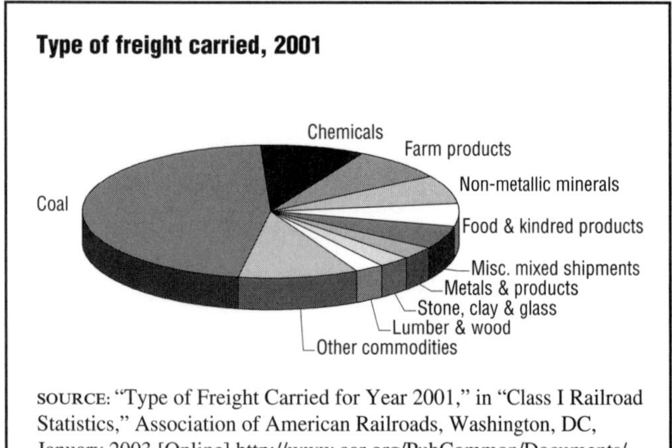

SOURCE: "Type of Freight Carried for Year 2001," in "Class I Railroad Statistics," Association of American Railroads, Washington, DC, January 2003 [Online] http://www.aar.org/PubCommon/Documents/AboutTheIndustry/Statistics.pdf [accessed April 21, 2003]

I railroads are required to report operating and financial data to the Surface Transportation Board. Table 2.1 shows that although the eight Class I railroads made up only 1.4 percent of the total number of railroads in 2001, they accounted for the vast majority of miles operated (68 percent), railroad employees (88 percent), and freight revenue (92 percent).

The Association of American Railroads (AAR), an industry trade organization, pointed out in its "The Impact of the Staggers Rail Act of 1980" report (January 2003) that freight rates fell significantly after the Staggers Rail Act partially deregulated the railroads. The AAR reports that in 2001 the railroads received 29 percent less in revenue per ton-mile (the movement of one ton of freight the distance of one mile) than in 1981 and 60 percent less in inflation-adjusted dollars, saving customers more than $10 billion. (See Figure 2.1.)

American railroads handled 1.091 trillion ton-miles of freight traffic in 1990 and reached a record high of 1.534 trillion ton-miles in 2000. (See Figure 2.2.) The AAR attributes the gain to an increase in the average length of haul.

In 1997 the average length of haul hit an all-time high of about 851 miles. That average declined slightly in 1998 and 1999 then rose again in 2000 (See Figure 2.3). Total tonnage shipped in 2001 was 1.74 million tons. (See Table 2.2.) Coal is the most important commodity shipped by rail, accounting for 46 percent of all railroad tonnage in 2001. (See Figure 2.4.) Chemicals and allied products ranked second, accounting for nearly 9.0 percent, and farm products ranked third at 7.9 percent.

Equipment

As anyone who has ever waited at a railroad crossing knows, a freight train can be very long. Those who amuse themselves by counting the number of cars on the train would have counted an average of 48 cars in 1929. The average number of cars grew steadily until 1985, when

FIGURE 2.5

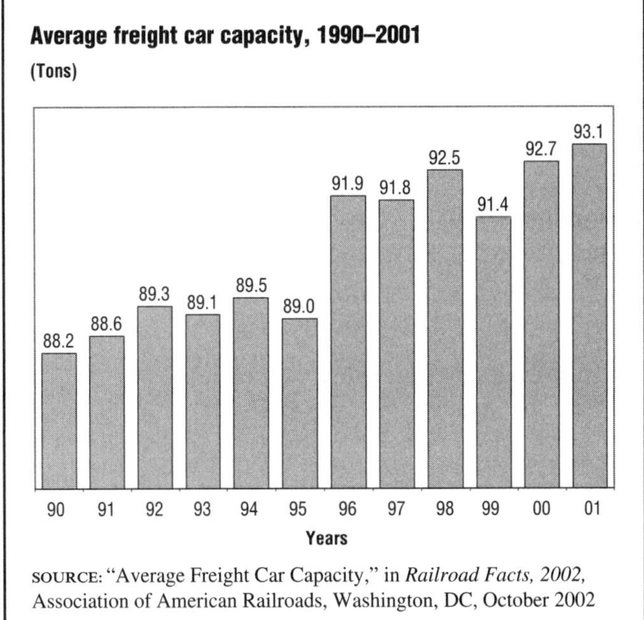

SOURCE: "Average Freight Car Capacity," in *Railroad Facts, 2002,* Association of American Railroads, Washington, DC, October 2002

FIGURE 2.6

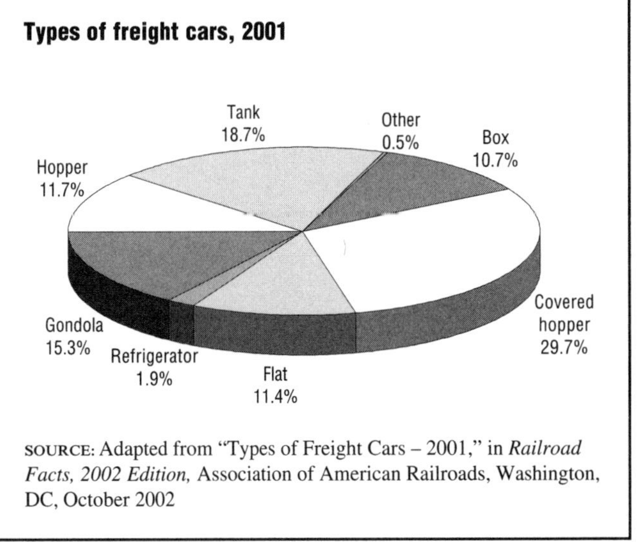

SOURCE: Adapted from "Types of Freight Cars – 2001," in *Railroad Facts, 2002 Edition,* Association of American Railroads, Washington, DC, October 2002

TABLE 2.3

Revenues and expenses, 2000–01

(Dollars in thousands)

	First quarter		
	2001	**2000**	**Change**
Operating revenues			
Freight	$8,254,511	$8,170,465	1.0%
Passenger	15,080	14,988	0.6
Passenger-related	225	177	27.1
All other operating revenues	245,712	223,261	10.1
Joint facility account	3,878	2,886	34.4
Total operating revenues	**$8,519,406**	**$8,411,777**	**1.3%**
Operating expenses			
Depreciation - road	$517,047	$476,868	8.4%
All other way and structures	767,010	836,076	-8.3
Total way and structures	1,284,057	1,312,944	-2.2
Depreciation - equipment	274,855	288,748	-4.8
All other equipment	1,542,262	1,631,137	-5.4
Total equipment	1,817,117	1,919,885	-5.4
Transportation - train and yard	2,957,520	2,833,967	4.4
Transportation - spec. serv. & admin.	418,102	394,724	5.9
General and administrative	846,598	816,896	3.6
Total operating expenses	**$7,323,394**	**$7,278,416**	**0.6%**

SOURCE: Adapted from "Revenues, Expenses and Income: U.S. Class I Railroads," in "Railroad Revenues, Expenses and Income: U.S. Class I Railroads: First Quarter 2001," R&E Series No. 785, Association of American Railroads, Washington, DC, 2001 [Online] www.aar.org [accessed April 22, 2003]

there were about 71 cars; in 1999, there was an average of 69 cars on a freight train. Today's average freight car is longer, larger, and carries almost twice as much freight as the old railroad cars. In 2001 the average car capacity was 93.1 tons. (See Figure 2.5). The average train carried about 2,947 tons of freight compared to an average trainload of only 804 tons in 1929.

According to the AAR, the average cost of a railroad car approaches $50,000 (Source: AAR Personal Communication, May 6, 2003). Figure 2.6 shows the types and percentages of cars in service in 2001. Boxcars carry nearly any kind of freight. Tank cars usually carry liquids. Hoppers, both open and closed, are easy to load and unload and carry coal, ore, cement, salt, flour, potash, and other types of bulk commodities. Gondola cars transport items that can be loaded by crane, magnet, or spout, such as scrap metal, logs, or steel. Refrigerator cars carry perishables. Flatcars carry truck trailers ("piggyback") or containers, two components of intermodal transportation.

Intermodal Freight Transportation

According to the AAR, the fastest growing segment of the U.S. freight railroad industry is intermodal traffic, which involves the movement of trailers or containers by rail and one or more other modes of transportation (usually a truck). Rail intermodal traffic rose 190 percent between 1980 and 2002, from 3.1 million trailers and containers in 1980 to more than 9 million in 2002. Intermodal service is more fuel-efficient and environmentally friendly than truck transport alone.

Operating Expenses

By far the largest category of operating expense for the railroad industry is transportation expenses (mainly train crews and fuel), which accounted for 44 percent of all operating costs in the first quarter of 2000 and 46 percent in the first quarter of 2001. (See Table 2.3.) Other expenses include the maintenance of train equipment, tracks, and rail yards, and general and administrative costs.

TABLE 2.4

Railroad finances, 2000–01

	2000	2001
Financial*		
Freight revenue (billion)	$33.1	$33.5
Operating revenue (billion)	$34.1	$34.6
Operating expense (billion)	$29.0	$29.2
Net income (billion)	$2.5	$2.7
Operating ratio	85.2%	84.3%
Return on average equity	7.95%	7.96%

* A change by one railroad in the 2001 accounting method for sister-company transactions added $0.37 billion in revenue and expenses.

SOURCE: Adapted from "Class I Railroads," in "Class I Railroad Statistics," Association of American Railroads, Washington, DC, January 2003 [Online] http://www.aar.org/PubCommon/Documents/AboutTheIndustry/Statistics.pdf [accessed April 21, 2003]

Financial Report

In 1999 the U.S. freight railroad industry posted one of its strongest financial results since World War II, reflecting the eighth consecutive annual increase in revenues. Class I operating revenue rose 1.1 percent in 1999 to $33.5 billion. Revenue declined slightly to $33.1 billion in 2000 and then rose 1.2 percent to $33.5 billion in 2001. (See Table 2.4.) Operating expenses rose 1.5 percent to $34.6 billion, up from $34.1 billion in 2000.

SHORT-LINE RAILROADS AND REGIONAL CARRIERS

A new segment of the railroad industry, short-line railroads, began to develop in 1980 when the Staggers Rail Act partially deregulated the railroads. With deregulation, large railroad companies could divest themselves of unwanted and unprofitable branch lines. New short-line railroad enterprises began to buy up the available properties.

Of the 573 railroads operating in the United States in 2001, 314 (55 percent) were local linehaul carriers (they operate less than 350 route miles). (See Table 2.1.) Local linehaul carriers accounted for 15 percent of all rail route miles, employed 2.7 percent of all rail workers, and generated 2.4 percent of all rail revenues. There were also 34 regional railroads in the United States. They are similar to but significantly smaller than Class I companies and operate at least 350 route miles. In 2001 regional railroads employed 10,302 people and reported revenues of $1.58 billion, approximately 4 percent of all rail revenues. Switching and terminal railroads operate in large cities and simplify the interchange of rail shipments among the railroads (usually Class I railroads) in their area. Frequently, Class I companies own carriers of this type.

The two top short-line railroad companies are RailAmerica, which in 2003 operated 49 railroads on approximately 12,900 route miles in the United States, Canada, Australia, Chile, and Argentina; and Genesee & Wyoming, Inc., which in 2003 operated more than 8,000 miles of track in the United States, Canada, Mexico, Bolivia, and Argentina. The companies buy old locomotives and maintain the tracks only to the level needed for the speeds at which their trains travel—sometimes a mere 20 miles per hour. Short-line railroads move freight and pursue the business of small shippers.

Supporters of short-line railroads believe the large-railroad mergers should create new opportunities for the short-lines to keep on growing, as Class I railroads continue to divest themselves of unwanted lines. They see the smaller carriers being able to create profitable, more customer-oriented operations because of their lower operating costs. On the other hand, some opponents warn that short-line railroads are a risky business. After all, the large railroad companies did not want these lines because they could not make money from them. They fear the short lines may find it hard to be profitable.

TODAY'S PASSENGER SYSTEM—AMTRAK

Amtrak, created by Congress with the Railroad Passenger Service Act of 1970, is the only significant long-distance passenger railroad left in the United States. By 1990, Amtrak looked very different from the fledgling passenger railroad started in the early 1970s. The system had progressed from trains heated by steam and purchased from 20 different bankrupt railroads to a major transportation company with 24,037 employees. By 2002 Amtrak's 23,000 employees operated a 22,000-mile network serving about 23.5 million intercity rail passengers over 43 routes in 46 states and the District of Columbia. (See Figure 2.7.) To achieve these successes, Amtrak improved service, reduced costs, and implemented an aggressive marketing campaign, pointing out the benefits and pleasures of train travel.

Struggling Since the '90s

Amtrak's financial condition has never been robust—operating expenses have always exceeded revenues. (See Figure 2.8.) In 1992, for the first time in over a decade, Amtrak revenues and passenger miles declined due to the national economic recession of the early 1990s. During those weak economic times, both business and discretionary travel fell, hurting all carriers. In addition, the airline industry responded with reduced fares, further undermining Amtrak ridership. Several important events occurred during 1992, however. After years of negotiations, agreements were reached with nearly all of Amtrak's 14 labor organizations. The year also began the transition to a new generation of train cars and locomotives that were

FIGURE 2.7

Amtrak's route network

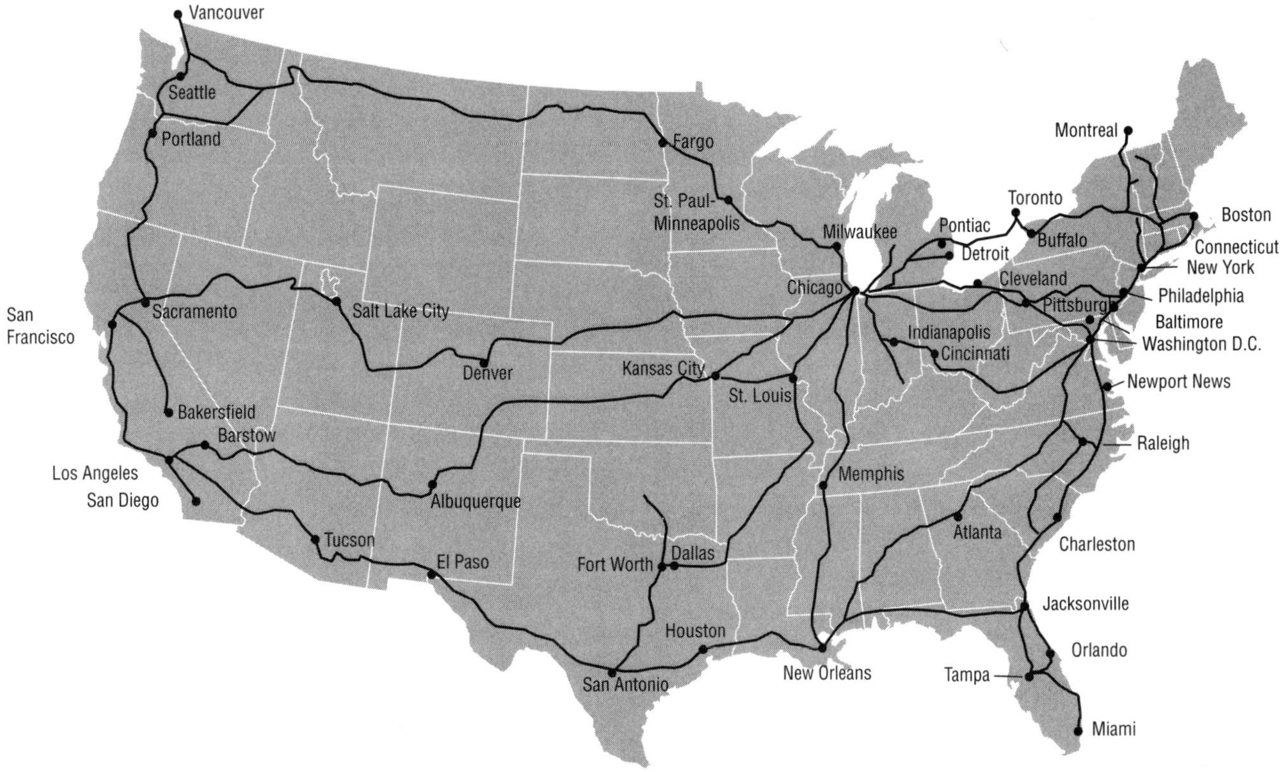

SOURCE: "Figure 1. Amtrak's Route Network" in *Intercity Passenger Rail, Assessing the Benefits of Increased Federal Funding for Amtrak and High-Speed Passenger Rail Systems,* U.S. General Accounting Office, Washington, DC, 1999

FIGURE 2.8

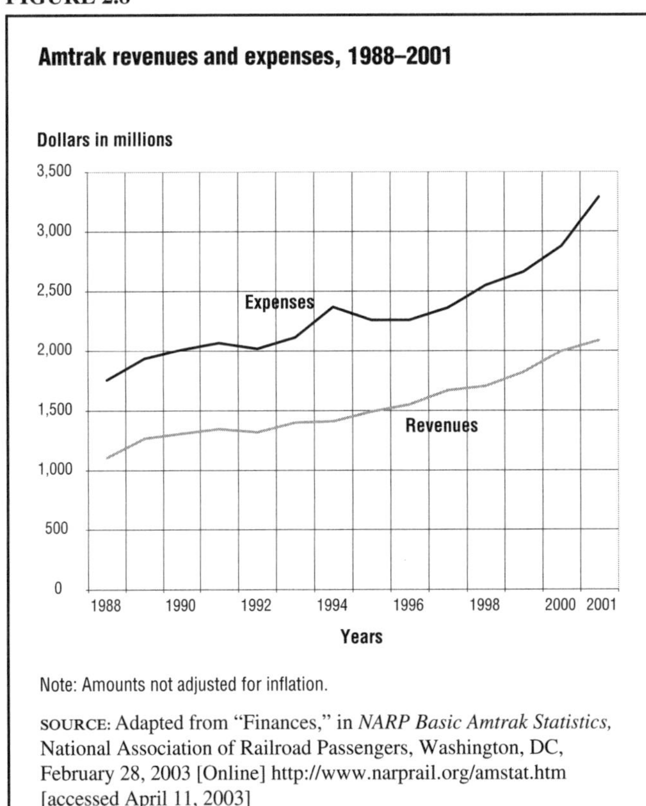

Note: Amounts not adjusted for inflation.

SOURCE: Adapted from "Finances," in *NARP Basic Amtrak Statistics,* National Association of Railroad Passengers, Washington, DC, February 28, 2003 [Online] http://www.narprail.org/amstat.htm [accessed April 11, 2003]

delivered in 1993 and 1994. This allowed Amtrak to retire most of its original fleet of 40-year-old Heritage cars and worn-out locomotives.

Amtrak also took steps intended to ensure its future as a viable carrier. The Department of Transportation and Related Agencies Appropriations Act (PL 102-388), approved in 1993, provided $700.1 million in federal funds to Amtrak for fiscal year 1993 ($331 million for operating purposes and the balance for capital acquisitions and improvements). That infusion of funds, however, was not enough. Like other major national intercity rail services in the world, Amtrak operates at a loss and it has always relied on government subsidies. Subsidies totaled nearly $25 billion over the period 1971–2001, compared with $225 billion for aviation systems and $607 billion for highways, according to a report from the General Accounting Office (GAO) (*Intercity Passenger Rail: Congress Faces Critical Decisions in Developing a National Policy,* General Accounting Office, GAO-02-522T, April 11, 2002). Despite an improving economy, financial difficulties for Amtrak worsened to the point that in 1995 Congress studied Amtrak's future and debated its long-term viability. Two years later it passed the Amtrak Reform and Accountability Act of 1997 (PL 105-103), which prohibited Amtrak from using federal funds for operating expenses after 2002. The act also required that Amtrak prepare and submit to Congress "an action plan for the complete liquidation" of the railroad if the Amtrak Reform Council created by the act should find that Amtrak required federal operating assistance after 2002.

Amtrak's financial condition continued to deteriorate. By 2001 its expenses were $3.2 billion but its revenues were only $2.08 billion. (See Figure 2.8.) That same year, Amtrak estimated that in order to maintain current levels of service, it would need a total of about $16 billion in federal funds for the years 2001 through 2020. Despite a boost in ridership after the September 11, 2001 terrorist attacks, in early 2002 Amtrak announced that in order to survive, it needed $1.2 billion in federal funds that year, double the amount it had previously requested for the year. If services were to be enhanced, Amtrak estimated that it would need an additional $14 billion (GAO-02-522T).

In September 2002 the GAO submitted a report to Congress suggesting that the entire process of funding intercity passenger rail be reexamined (*Intercity Passenger Rail: Potential Financial Issues in the Event That Amtrak Undergoes Liquidation,* GAO-82-871). While this complex matter is under consideration, temporary measures have been implemented. The DOT approved a loan of $100 million to Amtrak in July 2002 and $1.05 billion was appropriated for Amtrak in the 2003 fiscal year budget, together with flexibility on payback of the $100 million loan. Amtrak sought $1.812 billion in its 2004 budget request to Congress.

Amtrak and the federal government face difficult choices. Although Amtrak's business plans have helped to reduce net losses, significant challenges remain. As of fiscal year 2001 only one Amtrak route (the Metroliner service on the Northeast Corridor) earned sufficient revenue to cover operating costs. It seems likely that Amtrak will continue to need federal assistance in terms of operations and capital well into the foreseeable future, assuming that Congress decides to allow Amtrak to continue operating in its present form. Privatization is the alternative suggested by Joseph Vranich, who served on the Amtrak Reform Council, and Edward L. Hudgins ("Help Passenger Rail by Privatizing Amtrak," *Policy Analysis,* no. 419, November 1, 2001). The authors contend that Amtrak will never be self-sufficient and it is time for Amtrak to be liquidated and restructured.

HIGH-SPEED TRAINS

Fast Trains in the United States

In November 2000 Amtrak instituted high-speed rail service between New York City and Boston. The high-speed trains, called Acela, a combination of "acceleration" and "excellence," cut travel time between the two cities to 2 hours and 40 minutes by traveling at 150 miles per hour. The time gains were made possible through a $2 billion program that included electrifying the entire 470-mile stretch between Washington and Boston and straightening curves in the tracks. Moreover, the new trains had "tilt technology," enabling them to glide around corners by gently tilting into the bend. The ride is smooth and relatively quiet.

Acela has business-class and first-class seats with electrical outlets for laptop computer use, audio jacks, cars with conference tables, upgraded food and food service, and beer on tap. All this comes with a price, however. In 2002 the round-trip fare between New York and Boston was $254; New York to Washington was $314. This is still less than the walk-up airplane fare for these routes. Unfortunately, Acela has been plagued by mechanical problems that at times have caused the idling of the trains, resulting in the loss of millions of dollars in ticket revenue.

Nevertheless, the future of passenger rail will likely lie in high-speed trains, which could reduce travel time, relieve congestion in increasingly crowded skies and cities, and win a portion of the air travel market. This has already happened in the busy northeast corridor that links Washington, New York, and Boston. According to the Air Transport Association, an airline industry lobbying group, in the second quarter of 2001, air and rail passenger-miles were split 56 percent and 44 percent, respectively. A year later (post-September 11), those figures had reversed (*The Financial Times*, January 7, 2003).

High-speed trains are most practical for distances between 150 and 500 miles. For shorter distances, automobiles are preferred; for longer distances, airplanes might hold the advantage. Even at medium distances, trains would have to compete with airplanes, and to keep fares low enough to compete, subsidies would probably be needed. High-density corridors, where heavy passenger traffic occurs between several cities, are particularly well suited to high-speed train service. Prior to the introduction of Acela in 2000, the fastest U.S. train in service was Amtrak's Metroliner, which reached a maximum speed of about 125 miles an hour in its run between Washington and New York. Most Amtrak trains are much slower. The high-speed trains that are usually discussed for the American market are futuristic trains driven on magnetic cushions. Know as Maglev, these trains use powerful electromagnets that lift passenger cars about six inches above a guideway and then propel them at speeds up to 300 miles per hour.

Maglev

The 1998 Transportation Equity Act for the 21st Century provided up to $950 million for construction of Maglev trains beginning in 2003 if the technology was found to be feasible. In January 2001 the Federal Railroad

FIGURE 2.9

Designated high-speed rail corridors and Amtrak's northeast corridor

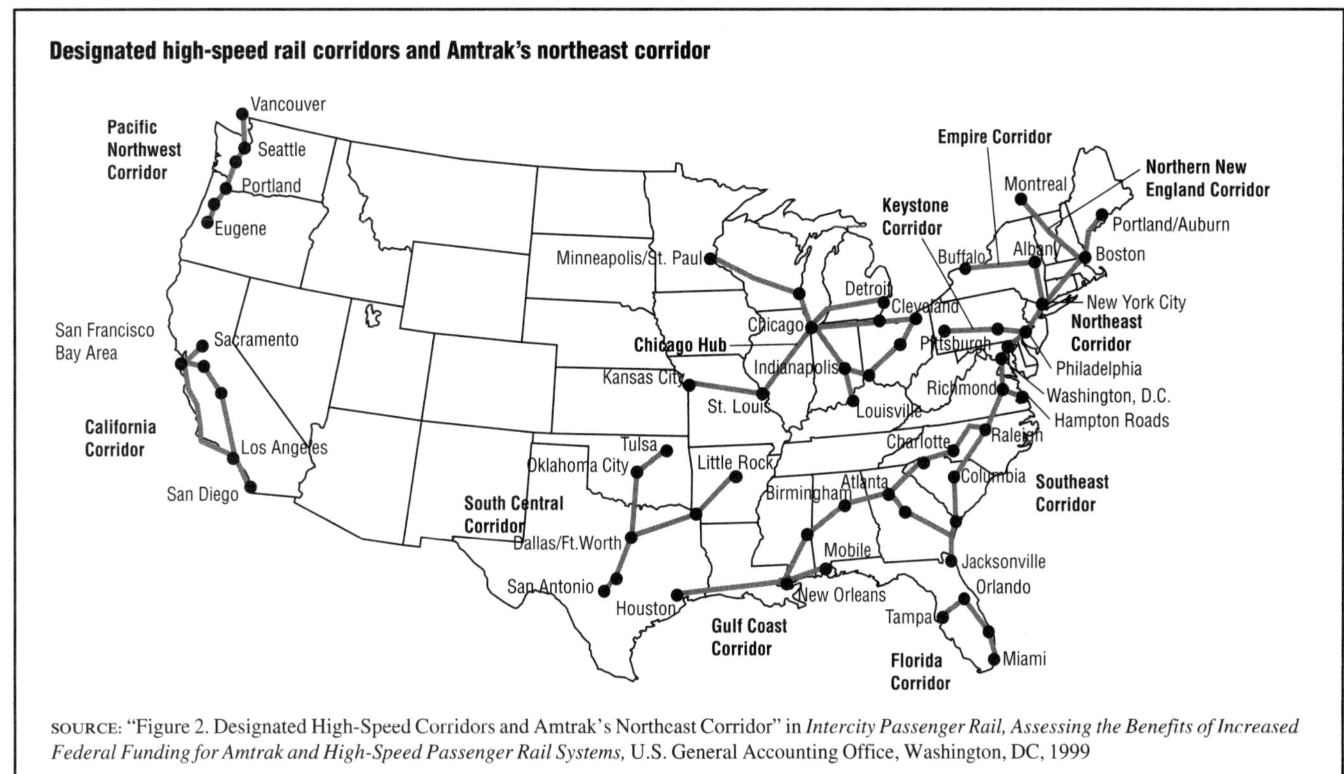

SOURCE: "Figure 2. Designated High-Speed Corridors and Amtrak's Northeast Corridor" in *Intercity Passenger Rail, Assessing the Benefits of Increased Federal Funding for Amtrak and High-Speed Passenger Rail Systems,* U.S. General Accounting Office, Washington, DC, 1999

Administration's Maglev Deployment Program named Pittsburgh and the Baltimore-to-Washington corridor as the two finalists for future development of magnetic levitation technology. Pittsburgh's project would connect the downtown and outlying suburbs to the city's busy airport and the Baltimore project would link downtown Baltimore and Baltimore-Washington International Airport with Washington, D.C. The projects will cost from $3 billion to $5 billion each, with state and private sources picking up the balance not covered by the $950 million federal grant. Critics say such a price for a project that will serve a limited number of people is simply too high. As of mid-2003 the projects were still looking for investors.

Fast Trains in Other Countries

EUROPE. Much of the technology and information about high-speed trains has come from Europe. Rail systems like the French TGV have been in use for many years. The primary reason for the popularity of high-speed rail in Europe is the severe congestion on Europe's roads and in the skies, a situation that America is also facing in its busiest metropolitan hubs. In European cities, short-distance flights are extremely expensive. The train costs less, takes only slightly longer, and carries passengers from downtown to downtown.

The TGV holds the world speed record at over 320 miles per hour and the TGV trains average about 185 miles per hour in regular service. Italy, Sweden, and Germany also use high-speed trains. Each system is being supported to some degree by its government. The 12 European nations have discussed linking their high-speed systems into one network that will span the continent, expanding 1,800 miles of lines into 18,000 and enabling average speeds of over 150 miles an hour. The 250-mile trip from Paris to London, using the Channel Tunnel (Chunnel), has been in operation since the mid-1990s and takes about three hours, often less than that of an air flight if ground time for the traveler is included.

The many nationalities, economic and political differences, diverse electrical systems, various languages, different visual rail signals, and other technical obstacles have complicated the European plan for a rail network. Some progress has been made, however. At the end of 2002 more than 3,200 miles of high-speed track traversed Europe and the figure is expected to increase to nearly 4,000 miles by 2010 (Gunther Ellwanger, "European HS network will double in size by 2010," *International Railway Journal,* vol. 42, October 2002).

JAPAN. Japan has had great success with its bullet-train system, the Shinkansen, which means "new trunk line." The Shinkansen started in 1964 between Tokyo and Osaka and carried 100 million passengers in its first 1,016 days of operation. Today the bullet trains generally run between 6 a.m. and midnight and are always crowded. In 1964 the trains traveled at 125 miles per hour; in 2003 the trains were travelling at nearly 200 miles per hour. Nevertheless, despite its success as a method of transportation,

FIGURE 2.10

Urban rail systems, 1975 and 2000

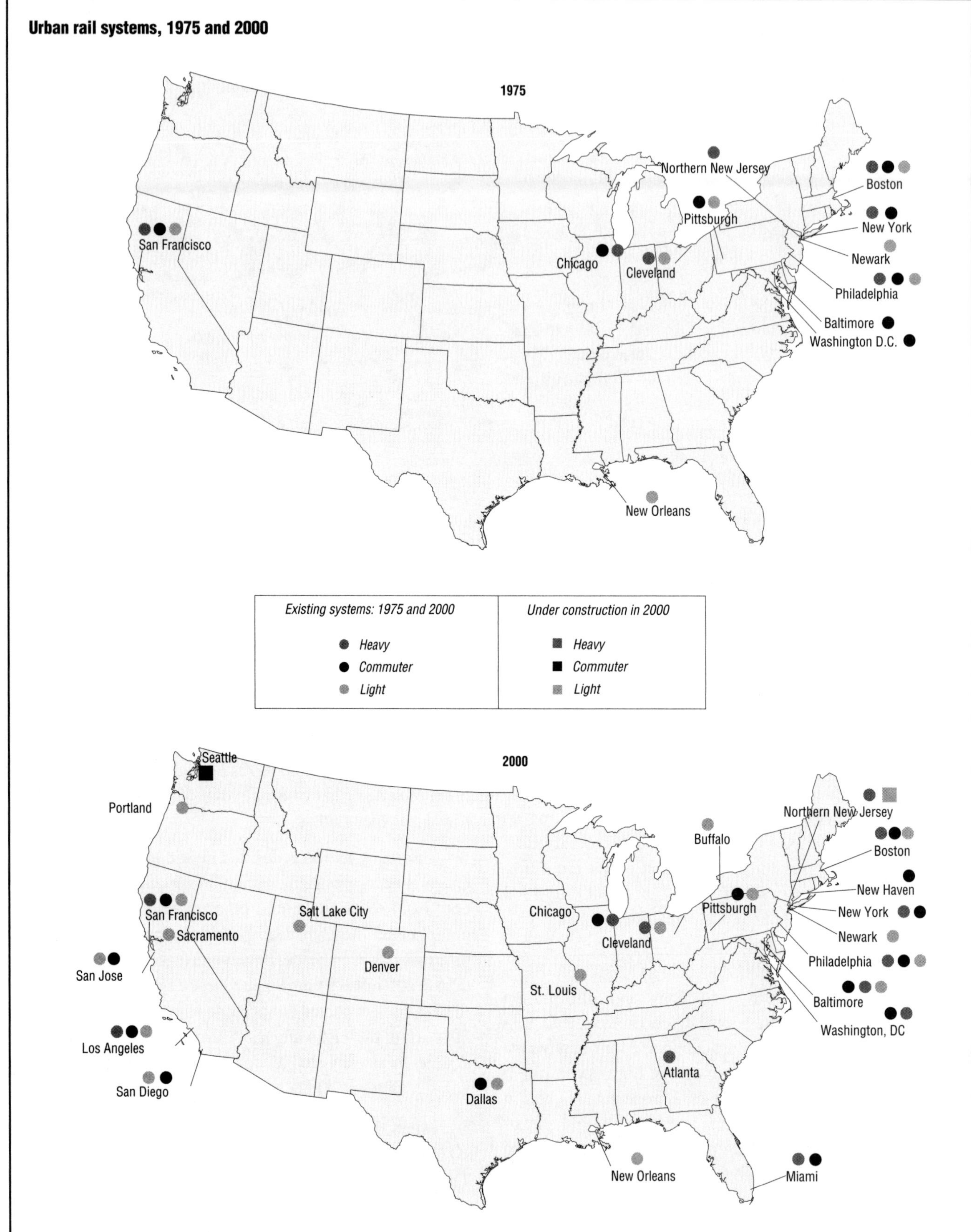

SOURCE: "Figure 2-11: Urban rail systems in the United States: 1975 and 2000," Chapter 2: "Growth, Deregulation, and Intermodalism," in *The Changing Face of Transportation,* U.S. Department of Transportation, Bureau of Transportation Statistics, BTS00-007, Washington DC, 2000

the Japanese rail system has had chronic, severe financial problems. A Japanese Maglev train had a successful trial run along an 11-mile test track in April 2003, but with estimated production costs three times higher than those for Shinkansen bullet trains, the future of Maglevs in Japan is uncertain.

Rail Projects in the United States

In 2003 there were 11 federally designated corridors in the United States that were in various stages of developing high-speed rail projects. (See Figure 2.9.) There were 12 corridors until January 1999, when Florida Governor Jeb Bush halted plans for a high-speed train intended to link the cities of Orlando, Tampa, and Miami. Bush said the project posed too much financial risk for taxpayers. Since then, voters approved an amendment to the Florida constitution in November 2000 that mandates the building of a system that operates at speeds in excess of 120 miles per hour. The new system will link the state's five largest urban areas and construction must begin by November 1, 2003.

According to the General Accounting Office report *Intercity Passenger Rail: Congress Faces Critical Decisions in Developing a National Policy,* the full cost to develop the 11 high-speed rail corridors is not yet known, but Amtrak has estimated that $50 billion to $70 billion would be needed over a 20-year period to fully implement the projects.

Although the current emphasis is on high-speed rail, since 1975 most of the growth in rail transit has been in light rail systems. (See Figure 2.10.) Federal, state, and local investment in transit systems increased 87 percent from 1988 to 1998, from $3.8 billion to $7.1 billion (*The Changing Face of Transportation,* Bureau of Transportation Statistics, Washington, D.C., 2000).

As of June 2002 there were more than 25 areas of the country that were considering some type of new commuter rail services (Van Wilkins, "Commuter Rail Update 2002," *Mass Transit,*, June 2002). This may reflect a growing awareness that increasing the livability of cities depends on decreasing congestion.

People in 10 metropolitan areas who did not have access to high-speed rail were surveyed by Global Strategy Group for the U.S. Conference of Mayors (*Traffic Congestion and Rail Investment,* January 17, 2001). The majority (79 percent) believed that traffic congestion had gotten worse in the last five years; 66 percent believed that if more roads are built, more people will drive, negating the benefits of new construction; and 80 percent favored the building of light rail and commuter rail systems that would link entire regions.

AMERICA'S PASSENGER RAIL SYSTEM POST 9/11

The 108th Congress (2003–04) will consider several pieces of legislation related to railroads, including the National Defense Rail Act (S 104) and the Rail Infrastructure Development and Expansion Act for the 21st Century (RIDE 21, HR 2950). These bills will test Congress's commitment to shoring up and expanding the nation's passenger rail system.

National Defense Rail Act

The National Defense Rail Act (S 104) authorizes:

- an annual federal investment of $4.6 billion for fiscal years 2004 to 2008 to develop a world-class, national passenger rail system
- a one-time $1.3 billion authorization in fiscal year 2004 for security needs and assessments
- an annual authorization of $1.55 billion to develop high-speed corridors outside of the Northeast Corridor
- $270 million annually for the development of short distance corridors between larger urban centers
- $580 million annually to preserve longer distance routes for communities lacking the population densities to justify air service
- $1.31 billion in annual funding for upkeep and expansion of passenger rail tracks in the Northeast Corridor

The bill requires that Amtrak implement several reform measures, including a new accounting and reporting system and a five-year financial plan. It requires that Amtrak apply any revenues from non-passenger-related business to satisfying system-wide liabilities and that Amtrak apply any net revenues from Northeast Corridor operations to capital needs in the Northeast Corridor. The bill was referred to the Senate Commerce Committee in January 2003.

Rail Infrastructure Development and Expansion Act for the 21st Century (RIDE 21)

The Rail Infrastructure Development and Expansion Act for the 21st Century (RIDE 21, HR 2950) calls for $59 billion for high-speed rail infrastructure, corridor development, rehabilitation, and improvement. RIDE 21 was referred to the House Transportation Committee for approval in April 2003.

Reconnecting America

The 108th Congress will for the first time ever simultaneously consider legislation to reauthorize federal programs for Amtrak, for the airline industry, and for highways and transit. Air travel has been especially hard hit by the terrorist attacks on September 11, 2001. Small and medium-size cities, in particular, can expect fewer transportation options as airlines cut back flight schedules and rail projects struggle. Many analysts believe that this presents a golden opportunity for the federal government to make drastic changes in the way it funds and regulates the nation's transportation system. In early 2003 Hank Dittmar, co-director of Reconnecting America, a nonprofit advocacy group for transportation reform, addressed Congress regarding this issue ("Improving the Link Between Air and Rail: A First Step Toward Reconnecting America," February 26, 2003). Testifying that the nation's intercity transportation system was in "crisis," Dittmar stated: "[T]he time is right to begin building an integrated intercity travel system for the 21st Century. Linking our air, rail and bus systems is the place to start."

In a March 15, 2003, gathering in Chicago, Scott Bernstein, another Co-Director of Reconnecting America, described a solution that would combine a high-quality intercity railroad service with a bus network that is capable of reaching the area between rail lines and linking the resulting rail/bus system with the existing air transportation infrastructure. Speaker Anthony Perl, author of *New Departures: Rethinking Rail Passenger Policy in the Twenty-First Century* (University Press of Kentucky, 2002), suggested that instead of continuing to cut services, airlines should "focus on high-volume, long distance routes and partner [with railroads] to build volume at hub airports" ("Experts Call for Focus on High Speed Rail to Create Travelports and Redefine Air Travel," *U.S. Newswire,* March 18, 2003).

CHAPTER 3
HIGHWAYS

The transportation system in the United States provides residents with a very high level of personal mobility. Americans use roads and highways more often than any other mode of transport. U.S. passenger and freight travel is dominated by the automobile, the truck, and the highway system, which accounts for more than 90 percent of all travel and more than 86 percent of the value of all goods and services shipped. The nation's productivity and international competitiveness depend on fast and reliable transportation, making the status of highways and bridges of paramount importance to the vitality of the U.S. economy.

EARLY ROADS

Before the arrival of Europeans, eastern America was crisscrossed by thousands of Indian trails that cut through forests, connecting villages and natural waterways. Colonial settlers were very dependent on these waterways. While they did expand some of the existing overland trails, most of their road-building was aimed at carrying goods to and from rivers and seaports. A few hard-surfaced roads were constructed near the larger cities.

As the colonies grew, Americans found they needed land as well as water routes. By the early 1700s, the government had established a land postal service between the main cities along the eastern seaboard. Foot carriers or horse-mounted riders delivered the mail, but they averaged only four miles an hour and did not work at night. Not surprisingly, a letter mailed in 1729 took four weeks to travel the 600 miles from Boston, Massachusetts, to Williamsburg, Virginia.

By 1750 enough roads were established that a regular stagecoach service was instituted between Philadelphia and New York City, and by the time of the American Revolution (1775–83), a stagecoach could travel from Philadelphia to Paulus Hook Ferry (now Jersey City), New Jersey, in two days. At today's speeds, the trip would take less than two hours.

NEW ROADS FOR A NEW NATION

The first intercity highway constructed in the newly independent United States connected Philadelphia and Lancaster, Pennsylvania. Built in 1793–94 with private funds, it was surfaced with stone and gravel and travelers were required to pay a toll to use it. In fact, almost all road-building during this period was done privately, with builders charging tolls for the use of their roads—a practice that would endure for the next 120 years.

The one major road financed with federal funds during this period was the famous Cumberland Road, or National Pike. Opened in 1818, it ran east-west, connecting Cumberland, Maryland, with Wheeling, West Virginia, and, later, Vandalia, Illinois. The road was heavily traveled by pioneers seeking to settle ever farther west, stimulating trade and linking the Midwest with the central government. Initially a free-access road, the Pike became subject to tolls as successive portions of it came under the control of the various states through which it passed.

Despite the construction of these new highways, most of the roads in the young nation were undeveloped, rutted, winding tracks, subject to damage by rain and snow. The new railroad industry and further development of local waterways and canals diverted attention away from road-building and maintenance. Slow, horse-drawn wagons and coaches, with their small capacity, could hardly compete economically with trains and barges.

A BOOST IN INTEREST

Ironically, the railroads were largely responsible for a renewed interest in road building. Because of their ability to haul large quantities of goods over long distances, the railroads were instrumental in opening up the territories west of the Mississippi River. Towns sprang up all along the western-bound tracks. Many settlers used the vast tracts of land for farming. While the railroads could haul produce from the rural town to the big city, they were of little use to the farmer whose wagon, loaded with agricultural produce, was stuck in a mud-filled, rutted road on the way to the station. Better roads were needed.

During this same period, roads gained an unlikely ally—the bicyclist. Bicycling rapidly became a popular national fad and Americans joined riding clubs for exercise and pleasure. Frustrated with the limited mileage and poor conditions of existing roads, these "wheelmen" banded together to establish "good roads." In fact, what became known as the Good Roads Movement was a major force in the development of our present-day system of roads and highways.

In 1891 the Good Roads Association was formed in Missouri and by 1901 more than 100 cycling organizations were vigorously campaigning for road expansion and improvement. These groups lobbied local and federal governments for financial aid and their spokesmen traveled throughout the country, promoting not only the need for better roads but also the idea that road improvement and new road construction would inevitably require new taxes.

The success of the Mecklenburg Road Law demonstrated the value of government support for roads. In 1879 Mecklenburg County, North Carolina, levied a road tax on all property in the county in an effort to improve the roads—a venture that would aid the many farmers and rural residents of the area. Soon Mecklenburg County had the best roads in the entire state.

While the federal government had been eager to offer incentives for railroad development, it did not immediately see the benefits of providing similar support for road-building. Nonetheless, the need for better roads could not be ignored forever. In response to the combined clamor of farmers and bicyclists, the U.S. Department of Agriculture created the Office of Road Inquiry in 1893. The role of the office was to investigate, educate, and distribute information on road building.

THE CAR IS BORN

It would be hard to overestimate the impact of the car on the development of U.S. society as a whole and on the field of transportation in particular. At the turn of the twentieth century, horses provided the main form of transportation. Then in 1908 Henry Ford introduced the Model T. Although it was not the first automobile, it was the first to be mass-produced and was relatively inexpensive. Automobile ownership was no longer limited to the wealthy, privileged few.

What had been a luxury quickly became a necessity. In 1910, 470,000 cars traveled the primitive American road system; by 1920 the number had swelled to over nine million. The existing roads were woefully inadequate for this amount of traffic.

In 1904 only 9 percent of the 2.4 million miles of road in the United States was surfaced. What little control existed over a road's location, size, and maintenance lay almost entirely in the hands of local authorities. A beautiful wide, paved road might end abruptly at a state line, simply because the neighboring state had different budgeting priorities. Largely owing to the efforts of the Good Roads Movement and other interested parties, however, the groundwork had already been laid for federal involvement and local governments turned to Washington for financial assistance.

FEDERAL INVOLVEMENT AND FEDERAL AID

It was not until 1916 that federal funds for road development became uniformly available to all states. The Federal Aid Road Act of 1916 provided partial funding and technical assistance to the states to build a network of new highways. All building projects had to be approved by the Federal Bureau of Public Roads. The states' responsibilities included project initiation, supplying the balance of the funding, and the administration and maintenance of finished roads within state boundaries. The roles and duties of the states and federal government established in the 1916 act have remained basically the same in all later highway legislation.

In 1944 Congress passed the Federal Aid Highway Act (70 Stat. 838) to create the 40,000-mile National System of Interstate and Defense Highways, although major funding did not become available until the passage of the Federal Aid Highway Act of 1956 (70 Stat. 374). While these two laws would eventually produce one of the most complete interstate highway systems in the world, the original rationale for the development of a highway network was to permit the rapid movement of troops and equipment around the country in case of war. From an original commitment of 50 percent, the federal government eventually provided nearly 90 percent of construction and repair costs for roads in the Federal Aid System.

Revenue for this increased federal spending came from the Highway Trust Fund, which was established by the Highway Revenue Act of 1956 (70 Stat. 374, Title II). Money for the fund came from highway taxes, equipment taxes (such as manufacturers' and car-sales taxes), and gasoline taxes. In 1987 Congress passed the Surface Transportation and Uniform Relocation Assistance Act (PL 100-17), which allocated another $87.9 billion over a five-year period to establish or continue federal highway and mass-transit programs.

In 1991 the Intermodal Surface Transportation Efficiency Act (ISTEA; PL 102-240) became law. The act established the Bureau of Transportation Statistics (BTS),

TABLE 3.1

Functional systems mileage, 2000

Functional system	Rural	% Change 1990-2000	Urban	% Change 1990-2000	Total	% Change 1990-2000	% of Total mileage
Interstate	33,150	-1.4	13,527	16.2	46,677	3.6	1.2
Other freeways/ Expressways	–	–	9,195	18.9	9,195	18.9	0.2
Other principal Arterial	99,013	18.0	53,554	2.6	152,567	12.4	3.9
Minor arterial	137,862	-4.9	90,301	20.3	228,163	4.0	5.8
Major collector	433,927	-0.8	–	–	433,927	-0.8	11.0
Minor collector	272,485	-7.5	–	–	272,485	-7.5	6.9
Collector	–	–	88,796	12.8	88,796	12.8	2.2
Local	2,115,297	-1.0	603,991	15.4	2,719,288	2.6	68.8
Total	**3,091,734**	**-1.3**	**859,364**	**14.8**	**3,951,098**	**2.1**	**100.0**

SOURCE: "Functional Systems Mileage," in *Our Nation's Highways–2000, Selected Facts and Figures,* U.S. Department of Transportation, Federal Highway Administration, Office of Highway Policy Information, Washington, DC, 2000

TABLE 3.2

Annual vehicle-miles of travel, 2000

(Millions)

Functional system	Rural	% Change 1990-2000	Urban	% Change 1990-2000	Total	% Change 1990-2000	% of Total Ttravel
Interstate	270,315	34.5	397,288	41.3	667,603	39.4	24.1
Other freeways/ Expressways	–	–	178,105	38.6	178,105	38.6	6.4
Other principal arterial	249,137	41.9	401,237	18.9	650,374	27.4	23.5
Minor arterial	172,780	10.5	326,855	37.5	499,635	27.5	18.1
Major collector	210,496	9.9	–	–	210,496	9.9	7.6
Minor collector	58,571	16.3	–	–	58,571	16.3	2.1
Collector	–	–	137,008	27.5	137,008	27.5	5.0
Local	128,332	31.0	237,239	23.5	365,571	26.7	13.2
Total	1,089,631	24.9	1,677,732	30.6	2,767,363	28.9	100.0

SOURCE: "Annual Vehicle–Miles of Travel (millions)," in *Our Nation's Highways–2000, Selected Facts and Figures,* U.S. Department of Transportation, Federal Highway Administration, Office of Highway Policy Information, Washington, DC, 2000

which collects data and studies freight activity and passenger travel throughout the country in order to improve the nation's highway system.

In June 1998 President Bill Clinton signed the largest public-works program in U.S. history—the Transportation Equity Act for the 21st Century (TEA-21; PL 105-178). TEA-21 reauthorized ISTEA, which expired in 1997. TEA-21 increased transportation spending in every state. The act committed $218 billion over the six-year period from 1998 to 2003 for transportation programs. The funds were to be spent on highway and bridge projects ($175 billion), mass transit ($41 billion), and safety programs ($2 billion). Significant features of TEA-21 included:

- Assuring a guaranteed level of federal funds for surface transportation through 2003
- Extending the Disadvantaged Business Enterprises program by providing minority and women-owned businesses nationwide with 10 percent participation in highway and transit contracting undertaken with federal funding
- Strengthening safety programs to increase the use of safety belts and encouraging the passage and enforcement of 0.08 percent blood-alcohol-level standards for drunk driving in every state
- Continuing the program structure established for highways and transit under ISTEA and adding new programs
- Investing in new research and development to help maximize the performance of the transportation system and emphasizing the development of Intelligent Transportation Systems to help improve the operation and management of transportation systems and vehicle safety

TABLE 3.3

Bridges by owner, 1996, 1998, and 2000

Owner	Number of bridges 1996	1998	2000
Federal	6,171	7,448	8,221
State	273,198	273,897	277,106
Local	299,078	298,222	298,889
Private	2,378	2,278	2,299
Unknown/unclassified	1,037	1,131	415
Total	581,862	582,976	586,930

SOURCE: "Exhibit 2-4. Bridges by owner, 1996, 1998, and 2000," in *2002 Status of the Nation's Highways, Bridges, and Transit: Conditions and Performance Report to Congress,* U.S. Department of Transportation, Federal Highway Administration, Washington, DC, 2002

TABLE 3.4

Bridges by functional system, 1996, 1998, and 2000

Functional system	Number of bridges 1996	1998	2000
Rural bridge			
Interstate	28,638	27,530	27,797
Other arterial	72,970	73,324	74,796
Collector	144,246	143,140	143,357
Local	211,059	210,670	209,415
Subtotal rural	456,913	454,664	455,365
Urban bridge			
Interstate	26,596	27,480	27,882
Other arterial	59,064	60,901	63,177
Collector	14,848	14,962	15,038
Local	24,441	24,969	25,684
Subtotal urban	124,949	128,312	131,781
Bridge total	581,862	582,976	587,146

SOURCE: "Exhibit 2-10. Bridges by Functional System, 1996, 1998, and 2000," in *2002 Status of the Nation's Highways, Bridges, and Transit: Conditions and Performance Report to Congress,* U.S. Department of Transportation, Federal Highway Administration, Washington, DC, 2002

Present Needs, Proposed Legislation

TEA-21 will expire on September 30, 2003, unless renewed by Congress. Part of the debate over reauthorization centers on the question of whether funds should be used to fix the current system or to build more roads. The U.S. Department of Transportation (DOT) assumes that a reauthorized transportation bill (TEA-3) will be for a six-year period and will build on the base established by ISTEA and TEA-21, with a post-September 11, 2001, emphasis on security. With reference to highways, the DOT assumes that funds will be devoted to intelligent systems such as pavement monitoring and remote sensing.

The National Highway System

ISTEA changed the way the federal government classified roads by introducing the National Highway System, or NHS. (The term "highway," as used here, refers not only to major highways but also to rural roads and urban streets that lead to or connect major roads and that collectively make up the highway network or system.) According to Rodney E. Slater, former head of the Federal Highways Administration, roads in the NHS carry more than 40 percent of all highway traffic, 75 percent of heavy truck traffic, and 90 percent of tourist traffic ("The National Highway System: A Commitment to America's Future," vol. 59, no. 4, spring 1996). The advantage of the NHS is that it identifies high-priority routes and allows states to concentrate on improving them with federal-aid funds.

The National Highway System Designation Act of 1995 (PL 104-59) provided a framework for the NHS consisting of about 160,000 miles of roads—or 4 percent of all public roads. In "The National Highway System" report on the U.S. Department of Transportation's Web site, the five components of the NHS are identified as:

1. The Eisenhower Interstate System of highways, which crisscross the country (totaling 46,617 miles in 2001, according to *The Pocket Guide to Transportation,* Bureau of Transportation Statistics, Washington, D.C., 2003)
2. Other principal arterials in rural and urban areas (114,700 miles in 2001)
3. The Strategic Highway Network (STRAHNET), which links major military installations and defense facilities designated by the Department of Defense
4. Major STRAHNET connectors
5. Intermodal connectors, which provide access between major intermodal facilities (airports, for example) and the other four subsystems that make up the National Highway System

TODAY'S HIGHWAY SYSTEM

The nation's highway network consists of more than 3.9 million miles of roads and streets, with most (78 percent) located in rural areas. (See Table 3.1.) This network accommodated more than 2.7 trillion vehicle miles of travel in 2000, a 29 percent increase over 1990. (See Table 3.2.) Bridges are a critical link in the nation's infrastructure (the basic facilities on which the growth of a community or state depends). In 2000 there were 586,930 bridges on the highway network, a 9 percent increase over 1996. (See Table 3.3.) Nearly 78 percent of these bridges were in rural areas. (See Table 3.4.) Also included in the network are 4,788 miles of toll roads, bridges, and tunnels, according to the Federal Highway Administration's "Total Toll Road, Toll Bridge, and Toll Tunnel Length in the United States in Operation as of January 1, 2001."

Highway Classifications

The more than 3.9 million miles of roads in the United States are functionally classified as arterials, collectors, or

TABLE 3.5

Ownership of roads and streets, 2000

Jurisdiction	Rural mileage	%	Urban mileage	%	Total mileage	%
State	663,755	21.5	111,539	13.0	775,294	19.6
Local	2,311,269	74.7	746,341	86.8	3,057,610	77.4
Federal	116,724	3.8	1,484	0.2	118,208	3.0
Total	3,091,748	100.0	859,364	100.0	3,951,112	100.0

SOURCE: "Ownership of U.S. Roads and Streets," in *Our Nation's Highways–2000, Selected Facts and Figures,* U.S. Department of Transportation, Federal Highway Administration, Office of Highway Policy Information, Washington, DC, 2000

local roads, depending on the type of service they provide. These categories are subdivided into rural and urban areas. (Table 3.1 shows highway mileage by function.)

Arterials, which are further classified as principal or minor, provide connections to other roads. They usually have higher design standards, with wider or multiple lanes. In rural areas, principal arterials are subdivided into interstate and other principal arterials (OPAs). In urban areas, principal arterials are subdivided into interstate, other freeways and expressways (OF&Es), and OPAs.

Collectors are usually two-lane roads that serve shorter trips. They collect and distribute traffic to and from the arterial systems. They often provide the fastest and most convenient way to reach a local destination. In rural areas, collectors are subdivided into major and minor collectors.

Most public road mileage is classified as local. Local roads provide the access between residential and commercial properties and the more heavily traveled highways.

Nationwide, states have jurisdictional responsibility for approximately 20 percent of the total public road and street mileage in the United States. The federal government owns and maintains only those roads on federal Indian reservations and in national parks—about 3 percent. Local governments control the remaining 77 percent. (See Table 3.5.) Of the nation's bridges, in 2000 the states owned and maintained 277,106, and the federal government owned 8,221. There were 298,889 bridges that were locally owned and maintained, while 2,299 were owned by private entities. (See Table 3.3.)

WHO PAYS WHAT?

Financing for roads and highways comes from both the public and private sectors. A variety of revenue sources finance the nation's highways, including direct user fees, such as license fees, tolls, and taxes on both gasoline and vehicles; and indirect fees, such as income taxes and local property assessments. Federal, state, and local

FIGURE 3.1

Highway funding and expenditures by governmental units, 1990 and 2000

(Billions of dollars)

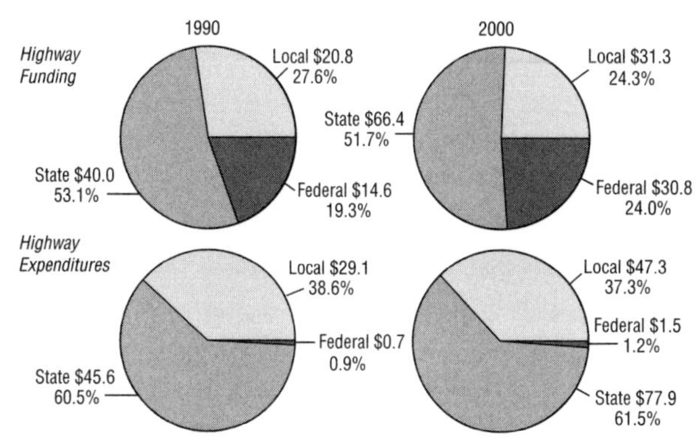

Note: Expenditures by the federal government only reflect direct expenditures by federal agencies, federal transfers are included with expenditures shown for state and local governments.

SOURCE: "Highway Funding and Expenditures by Governmental Unit (Billions of Dollars)," in *Our Nation's Highways–2000, Selected Facts and Figures,* U.S. Department of Transportation, Federal Highway Administration, Office of Highway Policy Information, Washington, DC, 2000

governments funded more than $128.5 billion in 2000, up from $35.3 billion in 1978 and $75.4 billion in 1990. (See Figure 3.1.)

The largest share of money used to finance highways comes from highway-user fees, including tolls, amounting to $75.5 billion over the period 1980 to 2000. (See Figure 3.2.) General funds accounted for $17.1 billion, while other taxes, investment income, and bond proceeds paid for the remaining $30.5 billion.

Highway construction, maintenance, and operating costs have risen dramatically—primarily because of inflation. Figure 3.1 shows the costs of keeping the nation's highways in shape, and Figure 3.2 illustrates the way capital is spent. Most road construction is devoted to improving existing highways and streets, through such projects as resurfacing, widening pavement, and minimizing curves. Most new roads are built by local governments to serve residential users only.

PROBLEMS FACING THE HIGHWAY SYSTEM

Highway Conditions

The Federal Highway Administration (FHWA) reported in *Status of the Nation's Highways, Bridges, and Transit: 2002 Conditions and Performance Report* that the ride quality of 86 percent of the nation's road mileage was rated "Acceptable" for 2000, up from 85.4 percent in 1999. Table 3.6 illustrates the percentage of interstate

FIGURE 3.2

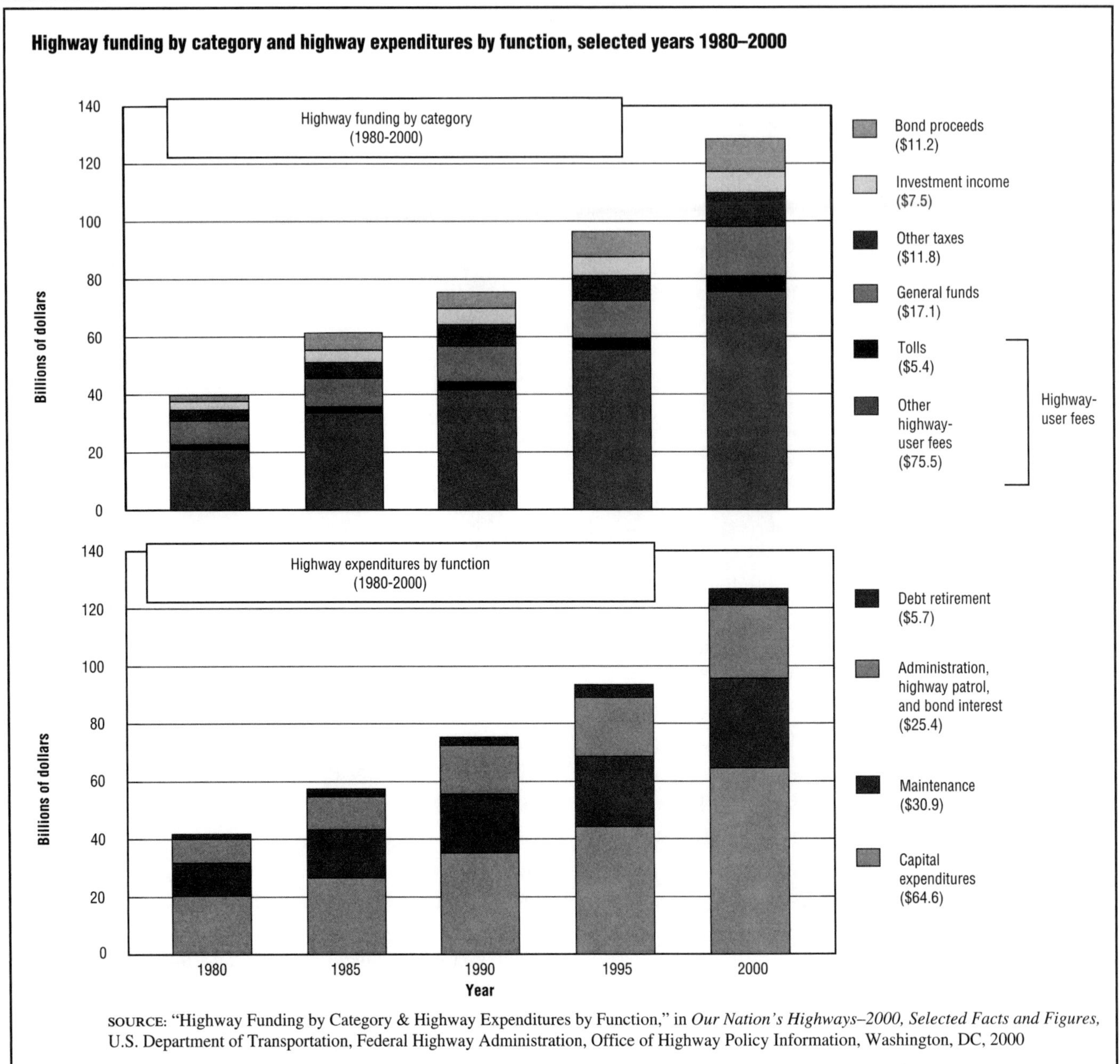

SOURCE: "Highway Funding by Category & Highway Expenditures by Function," in *Our Nation's Highways–2000, Selected Facts and Figures,* U.S. Department of Transportation, Federal Highway Administration, Office of Highway Policy Information, Washington, DC, 2000

highways that need improvement, according to the FHWA. The FHWA found that in 2001 about 41.8 percent of the interstate highways in the nation were in poor or mediocre condition. Approximately 28 percent of the nation's bridges were structurally deficient or functionally obsolete. (See Table 3.7.) Structurally deficient bridges are those that need significant maintenance, rehabilitation, or replacement. Functionally obsolete bridges are those that do not have lane widths, shoulder widths, or vertical clearances adequate for traffic demand.

The FHWA reported that the percentage of roadways in good paved condition has risen since the early 1990s. In 2000, 68.5 percent of rural interstates were in good or very good condition, up from 43 percent in 1994. Likewise, 48.2 percent of urban interstates were in good or very good condition in 2000, up from 33 percent in 1994. (See Figure 3.3.) The number of interstate bridges classified as deficient decreased, as did the number of faulty bridges on arterial and collector roads. Naturally, because of traffic loads and environmental conditions, roadways will continue to deteriorate, requiring ongoing rehabilitation programs to maintain the pavement structure in acceptable condition.

Traffic Congestion

Highway congestion continues to be a major concern for both urban and suburban areas of the nation. Population and business activities are by definition concentrated in metropolitan areas. Since 1980 the vast majority of the

TABLE 3.6

Condition of roadways, 1997–2001

Type of road	1997	1998	1999	2000	2001
Rural					
Interstate miles reported	**31,431**	**30,498**	**32,820**	**32,888**	**32,951**
Poor	3.6	4.1	2.4	2.1	1.9
Mediocre	19.1	16.5	14.0	12.2	11.7
Fair	20.7	17.8	18.1	16.9	15.4
Good	41.0	42.6	44.0	44.8	43.3
Very good	15.7	19.0	21.5	23.9	27.7
Urban					
Interstate miles reported	**12,477**	**12,321**	**13,109**	**13,139**	**13,261**
Poor	9.0	9.4	7.3	6.5	7.4
Mediocre	27.0	25.5	23.1	21.7	20.8
Fair	24.4	21.8	22.6	21.4	20.9
Good	32.9	32.0	34.9	37.1	35.9
Very good	6.7	11.4	12.0	13.3	14.9

Data are for the 50 states and the District of Columbia. Data in percent except where indicated.

SOURCE: Adapted from "Table 1-26: Condition of U.S. roadways by functional system," in *National Transportation Statistics 2002,* BTS02-08, U.S. Department of Transportation, Bureau of Transportation Statistics, Washington, DC, 2002

country's population growth has been in metropolitan areas, particularly in the suburbs. This tremendous growth has greatly exceeded the nation's highway development and has put an even greater demand on the already-strained urban highway system.

Most peak-hour congestion occurs in metropolitan areas with populations over 1 million. A 19-year study by the Texas Transportation Institute (TTI) looked at congestion in 75 urban areas, 40 of which had a population over 1 million (*2002 Urban Mobility Study,* College Station, TX). The TTI estimated a total congestion cost in 2000 of $67.5 billion, the value of 3.6 billion hours of delay and 5.7 billion extra gallons of gas consumed. The Federal Transit Administration (FTA) estimated in 1998 that traffic congestion cost U.S. businesses $40 billion a year in economic losses, a figure that would have been some $20 billion higher had it not been for the increase in mass transit over the preceding decade.

Table 3.8 shows the cost to individuals in terms of hours spent per year delayed in traffic in 1990 (19) and 2000 (27). Congestion grew in areas of every size, as did the average annual cost per person (from $267 to $507 in constant 2000 dollars).

Highway Safety

Highway safety is one of policymakers' top priorities. The federal government's primary involvement in highway safety is through the introduction of up-to-date highway designs and traffic-control devices. Also contributing greatly to improved highway safety are national programs discouraging alcohol and drug abuse, promoting proper use of seatbelts, and supporting various vehicle-safety programs (such as defensive-driving courses).

Highway fatality rates declined significantly in both rural and urban areas in the 1990s. This was partly due to changes in driving habits, such as the increased use of seat belts and the decline in drunk driving. Improvements in highway and vehicle design also contributed to declining highway fatality rates. Interstates are the safest type of highway, with the lowest fatality rates. Highway fatality rates declined on both arterial and collector roads, especially in rural areas, but the rate of decline was slower in urban areas.

The first motor vehicle death in the United States occurred in New York City on September 13, 1899. By 1955 a total of 3 million people had lost their lives in motor vehicle accidents; between 1966 and 1997, there were another 1.5 million fatalities. In 1979, 51,093 people died in motor vehicle accidents. The number dropped to 39,250 in 1992 but generally rose thereafter, reaching 42,387 in 2000, according to the Federal Highway Administration's "Motor Vehicle Fatalities and Travel" report. Considering the statistics per miles traveled, there were 1.5 deaths per 100 million vehicle miles traveled (VMT) in 2000—a 54 percent decrease since 1980. (See Figure 3.4.) The fatality rate (0.85) on the interstate system was a little more than one-half the rate on all highway systems. Because total travel is growing, the number of persons killed and injured may increase, although the rate was lower in the 1990s than in the 1980s. (See Figure 3.5.)

Alcohol-Related Fatalities

In December 2002 the National Highway Traffic Safety Administration (NHTSA) released a report documenting the relationship of alcohol to motor-vehicle fatalities in every state for the period 1982 to 2001 (*State Alcohol Related Fatality Rates Report,* DOT HS 809 528). In 2001 an estimated 41 percent of traffic fatalities (17,448) were alcohol-related, up from 40 percent in the three-year period 1997–99 and equal to the 2000 percentage. (See Figure 3.6.) The NHTSA and interested parties (organizations like Mothers Against Drunk Driving [MADD]) have set a goal to reduce the annual number of fatalities attributable to impaired driving to no more than 11,000 by the year 2005.

As part of the 2000 transportation appropriations bill, Congress required the states to adopt a 0.08 blood-alcohol level (BAC) as the standard for drunken driving by October 2003 or lose 2 percent of their federal highway aid each year from 2004 through 2006. As of April 2003,

TABLE 3.7

Condition of highway bridges, 1990–2001

	1990	1991	1992	1993	1994	1995	1996	1997	1998	1999	2000	2001
Urban bridges	108,770	112,363	115,312	117,488	121,141	122,537	124,950	127,633	128,312	130,339	133,384	133,401
Rural bridges	463,435	461,673	456,885	456,228	455,319	458,598	456,913	455,118	454,664	455,203	456,290	456,284
Total	**572,205**	**574,036**	**572,197**	**573,716**	**576,460**	**581,135**	**581,863**	**582,751**	**582,976**	**585,542**	**589,674**	**589,685**
Urban deficient bridges												
Structurally	16,847	17,032	16,323	15,932	15,692	15,205	15,094	14,846	14,073	12,967	12,695	12,705
Functionally	30,266	30,842	26,243	26,511	27,024	27,487	28,087	26,865	27,588	29,065	29,398	29,383
Total	**47,113**	**47,874**	**42,566**	**42,443**	**42,716**	**42,692**	**43,181**	**41,711**	**41,661**	**42,032**	**42,093**	**42,088**
Rural deficient bridges												
Structurally	121,018	117,502	102,375	96,048	91,991	89,112	86,424	83,629	78,999	75,183	70,881	70,890
Functionally	70,089	66,751	54,150	53,489	52,808	53,463	53,121	50,545	51,912	52,835	52,112	52,056
Total	**191,107**	**184,253**	**156,525**	**149,537**	**144,799**	**142,575**	**139,545**	**134,174**	**130,911**	**128,018**	**122,993**	**122,946**
All deficient bridges												
Structurally	137,865	134,534	118,698	111,980	107,683	104,317	101,518	98,475	93,072	88,150	83,576	83,595
Functionally	100,355	97,593	80,393	80,000	79,832	80,950	81,208	77,410	79,500	81,900	81,510	81,439
Total	**238,220**	**232,127**	**199,091**	**191,980**	**187,515**	**185,267**	**182,726**	**175,885**	**172,572**	**170,050**	**165,086**	**165,034**

Notes:

Structurally deficient bridges are defined as those needing significant maintenance attention, rehabilitation, or replacement.

Functionally deficient bridges are defined as those that do not have the lane widths, shoulder widths, or vertical clearances adequate to serve traffic demand, or the bridge may not be able to handle occasional roadway flooding.

Table includes: Rural-Interstate, principal arterial, minor arterial, major collector, minor collector and local roads; Urban-Interstate, other freeways or expressways, other principal arterial, minor arterial, collector, and local roads.

Data for 1990, 1992, 1997-99, and 2001 are as of December of those years; data for 1991 and 1994-96 are as of June of those years; data for 1993 are as of September of that year; data for 2000 are as of August of that year.

SOURCE: "Table 1-27: Condition of U.S. highway bridges," in *National Transportation Statistics 2002,* BTS02-08, U.S. Department of Transportation, Bureau of Transportation Statistics, Washington, DC, 2002

39 states and the District of Columbia had a 0.08 BAC law, according to MADD.

Preserving the System: Growth and Maintenance of Roads and Bridges

While travel on roads and highways has soared 1,000 percent since the mid-1940s, road mileage (the number of miles of roads) has grown only about 86 percent since the turn of the twentieth century. In 1904 there were about 2.1 million miles of rural public roads in the United States but only one tenth were surfaced. In 1960 there were 3.5 million miles of roads; in 2000 there were just under 4 million miles. (See Table 3.1 and Table 3.5.)

The increase in road travel naturally causes more wear and tear on the nation's road surfaces. Transportation experts agree that the nation's congested and decaying network of roads must be continually rebuilt and that the investment of billions of dollars pays for itself by promoting economic growth and productivity.

To pay for future needs, the Federal Highway Administration (FHWA) has developed two investment-requirement estimates for maintenance and new construction. The Cost to Maintain Conditions and Performance plan calculates the funds needed to keep the system running at its current level; the Cost to Improve Conditions and Performance calculates funds needed to improve the system. The FHWA estimated the average annual cost for the period 2001–2020 to maintain the 2000 level of highway and bridge conditions would be $75.9 billion, while the cost to improve the system was calculated to be $106.9 billion. (See Table 3.9.)

Both scenarios include the costs of repairing pavement and bridges in poor or fair shape, eliminating unsafe conditions, and adding capacity. Under the Cost to Maintain plan, some facilities will improve and some will worsen, but overall, the system will stay as it is. The estimates for Cost to Maintain are the lowest reasonable level of investment. Under the Cost to Improve scenario, all existing deficiencies will be improved. These estimates reflect the highest reasonable level of investment.

INTELLIGENT TRANSPORTATION SYSTEMS

Intelligent transportation systems combine automotive technology, computers, communications, and electronics to ease travel by reducing congestion and improving safety—all while remaining cost-efficient. Some examples of intelligent transportation systems include in-vehicle mapping systems, electronic message signs that give motorists traffic information, and sophisticated traffic-control centers. Under TEA-21, the DOT funded projects to develop systems that "talk and listen" to one another, allowing different technologies to work together.

FIGURE 3.3

Condition of pavement on rural and urban interstate highways, 2000

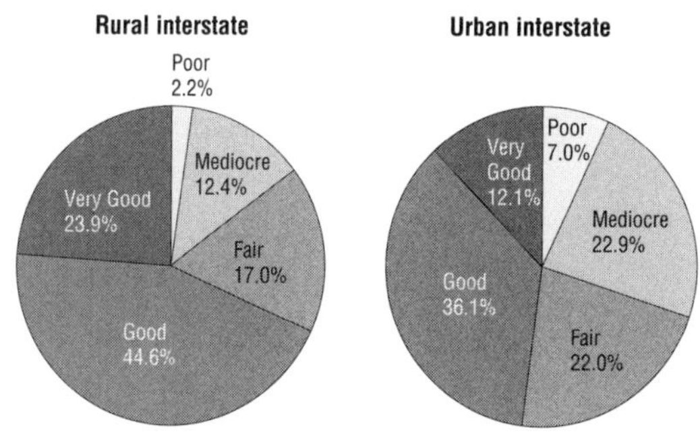

SOURCE: Adapted from "Exhibit 3-18. Rural Areas Pavement Condition by Functional Class, 2000," and "Exhibit 3-20. Urbanized Areas Pavement Condition by Functional Class, 2000," in *2002 Status of the Nation's Highways, Bridges, and Transit: Conditions & Performance Report to Congress,* U.S. Department of Transportation, Federal Highway Administration, Federal Transit Administration, Washington, DC, 2002

TABLE 3.8

Roadway congestion–hours of delay in traffic in seventy-five metropolitan areas, 1990 and 2000

	1990 delay per person	2000 delay per person	Percentage change 1990–2000	Annual growth rate 1990–2000
Very large areas	28	35	24	2.2
Large areas	12	22	88	6.5
Medium areas	6	14	120	8.2
Small areas	4	7	88	6.5
75-area average	**19**	**27**	**40**	**3.4**

Note:
Very large = over 3 million population (e.g., New York-northern NJ)
Large = 1 million to 3 million population (e.g., Atlanta)
Medium = selected areas with 500,000 to 1 million population (e.g., Memphis)
Small = selected areas with under 500,000 population (e.g., Colorado Springs)
The Texas Transportation Institute estimates delay indirectly by using traffic volumes and methodology developed by the Federal Highway Administration for estimating the effects of roadway incidents.

SOURCE: Adapted from "Table 15: Roadway hours of delay and congestion cost per person in 75 metropolitan areas: 1990 and 2000," in *Pocket Guide to Transportation,* U.S. Department of Transportation, Bureau of Transportation Statistics, Washington, DC, January 2003

FIGURE 3.4

Motor vehicle fatality rates per 100 million miles traveled, 1980–2000

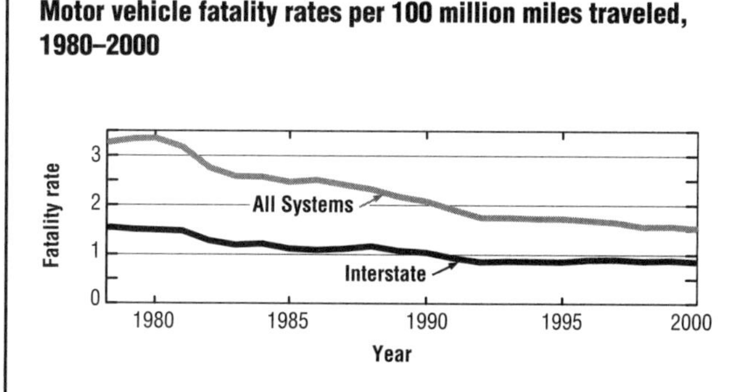

SOURCE: "Fatality Rates," in *Our Nation's Highways–2000, Selected Facts and Figures,* U.S. Department of Transportation, Federal Highway Administration, Office of Highway Policy Information, Washington, DC, 2000

Smart Roads—A Traffic Management System for the Future?

Not surprisingly, during peak traffic periods two-thirds of the cars on interstate highways are moving at less than 35 miles an hour. In cities such as New York, Los Angeles, Chicago, and Houston, many are barely moving at all. Simply put, the National Highway System has reached its capacity. But because of limited space in and around cities, building more roads is not always an option. In seeking a solution to the congestion, government, academic, and industry leaders are experimenting with an automated highway and driver-information system known as Intelligent Vehicle Highway Systems (IVHS) to route cars around bottlenecks, prevent tie-ups, and increase safety.

Other technological advances are also providing some possible solutions to the growing problem of highway congestion. A promising demonstration of some of these high-tech solutions—such as "smart cars," automated highways, and intelligent transportation systems—took place in 1997 at a short test track at Miramar College in California. An onboard computer with radar, video, and laser sensors led smart cars along radar-reflective tape, while other vehicles were guided by a series of magnets embedded every four feet along one lane. If implemented, this technology would allow a smart highway to take control of cars and move them along, bumper-to-bumper, at 70 miles per hour.

Such advanced technology is still years away from being employed on a large scale, but some high-tech methods of traffic management are currently in use across the country. Cameras, telecommunications, and sensors that make commuting easier and safer have been implemented in more than 384 public transit systems nationwide, per FCW Media Group's Web site, www.fcw.com (Megan Lisagor, "Smart Roads Could Help Homeland," September 23, 2002). In Seattle, for example, an experimental system uses electronic surveillance of freeway entrance ramps and synchronization of traffic lights to keep traffic moving steadily.

Commuters in New Jersey, New York, Massachusetts, Pennsylvania, Delaware, Maryland, and West Virginia are now using an electronic toll-taking system called E-Z Pass. The system uses radio waves to identify cars and automatically deducts tolls from prepaid accounts. Motorists do not have to stop but only slow down as they go through

FIGURE 3.5

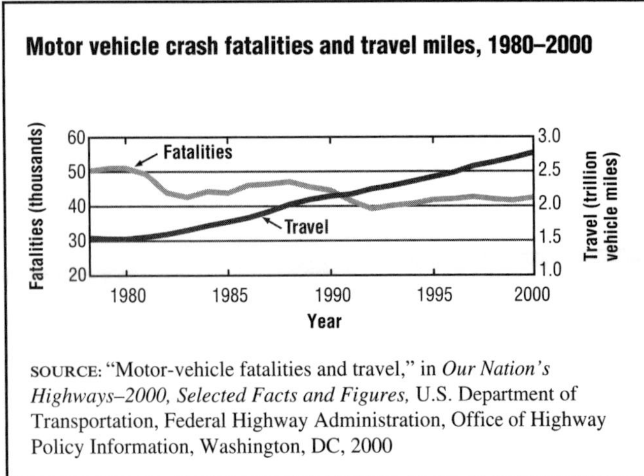

SOURCE: "Motor-vehicle fatalities and travel," in *Our Nation's Highways–2000, Selected Facts and Figures,* U.S. Department of Transportation, Federal Highway Administration, Office of Highway Policy Information, Washington, DC, 2000

FIGURE 3.6

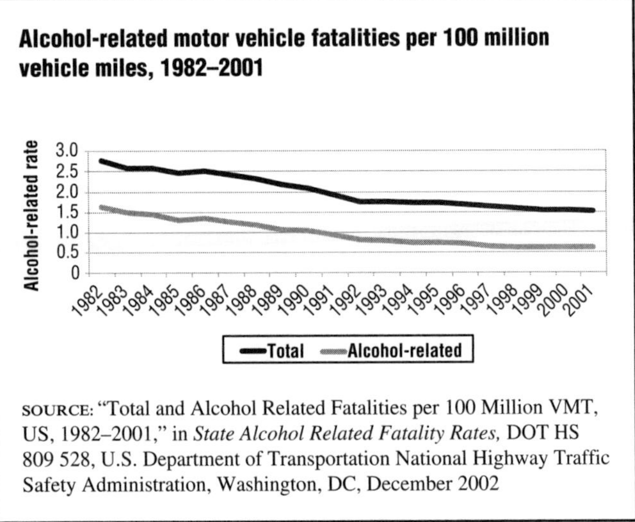

SOURCE: "Total and Alcohol Related Fatalities per 100 Million VMT, US, 1982–2001," in *State Alcohol Related Fatality Rates,* DOT HS 809 528, U.S. Department of Transportation National Highway Traffic Safety Administration, Washington, DC, December 2002

tollbooths. This technology is not without its glitches, though: several systems have malfunctioned, resulting in motorists being sent unwarranted violation citations in the mail.

California has an electronic toll-taking system called FasTrak™. As of 2003 the system was in use on all of the bridges in the San Francisco Bay area and on the Golden Gate Bridge; in southern California on Route 91 express lanes; in the Eastern, Foothill, and San Joaquin Hills toll facilities in Orange County; and on the Interstate 15 express lanes in San Diego County. Also in California, a private company has opened a toll road on a heavily congested section of State Route 91 that runs through Yorba Linda. Commuters can cruise through this former trouble spot at 65 miles an hour for an electronically collected fee that varies depending on the time of day.

High-Occupancy Vehicle Lanes

High-occupancy vehicle (HOV) freeway lanes are a concept introduced in the 1970s to relieve traffic congestion. HOV lanes are restricted during peak traffic hours to vehicles containing two or more passengers. They are intended to encourage carpooling, thereby relieving congestion, cutting gasoline consumption, and reducing air pollution. As of June 2002 there were major HOV projects in development and/or operating in 17 states according to the Federal Highway Administration's "Listing of Proposed Major Freeway/expressway HOV Facilities, June 2002."

Frustrated commuters have been known to violate the two-occupant limit and travel in the HOV lane anyway. Others buy lifelike dummies and place them in the passenger seat in order to make it appear that there are two people in the vehicle. These drivers are subject to large fines if they are caught: in California, violators must pay a minimum fine of $270. Critics feel that HOV lanes are underused and point out that the nine-to-five lifestyle for which they were planned is no longer valid since work hours for many commuters are frequently unpredictable. They complain that HOV lanes are fully used only a few hours a day. They also note that a number of cities have found their HOV programs ineffective and have returned their lanes to normal traffic flow.

Seeking new solutions to congestion, Congress created the Value-Pricing Pilot Program in the Transportation Equity Act for the 21st Century (TEA-21). Value pricing means charging motorists higher prices for traveling during peak periods. The pilot program provided technical and financial support for state and local efforts to plan, implement, manage, evaluate, and report on value-pricing initiatives. San Diego County, California, used TEA-21 funds to turn some of its HOV lanes into HOT (high-occupancy toll) lanes. Under the California plan, a vehicle with only one occupant could travel the HOV lanes for a fee of $50 a month.

When transit authorities convert previously untolled lanes to toll lanes, the issue of equity arises. A spokesperson for the FHWA presented the agency's solution to this problem—Fast and Intertwined Regular Lanes, or FAIR Lanes—at the 10th International Conference on High-Occupancy Vehicle Systems held in Dallas, Texas, in August 2000. FAIR Lanes separate congested freeways into two sections: fast lanes, which are electronically tolled with the toll varying by time of day, and regular lanes. Individuals using the regular lanes receive credits that can be saved and used as toll payments on the fast lanes or for transit fares or other related items.

Traffic congestion will not disappear anytime soon. Congress held a hearing on traffic congestion in May 2002 in connection with the reauthorization of TEA-21 (TEA-3). At the hearing FHWA Administrator Mary Peters noted that "Highway mileage increased only two percent during the period 1980–2000, while highway travel increased 80

TABLE 3.9

Average annual investment required to either maintain or improve highways and bridges, 2001–2020

(Billions of 2000 dollars)

	Average annual investment to maintain			Average annual investment to improve		
	Rural	Urban	Total	Rural	Urban	Total
System preservation						
Highway	9.6	14.0	29.7	13.3	17.2	39.1
Bridge	2.9	2.4	7.3	3.5	3.0	9.4
Total	12.5	16.4	37.1	16.8	20.2	48.5
System expansion	3.3	23.5	32.9	4.9	36.4	49.9
System enhancements	1.5	3.3	6.0	2.1	4.6	8.4
Total	**17.3**	**43.2**	**75.9**	**23.8**	**61.3**	**106.9**

SOURCE: Adapted from "Exhibit 7-2. Average Annual Investment Required to Improve Highways and Bridges, (Billions of 2000 Dollars)," and "Average Annual Investment Required to Maintain Highways and Bridges, (Billions of 2000 Dollars)," in *2002 Status of the Nation's Highways, Bridges, and Transit: Conditions & Performance Report to Congress,* U.S. Department of Transportation, Federal Highway Administration, Federal Transit Administration, Washington, DC, 2002

percent" ("Congestion & Lack of Capacity Threatens [sic] Nation's Roads, According to Highway Officials & User Groups," U.S. House of Representatives press release, May 21, 2002). Witnesses at the hearing proposed a variety of solutions in addition to providing more money for maintaining the existing system:

- add physical capacity to the highway system
- expand the use of Intelligent Transportation Systems
- streamline the environmental review process for highway projects to minimize delays
- set the federal motor fuels tax to rise and fall on an inflation-adjusted index (the federal gas tax was at the same level in 2002 as it was in 1993. That, and increasing fuel efficiency have combined to diminish the flow of tax revenues to the Highway Trust Fund)
- address Highway Trust Fund revenue that has been lost through ethanol subsidies (ethanol is taxed at a lower rate than gasoline)

Highway Safety Post-9/11

Safeguarding hazardous materials transported by trucks is a priority for the DOT, which launched an Intelligent Transportation Systems (ITS) operational test in September 2002 to measure the effectiveness of various safety and security technologies and procedures and to determine the costs and benefits of each. Over a two-year period, 100 trucks will be equipped with technologies such as biometric driver verification (which can automatically identify individuals based on behavioral and physiological characteristics), off-route vehicle alerts, stolen vehicle alerts, cargo tampering alerts, and remote vehicle disabling.

The ITS that was in place in Arlington, Virginia, on September 11, 2001, helped in the emergency evacuation of the area. The traffic management center in Arlington quarantined roads around the Pentagon, reversed High Occupancy Vehicle lane direction on Interstate 395, and regulated traffic signals to help improve traffic flow, according to C. Michael Walton, chairman of the Intelligent Transportation Society of America, who told FCW.com's Megan Lisagor that other technologies currently being used to relieve congestion can also be used for homeland security: smart cards and automatic vehicle location and map databases, for example.

CHAPTER 4

AUTOMOBILES

REVOLUTION ON THE ROAD

It would have taken a vivid imagination to envision the future potential of the first self-propelled land vehicle, created by Nicholas Cugnot in 1769. Powered by a steam engine, it could reach a maximum speed of three miles an hour and travel 15 miles without refueling. Twenty years later, in 1789, Oliver Evans patented a 42,000-pound, steam-powered carriage that could run on land or in the water.

The invention of the internal-combustion engine was a major development in automobile building. Gottlieb Daimler introduced the gasoline-powered car in Germany in 1887. The first successful American model was built by Charles and Frank Duryea in 1892–93, and by the turn of the century, eight thousand "horseless buggies" traveled the rough, unpaved roads of America.

The first factory devoted exclusively to the manufacture of automobiles was built by Ransom E. Olds in Detroit, Michigan, in 1899. Nine years later, Henry Ford's mass-produced, relatively inexpensive Model T transformed the automobile from a luxury into an affordable necessity. The nation's love affair with the car had begun.

The automobile rapidly changed Americans' way of life. Workers no longer had to live near the factories where they worked, so they moved into the newly developing suburbs. Industry did not have to be built on waterways or railroad lines because trucks could go anywhere there were roads. Shopping centers, fast-food restaurants, and motels are all the result of increased mobility brought about by the automobile. Drive-in franchise restaurants meant that a hamburger bought at a fast-food chain in Detroit would taste the same as one purchased at a drive-in from the same chain in Des Moines or Denver. From drive-in movies, popular in the 1950s and 1960s, to drive-through banks and cleaning establishments, Americans became accustomed to spending more time in their cars. For many people today, the car is a second home—a place where they can eat meals, listen to a CD, and talk on the phone as they drive.

As with many inventions, the automobile has been a mixed blessing. Along with giving people a previously unimagined degree of spatial freedom, it has contributed to urban sprawl, air and noise pollution, and a general decline in public transportation; it has also been responsible for millions of injuries and deaths. The car has changed family life dramatically, since the younger generation can now come and go much more freely. For most teenagers, receiving a driver's license is an important rite of passage and a symbol of independence.

THE AUTO INDUSTRY TODAY

The transportation system in the United States provides residents with the highest level of personal mobility—in terms of trips made and miles traveled—in the world. The automobile dominates U.S. passenger travel.

In 1950 there were 23 major U.S. car manufacturers; today, there are only two: General Motors Corporation and the Ford Motor Company. (In 1998, the Chrysler Corporation, the third member of the former "Big Three," merged with Daimler-Benz of Germany and is now known as DaimlerChrysler AG.) However, a number of foreign companies, including Honda, Toyota, Volkswagen, and BMW, now make many of their cars in this country. The economic health of the former "Big Three" has generally reflected that of the nation as a whole. The automobile market was weak during the early 1990s; a recovery started in 1992 and continued partway through 2001. The recession that began in March 2001 and has impacted the auto industry continued into 2003.

TABLE 4.1

U.S. Car and Truck Production Summary, 1991–2001

	Cars	% Total	Trucks	% Total	Total
2001	4,879,119	42.7	6,545,570	57.3	11,424,689
2000	5,542,217	43.4	7,231,497	56.6	12,773,714
1999	5,637,949	43.3	7,387,029	56.7	13,024,978
1998	5,554,373	46.3	6,448,290	53.7	12,002,663
1997	5,933,921	48.9	6,196,654	51.1	12,130,575
1996	6,082,835	51.4	5,747,322	48.6	11,830,157
1995	6,339,967	52.9	5,655,281	47.1	11,995,248
1994	6,601,220	53.9	5,638,068	46.1	12,239,288
1993	5,982,120	55.1	4,873,342	44.9	10.855,462
1992	5,666,891	58.5	4,024,552	41.5	9,691,443
1991	5,439,864	61.9	3,349,976	38.1	8,789,848

SOURCE: "U.S. Car and Truck Production Summary," in *Ward's Automotive Yearbook, 2002,* Ward's Communications, Southfield, MI, 2002, www.WardsAuto.com

FIGURE 4.1

Light vehicle market shares, sales periods 1976–2001

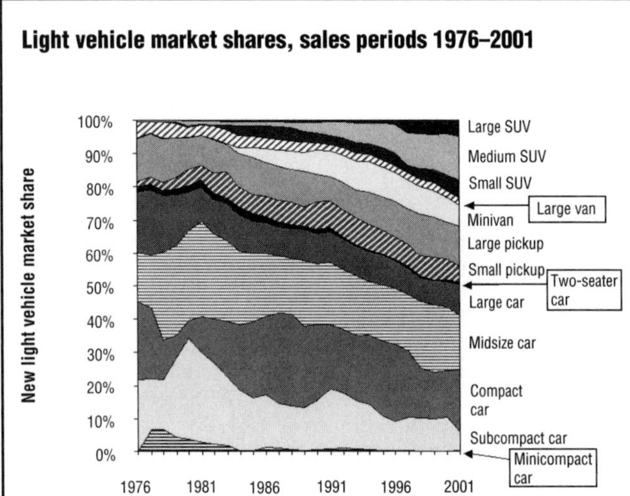

SOURCE: Stacy C. Davis and Susan W. Diegel, "Figure 7.1. Light Vehicle Market Shares, Sales Periods 1976–2001," in *Transportation Energy Data Book: Edition 22,* ORNL-6967, prepared by the Oak Ridge National Laboratory, Oak Ridge, TN, for the U.S. Department of Energy, Center for Transportation Analysis, September 2002 [Online] http://www-cta.ornl.gov/cta/data/Download22.html [accessed May 1, 2003]

TABLE 4.2

Retail sales of new cars and trucks, 1991–2001

(In thousands)

	Cars	Light trucks	Total
1991	8,175	4,123	12,298
1992	8,213	4,629	12,842
1993	8,518	5,351	13,869
1994	8,990	6,033	15,023
1995	8,635	6,053	14,688
1996	8,526	6,519	15,045
1997	8,272	6,797	15,069
1998	8,142	7,299	15,441
1999	8,698	8,073	16,771
2000	8,847	8,387	17,234
2001	8,423	8,598	17,021

SOURCE: Adapted from Stacy C. Davis and Susan W. Diegel, "Table 7.5. New Retail Automobile Sales in the United States, 1970–2001," and "Table 7.6. New Retail Sales of Trucks 10,000 Pounds GVW and Less in the United States, 1970–2001," in *Transportation Energy Data Book: Edition 22,* ORNL-6967, prepared by the Oak Ridge National Laboratory, Oak Ridge, TN, for the U.S. Department of Energy, Center for Transportation Analysis, September 2002 [Online] http://www-ctaornl.gov/cta/data/Download22.html [accessed May 5, 2003]

PRODUCTION AND SALES

The domestic production of automobiles and trucks hit an all-time high in 1999 at 13,024,978 units before dipping slightly in 2000 and falling 10.7 percent in 2001. (See Table 4.1.) The 11,424,689 units produced in 2001 were the lowest total since 1993. Trucks accounted for 57.3 percent of 2001 production (6.5 million); cars for 42.7 percent (4.8 million).

Sport utility vehicles (SUVs), which are classified as light trucks, were the fastest-growing sector of the motor-vehicle market in the 1990s. (See Figure 4.1.) According to the U.S. Department of Energy (*Transportation Energy Data Book: Edition 22,* September 2002), more than 3.8 million small, medium, and large SUVs were sold in 2001—an increase of 312 percent over 1990. For the sales period October 1, 2000, through September 30, 2001, SUVs accounted for 47.9 percent of sales of light trucks and 23.5 percent of all light vehicle sales (including automobiles).

In 1991 retail sales of new vehicles dropped to 12.3 million, the lowest level since 1983 (12.1 million). (See Table 4.2.) Not surprisingly, both were recession years in the United States. To lure consumers back into dealer showrooms, the automobile industry launched massive advertising campaigns and offered rebates and discounts to buyers. In 1993, helped by a recovering economy, U.S. retail sales rose to 13.8 million vehicles. Sales rose again in 1994 to 15.0 million units, dipped slightly to 14.7

TABLE 4.3

Top Cars and Trucks in the United States, 2001

Top 10 U.S. Car Sales

	Units	Percent change from 2000
Honda Accord	414,718	+2.5%
Toyota Camry	390,449	-7.7%
Ford Taurus	353,560	-7.5%
Honda Civic	331,780	+2.2%
Ford Focus	264,414	-7.6%
Toyota Corolla	245,023	+6.5%
Chevrolet Cavalier	233,298	-1.5%
Chevrolet Impala	208,395	+19.5%
Pontiac Grand Am	182,046	-15.3%
Chevrolet Malibu	176,583	-14.8%

Top-selling light trucks in 2001

Pickup		Sport/Utility		Van	
Ford F-series	865,152	Ford Explorer	415,921	Caravan	242,036
Chevy Silverado	701,699	Jeep Grand Cherokee	223,612	Windstar	179,595
Dodge Ram	344,538	Chevrolet Tahoe	202,319	Econoline	159,565
Ford Ranger	272,460	Ford Expedition	178,045	Town & Country	142,902

Top-selling cars by market segment in 2001

	Small	Middle	Large	Luxury
1st	Civic	Camry	LeSabre	DeVille
2nd	Focus	Accord	Intrepid	Avalon
3rd	Corolla	Taurus	Grand Marquis	BMW 3 series

U.S. light vehicle market share (includes each company's total import and domestic volumes)

2001
Total volume:
17,122,368

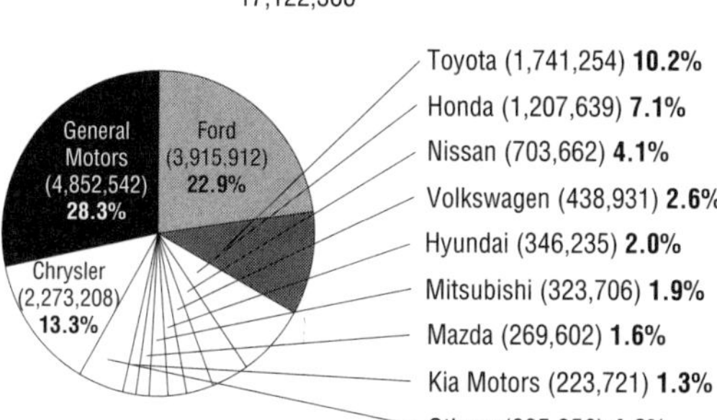

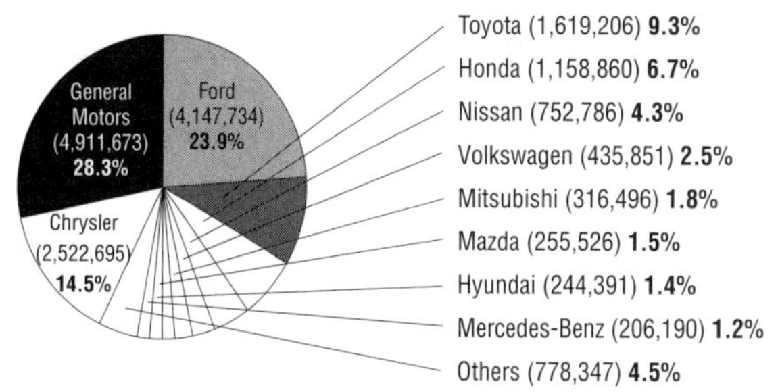

SOURCE: "U.S. Market Leaders–2001" in *Ward's Automotive Yearbook, 2002,* Ward's Communications, Southfield, MI, 2002, www.WardsAuto.com

million in 1995, and then continued climbing through 2001. Although 2001 was a recession year, sales exceeded 17.0 million after generous post-September 11 incentives lured customers back into showrooms. The 2001 sales marked the first time that light trucks (8.6 million) outsold cars (8.4 million).

With early 2003 sales lower than expected, by May of that year U.S. auto dealers faced a stockpile of nearly 4 million unsold cars and trucks, the largest such backlog in U.S. auto history (Jeffrey McCracken, "Vehicle Backlog Hits New Highs: Overproduction Could Bring Buyer Incentives," *Detroit Free Press*, May 14, 2003).

Buyer Preferences

In 2001 the top-selling cars were the Honda Accord, Toyota Camry, and Ford Taurus. Most people who chose pickup trucks purchased the Ford F-series, Chevrolet Silverado, or Dodge Ram. The most popular SUVs were the Ford Explorer, Jeep Grand Cherokee, and Chevrolet Tahoe. In the van category, the Dodge Caravan, Ford Windstar, and Ford Econoline were the top sellers. (See Table 4.3.)

Silver for cars and white for light trucks were the most popular colors among U.S. buyers in 2001. (See Figure 4.2.) According to a survey conducted by DuPont Automotive, silver was also the top choice in Europe, South America, and Asia. DuPont reported that yellow appeared in the top 12 in 2000 and 2001, signaling a "retro trend." Color is important, according to a report in the *Los Angeles Times* (Debra Beyer, "Your True Colors," 2003). Research indicates that 39 percent of American consumers would switch vehicle brands if they could not get their color of choice.

Auto Dealers

The number of new-car dealerships peaked at 51,000 in 1950. By January 2002 there were only 21,800 car dealers, according to the National Automobile Dealers Association

FIGURE 4.2

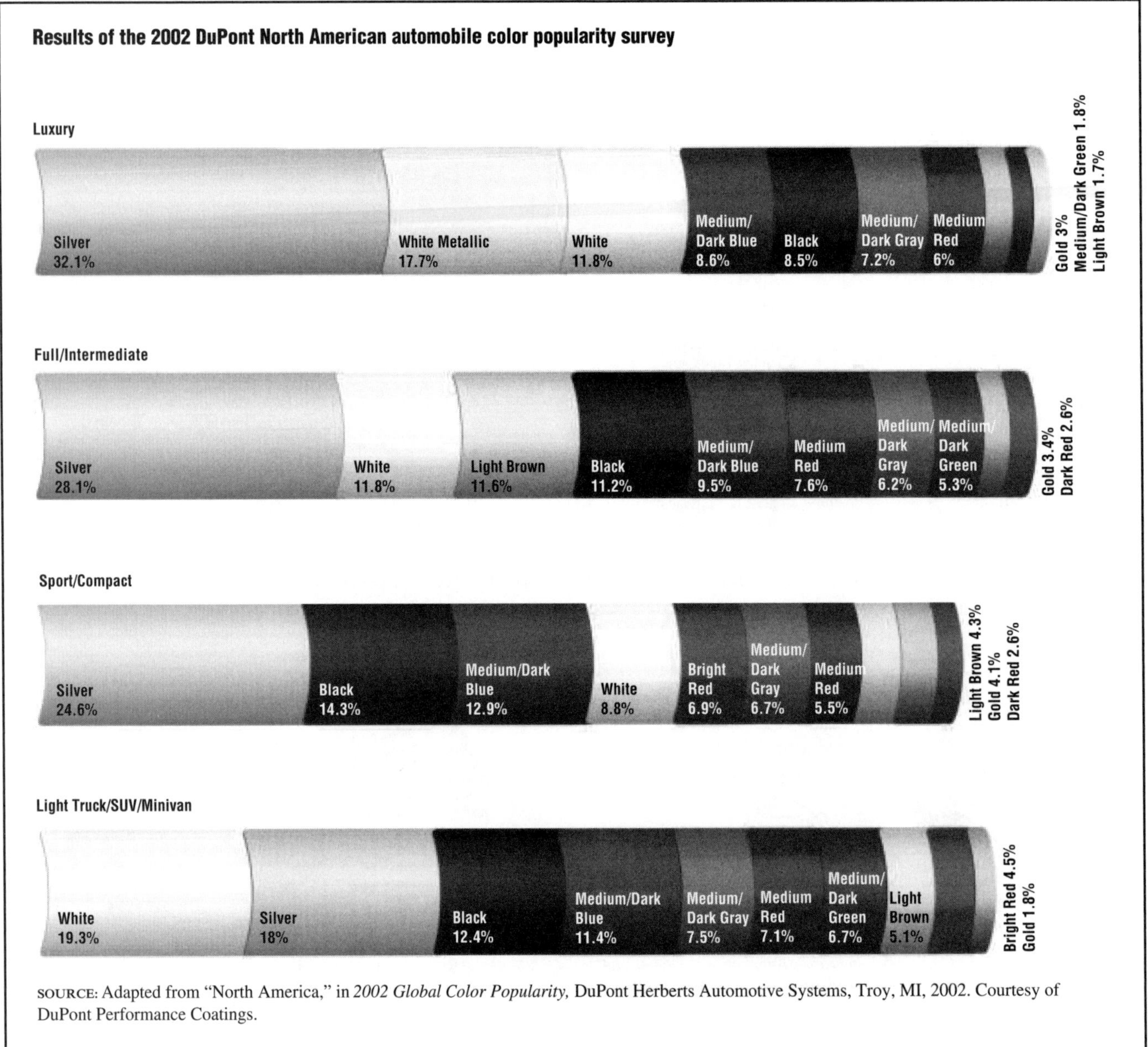

SOURCE: Adapted from "North America," in *2002 Global Color Popularity,* DuPont Herberts Automotive Systems, Troy, MI, 2002. Courtesy of DuPont Performance Coatings.

(NADA; http://www.nada.org). Two factors responsible for this decline are the increasing popularity of new-car leasing and the arrival of the high-volume auto "superstore," which sells not only new cars but also high-quality used and previously leased vehicles. Another change in the industry is the increasing number of car sales on the Internet. With online car sales luring away more and more customers, many dealers have created their own, state-of-the-art Web sites to compete with these Internet sellers.

Although there are fewer new-car dealerships today, more people are employed by dealers than ever before. In 1950 there were fewer than 800,000 employees. By 2001 that number had grown to an all-time high of more than 1.1 million people. Figure 4.3 shows the number of new-car dealership employees in 2001 by state. According to the NADA, in 2001 the average number of employees per dealership was 52.

The NADA reported that in 2001 new-car dealers sold more used cars (20.4 million) than new cars. There are three primary reasons for the growth in the used-car market. First, the average price of a new car approached $26,000, up drastically from the 1987 average of $13,000. A used car cost an average of $13,900 in 2001 (a record high). The second reason is that the increased popularity of leasing has expanded the supply of high-quality used cars. Many of these formerly leased cars are fitted with options that the new buyer cannot afford in a brand new vehicle. Finally, the overall quality of cars has improved to the point that a used car often offers excellent value for the money.

FIGURE 4.3

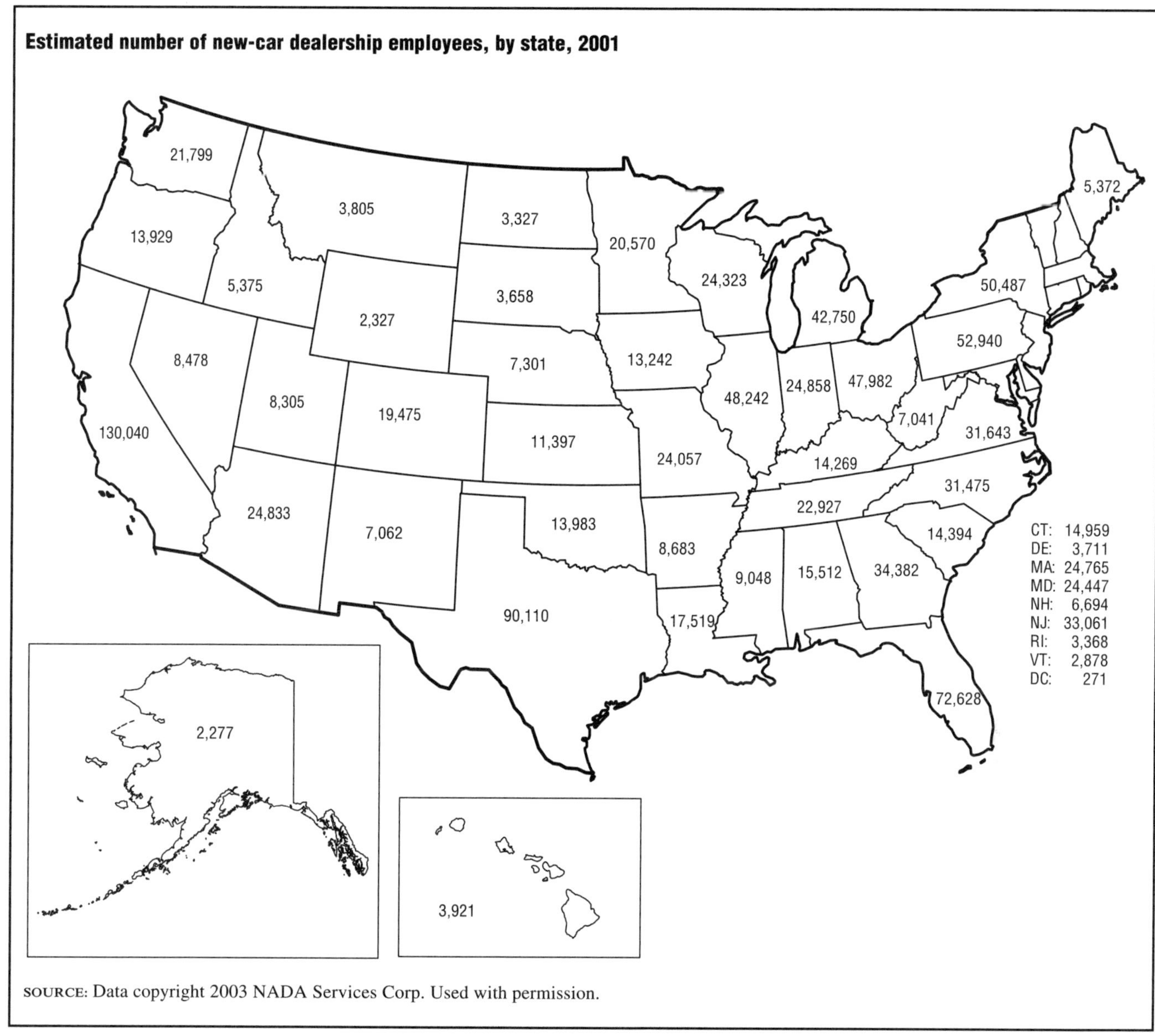

SOURCE: Data copyright 2003 NADA Services Corp. Used with permission.

Many potential new-car customers are choosing to either drive their old cars longer or head for the used-car lot. Industry analysts attribute this tendency to improvements in vehicle quality and engine technology. In 2002 the median age of cars on the road was 8.4 years, the highest since tracking began in the 1970s, according to R.L. Polk & Co. In 1996 the median age for trucks—including pickups, SUVs, and minivans—reached a record 7.5 years, but by 2002 that figure had declined to 6.6 years.

WORLD PRODUCTION

In 2000, 57.4 million cars, trucks, and buses were manufactured worldwide. (See Figure 4.4.) This was up significantly from 1997, when more than 38 million cars and 15 million trucks and buses were produced, then an all-time high. The United States' output in 2000 was 17.7 million units (the U.S. total excludes buses), besting every other nation, including Japan (10.1 million)—at one time the world's leader. Germany placed a distant third, with 5.5 million units. North America, Asia, and Western Europe each manufactured roughly one-third of the world's vehicles in 2000. Worldwide production declined 2.6 percent in 2001.

It is no longer an easy task defining the term "import"—particularly when it comes to cars. In the 1950s U.S. companies, with few exceptions, made cars in the United States and foreign cars were made in other countries. Today major foreign automakers such as Honda, Toyota, and BMW have manufacturing plants in the United States employing American workers and using many American-made parts. In addition, Chrysler, formerly one of the "Big Three" U.S. automakers, is now owned by DaimlerChrysler AG, of Germany, but Chrysler automobiles are still made in the United States. To add to the complexity, Ford Motor

FIGURE 4.4

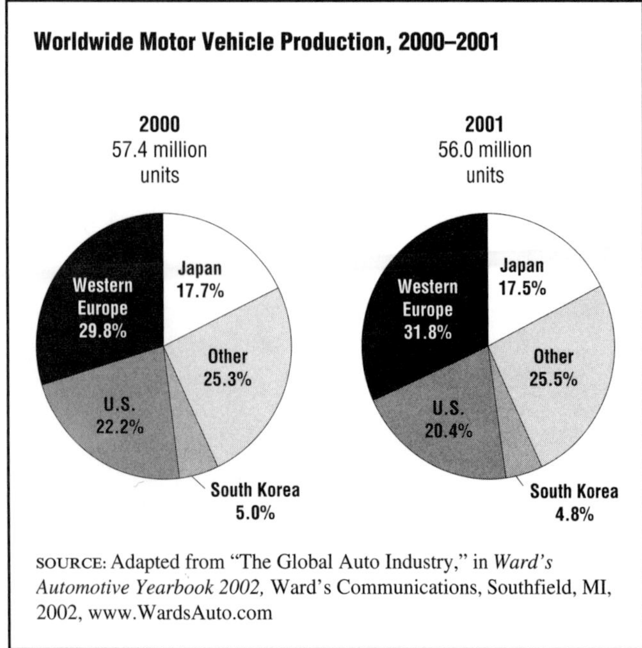

SOURCE: Adapted from "The Global Auto Industry," in *Ward's Automotive Yearbook 2002,* Ward's Communications, Southfield, MI, 2002, www.WardsAuto.com

Company, a U.S. company, has purchased controlling interests in Volvo, Mazda, Jaguar, Aston Martin, and Land Rover. Although owned by Ford, these companies still manufacture vehicles in their home countries. General Motors has also been active in overseas acquisitions, purchasing all or part of Isuzu, Suzuki, Subaru, Fiat, Saab, and Opel.

Japanese Imports Remain Strong

Because many Japanese do not own private vehicles—preferring instead to use public transportation to get to and from work—most vehicles made in Japan are sent abroad, especially to the United States. According to *Ward's Automotive Yearbook 2002*, in 2001 three of the five top-selling personal vehicles in the United States were Japanese: the Honda Accord (first place), Toyota Camry (second place), and Honda Civic (fourth place). (See Table 4.3.) Since 1997 domestic manufacturers have produced more trucks than cars. (See Table 4.1.) On the other hand, Asian and European manufacturers produce far more cars than trucks.

American Car Sales in Japan

While Japanese imports account for a large segment of the U.S. vehicle fleet, relatively few American cars are sold in Japan. U.S. car manufacturers long expressed frustration over their inability to make inroads into Japan's auto market. These manufacturers believed that the Japanese market was essentially closed to them because of the high import duties levied on many American cars and because of the difficulty of establishing dealerships in Japan.

The Japanese countered that the success of German auto manufacturers such as Mercedes-Benz, BMW, and Volkswagen in Japan was clear evidence that the American car manufacturers were not trying hard enough. It was suggested that Detroit was failing in its attempts to design cars specifically for the Japanese market: for instance, placing the steering wheel on the right instead of the left. In addition, none of the American companies built vehicles in Japan using Japanese workers.

In the early 1990s American automakers pressed the U.S. government to negotiate more favorable trade agreements with Japan. Talks between representatives of the Japanese and U.S. governments continued from 1993 to 1995. The two sides failed to work out a bilateral trade agreement and the talks finally broke down. On May 16, 1995, U.S. Trade Representative Mickey Kantor announced proposed tariffs of 100% on 13 models of Japanese cars imported into the United States. Trade talks resumed to avoid these tariffs, which could have hurt trade on both sides. On June 28, 1995, the proposed tariffs were avoided when the U.S. and Japan signed the Automotive Trade Agreement, which made it much easier for American-made cars to be sold in Japan. U.S. carmakers responded by starting to design cars tailored specifically to the needs of the Japanese market.

By 2001, though, American automakers had made few inroads in the Japanese market. According to *The Detroit News*, Japanese sales for General Motors and Ford Motor were down sharply in 2001, with both companies accounting for less than 1 percent of the Japanese market share (Mark Truby, "Detroit Automakers Seek Clues to Japanese Tastes," October 28, 2001). The only American car that piqued Japanese interest that year was the Ford Focus. At the 2001 Tokyo Auto Show, Japanese buyers also seemed enthusiastic about the Chrysler PT Cruiser.

According to *The Detroit News,* a car slightly bigger than a golf cart commands 27 percent of the Japanese market. American cars are perceived in Japan as too big, too expensive, consumers of too much gasoline, and of inferior quality. In the annual automobile quality survey conducted by J.D. Power and Associates, a global marketing information services firm, Toyota and Honda have consistently held the top spots among major auto makers in terms of the fewest problems reported per 100 vehicles. In the 2003 survey, Toyota, BMW, and Honda owners reported 115, 124, and 126 problems per 100 vehicles, respectively, while the top-ranked American manufacturer, General Motors, received 134 complaints. The industry average was 133 (Jamie Butters, "Honda, Toyota Drop in Quality," *Detroit Free Press*, May 7, 2003).

THE COST OF OWNING AND MAINTAINING A VEHICLE

Driving Is Not Cheap

The average new car cost nearly $26,000 in 2001, including optional equipment such as air conditioning and automatic transmission, as well as state taxes and title costs. In addition to the purchase price, the owner of a new car has considerable operating costs, including gas and oil, tires, and maintenance. The cost of driving a car varies by the size of the car. According to the American Automobile Association (AAA) in 2003, a small-car owner who drove 10,000 miles per year paid 11.5 cents in operating costs per mile; a midsize-car owner, 13.0 cents; and a large-car owner, 14.8 cents. Operating costs for the owner of a Chevrolet TrailBlazer LS (a midsize SUV) driven 10,000 miles per year were 13.5 cents per mile; for the owner of a Dodge Caravan SE (a minivan), 12.6 cents. In 2000 and 2001 the cost of gasoline was up over previous years, adding significantly to American drivers' operating costs.

Car-ownership costs include insurance; license, registration, and taxes; depreciation; and finance charges. In 2003 AAA reported annual ownership costs of $4,953 for a small-car owner who drives 10,000 miles; a midsize-car owner, $5,725; a large-car owner, $6,689; a Chevrolet TrailBlazer LS owner, $6,392; and a Dodge Caravan SE owner, $5,659. The total cost for a small car driven 20,000 miles in a year was $7,256; for a midsize car, $8,219; a large car, $9,685; an SUV, $9,297; and a van, $8,628.

AUTO INSURANCE. In 1927 Massachusetts became the first state to require drivers to carry auto liability insurance. Today all states require drivers to show some proof of financial ability to pay in case of an accident and most require drivers to show proof of liability insurance before they can register a vehicle or renew a vehicle registration. Not surprisingly, car insurance is big business. According to the Insurance Information Institute, Americans paid an average of $784 for auto insurance in 2002 and the amount was expected to rise 9 percent in 2003 to $855.

Insuring a car today is an expensive proposition. According to the Insurance Information Institute, in 2000 drivers in Washington, D.C. paid the most for car insurance—an average of $996.39 a year. New Jersey residents had the second-highest rates at $977.07, followed by Massachusetts at $945.61. At the other end of the scale, North Dakota drivers paid the least for car insurance ($477.28), followed by South Dakota, ($478.42), and Iowa ($478.75). The national average for 2000 was $686.71.

THE BEST ACCORDING TO DRIVERS AND EXPERTS

In 2002 *Consumer Reports* magazine selected the Volkswagen Passat as its top choice in the family-sedan and station-wagon categories. The Honda Civic EX was chosen best small car, while the hybrid gas-electric Toyota Prius, with an average fuel economy of 48 mpg, was selected best "green" (environmentally friendly) car. The Subaru Impreza WRX ranked as the most fun to drive. Among SUVs the Toyota Highlander was chosen as best midsize SUV, while the Toyota RAV4 was picked as best small SUV. The Toyota Tundra ranked as best pickup truck and the Honda Odyssey as best minivan. The BMW 530i was selected best car overall.

According to a 2002 survey of new car owners conducted by J.D. Power and Associates, Saturn owners were the happiest with the experience of buying their new vehicles. Saturn is the only car brand that offers nonnegotiable pricing. After Saturn, 8 of the next 10 in the sales satisfaction ranking were luxury vehicles produced by Cadillac, Lincoln, Lexus, Jaguar, and Mercedes-Benz.

GOVERNMENT REGULATION

The Corporate Average Fuel Efficiency (CAFE) Standards

In 1973 the Organization of Petroleum Exporting Countries (OPEC) imposed an oil embargo that provided a painful reminder to America of how dependent it had become on foreign sources of fuel. In 1972, the year before the embargo, the United States, with less than 6 percent of the world's population, consumed 31 percent of the world's oil and depended on foreign sources—particularly the Middle East—for 28 percent of that oil. The transportation sector uses 67 percent of the oil consumed in the United States, according to the U.S. Department of Energy (DOE). As a result of the embargo and in an effort to make the United States less dependent on foreign oil, Congress passed the 1975 Automobile Fuel Efficiency Act (PL 96-426), which set the initial Corporate Average Fuel Efficiency (CAFE) standards.

The CAFE standards required each domestic automaker—at the time, Ford, General Motors, Chrysler (now DaimlerChrysler AG), and American Motors (which merged with Chrysler)—to increase the average fuel economy of its new cars each year, until achieving 27.5 mpg by 1985. Under the CAFE rules, car manufacturers could still sell bigger, less efficient cars, but they also had to sell smaller, more efficient cars to meet the *average* fuel efficiency rates. Automakers that failed to meet each year's CAFE standards were required to pay fines. Those that managed to surpass the standards earned credits that they could use in years when they fell below the CAFE requirements.

Faced with the CAFE standards, American car companies became much more inventive, using innovations such as electronic fuel injection and front-wheel drive to make their cars—particularly their large, luxury models—more fuel-efficient. Ford's prestigious Lincoln Town Car achieved better mileage in 1985 than its tiny Pinto did in 1974.

The Persian Gulf War in the early 1990s reminded the United States of its continuing heavy dependence on

TABLE 4.4

Fuel economy standards for passenger cars and light trucks, model years 1978–2003
(Miles per gallon (mpg))

Model year	Passenger cars	Light tucks[1] Two-wheel drive	Four-wheel drive	Combined[2, 3]
1978	18.0[4]	...	...	...
1979	19.0[4]	17.2	15.8	...
1980	20.0[4]	16.0	14.0	...[5]
1981	22.0	16.7[6]	15.0	...[5]
1982	24.0	18.0	16.0	17.5
1983	26.0	19.5	17.5	19.0
1984	27.0	20.3	18.5	20.0
1985	27.5[4]	19.7[7]	18.9[7]	19.5[7]
1986	26.0[8]	20.5	19.5	20.0
1987	26.0[9]	21.0	19.5	20.5
1988	26.0[9]	21.0	19.5	20.5
1989	26.5[10]	21.5	19.0	20.5
1990	27.5[4]	20.5	19.0	20.0
1991	27.5[4]	20.7	19.1	20.2
1992	27.5[4]	...	...	20.2
1993	27.5[4]	...	...	20.4
1994	27.5[4]	...	...	20.5
1995	27.5[4]	...	...	20.6
1996	27.5[4]	...	...	20.7
1997	27.5[4]	...	...	20.7
1998	27.5[4]	...	...	20.7
1999	27.5[4]	...	...	20.7
2000	27.5[4]	...	...	20.7
2001	27.5[4]	...	...	20.7
2002	27.5[4]	...	...	20.7
2003	27.5[4]	...	...	20.7

[1] Standards for model year 1979 light trucks were established for vehicles with a gross vehicle weight rating (GVWR) of 6,000 pounds or less. Standards for model year 1980 and beyond are for light trucks with a GVWR of 8,500 pounds or less.
[2] For model year 1979, light truck manufacturers could comply separately with standards for four-wheel drive, general utility vehicles and all other light trucks, or combine their trucks into a single fleet and comply with the standard of 17.2 mpg.
[3] For model years 1982-1991, manufacturers could comply with the two-wheel and four-wheel drive standards or could combine all light trucks and comply with the combined standard.
[4] Established by Congress in Title V of the Motor Vehicle Information and Cost Savings Act.
[5] A manufacturer whose light truck fleet was powered exclusively by basic engines which were not also used in passenger cars could meet standards of 14 mpg and 14.5 mpg in model years 1980 and 1981, respectively
[6] Revised in June 1979 from 18.0 mpg.
[7] Revised in October 1984 from 21.6 mpg for two-wheel drive, 19.0 mpg for four-wheel drive, and 21.0 mpg for combined.
[8] Revised in October 1985 from 27.5 mpg.
[9] Revised in October 1986 from 27.5 mpg.
[10] Revised in September 1988 from 27.5 mpg.

SOURCE: "Table 1-1: Fuel Economy Standards for Passenger Cars and Light Trucks Model Years 1978 through 2003 (in MPG)" in *Automotive Fuel Economy Program: Annual Update Calendar Year 2001,* U.S. Department of Transportation, National Highway Traffic Safety Administration, Washington, DC, September 2002

foreign oil. In the war's aftermath, some members of Congress proposed raising the CAFE standards by as much as 40 percent, to 45 mpg for cars and 35 mpg for light trucks. Those in favor of raising the standards claimed that it would save about 2.8 million barrels of oil a day. They also noted that if cars became even more fuel-efficient, emissions of carbon dioxide—a "greenhouse" gas that has been identified as a primary contributor to global warming—would be significantly reduced. Moreover, the nation's millions of drivers would save money in gas costs. Despite some serious debate, these proposals gained little support.

Table 4.4 shows CAFE standards for 1978–2003. Under revised standards passenger cars should have averaged 27.5 miles per gallon by 1990. SUVs, which are classified as light trucks, are subject to a less stringent fuel economy standard of 20.7 mpg.

Table 4.5 shows CAFE averages for 1978–2001. In 2001 domestic and imported automobiles averaged 28.6 mpg and light trucks averaged 20.9 mpg, higher than the standards set by Congress. A May 2003 report (*Light-Duty Automotive Technology and Fuel Economy Trends: 1975 Through 2003*) from the Environmental Protection Agency (EPA) summarized fuel economy and technology usage trends for the years 1978–2003. The report indicated that new vehicle fuel economy peaked in 1987 and 1988 at 22.1 mpg and has been on a general downward trend since then. According to the EPA report, in model year 2003 all light vehicles averaged 20.8 mpg—6 percent lower than in 1988—with cars averaging 24.8 and light trucks, 17.7. Fuel economy declined primarily because of the increase in sales of less fuel-efficient light-duty trucks, especially SUVs.

When the 2003 war in Iraq again focused attention on America's dependence on foreign oil, SUVs came under attack. The Detroit Project, a group led by syndicated columnist Arianna Huffington, spearheaded a campaign that bought television ads claiming that driving an SUV aids terrorists by pouring money into Mid-East treasuries and suggesting that Americans stop buying the vehicles.

Another group, the Evangelical Environment Network, began its "What Would Jesus Drive?" campaign in February 2002 in an attempt to influence consumers to consider buying smaller, more fuel-efficient vehicles. This group's objections to SUVs include the vehicle's contribution to foreign oil dependence, environmental consequences, and human health issues.

ALTERNATIVE FUELS

The use of alternative, non-petroleum-based fuels is becoming an increasingly popular way to reduce vehicle emissions and overall energy use. Table 4.6 shows the variety of fuels that have been considered as alternative fuel sources for vehicles. According to the U.S. Department of Energy (DOE), there were 609,829 alternative-fuel vehicles available for sale in 2001. (See Table 4.7.) The DOE reported that 518,919 alternative-fuel vehicles were actually in use as of September 2002.

Ethanol

To help reduce the nation's dependence on imported oil, Congress in 1991 enacted the National Defense Authorization Act (PL 101-510). The law includes a provision directing federal agencies to purchase gasohol (gasoline containing 10 percent ethanol, a combustible

TABLE 4.5

Domestic and import passenger car and light truck fuel economy averages for model years 1978–2001
(Miles per gallon (mpg))

Model year	Domestic Car	Domestic Light truck	Domestic Combined	Import Car	Import Light truck[1]	Import Combined	All cars	All light trucks	Total fleet	Light truck share of fleet (%)
1978	18.7	...	...	27.3	...	...	19.9	...	...	...
1979	19.3	17.7	19.1	26.1	20.8	25.5	20.3	18.2	20.1	9.8
1980	22.6	16.8	21.4	29.6	24.3	28.6	24.3	18.5	23.1	16.7
1981	24.2	18.3	22.9	31.5	27.4	30.7	25.9	20.1	24.6	17.6
1982	25.0	19.2	23.5	31.1	27.0	30.4	26.6	20.5	25.1	20.1
1983	24.4	19.6	23.0	32.4	27.1	31.5	26.4	20.7	24.8	22.5
1984	25.5	19.3	23.6	32.0	26.7	30.6	26.9	20.6	25.0	24.4
1985	26.3	19.6	24.0	31.5	26.5	30.3	27.6	20.7	25.4	25.9
1986	26.9	20.0	24.4	31.6	25.9	29.8	28.2	21.5	25.9	28.6
1987	27.0	20.5	24.6	31.2	25.2	29.6	28.5	21.7	26.2	28.1
1988	27.4	20.6	24.5	31.5	24.6	30.0	28.8	21.3	26.0	30.1
1989	27.2	20.4	24.2	30.8	23.5	29.2	28.4	21.0	25.6	30.8
1990	26.9	20.3	23.9	29.9	23.0	28.5	28.0	20.8	25.4	30.1
1991	27.3	20.9	24.4	30.1	23.0	28.4	28.4	21.3	25.6	32.2
1992	27.0	20.5	23.8	29.2	22.7	27.9	27.9	20.8	25.1	32.9
1993	27.8	20.7	24.2	29.6	22.8	28.1	28.4	21.0	25.2	37.4
1994	27.5	20.5	23.5	29.7	22.0	27.8	28.3	20.8	24.7	40.2
1995	27.7	20.3	23.8	30.3	21.5	27.9	28.6	20.5	24.9	37.4
1996	28.1	20.5	24.1	29.6	22.2	27.7	28.5	20.8	24.9	39.7
1997	27.8	20.2	23.3	30.1	22.1	27.5	28.7	20.6	24.6	42.1
1998	28.6	20.5	23.3	29.2	22.9	27.6	28.8	21.1	24.7	44.5
1999	28.0	...	...	29.0	...	...	28.3	20.9	24.5	44.0
2000	28.7	...	...	28.3	...	...	28.5	21.3	24.8	44.6
2001	28.8	...	...	28.4	...	...	28.6	20.9	24.4	46.7

[1] Light trucks from foreign-based manufacturers.

NOTE: Beginning with model year 1999, the agency ceased categorizing the total light truck fleet by either domestic or import fleets.

SOURCE: "Table II-6: Domestic and Import Passenger Car and Light Truck Fuel Economy Averages for Model Years 1978-2001 (in MPG)" in *Automotive Fuel Economy Program: Annual Update Calendar Year 2001,* U.S. Department of Transportation, National Highway Traffic Safety Administration, Washington, DC, September 2002

liquid made from corn or other grains) when it is available at prices equal to or lower than those of gasoline. The fuel can be used in flexible-fuel vehicles produced by Ford, General Motors, and DaimlerChrysler. These flex-fuel systems, which can run on ethanol, gasoline, or a mixture of the two, are available on several regular-production models, such as the Ford Taurus, Ford Explorer, Dodge Caravan, Chrysler Voyager, and Chrysler Town and Country.

Federal agencies have taken a number of steps to encourage the use of gasohol. In 1991 Executive Order 12759 required federal agencies that operate more than 300 vehicles to reduce their gas consumption by 10 percent—an obvious incentive to use gasohol. State and federal governments spend about $1 billion each year supporting ethanol production. Despite these measures, however, use of gasohol has increased only slightly. Production of ethanol reached 2.13 billion gallons in 2002, up 20 percent over the previous year but far less than the 20 million barrels of oil that are consumed each day (Marianne Lavelle, "Living Without Oil," *U.S. News & World Report*, February 17, 2003).

A 2001 study by Cornell University scientist David Pimentel showed that it takes more energy to produce ethanol from grain than ethanol produces ("Ethanol Fuel from Corn Faulted as 'Unsustainable Subsidized Food Burning' in Analysis by Cornell Scientist," *Cornell News*, August 6, 2001). Pimental's calculations take into account the diesel and other fuels used to plant, grow, harvest, and process ethanol; the end result is that it costs about $1.74 per gallon to produce ethanol from corn compared with 95 cents to produce a gallon of gasoline.

In 2003 several Midwestern states (where most of the nation's grain is produced) lobbied Congress for a nationwide renewable fuels requirement of 5 billion gallons a year by 2012. California, New York, and Connecticut may soon substitute ethanol for the gasoline additive MTBE (methyl tertiary butyl ether) to conform to standards set by the 1990 Clean Air Act, which require an additive to gasoline used in areas with high levels of air pollution from ozone or carbon monoxide.

The U.S. Department of Energy (DOE) supports the production of ethanol from cellulosic biomass (agricultural waste products), a process that, when perfected, would require less energy than producing ethanol from grain. In December 2002 the DOE announced $75 million in grants for biomass ethanol research and development.

TABLE 4.6

Alternative transportation fuels, 2003

The U.S. Department of Energy classifies the following as "alternative fuels":

Biodiesel

A domestically produced, renewable fuel that can be manufactured from vegetable oils or recycled restaurant greases. Biodiesel is safe, biodegradable, and reduces serious air pollutants such as particulates, carbon monoxide, hydrocarbons, and air toxics (sic). Blends of 20 percent biodiesel with 80 percent petroleum diesel (B20) can be used in unmodified diesel engines, or biodiesel can be used in its pure form (B100), but may require certain engine modifications to avoid maintenance and performance problems.

Electricity

Can be used as a transportation fuel to power battery electric and fuel cell vehicles. When used to power electric vehicles or EVs, electricity is stored in an energy storage device such as a battery. EV batteries have a limited storage capacity and must be replenished by plugging the vehicle into a recharging unit. The electricity for recharging the batteries can come from the existing power grid or from distributed renewable sources such as solar or wind energy. Fuel cell vehicles use electricity produced from an electrochemical reaction that takes place when hydrogen and oxygen are combined in the fuel cell "stack." The production of electricity using fuel cells takes place without combustion or pollution and leaves only two byproducts, heat and water.

Ethanol

An alcohol-based alternative fuel produced by fermenting and distilling starch crops that have been converted into simple sugars. Feedstocks for this fuel include corn, barley and wheat. Ethanol can also be produced from "cellulosic biomass" such as trees and grasses and is called bioethanol. Ethanol is most commonly used to increase octane and improve the emissions quality of gasoline. In some areas of the United States, ethanol is blended with gasoline to form an E10 blend (10 percent ethanol and 90 percent gasoline), but it can be used in higher concentrations such as E85 or E95. Original equipment manufacturers (OEMs) produce flexible-fuel vehicles that can run on E85 or any other combination of ethanol and gasoline.

Hydrogen

Hydrogen gas (H_2) will play an important role in developing sustainable transportation in the United States because it can be produced in virtually unlimited quantities using renewable resources. Pure hydrogen and hydrogen mixed with natural gas (hythane®) have been used effectively to power automobiles. However, hydrogen's real potential rests in its future role as fuel for fuel cell vehicles. Hydrogen and oxygen fed into a proton exchange membrane (PEM) fuel cell "stack" produces enough electricity to power an electric automobile without producing harmful emissions.

Methanol

Also known as wood alcohol, has been used as an alternative fuel in flexible fuel vehicles that run on M85 (a blend of 85 percent methanol and 15 percent gasoline). However, it is not commonly used as such because automakers no longer are supplying methanol-powered vehicles. Methanol can also be used to make MTBE, an oxygenate that is blended with gasoline to enhance octane and create cleaner burning fuel. MTBE production and use has declined due to the fact that it has been found to contaminate ground water. In the future, methanol could possibly be the fuel of choice for providing the hydrogen necessary to power fuel cell vehicles.

Natural Gas (Compressed Natural Gas/Liquefied Natural Gas)

Domestically produced and readily available to end-users through the existing utility infrastructure, natural gas has become increasingly popular as an alternative transportation fuel. Natural gas is also clean burning and produces significantly fewer harmful emissions than reformulated gasoline. Natural gas can either be stored on board a vehicle in tanks as compressed natural gas (CNG) or cryogenically cooled to a liquid state, liquefied natural gas (LNG)

Propane (Liquefied Petroleum Gas)

A popular alternative fuel choice because an infrastructure of pipelines, processing facilities, and storage already exists for its efficient distribution. Besides being readily available to the general public, LPG produces fewer vehicle emissions than reformulated gasoline. Propane is produced as a by-product of natural gas processing and crude oil refining.

P-Series Fuel

A unique blend of natural gas liquids (pentanes plus), ethanol, and a biomass-derived cosolvent (MTHF). P-Series is made primarily from renewable resources and provides significant emissions benefits over reformulated gasoline.

Solar Energy

Solar energy technologies use sunlight to produce heat and electricity. Electricity produced by solar energy through photovoltaic technologies can be used in conventional electric vehicles. Using solar energy directly to power vehicles has been investigated primarily for completion and demonstration vehicles. Solar vehicles are not available to the general public and are not currently being considered by OEMs for production. However, solar vehicles have been developed and used in several competitions including the American Solar Challenge and the World Solar Challenge.

SOURCE: Adapted from "Alternative Fuels," U.S. Department of Energy, Alternative Fuels Data Center [Online] http://www.afdc.doe.gov/altfuels.html [accessed April 10, 2003]

Natural Gas and Propane

New Environmental Protection Agency emissions regulations that take effect in 2007 will require dramatically lower emissions from both conventionally fueled and alternatively fueled vehicles. Natural gas is one of the most readily available of the alternative fuels. Natural gas requires less refinery work than gas and is distributed around the continental United States; it also burns more cleanly than gasoline.

Chrysler began producing a natural gas version of its Dodge Ram pickup truck in 1997. Ford now produces several natural gas vehicles, including a Crown Victoria and the Ford F-150 light truck. Chevrolet offers a natural gas version of the Chevy Cavalier. These vehicles are designed as "bi-fuel users," which means that they can switch from natural gas to gasoline when needed. Honda introduced the first car powered solely by natural gas, the 2003 Honda Civic GX, described by *Test & Measurement World* (March 2003) as one of the "top 10 most technically sophisticated cars for 2003." The suggested starting price was $20,510.

Existing automobiles and trucks can also be converted to natural gas systems, at a cost of $3,000 to $5,000. A number of cities—including New York, Las Vegas, Long Beach, and San Francisco—have taxicab fleets that use natural gas, and some large cities have begun using natural gas in their bus fleets.

Drivers who choose to use natural gas as fuel for their vehicles face a dilemma: where to find a pump? Experts believe that any fueling system needs a large customer base and no one will buy cars that run on alternative fuel until

TABLE 4.7

Alternative fueled vehicles made available by both the original equipment manufacturers and aftermarket vehicle conversion facilites, 2001

Fuel type	Light duty total	Medium duty total	Heavy duty total	Grand total
Compressed Natural Gas (CNG)	4,711	4,396	2,014	**11,121**
Dedicated	1,974	1,518	2,014	**5,506**
Nondedicated	2,737	2,878	0	**5,615**
Electric (EVC) [1]	26,321	36	197	**26,554**
Nonhybrid	6,478	35	169	**6,682**
Hybrid	19,843	1	28	**19,872**
Ethanol, 85 Percent (E85) [2]	581,774	0	0	**581,774**
Dedicated	0	0	0	**0**
Nondedicated	581,774	0	0	**581,774**
Liquified Natural Gas (LNG)	0	0	393	**393**
Dedicated	0	0	393	**393**
Nondedicated	0	0	0	**0**
Liquified Petroleum Gas (LPG)	255	2,349	597	**3,201**
Dedicated	55	13	565	**633**
Nondedicated	200	2,336	32	**2,568**
Total	**613,061**	**6,781**	**3,201**	**623,043**
Dedicated and Nonhybrid	**8,507**	**1,566**	**3,141**	**13,214**
Nondedicated and Hybrid	**604,554**	**5,215**	**60**	**609,829**

[1] Includes gasoline/electric hybrid vehicles which are outside EPACT's definition of alternative fueled vehicle.

[2] The remaining portion of 85-percent ethanol is gasoline.

Notes:

Dedicated vehicles and nonhybrid electric vehicles are designed to operate exclusively on one alternative fuel.

Nondedicated vehicles and hybrid electric vehicles are configured to operated on more than one fuel, usually an alternative fuel and gasoline or diesel fuel.

Light Duty includes vehicles less than or equal to 8,500 GVWR.

Medium Duty includes vehicles 8,501 to 26,000 GVWR.

Heavy Duty includes vehicles 26,001 and over GVWR.

SOURCE: "Table 14: Summary of Onroad AFVs Made Available by Weight Class, Fuel Type and Vehicle Configuration Type, 2001" U.S. Department of Energy, Energy Information Administration [Online] http://www.eia.doe.gov/cneaf/alternate/page/datatables/atf114-20.html [accessed April 10, 2003]. Primary source: Energy Information Administration, Form EIA-886, "Annual Survey of Alternative Fuel Vehicles Suppliers and Users"

a fueling system has been set up. In 2000 Honda found a solution: The company bought a 20 percent stake in a Canadian producer of natural gas vehicle refueling units. The units allow drivers to fill their tanks from their home natural gas lines.

Gradually, compressed natural gas (CNG) fueling stations have been built across the county. According to the DOE, in 2002 there were about 110,000 CNG vehicles on the road and 1,280 natural gas refueling stations to serve them. In some cases, local natural gas companies build the CNG stations; large companies that have their own fleet of natural gas vehicles build others.

Propane, also called liquefied petroleum gas (LPG), has been the most successful alternative fuel as of mid-2003. According to the DOE, in 2002 there were 269,000 propane vehicles on the road and 3,353 propane refueling stations.

Hydrogen

For decades, advocates of hydrogen have promoted it as the fuel of the future abundant, clean, and cheap. A major obstacle to the development of hydrogen-powered cars has been solving the problems of fuel supply and distribution, though private companies (automakers, oil companies, and others) are working on solutions.

President George W. Bush has designated hydrogen development as a top energy priority. His 2003 Hydrogen Fuel Initiative proposed $1.2 billion for research over five years (including $181.7 million in the fiscal year 2004 budget request) to overcome hurdles standing in the way of a hydrogen-based economy. California Institute of Technology (Caltech) researchers warned in the June 2003 issue of *Science* that hydrogen leakage could damage the ozone layer, which protects the Earth from the ultraviolet rays that cause cancer. John Eiler, one of the authors of the Caltech study, acknowledged that further research might resolve the concerns raised in the report ("Hydrogen Economy Might Impact Earth's Stratosphere, Study Shows," Caltech Media Relations news release, June 12, 2003).

ALTERNATIVE VEHICLES

Electric Vehicles

In the early days of the automobile, electric cars outnumbered internal-combustion vehicles. With the introduction of technology for producing low-cost gasoline, however, electric vehicles fell out of favor. But as cities became choked with air pollution—much of it attributed to heavy urban traffic—the idea of an efficient electric car once again emerged. In order to make it acceptable to the public, however, several considerations had to be addressed: How many miles could an electric car be driven before needing to be recharged? How light would the vehicle need to be? And could the car keep up with the speed and driving conditions of busy freeways and highways?

In 1993 federal tax breaks became available for people who buy cars that run on alternative energy sources; these breaks are especially generous for purchasers of electric cars. The breaks are intended to compensate for the price difference between electric cars and the average gas-powered car. The breaks will be phased out by 2006 unless reinstated by Congress.

Several states have enacted laws that require a certain percentage of cars sold there to be low-emission vehicles such as electric cars. In California, for example, as of

2003 low-emission vehicles must make up 10 percent of cars sold. Generous incentives are granted by the state of California to buy or lease low-emission vehicles; they include grants totaling $9,000, free parking at Los Angeles International Airport, free recharging at participating agencies, and use of the state's 964 miles of carpool lanes with no requirement to carry a passenger.

Electric vehicles (EVs) come in three types: battery-powered; fuel cell; and hybrids, which are powered by both an electric motor and a small conventional engine.

BATTERY-POWERED VEHICLES. With a push from government mandates for cleaner cars, U.S. companies like General Motors (GM) and Ford began serious research into what they hoped would be the next generation of electric vehicles. In 1997 GM became the first American automaker to get an electric vehicle into production; EV1, a two-seater, was made available for the public to lease that year. In 1999 GM introduced its second-generation EV1, the Gen II. It used a lead-acid battery pack, had a driving range of approximately 95 miles, and was offered with an optional nickel-metal hydride battery pack, which increased its range to 130 miles. EV drivers had a charger installed at their home, allowing them to recharge the car overnight. GM discontinued its EV1 line in 2002; the need to recharge the battery every 100 miles was too inconvenient and the car did not sell. GM is now focusing on a hydrogen-powered sedan it calls Hy-Wire, which may be available in showrooms by 2010.

Ford produces a Ford Ranger in an EV model (available for lease only) and also manufactures electric trucks for the U.S. Postal Service.

FUEL-CELL VEHICLES. A fuel cell uses an electrochemical process that converts a fuel's energy into usable electricity. Some experts think that in the future, vehicles driven by fuel cells could replace vehicles with combustion engines. Fuel cells produce very little sulfur and nitrogen dioxide, and generate less than half the carbon dioxide of internal-combustion engines. Rather than needing to be recharged, they are simply refueled. Hydrogen, natural gas, methanol, and gasoline can all be used with a fuel cell, but attention through the early 2000s has focused on hydrogen.

DaimlerChrysler's Mercedes-Benz division introduced the first prototype fuel-cell car in 1999. The NECAR4 had zero-emissions and ran on liquid hydrogen. Unfortunately, the hydrogen had to be kept cold at all times, which made the design impractical for widespread use. DaimlerChrysler introduced a concept minivan, the Natrium, in 2002. It runs on hydrogen extracted from sodium borohydride, a compound derived from borax. It will be some time before hydrogen fuel-cell cars are commercially viable. General Motors' Vice President Larry Burns told *U.S. News & World Report*'s Marianne Lavelle that hydrogen cars may turn up in showrooms by 2015.

HYBRIDS. Hybrid cars have both an electric motor and a small internal-combustion engine. A sophisticated computer system automatically shifts from using the electric motor to the gas engine, as needed, for optimum driving. The electric motor is recharged while the car is driving and braking. Because the gasoline engine does only part of the work, the car gets very good fuel economy. The engine is also designed for ultra-low emissions.

As of 2003 there were three hybrids on the market in the United States: the Toyota Prius, the two-passenger Honda Insight, and a hybrid version of the Honda Civic. The cars were sold in Japan for a number of years before being introduced to the U.S. market. Americans purchased 36,000 Honda and Toyota hybrids in 2002, or 0.2 percent of the U.S. auto market share. America's entries in the hybrid market, the Chevy Silverado and GMC Sierra pickup trucks, were to go into production in 2003. A hybrid SUV, the Ford Escape, and a hybrid pickup, the Dodge Ram, will be available in 2004. (Stuart F. Brown, "Dude Where's My Hybrid?," *Fortune*, April 28, 2003).

Hybrid cars can cost up to $6,000 more than conventional gasoline-powered cars, which leads some industry analysts to believe there will never be a mass market for them (Jeff Plungis, "Hybrids Give Japan New Edge," *The Detroit News*, May 18, 2003).

SAFETY ON THE ROAD

According to the Federal Highway Administration (FHWA), there were 42,387 motor-vehicle fatalities in 2000. (See Table 4.8.) The number was up 2 percent over 1999 but down 5 percent from the 44,599 fatalities in 1990. The National Traffic Safety Administration estimated that 41,945 persons were killed in motor vehicle crashes in 2000 and 42,116 were killed in 2001. (See Table 4.9.) Approximately 3 million persons suffered nonfatal injuries in motor-vehicle accidents in 2001, down 4.9 percent from 2000.

Motor-vehicle fatalities tend to be concentrated most heavily among the youngest people who can legally drive and among the oldest segment of the population. According to the *2001 Annual Assessment of Motor Vehicle Crashes* (NHTSA, National Center for Statistics and Analysis, Washington, D.C., August 2002), fatalities and fatal crashes among persons aged 16–20 declined 0.4 percent and 1.0 percent, respectively, in 2000 and 2001. According to analyses of data from the federal Fatality Analysis Reporting System, in 2001, 6,719 people aged 65 years and older died in motor vehicle crashes, down less than 1 percent since 2000 but up 26 percent since 1975, and 5,582 people aged 13–19 died in crashes, down 36 percent since

TABLE 4.8

Motor vehicle fatalities and travel, 1990–2000

Year	Fatalities	Vehicle miles of travel (millions)
1990	44,599	2,144,362
1991	41,508	2,172,050
1992	39,250	2,247,151
1993	40,150	2,296,378
1994	40,716	2,357,588
1995	41,817	2,422,696
1996	42,065	2,484,080
1997	42,605	2,577,866
1998	42,029	2,631,522
1999	41,611	2,691,335
2000	42,387	2,767,363

SOURCE: Adapted from "Motor Vehicle Fatalities and Travel," U.S. Department of Transportation, Federal Highway Administration [Online] http://www.fhwa.dot.gov/ohim/onh00/line6.htm [accessed April 11, 2003]

TABLE 4.9

Persons killed and injured in motor vehicle crashes, 2000–01

	Year		Percent change
	2000	2001	
Persons killed	41,945	42,116	0.4
Persons injured	3,189,000	3,033,000	-4.9
Fatal crashes	37,526	37,795	0.7
Nonfatal crashes	6,356,000	6,285,000	-1.1
Injury crashes	2,070,000	2,003,000	-3.2
Property damage only	4,286,000	4,286,000	-0.1

SOURCE: "Persons Killed and Injured and Number of Crashes," in *2001 Annual Assessment of Motor Vehicle Crashes,* National Highway Traffic Safety Administration, National Center for Statistics & Analysis [Online] http://www-nrd.nhtsa.dot.gov/pdf/nrd-30/NCSA/Rpts/2002/Assess01.pdf [accessed May 8, 2003]

1975 ("Fatality Facts: Older People as of November 2002" and "Fatality Facts: Teenagers as of November 2002," Insurance Institute for Highway Safety, Arlington, VA, February 2003). There are fewer elderly people than younger people licensed to drive but their numbers have increased considerably as the population has aged. Older people do not have a greater tendency to get into crashes, but when they do, they are more susceptible to severe injuries.

What Makes a Safe Car?

As in the past, today's consumers are advised for reasons of safety to buy the largest car they can afford, with airbags and as many other safety features as possible. Experts advise buyers to look for features such as height-adjustable seat belts, antilock brakes, traction control, all- or four-wheel drive, and daytime running lamps. Car buyers are also advised to test-drive the car to make sure they can sit comfortably and use the gas and brake pedals with ease. It is also important, after buying the car, to read the owner's manual to learn how to use the various safety features.

Car manufacturers have sought to improve safety through a wide range of technological advances. Today's cars are designed not only to help prevent an accident, but to protect passengers if an accident should happen. Safety and car quality are foremost in the minds of many new-car buyers. A 2000 survey of consumer preferences, conducted by Maritz Marketing Research, found that prospective car buyers ranked safety sixth, behind reliability, durability, and value, and far higher than fuel economy (which ranked twenty-fifth).

Because of their inherent design, light trucks and SUVs often exhibit handling and balance inferior to that of a standard car. They often have a high profile and narrow base, making rollovers all too easy. Until recently, safety in the light-truck segment of the automobile market received less attention than safety in cars. However, as carmakers have come to recognize that "safety sells," and federal agencies have responded to citizen input, most new light trucks must now meet the same standards as cars. Some of the safety features already in use on SUVs and light trucks include air bags, side-impact protection, rollover protection, head restraints, and antilock brake systems.

Despite the stricter safety requirements, light trucks still pose serious safety issues. The NHTSA reported in 2003 that more than 10,000 people die every year in rollover crashes and the risk of dying is greater for SUV occupants. More than 60 percent of SUV occupants who were killed in 1999 died in crashes when their vehicle rolled over, compared to 23 percent for car occupants ("U.S. Transportation Secretary Slater Announces First Rollover Resistance Ratings," U.S. Department of Transportation press release, Washington, D.C., January 9, 2001).

In order to enable consumers to make informed choices, the NHTSA has since 2001 provided ratings of passenger vehicles' resistance to rolling over in a single vehicle crash. In this one- to five-star rating system, the lowest-rated vehicles (one star) are at least four times more likely to roll over than the highest-rated vehicles (five stars). When the first ratings were released in 2001, only one vehicle, the Honda Accord (a car), received five stars. Among SUVs rated in 2001, the highest rating was three stars (Chevrolet's Suburban, Tahoe, and Tracker; GMC's Yukon and Yukon XL; Honda's CR-V; and Suzuki's Vitara). As they become available, vehicle ratings are posted on the NHTSA Web site (http://www.nhtsa.dot.gov).

Other government studies have shown that SUVs can pose additional dangers to cars in collisions between the

TABLE 4.10

Restraint use rates for passenger car occupants in fatal crashes, 1991 and 2001

Type of occupant	1991	2001
Drivers	48	64
Passengers		
Front seat	46	63
Rear seat	31	47
5 years old and over	38	54
4 years old and under	55	74
All passengers	39	56
All occupants	**44**	**61**

SOURCE: "Table 3. Restraint use rates for passenger car occupants in fatal crashes, 1991 and 2001," in *Traffic Safety Facts 2001: Overview,* DOT HS 809 476, U.S. Department of Transportation, National Highway Traffic Safety Administration, Washington, DC, 2001

two. A September 1998 National Highway Traffic Safety Administration/University of Michigan Transportation Research Institute study (*Fatality Risks in Collisions Between Cars and Light Trucks,* Washington, D.C.) found that when an SUV strikes a passenger car in a frontal crash, the occupants of the car are nearly twice as likely to suffer fatal injuries as the occupants of the SUV. In collisions in which SUVs strike cars on the left side, the car drivers are up to 25 times more likely to die than the SUV drivers, depending on the location and type of the strike. In car-on-car left-side collisions, on the other hand, the risk of death to the driver of the car being struck is only 10 times likelier than that for the driver of the striking car.

SEAT BELTS/SHOULDER BELTS. In the press release announcing the new rollover ratings system, NHTSA Administrator Dr. Sue Bailey noted: "Your best chance of surviving a rollover is by buckling up. Eighty percent of the people killed in single vehicle rollovers were unbelted, and we know that belted occupants are about 75 percent less likely to be killed in a rollover crash than unbelted occupants." Seat belts have been standard equipment in cars for years. In 1984 New York became the first state to enact laws mandating their use. The old lap belt and shoulder restraints, however, have given way to newer, more effective devices. The "inertial reel" design favored by safety experts and most European carmakers allows a passenger to move around, but the reel pulls tight when the passenger sits upright.

As of 2003, 49 states and the District of Columbia have mandatory laws for the use of seat belts—New Hampshire is the lone exception—and all 50 states and the District of Columbia have laws mandating the use of child restraints. The FHWA estimated that 71 percent of Americans used shoulder belts in 2000, up from 58 percent in 1994, and that more than 74,000 lives had been saved because belts were used (*Status of the Nation's Highways, Bridges, and Transit: 2002 Conditions and Performance Report*, U.S. Department of Transportation, Washington, D.C., 2002).

In 2002 seat belt use reached an all-time high of 75 percent, according to the NHTSA. Table 4.10 compares restraint use rates among victims of fatal crashes in 1991 and 2001; only 61 percent of the victims were wearing restraints in 2001.

In 1998 President Clinton signed the six-year Transportation Equity Act for the Twenty-first Century (TEA-21; PL 105-178), reauthorizing the Intermodal Surface Transportation Efficiency Act (ISTEA; PL 102-240), which had expired in 1997. Under TEA-21, states were given incentives such as grants to improve transportation safety. One part of the incentive program allowed the transportation secretary to make grants to states that adopted "primary" safety-belt laws (which allow a law-enforcement officer to pull a driver over for not wearing a seat belt). In the report *Transportation: Invest in America: TEA-21 Reauthorization Policy Recommendations*, posted on the Web site of the American Association of State Highway and Transportation Officials in 2003, Norman Y. Mineta, U.S. Secretary of Transportation, urged that in reauthorizing TEA-21 Congress dedicate $1 billion per year to safety programs, including increasing seat belt use.

CHILD SAFETY SEATS. Despite recent increases in the use of child safety seats, motor-vehicle crashes remain the leading cause of injury death among U.S. children, according to the U.S. Department of Health and Human Service's report *Child Health USA 2002.* Of the 492 motor vehicle fatalities of children under 5 in 2001, fatality rates per 100,000 children were highest among children younger than age 1 (2.6) and among 2- and 4-year-old children (2.6) ("Fatality Facts: Children as of November 2002," Insurance Institute for Highway Safety, Arlington, VA, February 2003). According to the Insurance Institute for Highway Safety, because of loopholes in state laws, many children are exempt from either safety belt or child restraint use laws and therefore ride unrestrained.

According to the Center for Applied Behavioral and Evaluation Research, between 1975 and 1999, an estimated 4,500 lives were saved by the use of some type of child restraint (child safety seats or adult belts), and in 1999 alone, the lives of an estimated 307 children under age 5 were saved as a result of child restraint use (*Booster Seats: A Review of the Literature on Best Practices, Child Fatalities, Use and Misuse Rates, Reasons for Use and Non-Use, Current Strategies, and Perceived Information Needs,* June 2001). A campaign launched in 1997 by the NHTSA (Buckle Up America) resulted in a 12-percent decline in motor vehicle fatalities among children under age 5 by the end of 1999 ("America Buckles Up, But Could Do Better," NHTSA, July 2001). The NHTSA estimated that in 2002, 99 percent of infants under age 1, 94 percent of toddlers aged 1–4, and 83 percent of "booster age children" were restrained, a record level of compliance (*Child Restraint Use in 2002: Results from the 2002 NOPUS Controlled Intersection Study*, February 5, 2003). The NTSA reported that the percentage of infants who sat in the front seat of automobiles in 2002 (15 percent) was "alarming" and recommended that no child under the age of 13 sit in the front seat of an automobile.

Many parents do not install child safety seats correctly and often do not realize it until after a crash. Kelley Adams, a Ford Motor Company safety programs engineer, asserted that the confusion arises because child safety seats are secured using a vehicle's adult seat belt system (Mike O'Neill, "Ford Working to Protect Young Passengers," Boost America! news release, September 4, 2002). Ford installed LATCH systems (Lower Anchors and Tethers for Children) in its 2000 Windstar and Focus and on all Ford vehicles as of the 2002 model year. The system does not depend on the vehicle's belt system and could save up to 50 young lives a year. LATCH became mandatory on most child safety seats (but not booster seats) and vehicles manufactured after September 1, 2002.

Many parents are unaware that children under 80 pounds or 4 feet 9 inches in height should be restrained in booster seats. University of Washington researchers observed 2,880 children being picked up by their parents from schools or day-care centers and found that only 16 percent of the children were properly restrained and only 21 percent of children who should have been in booster seats were restrained in booster seats (two-thirds were strapped into an adult seat belt instead) (K.L. Capozza, "Confusion Leads to Underuse of Booster Seats," HealthDayNews online, April 7, 2003).

ERGONOMICS. Ergonomics, as it relates to cars, is the science of design to promote easy visibility and driving. In the past there was a trend toward unnecessary lights and controls on the dashboard. People spent too much time searching dashboard dials to find the gas gauge or the button to turn on the radio. In a car traveling 65 miles an hour, such distractions can cause major problems, including fatal accidents. To address this problem, manufacturers are trying to simplify driving; controls and displays are now generally well placed and easy to see and access, thus reducing the need for drivers to take their eyes off the road.

AIR BAGS. Frontal collisions are the cause of more than half of all vehicle fatalities, according to the Insurance Institute for Highway Safety, and air bags are designed to protect people involved in serious frontal collisions. The federal government mandated that as of 1995 every new car, domestic and imported, had to offer air bags as an option. Beginning with model year 1998, all new passenger cars were required to have driver and passenger air bags along with safety belts. These laws applied to light trucks beginning in model year 1999.

The NHTSA reported that as of October 1, 1999, the lives of an estimated 4,011 drivers and 747 passengers had been saved by airbags. However, 84 children and 56 adults lost their lives, in most cases because the victim was too close to the airbag ("Safety Fact Sheet," November 2, 1999). Because of the demonstrated risks that air bags posed to infants, children, and other occupants, especially in low speed crashes, in 1998 automakers began installing less powerful bags, which lowered the number of deaths and injuries related to airbags without compromising safety, according to a study by the Washington, D.C.–based Alliance of Automobile Manufacturers (Dee-Ann Durbin, "Air Bag Injuries, Deaths Fall," *Detroit Free Press*, April 8, 2003). Government regulations required that beginning with model year 2003, 20 percent of all vehicles sold had to be equipped with advanced air bag systems that reduce the risk of injuries to drivers and young children. The percentage increases to 35 percent for model year 2004.

The new generation of "smart" air bags features sensors that can deactivate the airbag when the presence of a child weighing under 56.5 pounds is detected. The auto industry is working on other advanced air bag technologies that measure variables such as the severity of the crash, the posture of the vehicle occupant, safety belt usage, and how close the occupants are to the air bag module before the bag is deployed. DuPont is working on a low-profile, plastic bladder-like airbag that unfolds rather than inflates in the event of a serious crash. The technology will be incorporated into floor mats, driver seats, and doors, and will protect a driver's lower legs, thorax, and head.

ANTILOCK BRAKE SYSTEMS. Next to seat belts and air bags, antilock braking systems (ABS) are probably the most important recent innovation in auto technology. Skids are caused when tires lose their grip on the road and "lock up" (stop spinning). Antilock brakes help to prevent wheel lockup and help maintain steering control on slippery surfaces and during sudden stops and evasive maneuvers. As with air bags, ABS is now a standard feature on most new cars—even on many inexpensive, entry-level models.

A British study reported in the March 2, 2002, *New Scientist* found that ABS did not reduce the number of accidents. Nearly 21,000 drivers of modern cars were questioned about the number of accidents they had been involved in; there was little difference in accident rates between those who had ABS and those who did not. An earlier study by the Insurance Institute for Highway Safety (December 1996) found that cars with ABS were more likely than cars without ABS to be in fatal crashes, many of which involved only a single vehicle. Experts found this

FIGURE 4.5

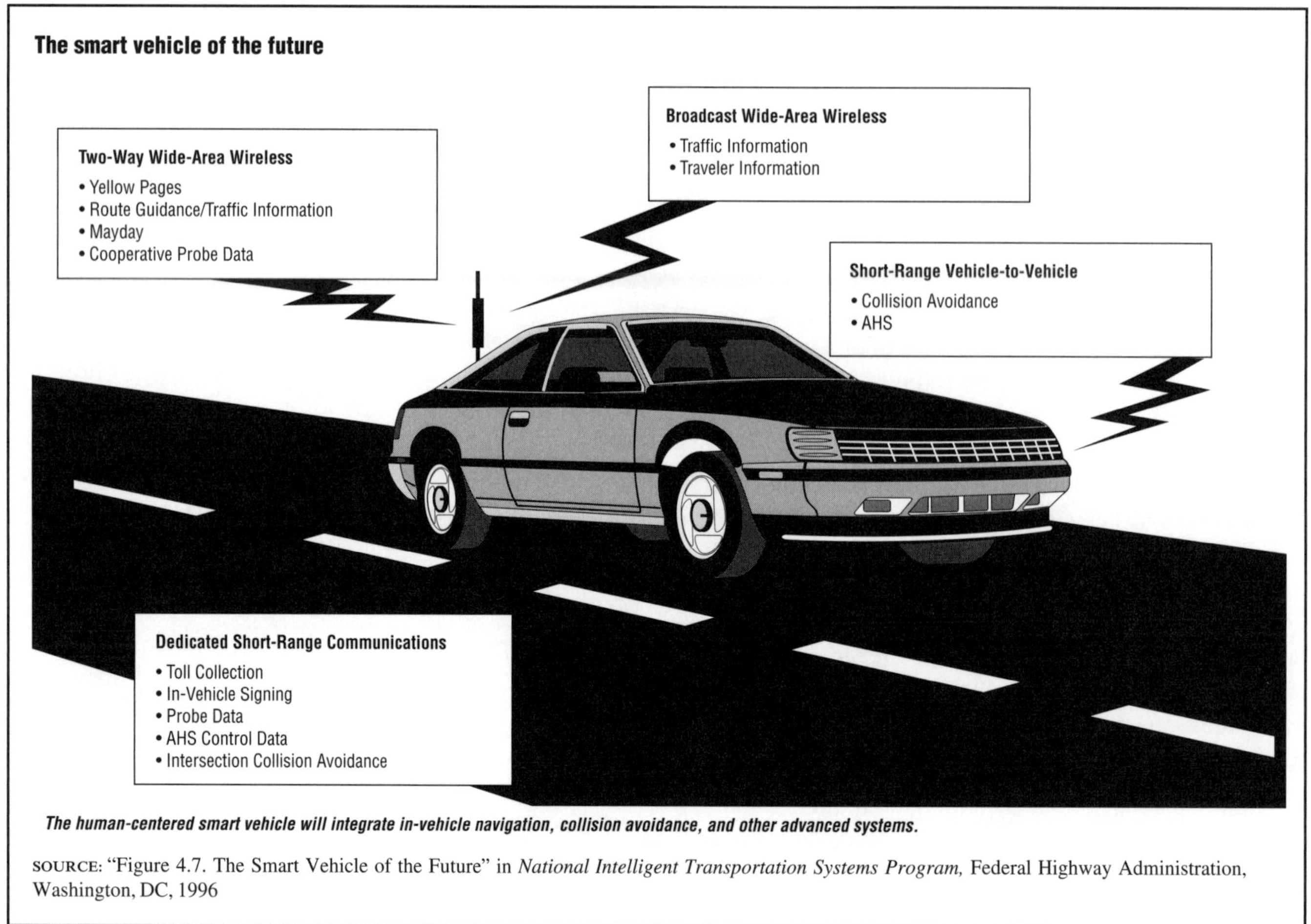

The human-centered smart vehicle will integrate in-vehicle navigation, collision avoidance, and other advanced systems.

SOURCE: "Figure 4.7. The Smart Vehicle of the Future" in *National Intelligent Transportation Systems Program,* Federal Highway Administration, Washington, DC, 1996

puzzling but suggested that drivers may take more risks with antilock brakes or do not use them properly. Antilock brakes need hard, continuous pressure to engage, rather than the pumping action that many drivers learned when they first started driving.

FRONT-WHEEL, REAR-WHEEL, AND FOUR-WHEEL DRIVE. In a car, not every wheel is created equal. Most cars are equipped to send power from the engine to either the wheels in the front (front-wheel drive) or to the ones in the back (rear-wheel drive). Some deliver power to all four wheels at once (four-wheel or all-wheel drive). All have different advantages.

Front-wheel drive vehicles have the weight of the engine pushing down on the tires, thus improving traction on slippery roads. Large-car owners prefer rear-wheel drive. If a car is towing a boat or trailer, rear-wheel drive puts extra force on the rear axle, which creates extra traction. Also, rear-wheel drive is called the "driver-friendly" option. When the driver pushes down on the gas pedal, the weight is transferred to the rear wheels, allowing faster starts, which makes this option popular with sports-car owners and other high-performance drivers. Spreading the power to all four wheels (four-wheel drive) provides a better grip on the road, an important safety feature for driving on snow, ice, or unpaved roads.

A relatively new alternative is the Traction Control System (TCS), a variant of ABS. When a wheel begins to spin while accelerating, TCS gently brakes only the spinning wheel, thus slowing it down until it regains traction. The technology of TCS is simpler than that of four-wheel drive, and uses less fuel. In the future, TCS may become a popular and cheaper option for new-car buyers.

ELECTRONIC STABILITY PROGRAMS. Electronic stability programs (ESP) are considered by auto industry analysts to be a particularly promising technology. Popular in Europe, ESPs have yet to make a significant inroad in the American market. ESPs use sensors and actuators from ABS and traction control systems to take brake pressure and other readings in order to determine the traction necessary to turn a corner; gyroscopes and other sensors judge when a vehicle is starting to tip on its side. The system then ensures the optimum amount of stability and grip. As of 2003 ESPs were installed in more than half of cars produced in Germany, 20 percent of cars produced in France, and in fewer than 10 percent of cars produced in Japan and the United States (Edmund Chew, "Bosch:

ESP Beats the Airbag in Saving Lives," *Automotive News*, April 21, 2003).

SPACE-AGE TECHNOLOGY—SMART CARS. With the help of a technology known as Intelligent Vehicle Highway Systems (IVHS), the cars of the future will largely be mobile computers and will provide safety features that not only reduce accidents but also provide even more driver comfort. (See Figure 4.5.) High-tech equipment is already available in many luxury cars today. Some of these "extras" include onboard navigational systems to guide drivers around traffic jams and bad weather; "adaptive cruise control" that uses radar or lasers to "sense" when traffic is getting too close and makes the car slow down; systems that automatically call for help if an air bag deploys; tires that can run for 50 miles after they've gone flat; and sensors that automatically turn on the wipers when they detect rain on the windshield. Night vision technology allows drivers of the Cadillac DeVille to "see" images beyond the reach of headlights; the system uses thermal imaging to track heat sources. Global positioning system (GPS) satellites may soon be able to track around curves and adjust a car's speed to traffic conditions.

Researchers at the University of Michigan are working on a crash avoidance system that will alert drivers when their car is in danger of driving off the road (Road Departure Crash Warning). The system will alert speeding drivers of an approaching curve. Other projects are being developed by the NHTSA in cooperation with industry and academia. They include:

- Research into how drivers use wireless phones while driving to determine whether hands-free wireless telephones are warranted
- Lane-tracking systems that will help alert and prevent a driver from drifting into the next lane or off the highway
- A cooperative intersection that will communicate data on traffic signals and oncoming vehicles, reducing the risk of intersection collisions
- Automated collision-notification systems that will guide emergency service personnel to the scene of an accident

Engineers in the United States, Europe, and Japan are developing "smart cars" capable of driving themselves. These cars enable a driver to enter a freeway, turn the driving responsibilities over to the car, and read the morning paper on the way to the office. In 1997 a combination of "smart cars," automated highways, and "intelligent" transportation systems was demonstrated in California. Cars followed along highway lanes, automatically slowing down and speeding up in response to traffic flow. The vehicles were directed by a combination of radar, video, and laser sensors commanded by an onboard computer. The National Automated Highway System Consortium sponsored the demonstration.

At many car-rental agencies across the United States, drivers can rent "smart cars" equipped with microcomputers, multiple antennas, a cellular phone, and a transponder that communicates with global-positioning satellites, providing the driver with information about traffic trouble spots and sightseeing attractions. In California, New Jersey, Texas, and other states, drivers on certain toll roads do not have to stop and pay tolls. A scanner reads a barcode sticker on the windshield, identifies the car, and automatically debits the driver's account. Oklahoma has electronic collections systems on each of its 10 toll roads. Similar systems are also used overseas.

What Makes an Unsafe Driver?

Based on a 1996 study, the NHTSA estimated that driver distraction of all types probably contributes to between 20 percent and 30 percent of all crashes ("Statement of L. Robert Shelton, Executive Director, National Highway Traffic Safety Administration Before the Subcommittee on Highways and Transit Committee on Transportation and Infrastructure, U.S. House of Representatives," May 9, 2001). Although auto manufacturers continue to build safer and safer cars, it is primarily the driver who ultimately determines whether or not a car or truck will be involved in an accident. Many factors play a part in traffic fatalities, including the amount of alcohol consumed before getting behind the wheel, the age of the driver, and the speed of the vehicle. When other factors are controlled, driver characteristics far outweigh vehicle factors in predicting a crash.

ALCOHOL IMPAIRMENT. The use of alcohol as a contributing factor in fatal traffic accidents has been steadily decreasing since 1982—most likely because of tougher enforcement of liquor and DWI ("driving while intoxicated") laws in most states and the elevation of the drinking age to 21. In 1982 about 46 percent of all traffic fatalities involved an intoxicated "active participant." In 2000 the NHTSA reported that 31 percent of all traffic deaths involved a driver or nonoccupant of the vehicle who was legally intoxicated. This amounts to nearly 11,000 alcohol-related fatalities (*Alcohol Involvement in Fatal Crashes 2000*, March 2002).

The highest rates of intoxication were for drivers in their early twenties. In 2000 about 27 percent of all drivers aged 21–24 involved in a fatal accident were legally drunk; 15 percent of drivers aged 16–20 were legally drunk.

TEA-21 (1998 Transportation Equity Act for the 21st Century) provided incentive grants from a $500 million fund to states that enacted and enforced laws that lowered the legal-intoxication limit from 0.10 to 0.08 blood

FIGURE 4.6

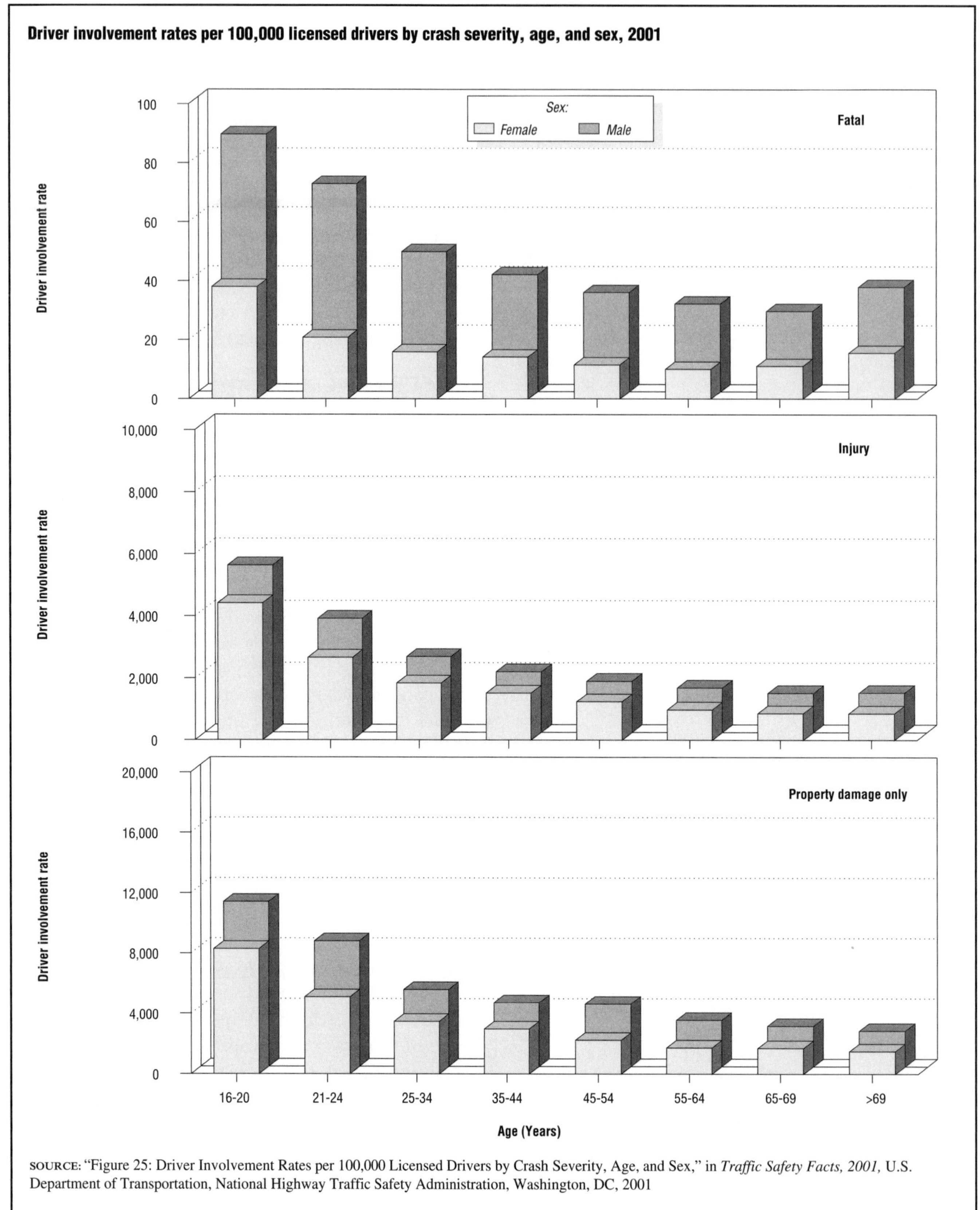

SOURCE: "Figure 25: Driver Involvement Rates per 100,000 Licensed Drivers by Crash Severity, Age, and Sex," in *Traffic Safety Facts, 2001,* U.S. Department of Transportation, National Highway Traffic Safety Administration, Washington, DC, 2001

alcohol content (BAC). As further incentive, in October 2000 Congress passed the Transportation Appropriations Bill, which contains a mandate for 0.08 BAC as the national standard for impaired driving. According to the bill, states that do not enact 0.08 BAC laws by 2004 will have 2 percent of certain federal highway-construction funds withheld, with the penalty increasing to 8 percent by 2007. As of April 2003, 39 states and the District of Columbia had adapted 0.08 BAC laws, according to the Insurance Institute for Highway Safety Web site.

CELL PHONES. At any given time, an estimated 600,000 drivers are using their cell phones, according to data collected in 2000 (Dennis Utter, "Passenger Vehicle Driver Cell Phone Use Results from the Fall 2000 National Occupant Protection Use Survey," Peter R. Thom and Associates Newsletter, Fall 2001). A 2001 NHTSA survey found that 54 percent of drivers usually have a cell phone in their vehicles when they drive; almost 80 percent leave their cell phone turned on while driving and 73 percent have at some point talked on the phones while driving ("Statement of L. Robert Shelton," cited above).

Although the NHTSA agrees that cellular telephone use increases the risk of a collision, it points out that there are benefits of having a cell phone available in motor vehicles. It reported that cell phone users place more than 98,000 calls for emergency assistance each day and that in many instances cellular phones reduced response time to automobile accidents, thus saving lives. Several states have placed restrictions on drivers' use of hand-held cell phones and as of 2002 a few jurisdictions had banned their use.

YOUNG DRIVERS AND ACCIDENTS. The youngest drivers, those under age 20, are the most likely to be involved in motor-vehicle accidents. After age 20, accident rates decrease—a notable exception being drivers over the age of 69 who are involved in traffic fatalities. (See Figure 4.6.) Drivers between the ages of 16 and 24, particularly males, are disproportionately high contributors to traffic accidents and highway deaths. Young drivers also pose the greatest loss for insurers. According to the American Automobile Association (AAA) Foundation for Traffic Safety, the majority of all citations issued to young drivers are for speeding.

Young males consistently have the costliest insurance claims. Because of this, many insurance companies refer young drivers to "high-risk" insurers, thus reducing the number of young policyholders they have to carry.

Many young people object to being penalized with high insurance rates and have proposed "age-free" insurance policy programs. Under such policies, young drivers would be required to pass rigorous driver-education courses and sign a contract agreeing to abide by safety-belt laws, drinking-and-driving laws, and other safety regulations. In return, they would pay higher premiums for a specified time and then be eligible for refunds if they lived up to the terms of the contract.

Citing inadequate driver training as a primary contributor to poor driving skill among teenagers, several organizations, such as the NHTSA, the Insurance Institute for Highway Safety, and the National Association of Independent Insurers, advocate a "graduated licensing" program. Under such a program, teens do not go directly from learner's permit to adult license. Rather, there is an intermediate stage, involving more restrictions and greater supervision, during a teen's most dangerous driving years: 16–18. According to the NHTSA, in 2003, 17 states had licensing systems with several of the recommended components of a graduated licensing system.

OLDER DRIVERS AND ACCIDENTS. As the U.S. population matures, an increasing number of elderly drivers will be on the road. Given the number of miles they drive, elderly persons are disproportionately involved in collisions—particularly two-vehicle collisions. The National Safety Council has found that there are definite crash patterns among older drivers. They often fail to yield the right-of-way and sometimes do not pay attention to or do not see signs and signals.

Senior citizens' driving skills may diminish in other ways, including functional losses in vision, reaction time, and information processing. They often have more difficulty with backing and parking maneuvers. Older drivers also have the most accidents making left turns across traffic. The AAA's Foundation for Traffic Safety notes, however, that it is not chronological age but the driver's overall functional ability that predicts difficulties. This means that one cannot assume that a driver who is 60 is necessarily more able to drive than one who is 75.

Older people enjoy the freedom and independence of driving their own cars as much as anyone else. Looking toward the future, when many more senior citizens will be on the road, the AAA developed guidelines for a "grade" licensing program—a license that carries some restrictions. Several states have already experimented with this type of program, which attempts to balance the risks and safety needs of older drivers and others. For example, as of 2001, 11 states mandated a shorter license period before renewal as a driver ages ("Older Driver Relicensing Laws: The State of the States" MIT Age Lab, October 2001). The ultimate goal, however, is to help elderly drivers maintain their mobility for as long as they can safely do so.

ACCIDENTS AND DRIVER ERROR. Most accidents on the road result from the interaction of three factors: driver, vehicle, and road conditions. While motorists have little or no control over highway conditions and usually cannot predict whether their vehicles will perform correctly, they can control the way they drive. Table 4.11 lists the various types of improper driving that resulted in injuries or fatal accidents in 1999 and in 2000.

Right-of-way mistakes and speeding caused the most accidents and fatal injuries. The National Safety Council estimated that in 2000, driver error (improper driving) contributed to 57.8 percent of all accidents. (See Table 4.11.) Of collisions between motor vehicles, angle

TABLE 4.11

Improper driving as a factor in accidents, 1999 and 2000

Kind of improper driving	Fatal accidents 1999	Fatal accidents 2000	Injury accidents 1999	Injury accidents 2000	All accidents 1999	All accidents 2000
Improper driving	72.6%	61.6%	67.2%	60.3%	62.2%	57.8%
Speed too fast or unsafe	23.0	23.7	13.0	16.3	10.6	13.6
Right of way	20.1	18.6	25.8	19.9	22.9	20.1
Failed to yield	10.8	10.1	19.2	15.0	13.8	12.7
Passed stop sign	4.6	3.8	1.7	1.3	3.2	2.2
Disregarded signal	4.7	4.6	4.9	3.6	5.9	5.3
Drove left of center	9.6	8.2	1.7	1.1	1.3	1.0
Improper overtaking	1.1	0.9	0.9	0.6	1.2	0.9
Made improper turn	1.2	0.7	2.4	2.0	3.0	2.4
Followed too closely	0.5	0.5	3.4	4.3	6.3	5.7
Other improper driving	17.1	9.0	20.3	16.1	16.9	14.1
No improper driving stated	27.4	38.4	32.8	39.7	37.8	42.2
Total	100.0%	100.0%	100.0%	100.0%	100.0%	100.0%

Note: Based on reports from 7 state traffic authorities.

SOURCE: National Safety Council, *Injury Facts, 2001 Edition.* National Safety Council, Itasca, Illinois, 2001

collisions (collisions that are not head-on, rear-end, rear-to-rear, or sideswipe) caused the most deaths, while rear-end collisions caused the most nonfatal injuries and injury accidents.

ROAD RAGE AND AGGRESSIVE DRIVING. "Aggressive" driving is erratic and dangerous driving characterized by speeding, tailgating, failing to yield, weaving in and out of traffic, passing on the right, making improper lane changes, and running stop signs and lights. The NHTSA estimated in 1997 that about one-third of all highway crashes, and about two-thirds of highway fatalities, can be blamed on aggressive driving ("Statement of The Honorable Ricardo Martinez, M.D., Administrator, NHTSA," July 17, 1997).

Sometimes, aggressive driving, a traffic offense, escalates into road rage, a crime. A driver becomes enraged at another driver for tailgating, cutting them off, or some other real or imagined offense. The raging driver may make hand and facial gestures, scream, honk, flash headlights, or even try to intercept and confront the other driver. There have been many documented cases of enraged drivers running other cars off the road, shooting at vehicles, or even getting out of their cars to beat up or kill another driver.

Reported incidents of aggressive driving soared in the 1990s. According to one of the most recent studies of aggressive driving fatalities, which was carried out by the AAA, almost 13,000 people were injured or killed between 1990 and 1997 by aggressive driving. The AAA studied 10,037 aggressive-driving incidents and found that the majority of aggressive drivers were men between the ages of 18 and 26. However, the AAA also found that there were hundreds of cases involving older men and women who just "snapped" (*Aggressive Driving: Three Studies*, AAA Foundation for Traffic Safety, Washington, D.C., March 1997).

Growing concern about these drivers and the problems they cause on the roads led the NHTSA to develop a number of programs to combat aggressive driving, including an education-and-awareness program and a demonstration project to study effective enforcement. Arizona was the first state to pass a law that makes aggressive driving a misdemeanor offense; the law was enacted May 26, 1998. The NHTSA Web site provides a table that summarizes the aggressive driving laws that have been passed in the states ("Summary Table on Aggressive Driving Laws").

UNLICENSED DRIVERS. Studies by the AAA Foundation for Traffic Safety have identified unlicensed drivers as being responsible for a significant percentage of fatal crashes, pointing to a need for the states to address the handling of unlicensed drivers (*Unlicensed to Kill: The Sequel*, Washington, D.C., January 2003). In the period studied, 1993–99, unlicensed drivers were involved in 20 percent of fatal crashes. Percentages varied widely by state, ranging from a low of 6.1 percent in Maine to a high of 23.1 percent in New Mexico. Drivers with suspended licenses were involved in 4.5 percent of fatal crashes in 1993 and 5 percent in 1999.

AUTO CRIME

Thefts

Motor vehicle theft increased by nearly two-thirds between the early 1980s and early 1990s, peaking at 1.66 million incidents in 1991. After that, motor vehicle theft decreased each year until 1999 (1.15 million), then began to rise again, with approximately 1.2 million vehicles stolen in 2001, a 5.7 percent increase over 2000, according to the FBI's *Uniform Crime Reports*. Thanks to theft-prevention devices in many vehicles, there are fewer casual thieves, although there are still many professionals. When a professional auto thief steals a vehicle, it is either quickly stripped for parts or shipped out of the country. In 2001, 53 percent of stolen vehicles were recovered.

A June 10, 2003, press release from the National Insurance Crime Bureau (NICB), an Illinois-based nonprofit organization that studies vehicle theft and insurance fraud, reports that about 200,000 stolen vehicles are shipped out of the country or driven across international borders each year ("Port and Border Areas Special Targets for Vehicle Theft; People Should be More Vigilant Than Ever, Warns NICB,"). For this reason, border cities like Detroit, Phoenix, and Miami tend to have high auto-theft rates.

The NICB reported that in 2001 the three most frequently stolen automobiles were the Toyota Camry, Honda Accord, and Honda Civic. These cars have long been popular with car thieves, mainly because they're plentiful and many of their parts are interchangeable across different model years. But cars are not the only targets. In 2001 nearly one-third (17) of the top 50 most frequently stolen vehicles were SUVs, pickup trucks, and vans or minivans. The most popular of these were the Jeep Cherokee and Grand Cherokee, Chevrolet Full-Size C/K Pickup, Ford F-150, and Dodge Caravan.

Air-Bag Theft

The NICB estimates that more than 50,000 air bags are stolen each year nationwide. As air bags have become more common in cars and light trucks, they have also become more popular with thieves. Police estimate that half of all recovered stolen vehicles are missing at least one air bag. Air bags—particularly those on the driver side—are easy to steal because they are held in place with only a few nuts and bolts. Stolen air bags can be sold for $50–$200, or, if passed off as new, for as much as $1,000, according to information available on the NICB's Web site in July 2003.

Carjacking

Carjacking is the theft of a motor vehicle by force or threat of force. National statistics on carjacking are not available; the crime is usually identified as "auto theft" or "armed robbery." According to a special report prepared by the Bureau of Justice Statistics, an average of about 49,000 completed or attempted nonfatal carjackings took place each year between 1992 and 1996, the most recent years for which data are available (Patsy Klaus, "Carjacking in the United States," revised May 1999). Most completed carjackings occurred in the daytime, and 40 percent took place in open, public locations such as near a bus stop or subway or train station.

About 9 in 10 (92 percent) completed carjackings involved a weapon, compared with 75 percent of all attempted carjackings. About one-fourth (23 percent) of all completed carjackings involved injury to the victim, compared with 10 percent of all attempted carjackings. While all completed carjackings were reported to the police, only 57 percent of attempted carjackings were reported.

In many carjackings, the criminal is a young male who is after the vehicle or its expensive, flashy accessories. The carjacker may accost the person sitting in the vehicle, eject the victim, and then take off with the car. Some police officials believe that because of the effectiveness of newer anti-theft devices, many thieves actually find it easier to steal cars at gunpoint.

GOVERNMENT ACTION AGAINST CARJACKING. In October 1996, President Bill Clinton signed the Carjacking Correction Act of 1996 (PL 104-217), which made carjacking a federal offense. The law stipulates that if bodily injury is inflicted on the victim, the maximum sentence can be increased from 15 to 25 years. When Clinton signed the act, he said he hoped that it would increase the security of all Americans—particularly women. The vast majority of carjacking cases are handled under state laws, however.

In August 1997 Louisiana passed a controversial state law popularly referred to as the "Shoot the Carjacker" law, giving motorists in that state the authority to use deadly force against their assailants. Although there are laws throughout the United States that permit self-defense, this is the first law that specifically focuses on self-defense against carjacking.

CHAPTER 5

BICYCLES, MOTORCYCLES, AND RECREATIONAL VEHICLES

BICYCLES

Bicycles played an important role in the development of roads in America. In the early 1900s, the bicycle was a form of transportation as well as recreation. However, the growing number of cars (and the increasing hazards for cyclists) led to a decline in the use of bicycles as a serious mode of transportation. Today, most bicycling is done for recreation or fitness. *Bicycle Retailer and Industry News* reported that in 2001 the retail bicycle market was a $4.2 billion industry. It also noted that most of the bicycles sold in America are imported (95 percent in 2001). As of 2003 there were only a handful of companies still manufacturing bicycles in the United States, including American Bicycle Group, Cannondale, Huffy, and Trek.

Who Rides Bikes?

The National Sporting Goods Association (NSGA) reported in its *Sports Participation in 2002* report that 41.4 million Americans aged 7 and over rode a bicycle at least once in 2002. While this number was up 6.1 percent over 2001, bicycle riding over the ten-year period 1991–2001 was down 27.7 percent. Bicycling ranked as the seventh most popular recreational activity in the United States in 2002, down from a third place ranking in 1998.

The results of a U.S. Department of Transportation (DOT) survey of people of driving age (*National Survey of Pedestrian & Bicyclist Attitudes and Behaviors: Highlights Report*) were released on May 4, 2003. About one-quarter (27.3 percent) of respondents rode a bicycle at least once during the summer of 2002 (May–August), compared with nearly 80 percent who took at least one walk lasting 5 minutes or longer. (See Figure 5.1.) The survey revealed that more men (34 percent) than women (21.3 percent) rode bicycles. Hispanics (29.4 percent) were more likely than non-Hispanic whites (27.8 percent) and blacks (22.5 percent) to have ridden a bicycle. After age 44, bicycle ridership declined steeply as people aged.

FIGURE 5.1

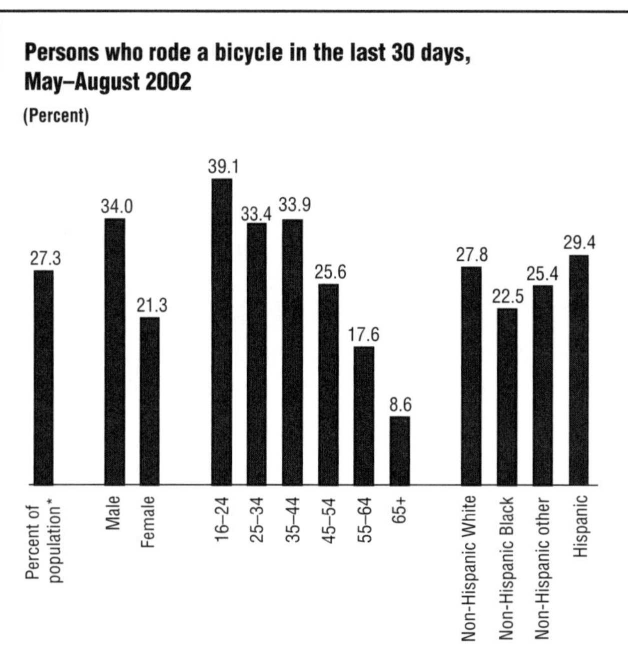

* Estimates reflect total U.S. population age 16 or older in the 50 states and the District of Columbia.

SOURCE: "Figure 1: Percentage Bicycling in Past 30 Days by Gender, Age, Race/Ethnicity," in *National Survey of Pedestrian & Bicyclist Attitudes and Behaviors: Highlights Report,* U.S. Department of Transportation, National Highway Traffic Safety Administration and Bureau of Transportation Statistics [Online] http://www.bicyclinginfo.org/pdf/FinalBikePedSurveyHighlightsReport_v2.pdf [accessed May 15, 2003]

More than a quarter of the bicyclists (26.0 percent) reported that recreation was the purpose of their trip. Exercise or health reasons were reported by 23.6 percent.

COMMUTERS. About 5 percent of bicyclists in the DOT survey indicated that they used a bicycle to commute to school or work. In a 1997 survey of bicycle commuters, the most recent survey to provide a wealth of detail, it was revealed that 41 percent of bicycle commuters lived in only

TABLE 5.1

Specialty bicycle sales by year, 2000–02

Category	2002	2001	2000	Average price 2002
Mountain	33.8%	36.8%	41.0%	$450.30
Youth	28.3	26.1	28.5	197.49
Comfort	20.6	20.8	13.6	339.15
Hybrid	9.4	8.8	10.2	404.66
Road	5.3	4.4	3.6	1,194.68
Cruiser	2.2	2.8	2.8	275.17
Tandem	0.15	0.11	0.12	887.91

SOURCE: "Specialty Bicycle Sales By Year, 2000–2002," in *2002 NBDA Statpak,* National Bicycle Dealers Association, Costa Mesa, CA, 2002

TABLE 5.2

Bicycles sold, 1973–2002

Year	Bicycles sold (millions), 20" and up wheel sizes	Bicycles sold (millions), all wheel sizes
2002	13.6*	19.5*
2001	11.3*	16.7*
2000	11.9*	20.9
1999	11.6*	17.5*
1998	11.1*	15.8*
1997	11.0*	15.2*
1996	10.9	15.4
1995	12.0	16.1
1994	12.5	16.7
1993	13.0	16.8
1992	11.6	15.3
1991	11.6	
1990	10.8	
1989	10.7	
1988	9.9	
1987	12.6	
1986	12.3	
1985	11.4	
1984	10.1	
1983	9.0	
1982	6.8	
1981	8.9	
. . .1973	15.2 (record high)	

*Indicates projected figures.

SOURCE: "A Look at the Bicycle Industry's Vital Statistics," in *2002 NBDA Statpak,* National Bicycle Dealers Association, Costa Mesa, CA, 2002. Primary source: Bicycle Manufacturers Association, and apparent market consumption based on U.S. Department of Commerce import statistics, and estimates of domestic market production by National Bicycle Dealers Association Retail Data Capture program

5 states: California, Hawaii, Idaho, Oregon, and Washington (William E. Moritz, "A Survey of North American Bicycle Commuters," University of Washington, Seattle, January 24, 1997). Most bicycle commuters surveyed (81 percent) were male, their average age was 39 years, and 69 percent were between the ages of 26 and 45. The majority of these bicycle riders (58 percent) described themselves as professionals, 63 percent had a household income of at least $45,000, and 44 percent owned a car. (Note that most [66 percent] of the respondents submitted their answers by way of the Internet.) Most (95 percent) of the bicycle commuters listed health/fitness as their reason for commuting, and 82 percent reported that their health had improved somewhat or greatly since they began commuting.

Many of the respondents indicated that facilities were available at their destination for storing bicycles: bike racks (69 percent), bike lockers (15 percent), or locked rooms/cages (19 percent). In addition to these accommodations offered by employers, many communities are developing incentives for bicycle commuters, thanks in part to a variety of federally funded programs developed to encourage Americans to ride their bicycles. In some West Coast cities (Berkeley, Long Beach, and Palo Alto, California, and Seattle, Washington), Bikestation franchises offer secure parking and bike rentals. Some stations also offer repairs and changing rooms for commuters.

MOUNTAIN BIKERS. Mountain biking officially took off as a sport in 1971 and became an Olympic event in 1996. The mountain bike has upright seating, 26-inch wheels, and larger tires that are more shock-absorbent than traditional road bike tires, making the ride more comfortable. Its range of gears allows for more versatility. According to the National Bicycle Dealers Association, mountain bikes made up 33.8 percent of specialty bicycles sold in 2002, down from 41.0 percent in 2000. (See Table 5.1.) Mountain bikes are now considered to be a maturing segment of the industry. The declining sales of mountain bikes may be in part a reflection of an emerging market for what are being called "comfort" bicycles, which look very much like mountain bikes, but have soft saddles, a more upright seating position, and easier gearing. Comfort bicycles accounted for 20.6 percent of specialty bicycle sales in 2002, up 51 percent since 2000.

Industry Outlook

Bicycle sales have experienced a series of ups and downs since the 1980s. A dramatic increase in gasoline prices in the 1970s and a growing concern over health and fitness combined to produce record overall sales of about 15.2 million bicycles in 1973. (See Table 5.2.) Sales then tumbled to 6.8 million in 1982, rose to 12.6 million in 1987, fell sharply to 9.9 million the following year, and reached 13 million in 1993. Nearly 17 million bicycles of all wheel sizes were projected to be sold in 2001, down 20 percent from projected sales in 2000, but in 2002 bicycle sales were projected to be on the rebound, rising to 19.5 million.

Bicycle sales are generally linked to two factors: market saturation and changing demographics. To continue the growth that bicycle sales enjoyed at their peak, owners would have to replace their bikes every three years. Currently, however, the average bike lasts longer than three years.

TABLE 5.3

Nonoccupant traffic fatalities, 1991–2001

Year	Pedestrian	Pedalcyclist	Other	Total
1991	5,801	843	124	6,768
1992	5,549	723	98	6,370
1993	5,649	816	111	6,576
1994	5,489	802	107	6,398
1995	5,584	833	109	6,526
1996	5,449	765	154	6,368
1997	5,321	814	153	6,288
1998	5,228	760	131	6,119
1999	4,939	754	149	5,842
2000	4,763	693	141	5,597
2001	4,882	728	120	5,730

SOURCE: "Table 5: Nonoccupant Traffic Fatalities, 1991–2001," in *Traffic Safety Facts 2001: Overview,* DOT HS 809 476, U.S. Department of Transportation, National Highway Traffic Safety Administration, Washington, DC, 2001 [Online] http://www-nrd.nhtsa.dot.gov/pdf/nrd-30/NCSA/TSF2001/2001overview.pdf [accessed April 14, 2003]

Companies are making a wider variety of cycles. Constant improvements are being made in design and materials, including aerodynamic handlebars and disc wheels. Indoor fitness equipment has also become an important part of the bicycle industry. Exercise bicycles and associated accessories have provided another path through which the bicycle industry can sell to people committed to physical fitness. Since cycling does not subject people to the pounding of some other sports, it can be a lifetime activity. Many bicycle stores in the United States sell some indoor exercise equipment.

The Imports

In 1979 American manufacturers heavily dominated the U.S. bicycle market, but in the 1990s the situation changed. In 1991 imports accounted for 43 percent of American bicycle sales; only 9 years later, imports accounted for 97 percent, according to the International Bicycle Fund. Declining interest in bicycling in the 1990s (which some analysts attribute to increased interest in inline skating) forced many U.S. manufacturers to close their plants. Most imported bicycles come from the People's Republic of China (mainland) and from the Republic of China (Taiwan), where production costs are cheaper.

Bikes and Accidents

Bicycle riding can be a hazardous activity. According to a report (Gregory B. Rodgers, *Part I. An Overview of the Bicycle Study*) available on the Consumer Product Safety Commission's Web site in 2003, every year almost half a million bicycle injuries are serious enough to require medical treatment. According to the Centers for Disease Control and Prevention, between July 2000 and June 2001, 337,499 children under age 15 were treated in emergency departments for bicycle injuries; 70 percent were boys and 30 percent were girls (*Morbidity and Mortality Weekly Report*, August 23, 2002). The National Highway Traffic Safety Administration (NHTSA) reported that 728 pedalcyclists were killed in 2001, up from 693 in 2000, representing nearly 13 percent of pedestrian/pedalcyclist traffic fatalities. (See Table 5.3.)

TABLE 5.4

Pedalcyclists killed, by related factors, 2001

Factors	Number	Percent
Failure to yield right of way	134	18.4
Riding, playing, working, etc., in roadway	112	15.4
Improper crossing of roadway or intersection	102	14.0
Failure to obey (e.g., signs, control devices, officers)	45	6.2
Not visible	38	5.2
Operating without required equipment	35	4.8
Failure to keep in proper lane or running off road	33	4.5
Inattentive (talking, eating, etc.)	31	4.3
Darting into road	25	3.4
Making improper turn	19	2.6
Failing to have lights on when required	17	2.3
Riding on wrong side of road	12	1.6
Improper lane changing	10	1.4
Improper entry to or exit from trafficway	4	0.5
Erratic, reckless, careless, or negligent operation	4	0.5
Other	46	6.3
None Reported	241	33.1
Unknown	20	2.7
Total Pedalcyclists	728	100.0

Note: The sum of the numbers and percentages is greater than total pedalcyclists killed as more than one factor may be present for the same pedalcyclist.

SOURCE: "Table 103: Pedalcyclists Killed, by Related Factors," in *Traffic Safety Facts 2001,* DOT HS 809 484, U.S. Department of Transportation, National Highway Traffic Safety Administration, Washington, DC, December 2002

The demographics of bicycle fatalities underwent a change between 1975 and 1998, according to an analysis done by Riley R. Geary of the Institute for Traffic Safety Analysis in Arlington, Virginia. Whereas in 1975 nearly 70 percent of bicycle deaths involved juveniles (under age 16), by 1998 only 30 percent involved juveniles. According to the Insurance Institute for Highway Safety (IIHS), by 2001 persons aged 16 and older accounted for 78 percent of all deaths from bicycle accidents.

Of fatal bicycle collisions that occurred in 2001, the IIHS reported that males (652) were far more likely to be involved than were females (72). Table 5.4 shows data relating to pedalcyclist deaths in 2001. Police reported one or more errors related to the cyclists' behavior for 64.2 percent of the pedalcyclists killed. Riding, playing, and working in the roadway (15.4 percent), failure to yield the right-of-way (18.4 percent), and improper crossing (14.0 percent) accounted for nearly half (47.8 percent) of the deaths.

Two factors affect cycling and safety. First, unlike the car driver, bicyclists are not surrounded by two or three tons of metal to help protect them in a crash or a fall.

TABLE 5.5

Teens and helmets, 2001

When you rode a motorcycle during the past 12 months, how often did you wear a helmet?

	All teens (13,357)
Did not ride a motorcycle	74.7%
Never wore a helmet	7.1
Rarely wore a helmet	2.3
Sometimes wore a helmet	2.5
Most of the time wore a helmet	3.3
Always wore a helmet	10.1

When you rode a bicycle during the past 12 months, how often did you wear a helmet?

	All teens (13,357)
Did not ride a bicycle	34.9%
Never wore a helmet	50.1
Rarely wore a helmet	5.0
Sometimes wore a helmet	3.3
Most of the time wore a helmet	2.9
Always wore a helmet	3.8

SOURCE: Adapted from "2001 National School-based Youth Risk Behavior Survey Public-use Data Documentation," U.S. Centers for Disease Control and Prevention, Atlanta, GA, 2002 [Online] http://www.cdc.gov/nccdphp/dash/yrbs/data/2001/yrbs2001.pdf [accessed April 14, 2003]

Second, many bicyclists do not wear protective helmets while riding. According to the IIHS, an estimated 82 percent of bicyclists who were killed in 2001 were not wearing helmets.

BIKE HELMETS MAKE SENSE. In "Bicycle Injuries and Safety Helmets in Children: Review of Research" (*Orthopaedic Nursing*, Jan-Feb 2003), Sherrilyn Coffman asserted that 10 percent of trauma deaths among children are related to bicycle injuries. She cited research demonstrating that in 1998, 76 percent of head injuries and 41 percent of deaths from head injury occurred among children younger than 15 years of age. Bicycle crashes were the most common cause of serious head injuries in children. Many of those injuries could have been avoided if the children had been wearing helmets. Coffman noted that in a national survey of parents carried out in 1995, fewer than one-quarter (23.1 percent) reported helmet use by their children; she also noted that other research has shown that parents tend to overestimate helmet use by their children.

There is no federal law mandating the use of bicycle helmets. According to the Bicycle Helmet Safety Institute, as of May 1, 2003, there were bicycle helmet laws of some kind in 31 states plus the District of Columbia. There were 19 state laws and 90 laws governing localities, with the majority being age-specific. For example, in California, all riders under age 18 and passengers under age 5 must wear a bicycle helmet.

In 2001 a national survey conducted by the Centers for Disease Control and Prevention asked teens how often they wore a helmet when riding a bicycle or motorcycle. (See Table 5.5.) More than half (50.1 percent) of teenagers claimed they never wore a helmet when riding a bicycle and 5 percent used their helmets "rarely." Only 3.8 percent wore their helmets all of the time, 2.9 percent wore one most of the time, and 3.3 percent wore a helmet some of the time. In January 2000 the NHTSA estimated that if all children ages 4 to 15 would wear helmets, 39,000 to 45,000 head injuries and 18,000 to 55,000 scalp and facial injuries would be prevented every year.

Governmental Support for Bicycles

Federal funds were made available for bicycle and pedestrian projects with the passage of the 1991 Intermodal Surface Transportation Efficiency Act (ISTEA; PL 102-240). ISTEA's successor, the Transportation Equity Act of 1998 (TEA-21), continued funding for bicycle projects, which typically involved the construction of transportation facilities (such as bike racks and lockers) and trails as well as the production and distribution of maps, safety brochures, etc.

The Safe, Accountable, Flexible, and Efficient Transportation Efficiency Act of 2003 (SAFETEA) is a proposed reauthorization of TEA-21. If approved by Congress, SAFETEA will make safety the priority in the allocation of nearly $250 billion in transportation funding for the period 2004–09. The states may dedicate the funds apportioned to them for "any safety improvement project on any public road or publicly owned bicycle or pedestrian pathway or trail." (The text of the bill is available online at http://www.fhwa.dot.gov/reauthorization/safetea.htm.)

RAILS-TO-TRAILS. Rails-to-Trails is part of a government program that was started in 1986 to make use of hundreds of miles of unused, scenic railway corridors. The Surface Transportation Board (part of the DOT) approves the abandonment of a line after service has been discontinued. Then a voluntary agreement, called railbanking, may be entered into between the railroad company and a park agency, allowing the rail corridor to be used as a trail until the railroad company might need the corridor for service again.

By January 2003 Rails-to-Trails had turned more than 12,000 miles of tracks in all states into public recreation trails for bikers, hikers, and horseback riders. The most heavily used trails are in Massachusetts, Virginia, Florida, Washington, Rhode Island, Illinois, Maryland, and Utah as noted on the organization's Web site in 2003. The Rails-to-Trails Conservancy hopes an additional 15,000 miles will be built by 2005. Much of the funding for Rails-to-Trails conversions was provided by ISTEA. The preservation and conversion of abandoned railway corridors was one of 10 specific nonhighway projects for which ISTEA set aside $3.3 billion. TEA-21 continued to dedicate funds to improving bicycle access through more Rails-to-Trails. The Department of Transportation also contributes money ($30 million annually) through its Recreation Trails Trust Fund.

International Bicycle Use

In countries with high automobile ownership, the extent of bicycle use has varied depending upon public policy and popular attitudes. According to a Worldwatch Institute news release, strong support from citizens and governments in the 1990s resulted in a burgeoning use of bicycles as a way of reducing pollution and congestion (Gary Gardiner, "Cities Turning to Bicycles to Cut Costs, Pollution, and Crime," August 26, 1998). Particularly in big cities in Germany, Denmark, and the Netherlands, bicycles account for up to 30 percent of trips, compared with only 1 percent in the United States.

CHINA. Before 1979 the Chinese government rationed bicycles and only one person in four or five had a bicycle. Following government reforms of 1979, rationing ended and one-third of the road space was set aside for cyclists. By 2001 there were 540 million bicycles in China and residents of Beijing made 40 percent of their daily trips on a bicycle (Philip P. Pan, "Bicycle No Longer King of the Road in China," *The Washington Post,* March 12, 2001).

GREAT BRITAIN. In Great Britain a project called Sustrans (sustainable transport), which began in 2001, has established a National Cycle Network. As of 2003 Sustrans reported that its network consisted of 6,500 miles of traffic-free and traffic-calmed routes for cyclists and for walkers throughout the United Kingdom, with a total goal of 10,000 miles by 2005. The project is funded by the national lottery, local authorities, and donations; it aims to reduce the emissions that contribute to global warming. Safe routes to schools and train stations are planned.

FINLAND. The city of Helsinki, Finland, instituted a policy aimed at doubling the number of trips residents made on bicycles, from 6 percent in 1995 to 12 percent by 2005, in order to benefit both city traffic and public health. The city also set a goal to reduce the number of cycling accidents by one-third. City planners created bike lanes, bike parking, and bike-and-ride transit opportunities to facilitate the use of pedal transportation, along with marketing efforts to educate the public on the benefits of cycling. Officials expected millions of dollars in savings on road surfacing and infrastructure, parking spaces, reduction of noise, congestion, and emissions. They also expected a reduction in healthcare costs due to increased fitness, according to a report available on the Internet on the European Local Transport Information Service Web site (www.eltis.org). A study by Dr. Eero Pasanen ("The Risks of Cycling," Helsinki City Planning Department, 1999) found an unintended consequence of the city's encouragement of bicycling: cyclists traveling on the city's new two-way bike paths were more likely to be injured than cyclists traveling on streets with motor traffic.

New Kinds of Cycles

Bicycle innovators are constantly working on new developments for the industry. Recent attention has focused on electric bicycles. Although they are more popular abroad, the United States has several models of electric-powered bicycles on the market. The eGo, for example, requires no pedaling (unlike most electric bicycles), uses no gasoline, reaches a top speed of 23 miles per hour, and runs for 25 miles on a battery that charges in five hours. The Chinese introduced the world's first no-pollution battery electric bicycle in December 2002; its zinc-air battery, unlike a lead battery, emits no waste after disposal. According to Electric Bikes Northwest, a leading electric bicycle dealer, 200,000 electric bicycles were sold in Japan in 2002 and 50,000 were sold in Europe. U.S sales are predicted to surpass European sales by 2005, according to Seattle's Electric Bikes Northwest Web site in 2003.

Electric bike manufacturers are targeting commuters, environmentalists, college students, messengers, and older riders, or anyone who enjoys riding a bike but would like a little help on the hills. The electric bicycle models cost from around $600 to $1,900. Manufacturers are also making kits that can be installed on any bicycle to turn it into an electric bike for half the cost of a ready-made model.

MOTORCYCLES

Motorcycling is both a popular recreational activity and a source of transportation. Industry and government agencies use motorcycles in such varied activities as law enforcement, agriculture, and land resource management. According to the Motorcycle Industry Council, Inc., a non-profit, national trade association that represents the motorcycle industry, there were about 6.6 million motorcycles and scooters in use in 2001 ("Impaired Motorcycle Riding: Law Enforcement Officers Focus Group Results," NHSTA, February 2001).

Information available on the NHTSA's Web site in 2003 ("Introduction to Motorcycles") defined "current street-legal" motorcycles as follows:

- Traditional—designed as basic transportation, with few frills
- Cruiser—today's most popular model, featuring a long profile with a low saddle height and emphasizing style over performance
- Sportbike—today's second most popular model, featuring a streamlined body, and emphasizing handling, acceleration, speed, braking, and cornering ability

FIGURE 5.2

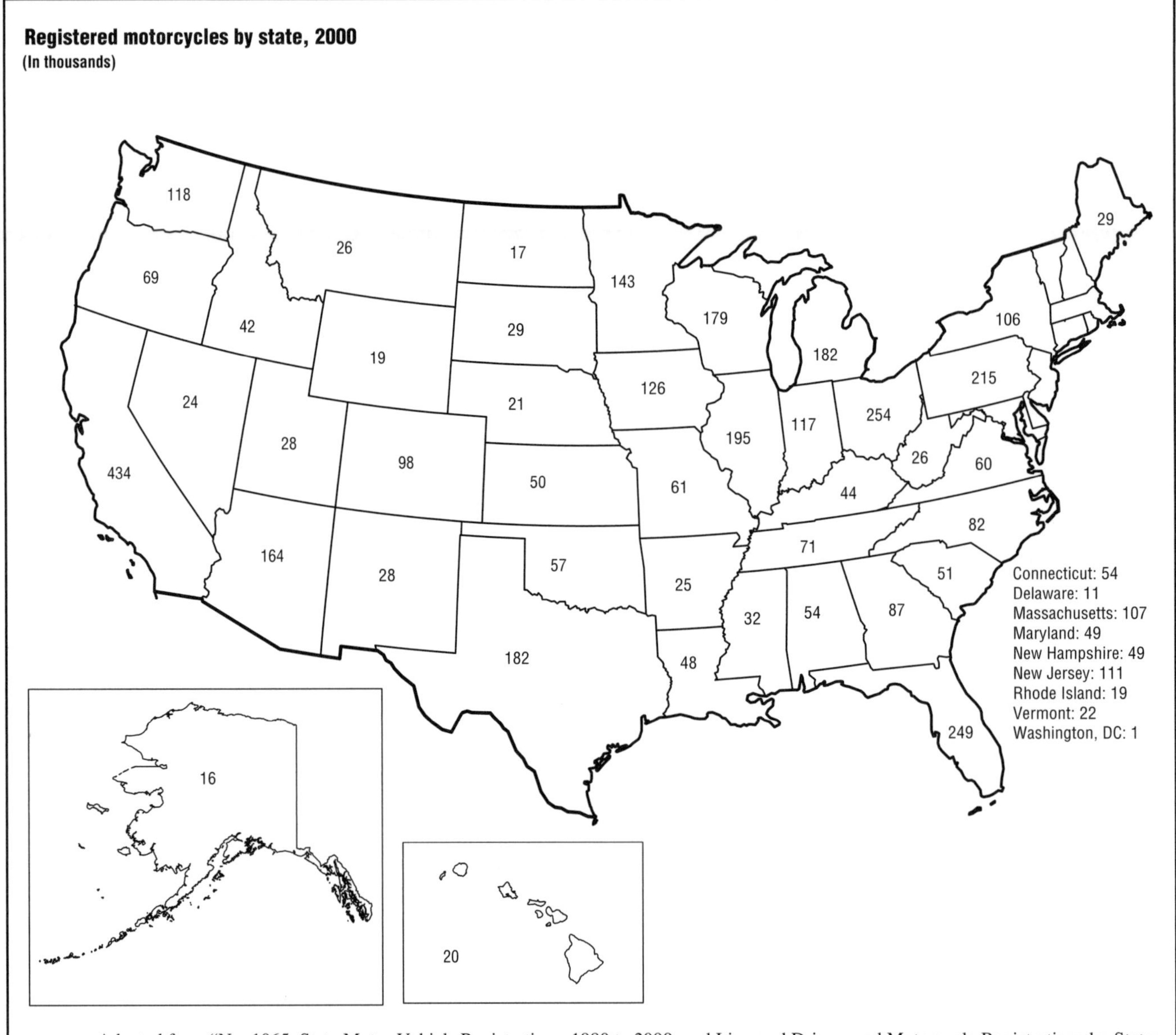

Registered motorcycles by state, 2000
(In thousands)

SOURCE: Adapted from "No. 1065. State Motor Vehicle Registrations, 1980 to 2000, and Licensed Drivers and Motorcycle Registrations by State: 2000," in *Statistical Abstract of the United States: 2002,* U.S. Census Bureau, December 2002

- Touring—today's third most popular model, a large bike with amenities for traveling long distances in comfort
- Sport-Touring—a combination of the handling of sportbikes and the comfort and some of the luggage capacity of touring bikes, designed for medium- and long-distance travel on curving roads
- Dual-Purpose—designed for use on- and off-road, featuring a tall, narrow, lightweight body
- Scooters—small, lower-power vehicles suitable for travel on urban surface streets
- Mopeds and Nopeds—lightweight, low-power vehicles that resemble bicycles
- Sidecar—a one-wheel device that can be attached to the side of a motorcycle to carry a passenger or cargo
- Trike—a three-wheel motorized vehicle created by grafting the front of a motorcycle to the back of a car or by adding a rear axle to the rear of a motorcycle

Federal regulations define highway motorcycles as "any motor vehicle with a headlight, taillight, and stoplight and having: two wheels, or three wheels and a curb mass less than or equal to 793 kilograms (1749 pounds)" ("Proposed Emission Standards for New Highway Motorcycles and Recreational Boats," Environmental Protection Agency, Washington, D.C., July 2002). Federal Motor Vehicle Safety Standards regulate motorcycle manufacturing standards, but the 50 states govern their operation, registration, and licensing.

FIGURE 5.3

Retail sales of new motorcycles, 1970–2000

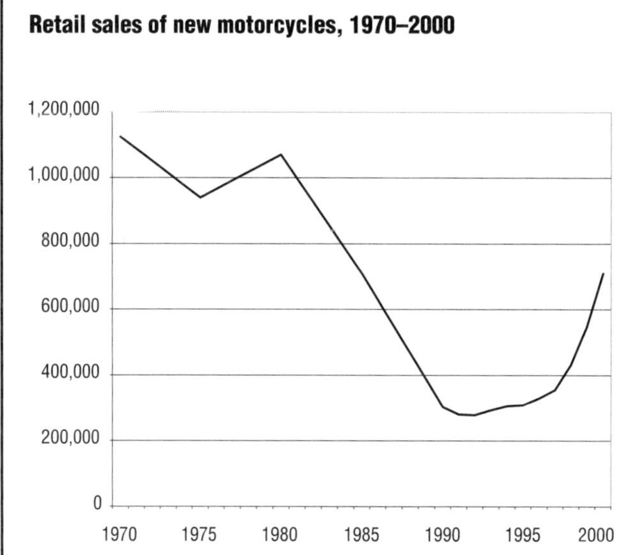

Notes: Data for 1971–1974, 1976–1979, 1981–1984, and 1986–1989 are interpolated. Data for 1999 is revised. Retail sales of new motorcycles includes domestic and imported vehicles. Prior to 1985, all terrain vehicles (ATVs) were included in the motorcycle total. In 1995, the Motorcycle Industry Council revised its data for the years 1985 to present to exclude ATVs from its totals.

SOURCE: Adapted from "Table 1-12: Sales or Deliveries of New Aircraft, Vehicles, Vessels, and Other Conveyances," in *National Transportation Statistics 2002,* Bureau of Transportation Statistics [Online] http://www.bts.gov/publications/national_transportation_statistics/2002/html/table_01_12.html [accessed May 19, 2003]

Numbers

The U.S. Census Bureau reported that in 2000 there were 4.3 million registered motorcycles in the United States, up 4.9 percent from 1999. Regionally, California has traditionally led the nation in motorcycle population. In 2000 there were 434,000 registered motorcycles in California, or 10 percent of the total. (See Figure 5.2.) Ohio ranked second with 5.9 percent of total registrations and Florida ranked third at 5.8 percent.

Motorcycle sales peaked in 1970, when more than 1.1 million new units were sold. (See Figure 5.3.) In 1985, 500,000 motorcycles were sold; the number then declined through the rest of the decade. The industry recovered strongly during the 1990s, with sales growing 66 percent from 1992 to 1998. Sales of scooters, in particular, rose dramatically, from about 12,000 in 1997 to 50,000 in 2001 (Matt Nauman, "Scooters Zooming in Popularity," *Knight Ridder/Tribune News Service,* May 20, 2002). In 2002 the motorcycle industry marked its tenth consecutive year of rising sales, with more than 937,000 new units sold, up 9.4 percent over the 2001 figure of more than 850,000. (Jean Halliday, "Motorcycle Makers Face Aging Clientele; BMW, Others Launch Efforts to Lure Young," *Advertising Age,* April 14, 2003).

A Global Industry

Just like the automobile industry, the motorcycle industry is a global enterprise. In countries as far-flung as Australia, Italy, Germany, Mexico, and Japan, the motorcycle is a method of transportation, a form of fun and sport, and an important economic sector. According to *Advertising Age*, the top-ranked motorcycles in terms of U.S. sales in 2002 were produced by Harley-Davidson (American) and three Japanese companies, Yamaha, Honda, and Suzuki.

Harley-Davidson, based in Wisconsin, exports more than 50,000 motorcycles each year, according to a Wisconsin Department of Commerce press release dated May 13, 2003. U.S. government export data show that motorcycle and motorcycle parts exports to Mexico increased 170.1 percent between 2001 and 2002; exports to Australia were up 59.6 percent; and exports to Belgium were up 40.3 percent ("Top 20 U.S. Export Destinations for Motorcycles and Parts," International Trade Administration, U.S. Department of Commerce, Washington, D.C., 2003). In that same period, imports from Brazil were up 218.0 percent, imports from China were up 55.5 percent, and imports from Denmark were up 175.4 percent ("Top 20 U.S. Import Sources for Motorcycles and Parts," International Trade Administration, U.S. Department of Commerce, Washington, D.C., 2003).

The Motorcycle Owner—A Profile

According to a frequently cited Motorcycle Industry Council survey, in 1998 the average motorcycle owner was 38 years old and married, with a high school diploma or more and a median household income of $44,100. The greatest percentage of motorcycle owners were male (92 percent), but the percentage of female owners reached 8 percent in 1998, up from 6 percent in 1990 and 1 percent in 1960 ("Motorcycle Ownership Profile by Age, Marital Status, Education, Occupation and Income: 1980, 1985, 1990 and 1998," Motorcycle Industry Council, 1999).

Harley-Davidson manufactures cruisers, which are especially popular with Baby Boomers. Of the more than 261,000 cruisers sold in 2001, Harley-Davidson's share of the market was 45 percent (117,742) (Don J. Brown, "2001 Market Recap: There It Is!" *Dealernews*, vol. 38, January 2002). Harley-Davidson purchasers are older and wealthier than the typical motorcycle owner, according to the 2001 Motorcycle Industry Council survey. The median age of a Harley buyer was 45.6 years and his median household income was $78,300. More than one quarter (28 percent) of purchasers were either new to motorcycles or had not owned a motorcycle in the past 5 years.

Safety Record

The fatality record for motorcycles improved between 1991–97. (See Table 5.6.) In 1991, 2,806 people were

TABLE 5.6

Motorcyclist fatalities and injuries and fatality and injury rates, 1991–2001

Year	Fatalities	Registered vehicles	Fatality rate [1]	Vehicle miles traveled (millions)	Fatality rate [2]
1991	2,806	4,177,365	6.7	9,178	30.57
1992	2,395	4,065,118	5.9	9,557	25.06
1993	2,449	3,977,856	6.2	9,906	24.72
1994	2,320	3,756,555	6.2	10,240	22.66
1995	2,227	3,897,191	5.7	9,797	22.73
1996	2,161	3,871,599	5.6	9,920	21.78
1997	2,116	3,826,373	5.5	10,081	20.99
1998	2,294	3,879,450	5.9	10,260	22.31
1999	2,483	4,152,433	6.0	10,584	23.46
2000	2,862	4,346,068	6.7	10,479	27.65
2001	3,181	—	—	—	—
Year	**Injuries**	**Registered vehicles**	**Injury rate [1]**	**Vehicle miles traveled (millions)**	**Injury rate [2]**
1991	80,000	4,177,365	193	9,178	876
1992	65,000	4,065,118	160	9,557	681
1993	59,000	3,977,856	149	9,906	600
1994	57,000	3,756,555	153	10,240	561
1995	57,000	3,897,191	147	9,797	587
1996	55,000	3,871,599	143	9,920	557
1997	53,000	3,826,373	137	10,081	526
1998	49,000	3,879,450	126	10,260	477
1999	50,000	4,152,433	120	10,584	472
2000	58,000	4,346,068	133	10,479	551
2001	60,000	—	—	—	—

[1] Rate per 10,000 registered vehicles
[2] Rate per 100 million vehicle miles traveled
— = not available

SOURCE: "Table 1. Motorcyclist Fatalities and Injuries and Fatality and Injury Rates, 1991–2001," in *Traffic Safety Facts 2001: Motorcycles,* U.S. Department of Transportation, National Highway Traffic Safety Administration, DOT HS 809 473 [Online] http://www-nrd.nhtsa.dot.gov/pdf/nrd-30/NCSA/TSF2001/2001mcycle.pdf [accessed May 19, 2003]

FIGURE 5.4

Previous driving records of drivers involved in fatal traffic accidents by type of vehicle, 2001

(Percent)

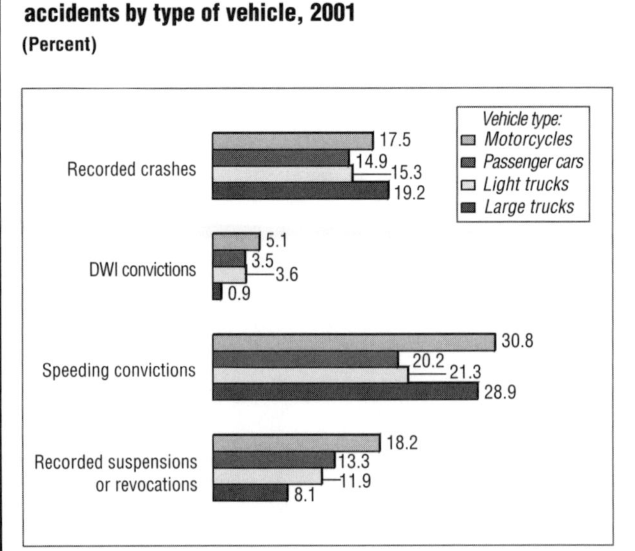

SOURCE: "Figure 1. Previous Driving Records of Drivers Involved in Fatal Traffic Crashes, by Type of Vehicle, 2001," in *Traffic Safety Facts 2001: Motorcycles,* U.S. Department of Transportation, National Highway Traffic Safety Administration, DOT 809 473 [Online] http://www-nrd.nhtsa.dot.gov/pdf/nrd-30/NCSA/TSF2001/2001mcycle.pdf [accessed May 19, 2003]

killed on motorcycles. By 1997 this number dropped 25 percent to 2,116. Fatalities then began to climb again, rising 39 percent from 1998–2001. While the number of vehicle miles traveled generally climbed, the fatality rate per 100 million vehicle miles traveled dropped from 30.57 in 1991 to 27.65 in 2000.

The total number of motorcycle injuries fell 27.5 percent between 1991 (80,000) and 2000 (58,000) and then rose 3.4 percent in 2001 (60,000). The injury rate tumbled from 876 injuries per 100 million miles traveled in 1991 to 472 in 1999 and then rose 16.7 percent in 2000 (551). (See Table 5.6.)

The Motorcycle Industry Council attributes part of the decline in fatalities and injuries in the 1990s to increased participation in *RiderCourse* education and training programs developed by the Motorcycle Safety Foundation. These programs, designed for both beginning and experienced riders, are generally supported by state funding and administered by state agencies. According to the American Motorcycle Network's Web site, between 1974 and 2002 more than 2.5 million riders graduated from *RiderCourse* programs. Safety helmet laws and a greater recognition of the dangers of drinking and driving were also believed to have contributed to the decline.

Several theories have been advanced to explain the more than 50 percent increase in fatalities between 1997 and 2001. They include more motorcycles on the road, the repeal of helmet laws in some states, and the rising number of older riders. According to the IIHS, in 1990, 14 percent of motorcyclists killed (438 of 3,128) were age 40 or over; by 2000 the age 40+ share of motorcycle fatalities was 40.4 percent (1,127 of 2,789) ("Fatality Facts: Motorcycles as of November 2002," Arlington, VA, 2003).

When a motorcycle is involved in an accident, the rider's chances of being seriously hurt or killed are much higher than if he or she were riding in a vehicle that afforded more protection. Motorcycles made up 2 percent of all registered vehicles in the United States in 2001 and accounted for only 0.4 percent of all vehicle miles traveled, according to the NHTSA. But motorcycles accounted for 8 percent of total traffic fatalities in 2001, and per vehicle mile, motorcyclists were 21 times as likely as occupants of cars to die in a traffic crash.

Many cyclists involved in fatal accidents have little or no professional instruction or training. More than

FIGURE 5.5

Intoxication rates for motorcyclists killed in traffic accidents by time of day, 2001

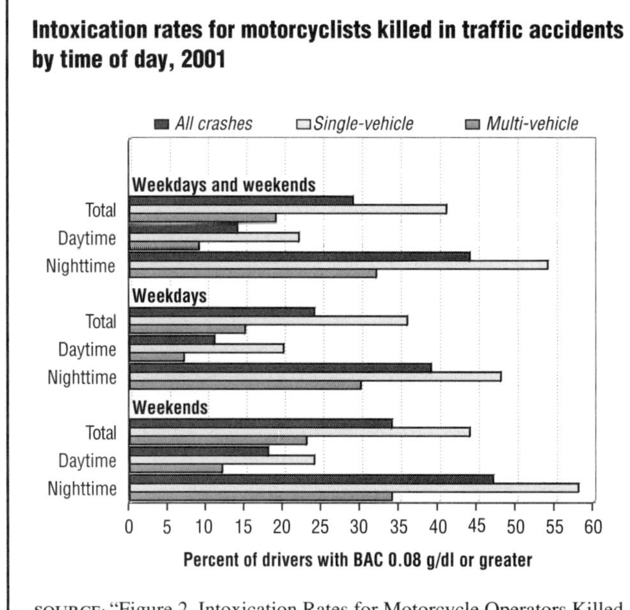

SOURCE: "Figure 2. Intoxication Rates for Motorcycle Operators Killed in Traffic Crashes, by Time of Day, 2001," in *Traffic Safety Facts 2001: Motorcycles,* U.S. Department of Transportation, National Highway Traffic Safety Administration, DOT 809 473 [Online] http://www-nrd.nhtsa.dot.gov/pdf/nrd-30/NCSA/TSF2001/2001mcycle.pdf [accessed May 19, 2003]

FIGURE 5.6

Motorcycle helmets

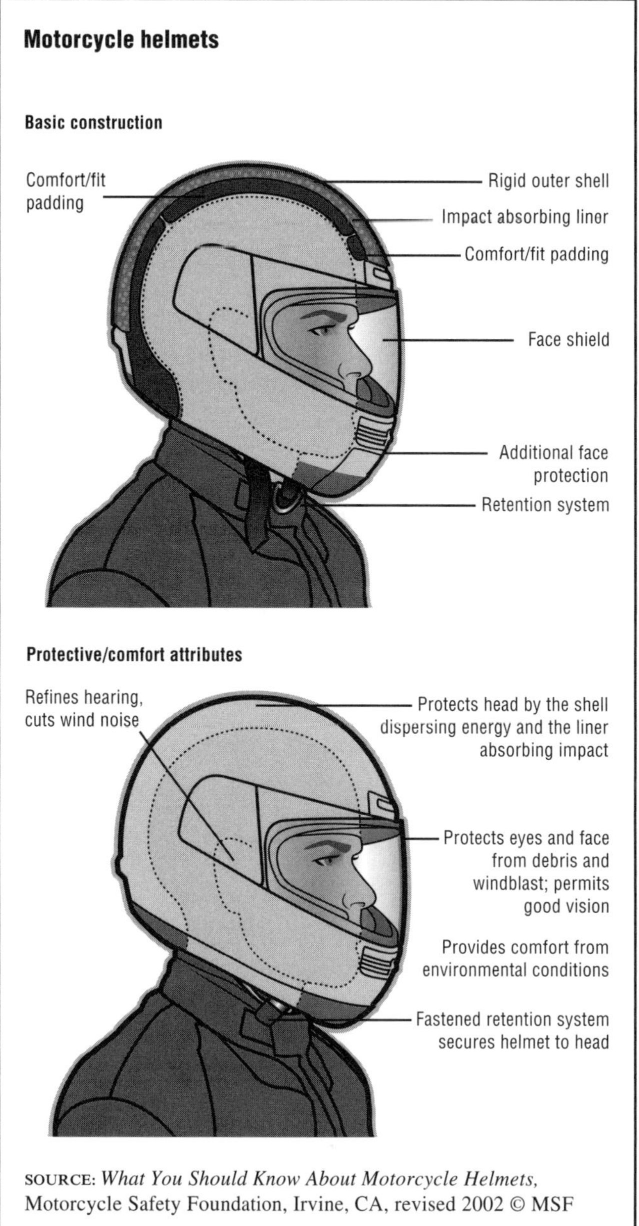

SOURCE: *What You Should Know About Motorcycle Helmets,* Motorcycle Safety Foundation, Irvine, CA, revised 2002 © MSF

one-quarter of those killed in 2001 (27 percent) did not have valid operating licenses, and nearly 1 in 5 (18.2 percent) had records of suspended or revoked licenses. (See Figure 5.4.) Nearly one-third (30.8 percent) had been convicted of speeding, 5.1 percent had been convicted for driving while intoxicated, and 17.5 percent had been involved in crashes before.

Severity of injury is directly related to speed, motorcycle size, and the amount of alcohol involved. In 41 percent of deaths of cyclists in single-vehicle motorcycle crashes in 2001, the drivers had blood alcohol concentrations at or above 0.08 percent, the national standard for impaired driving in most states. (See Figure 5.5.) The majority (58 percent) of cyclists killed in single-vehicle crashes on weekend nights were intoxicated.

The Helmet Issue

One of the things that makes motorcycling attractive to some people is the freedom of riding in the open air, although this can have its drawbacks, such as bad weather, insects flying into the driver's face, and debris flying up from the road. As a result, motorcycle gear was invented to offer riders comfort and protection.

The most important piece of equipment for a motorcyclist is a helmet. (See Figure 5.6.) Helmets protect the head in two ways. The outer shell resists penetration and abrasion, while the inner portion absorbs the shock by slowly collapsing on impact. Both the outer shell and the inner liner spread the force of an impact throughout the entire helmet. When a rider collides with the pavement while wearing a protective helmet, it should be not unlike landing head first on a thick cushion.

In addition, a motorcycle helmet reduces wind noise and windblast and deflects insects and pebbles that fly into the rider's face. The helmet with an ANSI or Snell sticker means that it conforms to the standards of the American National Standards Institute or the Snell Memorial Foundation.

As of 2001, 20 states, the District of Columbia, and Puerto Rico required helmet usage by all motorcycle operators and passengers, down from 21 states in 1999. (See Table 5.7.) Florida repealed its helmet law effective July 1, 2000, and Massachusetts was considering a bill introduced

TABLE 5.7

State motorcycle helmet use requirements, as of 2001

State	Original law	Subsequent action, date(s) and current status
AL	11/06/67	Helmet use required for all riders.
AK	01/01/71	Repealed effective 7-1-76 except for persons under 18 years of age, and all passengers.
AZ	01/01/69	Repealed effective 5-27-76 except for persons under 18 years of age.
AR	07/10/67	Helmet use required for all riders. Repealed effective 8/1/97 except for riders under 21 years of age.
CA	01/01/85	Helmet use required by riders under 15 1/2 years of age. Effective 1-1-92 helmet use required for all riders.
CO	07/01/69	Repealed effective 5-20-77. No helmet use requirement.
CT	10/01/67	Not enforced until 2-1-74. Repealed effective 6-1-76. Effective 1-1-90 adopted requirement for helmet use by persons under 18.
DE	10/01/68	Repealed effective 6-10-78 except for persons under 19 years of age. Also requires that a helmet be carried on the motorcycle for persons 19 and older.
DC	10/12/70	Helmet use required for all riders.
FL	09/05/67	Repealed effective 7-1-2000 except for riders under 21 years old and those without $10,000 medical insurance covering injuries resulting from a motorcycle crash.
GA	08/31/66	Helmet use required for all riders.
HI	05/01/68	Repealed effective 6-7-77 except for persons under 18 years of age.
ID	01/01/68	Repealed effective 3-29-78 except for persons under 18 years of age.
IL	01/01/68	Repealed effective 6-17-69 after being declared unconstitutional by the State Supreme Court on 5-28-69. No helmet use requirement.
IN	07/01/67	Repealed effective 9-1-77. Effective 6-1-85 adopted requirement for helmet use by persons under 18.
IA	09/01/75	Repealed effective 7-1-76. No helmet use requirement.
KS	07/01/67	7-1-67 to 3-17-70 for all cyclists. 3-17-70 to 7-1-72 only for cyclists under 21 years of age. 7-1-72 to 7-1-76 for all cyclists. 7-1-76 to 7-1-82 applied only to persons under 16 years of age. After 7-1-82 applies only to persons under 18 years of age.
KY	07/01/68	Repealed effective 7-15-98 except for riders under 21 years old, riders operating with instruction permit, riders with less than 1 year experience and/or riders not providing proof of health insurance. Insurance provision repealed effective 7-15-2000.
LA	07/31/68	Repealed effective 10-1-76 except for persons under 18 years of age. Readopted for all cyclists effective 1-1-82. Repealed effective 8-15-99 except for riders under age 18 and those without $10,000 medical insurance; proof of insurance policy must be shown to law enforcement officer upon request.
ME	10/07/67	Repealed effective 10-24-77. Amended effective 7-3-80 to require use by cyclists under 15 years of age, novices, and holders of learner's permits.
MD	09/01/68	Repealed effective 5-29-79 except for persons under 18 years of age. Effective 10-1-92 helmet use required for all riders.
MA	02/27/67	Helmet use required for all riders.
MI	03/10/67	Repealed effective 6-12-68. New law adopted effective 9-1-69. Helmet use required for all riders.
MN	05/01/68	Repealed effective 4-6-77 except for persons under 18 years of age.
MS	03/28/74	Helmet use required for all riders.
MO	10/13/67	Helmet use required for all riders.
MT	07/01/73	Repealed effective 7-1-77 except for persons under 18 years of age.
NE	05/29/67	Never enforced. Declared unconstitutional by State Supreme Court and repealed effective 9-1-77. Effective 1-1-89 helmet use required for all riders.
NV	01/01/72	Helmet use required for all riders.
NH	09/03/67	Repealed effective 8-7-77 except for persons under 18 years of age.
NJ	01/01/68	Helmet use required for all riders.
NM	05/01/67	Initial law applied only to cyclists under 18 years of age and to all passengers. Law requiring helmet use by all cyclists adopted effective 7-1-73. Repealed effective 6-17-77 except for persons under 18 years of age.
NY	01/01/67	Helmet use required for all riders.
NC	01/01/68	Helmet use required for all riders.
ND	07/01/67	Repealed effective 7-1-77 except for persons under 18 years of age.
OH	04/02/68	Repealed effective 7-1-78 except for persons under 18 years and first year novices.
OK	04/27/67	4-27-67 to 4-7-69 helmet use required for all motorcyclists. From 4-7-69 to 5-3-76 for cyclists under 21 years of age. 5-3-76 for cyclists under 18 years of age.
OR	01/01/68	Repealed effective 10-4-77, except for persons under 18 years of age. Effective 6-16-89 helmet use required for all riders.
PA	09/13/68	Helmet use required for all riders.
RI	06/30/67	Repealed effective 5-21-76 except for passengers on motorcycles. Effective 7-01-92 helmet use required for operators under 21 years of age, all passengers, and first year novices.
SC	07/01/67	Repealed for ages 21 and over effective 6-16-80. Required for riders under 18 years old.
SD	07/01/67	Repealed effective 7-1-77 except for persons under 18 years of age.
TN	06/05/67	Helmet use required for all riders.
TX	01/01/68	Repealed effective 9-1-77 except for persons under 18 years of age. Effective 9-1-89 helmet use required for all riders. Effective 9-1-97 helmets required for riders under 21, those who have not completed a rider training course, and those without $10,000 medical insurance.
UT	05/13/69	Helmets required only on roads with speed limits of 35 mph or higher. Effective 5-8-77 law changed to require helmet use only by persons under 18 years of age.
VT	07/01/68	Helmet use required for all riders.
VA	01/01/71	Helmet use required for all riders.
WA	07/01/67	Repealed effective 7-1-77. 7-1-87 helmet use required for riders under 18. Effective 6-8-90 helmet use required for all riders.
WV	05/21/68	Helmet use required for all riders.
WI	07/01/68	Repealed effective 3-19-78 except for persons under 18 years of age, and for all holders of learner's permits.
WY	05/25/73	Repealed effective 5-27-83 except for persons under 18 years of age.
PR	07/20/60	Helmet use required for all riders.

- 20 states plus the District of Columbia and Puerto Rico require helmet use for all riders.
- 27 states require helmet use for certain riders.
- 3 states do not require helmet use for riders.

SOURCE: "Table 124: Status of State Motorcycle Helmet Use Requirements," *Traffic Safety Facts, 2001,* Department of Transportation, National Highway Traffic Safety Administration, Washington, DC, December 2002

FIGURE 5.7

RV types and terms, 2003

Recreation vehicle/RV (AR'-Vee)n.— A recreation vehicle, or RV, is a motorized or towable vehicle that combines transportation and temporary living quarters for travel, recreation, and camping. RV's do not include mobile homes, off-road vehicles or snowmobiles. Following are descriptions of specific types of RV's and their average retail price.

Towables

RV's designed to be towed by a motorized vehicle (car, van or pickup truck) and of such size and weight as not to require a special highway movement permit. Towable RV's do not require permanent on-site hook-up.

$5,483
Folding camping trailer
A lightweight unit designed for towing by most motorized vehicles, even some small compact cars. It ranges from 15 to 23 feet in length (when opened) with sides that collapse for towing and storage.

$14,308
Truck camper
A unit ranging from 18 to 21 feet in length designed to be loaded onto or affixed to the bed or chassis of a pickup.

$15,336
Travel trailer
A unit ranging from 12 to 35 feet in length designed to be towed by a car, van, or pickup by means of a bumper or frame hitch.

$25,838
Fifth-wheel travel trailer
A unit ranging from 21 to 40 feet in length designed to be affixed and towed by a pickup equipped with special hitch in the truck bed.

Motorized

RV's built on or as an integral part of a self-propelled motor vehicle chassis, combining transportation and living quarters in one unit.

$130,483
Conventional (Type A)
The living unit has been entirely constructed on a bare, specially designed motor vehicle chassis.

$57,146
Van camper (Type B)
A cargo van that has been customized to include temporary sleeping, eating, and bathroom facilities.

$56,474
Mini (Type C)
A scaled-down unit built on an automotive manufactured van frame with an attached cab section.

SOURCE: Recreation Vehicle Industry Association [Online] http://www.rvia.org/consumers/recreationvehicles/types.htm [accessed April 10, 2003]

in May 2003 that would permit motorcyclists over age 21 to ride without helmets. In 27 states, only minors (drivers under 18 or 21) were required to wear helmets. Three states (Colorado, Illinois, and Iowa) had no laws requiring helmet use.

A Study of Helmet Use

In 1997 Arkansas and Texas amended their helmet laws, which had mandated universal use of helmets, to then require only that motorcycle drivers under 21 wear helmets. Researchers for the NHTSA conducted a study of the consequences of these changes in laws (*Evaluation of Motorcycle Helmet Law Repeal in Arkansas and Texas,* Washington, D.C., September 2000). By May 1998 helmet use had fallen to 52 percent in Arkansas and 66 percent in Texas. In 1998 motorcyclist fatalities increased by 21 percent in Arkansas and by 31 percent in Texas compared with 1996.

The NHTSA report quoted a General Accounting Office finding that

> "helmet use reduces fatality rates and reduces injury severity among survivors of motorcycle accidents" and that "universal helmet laws have been very effective in increasing helmet use, virtually doubling use compared with experience without a law or with a limited law applying only to young riders. Under universal helmet laws, most states experienced 20 to 40 percent lower fatality rates than during periods without laws or under limited laws." Several studies conducted since 1991 provide more recent evidence of the same effects.

The Bureau of Transportation Statistics reported that helmets saved the lives of 674 people in 2001; a total of

TABLE 5.8

Recreational/conversion vehicles shipments data, 1978–2002

	Recreation vehicles			Conversion vehicles		
Year	RV unit shipments (in 000)	% Change from prior year	RV retail value (in billions)	CV unit shipments (in 000)	% Change from prior year	CV retail value (in billions)
1978	389.9	- 5.8	4.077	136.4	+ 13.6	$1.606
1979*	199.2	- 48.9	2.123	108.5	- 20.5	1.458
1980*	107.2	- 46.2	1.168	71.3	- 34.3	.783
1981	133.6	+ 24.6	1.253	99.8	+ 4.0	1.448
1982	140.6	+ 5.2	1.879	111.3	+ 11.5	1.539
1983	196.6	+ 39.8	3.485	104.2	- 6.4	2.837
1984	215.7	+ 9.7	4.393	175.3	+ 68.2	3.340
1985	186.9	- 13.4	3.936	164.8	- 6.0	3.093
1986	189.8	+ 1.6	4.031	181.9	+ 10.4	3.533
1987	211.7	+ 11.5	4.660	181.9	0.0	3.740
1988	215.8	+ 1.9	4.955	204.2	+ 12.3	4.233
1989	187.9	- 12.9	4.589	200.4	- 1.9	4.438
1990	173.1	- 7.9	4.113	174.2	- 13.1	4.110
1991	163.3	- 5.7	3.614	130.4	- 25.1	3.124
1992	203.4	+ 24.6	4.411	179.3	+ 37.5	4.492
1993	227.8	+ 12.0	4.713	192.4	+ 7.3	4.805
1994**	259.2	+ 13.8	5.691	259.6	+ 35.0	6.505
1995	247.0	- 4.7	5.894	228.2	- 12.1	6.210
1996	247.5	+ 0.2	6.328	219.3	- 3.9	6.038
1997	254.5	+ 2.8	6.904	184.3	- 16.0	5.024
1998	292.7	+15.0	8.364	148.6	-19.4	4.393
1999	321.2	+9.7	10.413	152.6	+2.7	4.964
2000	300.1	-6.6	9.529	118.2	-22.5	4.133
2001	256.8	-14.4	8.598	64.2	-45.7	2.272
2002	311.0	+21.1	10.960	67.7	+5.5	2.537

* Gas & Credit Crunch
** Beginning in 1994, CV shipment figures include truck and sport-utility vehicle conversions.

SOURCE: "RV Shipments Data: Shipments History," Recreation Vehicle Industry Association [Online] http://www.rvia.org/media/ShipmentsData.htm [accessed April 14, 2003]

18,461 lives were saved by helmet use between 1975 and 2001. Table 5.5 shows that of more than 13,000 teens surveyed in 2001, only 10.1 percent reported always wearing a helmet when riding a motorcycle.

RECREATIONAL VEHICLES

Recreational vehicles (RVs) come in a variety of shapes and sizes, suited to the various needs of those who want to take the comforts of home with them when they travel. The Recreation Vehicle Industry Association (RVIA) recognizes two categories of RVs: towables and motorized vehicles. (See Figure 5.7.) Motorized vehicles combine transportation and living quarters in a single unit. Towables, as the name implies, must be towed by a motorized vehicle.

Many RVs have comfortable beds, modern kitchens and bathrooms, and dining and living rooms. Many offer homelike luxuries, such as televisions, air conditioning, and microwave ovens. Among the most popular electronic extra features included in RVs are surround-sound stereos, CD players, TVs, VCRs, and video game systems. New high-tech options include bedrooms that convert into offices, featuring a dedicated spot for computer and Internet jacks, and moving walls that expand the interior living space for added comfort once the RV is parked. Known as a slideout, this feature allows the owner to electronically push a portion of the RV's exterior wall outward up to three and one-half feet to enlarge the living, dining, sleeping, or kitchen area. The only limitation on such amenities is cost. In 2003 costs for standard RVs ranged from an average of $5,483 for a folding camping trailer to $130,483 for a large motor home, according to the RVIA. (See Figure 5.7.)

Special luxury RVs, including buses designed for people to live in for extended periods, can be very expensive. The Me2 by Travel Supreme, a 41-foot luxury motor home, cost $325,000 in 2003; it includes a built-in garage for storing a small car to be used for short trips (Julie Rawe, "Not Your Dad's RV," *Time*, April 7, 2003). Other, even more expensive models might feature a 51-inch projection screen TV, global positioning equipment, air-operated pocket doors (similar to those seen on "Star Trek"), and a monitor that permits the owner to see who is at the front door.

Recreational Vehicles Sales

A "gas and credit crunch" in 1979 and a general recession in 1980 explained a steep decline in deliveries of recreation and conversion vehicles (CVs) (to 178,500 units in 1980). (See Table 5.8.) The industry began to recover in 1981, and deliveries climbed until 1989, when they reached more than 388,000 units.

The economic downturn of the early 1990s reversed the growth trend; sales slipped 30 percent between 1988 and 1991, to only 293,700 RVs and CVs purchased. (See Table 5.8.) By almost every measure, 1994 marked an exceptional year for the RV industry. Total RV deliveries grew to 518,800, the highest since 1978 (beginning in 1994 shipment figures included truck and sport-utility vehicle conversions). Retail value of 1994 shipments was $12.2 billion, the largest sales volume ever to that date. In 1995, 475,200 RVs and CVs were delivered. Shipments of RVs climbed from 1995–99, but shipments of CVs generally dropped off, except for a rise in 1999. In 2000, 418,300 RVs and CVs, with a record high retail value of $13.7 billion, were shipped. A weak economy saw shipments fall in 2001 but shipments then rose dramatically in 2002. Industry analysts attribute the upturn, which began in late 2001, to the events of September 11, 2001.

In an April 2003 press release, the RVIA predicted a 2 percent increase in 2003 RV sales over 2002. According to RVIA President David J. Humphreys:

Helping drive RV sales are the vast baby boomer market and the surging popularity of driving vacations in the United States. Families want to escape to America's outdoors in these uncertain times, spend quality time together, and avoid hassles associated with flying—all long-term trends likely to sustain continued RV market growth.

Who Owns RVs?

An RVIA press release dated April 26, 2002 describes a 2001 University of Michigan study showing that an RV could be found that year in a record 1 in 12 vehicle-owning households in the United States—nearly 7 million households. That number is predicted to rise to nearly 8 million by 2010. In the age group 35 to 54, 8.9 percent of people owned an RV, compared with 10 percent of individuals over the age of 55. With a median age of 49, the average RV owner was married, owned a home, and had an annual household income of $56,000.

Wooing the "Mature" Consumer

The number of Americans age 55 and older is expected to increase by 27 percent from 2000 to 2010, as the early Baby Boomers reach their mature years. This age group will represent about 25 percent of all Americans—75.1 million citizens—by 2010.

The RVIA hopes to capitalize on this increase in the number of older Americans, who traditionally have larger net worth and higher disposable incomes. Some in this older age group will enjoy early retirement and a more flexible schedule, which permits more leisure activity.

Younger, More Diverse Prospects

An undated RVIA press release ("Families Remain Hot RV Prospects, As Market Becomes Younger, More Affluent") describes a 2001 study showing that prospective RV buyers were younger and more ethnically diverse than was previously believed. These "prime" buyer prospects were revealed to have an average age of 41 and to be well educated and affluent. Families with two or more children under 18 were considered to be particularly likely buyers.

CHAPTER 6
THE TRUCKING INDUSTRY

Unlike boats, which must travel through water, and railroads, which must follow steel tracks, trucks can go anywhere there is a road. While they may not be able to carry as much freight as barges or railway cars, trucks can reach almost any destination, connecting coast to coast and border to border.

In 2002 trucks transported 87 percent of the nation's general freight business (in terms of revenues), representing 68 percent of total freight tonnage, according to the American Trucking Associations (ATA). This accounted for about 5 percent of the country's gross domestic product, or $585 billion (John D. Schulz, "Hit the Pavement Running," *trafficWORLD*, March 10, 2003). The ATA predicted in March 2003 that the trucking industry's share of freight tonnage will increase to 68.2 percent by 2008.

Although intercity trucking accounts for the majority of trucking industry revenues, some of the demand for truck transport can be attributed to increased trade with Canada and Mexico, the result of the 1992 North American Free Trade Agreement (NAFTA). In 2001 trucks transported 64.4 percent of all goods traded with Canada and Mexico (in terms of value) and 31.5 percent in terms of weight (*Pocket Guide to Transportation*, Bureau of Transportation Statistics, Washington, D.C., 2003).

TYPES OF CARRIERS

The ATA identifies three broad categories of motor carriers: 1) Class I, II, and III intercity carriers, 2) owner-operators, and 3) private motor carriers. Intercity carriers are trucking companies that maintain fleets of trucks and employ people to drive them. Owner-operator carriers are independent truckers who own their trucks and operate for hire. These operators enter and exit the market at will, making it difficult to obtain data on their operations. Private carriers are owned and operated by companies for the purpose of hauling only their own materials and products. Class I carriers are those with annual gross operating revenues of $5 million or more; Class IIs have revenues between $1 million and $5 million; and Class IIIs, which make up the majority of carriers, have revenues of less than $1 million.

TYPES OF TRUCKS

The trucking industry includes all trucks hired to transport goods from one point to another. A truck can be one of hundreds or thousands owned and operated by a major freight-hauling company, or it may be the single tractor-trailer of an independent operator. These include straight trucks; 3-, 4-, and 5-axle semitrailers; flatbed trailers; Rocky Mountain doubles; and mammoth turnpike doubles. (See Figure 6.1 for typical types and dimensions.)

Every truck, trucker, and trucking company plays a vital role in the nation's economy and lifestyle. Trucks connect raw materials to factories, factories to stores, and stores to homes. Thanks to trucks, Oklahomans eat California lettuce, Nebraskans dine on Gulf shrimp, and Texans consume Florida corn. Works of art are enjoyed by millions of people as exhibits travel by truck from city to city. Cars manufactured in Detroit are brought by truck to the dealer's lot in Maine.

Big Rigs: Blessing or Curse?

The largest trucks on the highways are often called "truck trains" or "monster trucks." They are triple trailers, measuring just under 100 feet, and turnpike doubles, which are twin 45- to 48- foot trailers. The larger trucks are also called longer combination vehicles (LCVs), or extra-long vehicles (ELVs). (See Figure 6.1.)

These trucks are much bigger, longer, and heavier than the standard, five-axle 18-wheeler that motorists have become accustomed to. A triple-trailer rig stretches about one-third the length of a football field. Each type of large

FIGURE 6.1

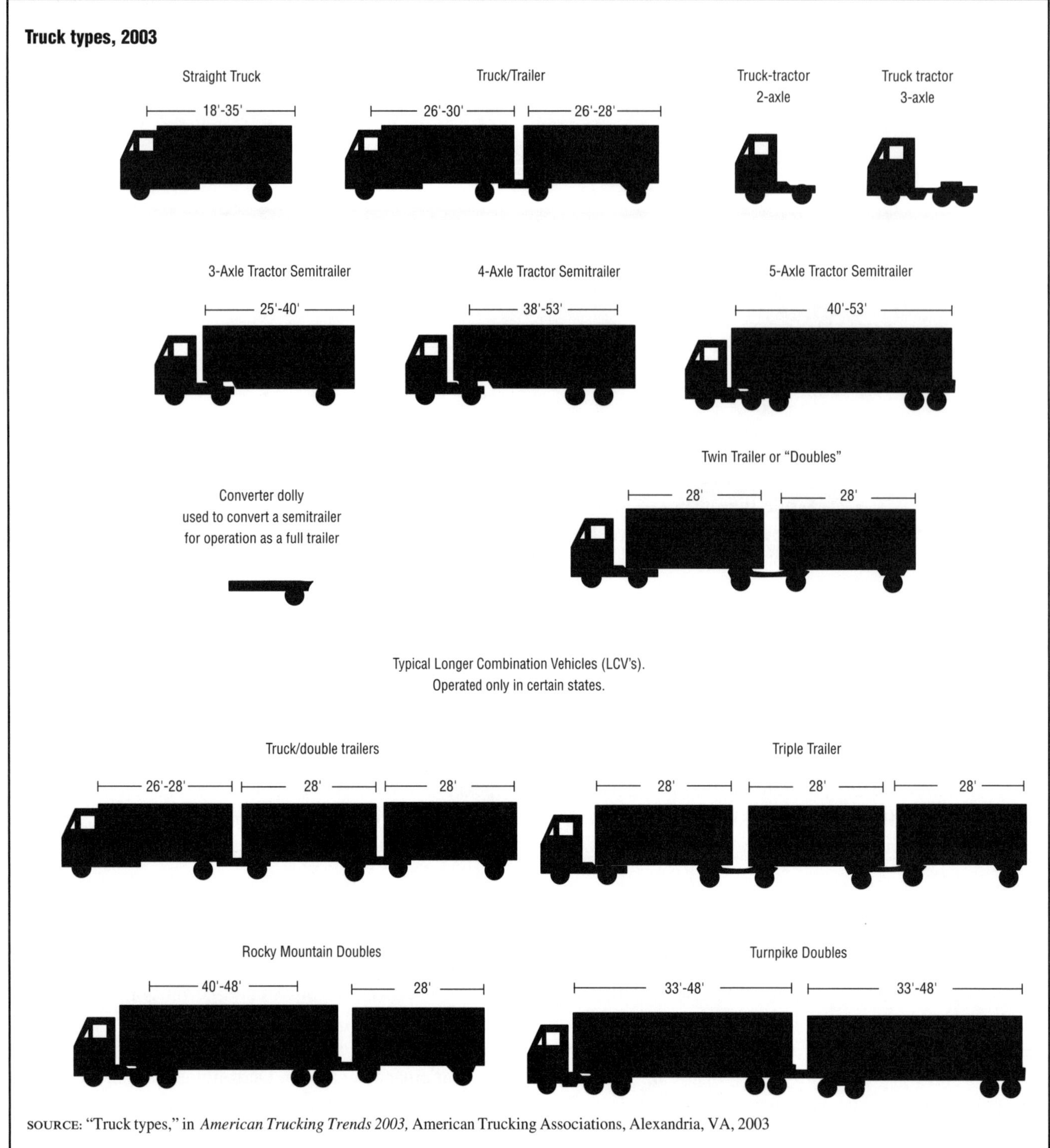

SOURCE: "Truck types," in *American Trucking Trends 2003,* American Trucking Associations, Alexandria, VA, 2003

truck weighs about 125,000 pounds. By comparison, the average family sedan is about 16 feet long and weighs 3,500 pounds.

PROPONENTS OF BIG RIGS. According to Americans for Safe and Efficient Transportation (ASET), a coalition of shippers, motor carriers, and manufacturers that lobbies to raise permissible truck weight to 97,000 pounds, big trucks provide a more efficient way to move goods, and they cut fuel consumption, congestion, and pollution because there are fewer trucks on the road. The trucking industry believes that the bigger rigs make sense—not only for their companies, but also for their customers, and are the only way to meet demand. Trucking company officials also claim that they take very strict measures to ensure that the trucks are operated safely and that only the most qualified drivers are allowed to operate LCVs.

TABLE 6.1

U.S. Retail Truck Sales, 1990–2002

Year	Class 1	Class 2	Class 3	Class 4	Class 5	Class 6	Class 7	Class 8	Total
1990	3,450,958	1,096,866	20,873	27,453	5,055	38,210	85,444	121,304	4,846,163
1991	3,246,128	876,257	21,256	23,829	3,301	22,463	72,596	98,714	4,364,544
1992	3,608,493	1,021,088	25,519	25,631	3,589	27,728	73,229	119,054	4,904,331
1993	4,132,433	1,213,008	32,680	33,317	4,288	26,642	80,741	157,886	5,680,995
1994	4,526,902	1,505,899	35,260	44,485	4,137	20,313	98,165	185,696	6,420,857
1995	4,421,891	1,631,303	39,890	52,623	4,291	23,336	106,724	201,303	6,481,361
1996	4,828,871	1,689,739	51,820	58,722	7,267	19,403	103,528	170,009	6,929,359
1997	5,084,800	1,712,043	52,804	56,526	9,262	18,111	113,689	178,551	7,225,786
1998	5,263,152	2,035,637	102,497	43,357	25,189	31,586	114,665	209,483	7,825,566
1999	5,707,182	2,365,664	122,408	49,423	30,353	48,115	130,983	262,316	8,716,444
2000	5,965,085	2,421,451	116,594	47,417	29,165	51,169	122,614	211,553	8,965,048
2001	6,090,543	2,516,423	92,778	52,037	24,362	42,430	91,564	139,616	9,049,753
2002	6,068,352	2,564,745	80,042	37,827	24,003	45,095	69,328	146,031	9,035,423

SOURCE: Ward's Communications, Southfield, MI, www.WardsAuto.com

OPPONENTS OF LCVS. Many people have reservations about the safety of the massive trucks on the highways. Organizations opposing LCVs are concerned about the danger they represent to other drivers. A brochure prepared by Citizens for Reliable and Safe Highways (CRASH) included a photo of a school bus crushed like a soda can by an LCV. Although the accident rate for LCVs is lower than that of other freight carriers, an accident involving a monster truck is often worse because of the size and weight of the vehicle. The railroads oppose LCVs because they consider these trucks to pose serious competition to their market niche. The Association of American Railroads has released printed and television material opposing LCVs. In 2003 the AAR's Web site asserted that if more shippers were to begin depending on double and triple trucks, it could cost the railroad industry from $3 to $7 billion a year.

Laws Regulating Size and Weight

The federal government began regulating the size and weight of trucks in 1956 to preserve the nation's investment in the then-new interstate highway system, but states that already had higher weight limits were "grandfathered"—allowed to keep their previous levels. With the Surface Transportation Assistance Act (STAA) of 1982 (PL 97-424), Congress required states to adopt the federal weight limits on interstate highways. In 1991 the Intermodal Surface Transportation Efficiency Act (ISTEA; PL 102-240) prohibited states from allowing any expansion of LCV carriers. ISTEA expired on September 30, 1997, and a new bill reauthorizing ISTEA for six more years was passed in May 1998. TEA-21 (PL 105-178) continued the same provisions of ISTEA but required the Transportation Research Board (TRB) to conduct a broad study of the impacts of federal size and weight laws for trucks. The TRB is a coalition of engineers, scientists, and transportation researchers that advises the federal government.

Before the TRB report was completed, in August 2000 the Department of Transportation (DOT) submitted to Congress the *Comprehensive Truck Size and Weight Study*, which examined several scenarios for truck size and weight restrictions in an effort to determine potential damage to the highway system and danger to the public. Although it was noted that heavier trucks effectively shorten the life of a highway, no definitive figures were given for damages. Similarly, no statistics were given for accidents related to large trucks; however, the study did show that some larger, heavier trucks are more prone to rollover and less able to avoid sudden obstacles at highway speeds than smaller, lighter trucks.

The TRB released its report *Regulation of Weights, Lengths, and Widths of Commercial Motor Vehicles* in 2002. The report recommended that the states be authorized to allow big trucks to operate on interstate highways.

Supporters of the bigger trucks continue to press for raising the limits on truck size. In anticipation of Congressional hearings on the reauthorization of TEA-21, the ATA summarized the trucking industry's position in *Transportation Reauthorization Policy Statements: Preliminary Report* (Alexandria, VA, February 2002). Specifically, ATA recommended that Congress reform "outdated federal laws restricting the operation of more productive vehicles. Let States, on a limited and strictly controlled basis, allow the expanded operation of longer and heavier trucks on their highways."

PAYING THEIR SHARE?

Trucks cause considerable damage to road surfaces because they are very heavy and travel a great number of miles. Truck owners are taxed to help pay their share of road repair and maintenance. *Modern Bulk Transporter* reported ATA statistics showing that in 2000 commercial trucks paid $15.3 billion in federal highway user taxes and

TABLE 6.2

Number of truck drivers, 1990–2001

In thousands

Year	Total drivers	Women	Minority
1990	2,607	3.9%	21.9%
1991	2,666	4.1%	22.8%
1992	2,694	4.6%	22.1%
1993	2,786	4.5%	21.1%
1994	2,815	4.5%	23.1%
1995	2,861	4.5%	23.0%
1996	3,019	5.3%	22.7%
1997	3,075	5.7%	24.5%
1998	3,097	5.3%	26.9%
1999	3,116	4.9%	26.8%
2000	3,088	4.7%	26.9%
2001	3,156	5.3%	26.6%

SOURCE: "Table 1-3: Number of truck drivers," in *American Trucking Trends*, American Trucking Associations, Alexandria, VA, 2000; 2000-01 data from "Number of truck drivers," in *American Trucking Trends 2003*, American Trucking Associations, Alexandria, VA, 2003

$16.5 billion in state taxes. Whether this is a fair share of highway costs based on the amount of damage trucks do to roadways is a matter of debate.

In a February 20, 2002, press release, ATA President William J. Canary expressed his view on the fair share issue in connection with a proposal to build mandatory trucks-only lanes on Interstate 81 in Virginia, on which tolls would be imposed: "the trucking industry already pays its fair share of highway taxes and it is unacceptable to ask this industry to pay twice for the use of this interstate" ("ATA, Virginia Association Fight I-81 'Double Taxation' Toll Plan"). However, a May 2000 addendum to a 1997 Department of Transportation Highway Cost Allocation Study reported that

> only the very lightest combination trucks pay their share of Federal highway cost responsibility. The most common combination vehicles, those registered at weights between 75,000 and 80,000 pounds, now pay only 80 percent of their share of Federal highway costs and combinations registered between 80,000 and 100,000 pounds pay only half their share of Federal highway costs.

TRUCK SALES

The 1990–91 recession led to a temporary drop in the sale of large trucks. In 1991 total truck sales were 4.3 million. (See Table 6.1.) Sales then increased with the improving economy, and by 1998 sales had nearly doubled to 7.8 million. In 1999, 8.7 million trucks were purchased. Sales exceeded 9 million in 2001 before declining slightly in 2002 (9.035 million). There were more than 87 million registered trucks on American roads in 2000, including pickups, panels, and delivery vans ("No. 1062. State Motor Vehicle Registrations: 1980 to 2000" in *Statistical Abstract of the United States: 2002,* U.S. Census Bureau, Washington, D.C., 2002).

TRUCKING EMPLOYMENT

Although the drivers of heavy-duty trucks are the most visible to the public, they made up only 3.1 million of the 9.7 million persons employed in the trucking industry in 1999, according to ATA estimates. (See Table 6.2.) Other employees included mechanics and administrative personnel. Women were only 5.3 percent of the drivers in 2001, down from a high of 5.7 percent in 1997. Minorities made up 26.6 percent of the total number of heavy-duty drivers in 2001, up from 21.9 percent in 1990.

According to Bureau of Labor Statistics estimates, in 2001, 1.5 million people were employed as drivers of heavy trucks or tractor-trailers, and another 996,000 people drove light trucks or delivery vans.

Truck Driver Testing, Training, and Certification

Until the terrorist attacks of September 11, 2001, forced the federal government to reevaluate the regulation of the nation's transportation system, no federal or state laws required truck drivers to receive specific, formal training. They were, however, required to have a commercial driver's license (CDL). Disturbed by the studies that cited driver error as a major cause of truck accidents, Congress passed the Commercial Motor Vehicle Safety Act of 1986 (PL 99-570). The act's goals were to improve driving ability, remove problem truck drivers from the road, and establish a uniform, standardized licensing system. In 1988 the Federal Highway Administration (FHWA) issued a ruling establishing minimum federal standards for states to implement in testing commercial drivers, including all truck drivers. Since 1992 all truck drivers have had to pass both written exams and driving tests that meet federal standards. The test is considered much more difficult than the standard exam for an automobile license. The federal manual to help prepare truck drivers for the required test is 120 pages in length.

Most truck drivers learn to drive their large rigs either through formal training in truck driver training schools or community colleges, through their companies, or informally from friends and relatives. In the mid-1980s the trucking industry created the Professional Truck Drivers Institute (PTDI) to improve truck-driver training by offering PTDI-certified classes; in 1989 the first eight training schools began offering certified classes. As of May 28, 2003, PTDI-certified courses were offered at 64 schools in 27 states and Canada (Source: Personal Communication, PTDI). According to information on the PTDI Web site in May 2003, there are 2.9 million trained truck drivers on the nation's roads. PTDI strongly urges prospective drivers to take certified classes to ensure that they are being trained

FIGURE 6.2

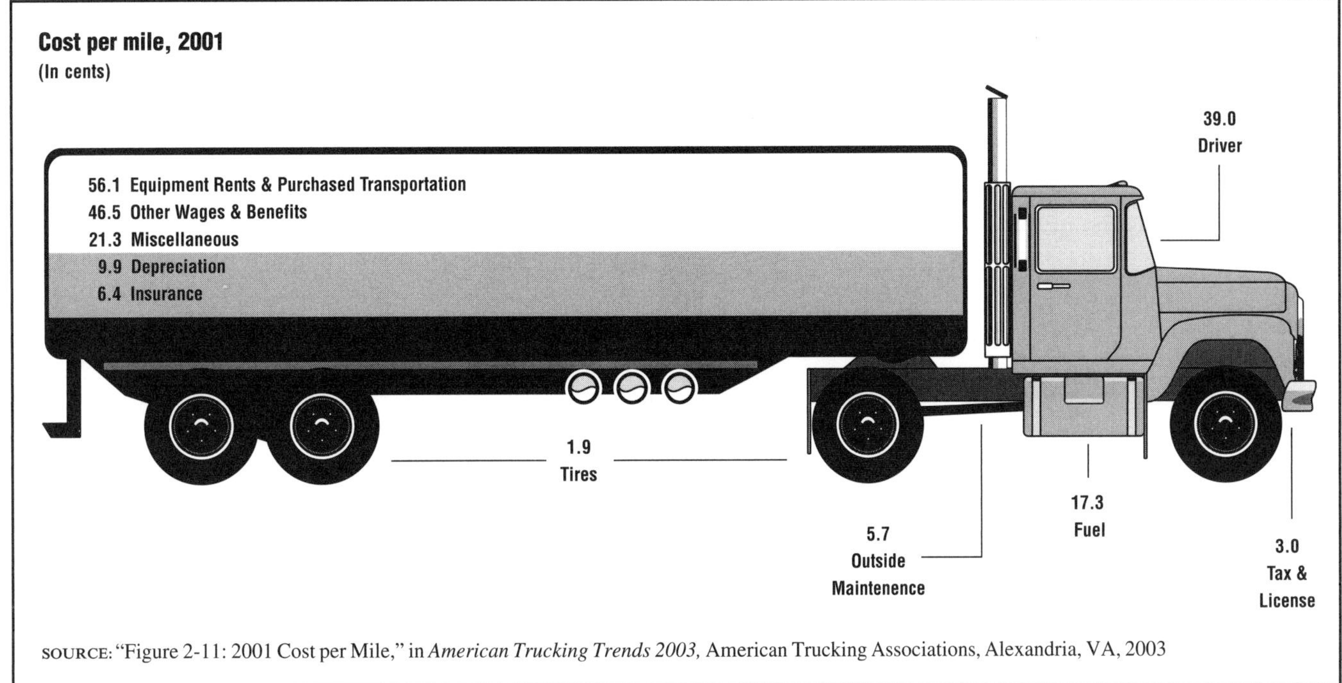

SOURCE: "Figure 2-11: 2001 Cost per Mile," in *American Trucking Trends 2003,* American Trucking Associations, Alexandria, VA, 2003

properly and to increase their chances of being hired by a trucking company, but there is no legal requirement that they do so. Some trucking companies have their own specific driver training requirements.

NEW RULES. The USA PATRIOT Act (PL 107-56), enacted October 25, 2001, required the DOT and the Transportation Security Administration (TSA) to formulate new rules governing truck drivers who are certified to haul hazardous materials (HAZMAT), which include paints, household cleaning chemicals, and explosives, among other materials. The new (interim final) rules were published in the *Federal Register* on May 5, 2003, and took effect immediately. According to the Air & Expedited Motor Carriers Association Web site in 2003, the rules affect approximately 3.5 million commercial drivers who have HAZMAT endorsements.

HAZMAT drivers are now required to undergo background records checks that include fingerprinting and a review of criminal, immigration, and FBI records. Any applicant who has been convicted in military or civilian courts of certain violent felonies in the preceding seven years (such as acts of terrorism), or who has been found mentally incompetent, will not be permitted to obtain or renew the HAZMAT endorsement (a waiver may be issued to persons rejected for mental incompetence who can prove they are rehabilitated). The checks must verify that a driver is a U.S. citizen or a lawful permanent resident.

A companion rule was issued by the Federal Motor Carriers Safety Administration (FMCSA) that prohibits states from issuing, renewing, transferring or upgrading a CDL with a HAZMAT endorsement, unless the TSA has conducted a background check and determined that the applicant does not pose a security risk.

Under a final rule published March 25, 2003, in the *Federal Register* by the DOT Research and Special Programs Administration, shippers and carriers of certain highly hazardous materials must devise security plans and provide security training for employees beginning in September 2003.

In an example of industry-government cooperation, the DOT provides funding for the voluntary Highway Watch Program, which is administered by the ATA. Truck drivers in 18 states (as of May 2003) are specially trained and equipped to report accidents, breakdowns, hazardous road conditions and other highway dangers to the appropriate authorities. A truck driver (or any other civilian) who reports a tip that prevents a terrorist attack may be eligible for a reward under the Rewards for Justice Program administered by the U.S. Secretary of State.

Truck Drivers, Drugs, and Accidents

In 1988 the U.S. Department of Transportation (DOT) issued regulations on drug-testing policies for safety-sensitive airline, railroad, motor carrier (trucking), and shipping employees. Since 1989 tests have been given before employment, after accidents, periodically, when there is reasonable suspicion, and randomly. Employers must conduct unannounced drug tests on 50 percent of their employees each year. The random-testing rule initially caused considerable controversy, mainly over the irregular

FIGURE 6.3

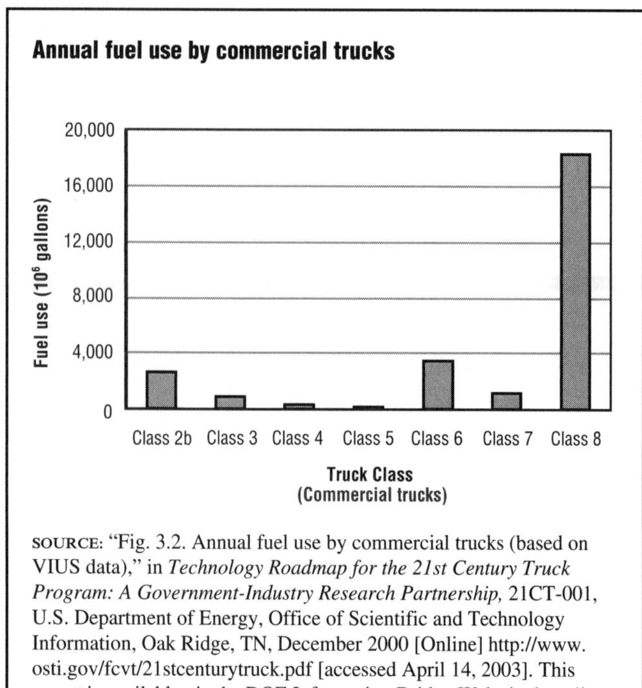

SOURCE: "Fig. 3.2. Annual fuel use by commercial trucks (based on VIUS data)," in *Technology Roadmap for the 21st Century Truck Program: A Government-Industry Research Partnership,* 21CT-001, U.S. Department of Energy, Office of Scientific and Technology Information, Oak Ridge, TN, December 2000 [Online] http://www.osti.gov/fcvt/21stcenturytruck.pdf [accessed April 14, 2003]. This report is available via the DOE Information Bridge Web site http://www.doe.gov/bridge

FIGURE 6.4

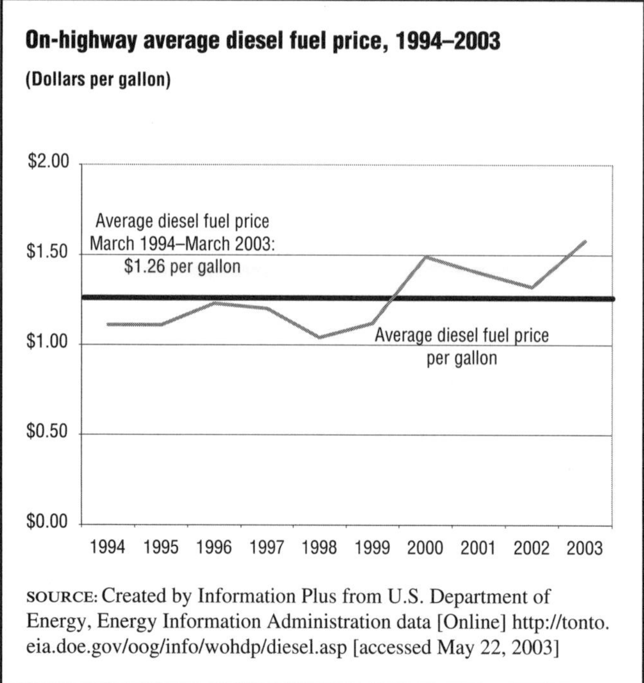

SOURCE: Created by Information Plus from U.S. Department of Energy, Energy Information Administration data [Online] http://tonto.eia.doe.gov/oog/info/wohdp/diesel.asp [accessed May 22, 2003]

testing schedule of independent truckers, which is difficult to enforce and expensive for the industry.

The FHWA also issued regulations under the 1986 Commercial Motor Vehicle Safety Act (see above) that prohibit truck drivers from driving under the influence of alcohol or any illegal drug. The first violation results in a one-year suspension from driving a commercial motor vehicle; the second infraction is justification for permanent disqualification as a driver. Truck drivers are also required to undergo a medical checkup every two years, to evaluate both mental and physical fitness.

According to an undated study of interstate tractor-trailer drivers conducted by the Insurance Institute for Highway Safety (IIHS), evidence of alcohol or drugs, including marijuana, cocaine, and prescription or over-the-counter stimulants, or a combination of these substances, was found in either the blood or urine of 29 percent of drivers tested. The IIHS referred to a National Transportation Safety Board investigation of fatal truck crashes in which it was found that stimulants were present in 15 percent of cases and were the most frequently identified drug class among deceased drivers.

The Bureau of Labor Statistics reported that in 2000 truck drivers had more workplace injuries and illnesses involving time away from work than any other occupation.

TRUCKING INDUSTRY COSTS

The average tractor-semitrailer is very expensive to operate. According to 2001 statistics from the ATA, the typical "big rig" got only 5 to 8 miles per gallon, traveled 80,000 to 100,000 miles per year, and cost the typical trucking company about $2.07 per mile to operate. The major expenditures were wages and employee benefits (not including the driver), 46.5 cents per mile; purchasing or renting the trucks, 56.1 cents; and driver's salary, 39 cents. (See Figure 6.2.) Fuel is a major expense. Figure 6.3 shows annual fuel use by commercial trucks. The big Class 8 trucks (for example, a Mack or a Peterbilt) use 18 billion gallons per year, far in excess of fuel usage by any other class of truck. Figure 6.4 shows trends in the price of on-highway diesel fuel. Prices were up in 2003 because of the tense situation in the Middle East. According to the ATA's William Canary, as cited on the ATA Web site in 2003: "[W]ith every 10-cent increase in the price of diesel fuel, on average, 1,000 motor carriers with five trucks or more in their fleet will file for bankruptcy; this excludes the potentially thousands of smaller truckers that will fail in the same environment."

21st Century Truck Program

Maximizing fuel economy to reduce pollution and dependence on foreign oil are major transportation goals. On the assumption that "trucks are the mainstay for trade, commerce, and economic growth in the United States," the 21st Century Truck Program was announced in April 2000. It is a partnership between the truck and bus industries and their supporting industries and the federal government

FIGURE 6.5

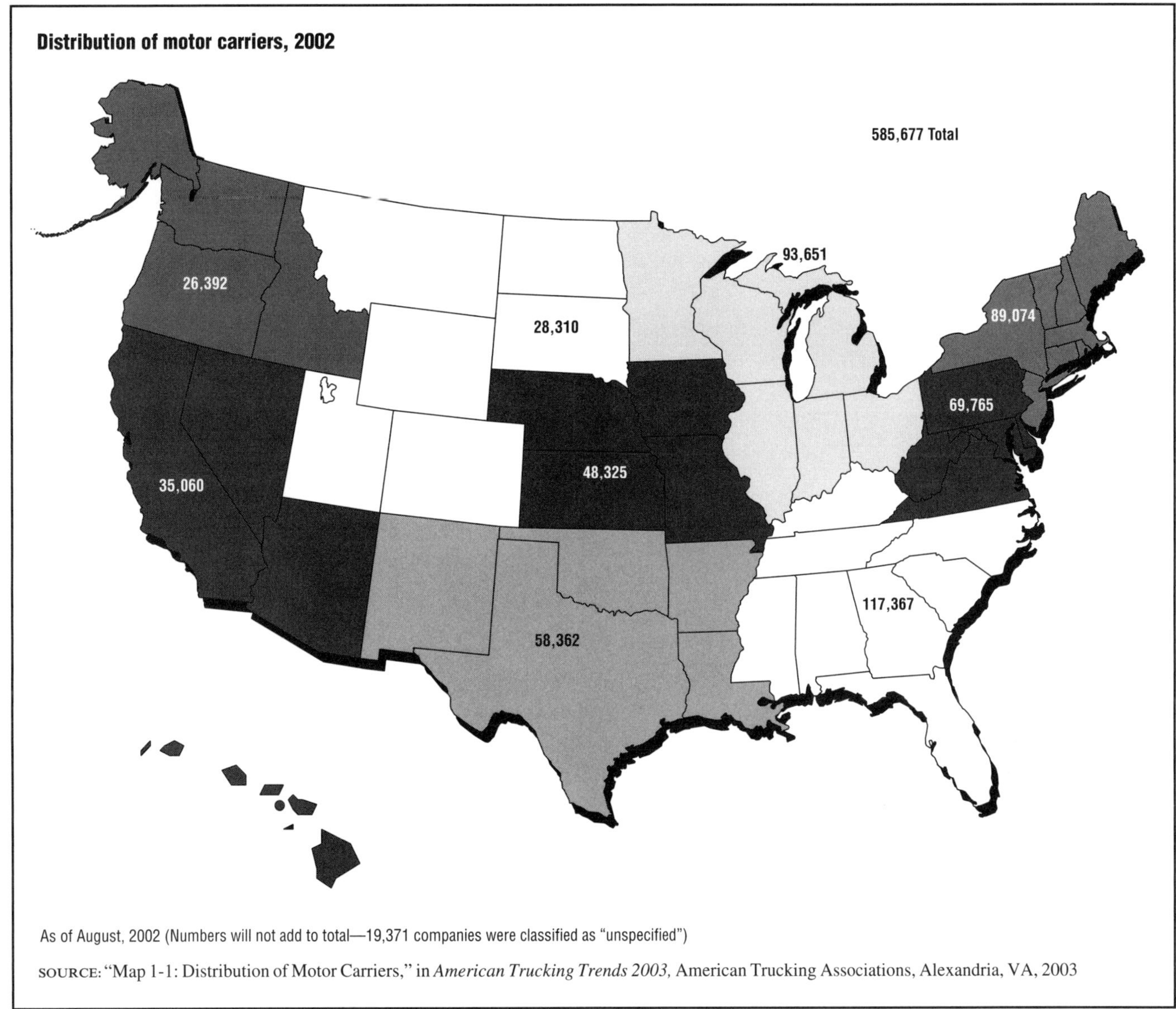

SOURCE: "Map 1-1: Distribution of Motor Carriers," in *American Trucking Trends 2003,* American Trucking Associations, Alexandria, VA, 2003

for research and development of technologies that will, by 2010:

- Double or triple fuel efficiency on a tons-per-gallon basis (depending on the class of truck)
- Reduce emissions
- Reduce truck-related fatalities by 50 percent
- Enhance affordability while maintaining or enhancing performance

Already being implemented are advanced technologies that allow trucking companies to gather "real-time" data on fleet movement, location, driver and fleet performance, etc. (called "telematics"), resulting in better fuel economy among a host of other benefits. Ongoing research is being conducted on engines and motors, materials, supercomputing, and vehicle intelligence systems.

THE EFFECTS OF DEREGULATION

Following years of government controls, Congress passed the Airline Deregulation Act of 1978 (PL 95-504), the Staggers Act of 1980 (railroads; PL 96-448), the Motor Carrier Act of 1980 (PL 96-296), and the Trucking Industry Regulatory Reform Act of 1994 (PL 103-311), which lifted many restrictions on market entry and exit, pricing, scheduling, and routing in the transportation industry.

The arguments for and against deregulation followed a similar pattern in all areas of transportation. Supporters argued that deregulation would benefit both the industry and the consumer by stimulating competition. Competition would, in turn, result in lower rates and better service for the consumer, eliminate poorly managed companies, and increase industry profits.

Opponents of deregulation were concerned that a lack of controls would allow the major players with the most

TABLE 6.3

Fatalities and injuries in crashes involving large trucks, 2001

Type of fatality	Number	Percentage of total
Occupants of large trucks	704	14
Single-vehicle crashes	471	9
Multiple-vehicle crashes	233	5
Occupants of other vehicles in crashes involving large trucks	3,940	78
Nonoccupants (Pedestrians, pedalcyclists, etc.)	438	9
Total	**5,082**	**100**
Type of injury	**Number**	**Percentage of total**
Occupants of large trucks	29,000	23
Single-vehicle crashes	13,000	10
Multiple-vehicle crashes	16,000	12
Occupants of other vehicles in crashes involving large trucks	99,000	75
Nonoccupants (Pedestrians, pedalcyclists, etc.)	3,000	2
Total	**131,000**	**100**

SOURCE: "Table 4. Fatalities and Injuries in Crashes Involving Large Trucks, 2001," in *Traffic Safety Facts 2001: Overview,* DOT HS 809 476, U.S. Department of Transportation, National Highway Traffic Safety Administration, Washington, DC, 2001 [Online] http://www-nrd.nhtsa.dot.gov/pdf/nrd-30/NCSA/TSF2001/2001overview.pdf [accessed April 14, 2003]

resources to gain the bulk of the consumer market, forcing even well-managed smaller companies out of business. Another fear was that the small or out-of-the-way consumer might be left out as companies concentrated on high-volume, highly profitable market segments.

Trucking Profitability, Drivers' Wages Decline

After the trucking industry was deregulated, thousands of new companies sprang up, hoping to take advantage of the new ease of entry into the market and the ability to set their own prices. In addition, many existing companies quickly expanded and entered new markets. According to Wayne K. Talley ("Wage Differentials of Transportation Industries: Deregulation Versus Regulation," *Economic Inquiry*, July 2001), the number of carriers more than doubled between 1980–1987; many of the new ventures ended in bankruptcy. Union membership declined and competition from nonunion motor carriers drove wages down. According to Cynthia Engel ("Competition Drives the Trucking Industry," *Monthly Labor Review*, April 1998), by 1996 only 23 percent of truckers were union members, down from 62 percent in 1973, and real average hourly earnings fell by 40 percent between 1978 and 1996. Heavier workloads in the rush to be competitive led to cost-saving measures that kept drivers on the road for the better part of a week at a time. This, combined with relatively unattractive pay, led to a high driver turnover rate and driver shortages.

A DOT-sponsored study of the effects of deregulation covering the period 1991–97 found that trucking firms' profitability declined overall, but smaller firms had higher profitability than large firms (Alex P. Tang, *Impacts of Deregulation on the Performance of Trucking Firms,* August 1999). But the most successful companies in the new world of deregulation were the four trucking "giants"—ABF Freight System, CF Motor Freight (formerly Consolidated Freightways), Roadway Express, and Yellow Corp. (formerly Yellow Freight System). When other companies went out of business, the larger corporations were able to buy terminals and equipment at bargain prices. They also hired the best of their bankrupt competitors' drivers and acquired the failed enterprises' customers. This helped consolidate their dominance in the industry. Millions of dollars were invested in technology, and as of June 2003 three of the four continued to dominate the trucking industry. CF Motor Freight, on the other hand, filed for bankruptcy in 2002.

The FMCSA reported 592,909 registered interstate motor carriers as of November 2001. Figure 6.5 shows the distribution of motor carriers by region as of 2000, according to data from the ATA.

SAFETY OF TRUCKS

The National Highway Traffic Safety Administration reported that in 2001, 131,000 people were injured in crashes involving large trucks (gross vehicle weight rating greater than 10,000 pounds), and 5,082 people died (which amounts to 12 percent of the motor vehicle fatalities [42,116] for that year). (See Table 6.3.) In the vast majority of cases, it was not the truck driver but the occupant of the other vehicle who suffered injury (75 percent) or death (78 percent).

Table 6.4 shows the vehicle configurations of large trucks involved in crashes in 2001: 4,793 were involved in fatal crashes, 38,061 were involved in injury crashes, and 42,259 were involved in property-damage-only crashes. Truck tractors pulling semi-trailers accounted for the majority (62 percent) of the fatal crashes, nearly half (47.4 percent) of the injury crashes, and more than half (51.5 percent) of the property-damage-only crashes. The largest trucks accounted for only a small percentage of the fatal crashes—doubles (truck tractors pulling a semi-trailer and a full trailer) for 3.5 percent and triples (tractors pulling three trailers) for 0.2 percent. (See Table 6.1 for illustrations of doubles and triples.)

Table 6.5 shows characteristics of 4,749 drivers of large trucks involved in fatal crashes in 2001. In more than two-thirds (67.9 percent) of the fatal single-vehicle crashes that involved large trucks, accident records showed the truck driver had committed some type of error. (See Table 6.5.) In 43.3 percent of those incidents, the driver was either exceeding the speed limit, driving too fast for the road conditions, or had run off the road. When multiple vehicles

TABLE 6.4

Large trucks in crashes by vehicle configuration, 2001

	Fatal		Injury		Towaway	
Vehicle configuration	**Number**	**Percent**	**Number**	**Percent**	**Number**	**Percent**
Single-Unit, 2 Axles	613	12.8%	5,409	14.2%	5,284	12.5%
Single-Unit, 3+ Axles	535	11.2%	4,122	10.8%	3,829	9.1%
Single-Unit, Axles Unknown	183	3.8%				
Truck/Trailer(s)	53	1.1%	4,220	11.1%	4,669	11.0%
Truck Tractor (Bobtail)	113	2.4%	1,203	3.2%	1,208	2.9%
Tractor/Semi-trailer	2,977	62.1%	18,053	47.4%	21,743	51.5%
Tractor/Double	166	3.5%	713	1.9%	1,475	3.5%
Tractor/Triple	10	0.2%	47	0.1%	72	0.2%
Unknown	143	3.0%	1,039	2.7%	784	1.9%
Missing			3,255	8.6%	3,195	7.6%
Total	**4,793**	**100.0%**	**38,061**	**100.0%**	**42,259**	**100.0%**

Note: A large truck is defined as a truck with a gross vehicle weight rating (GVWR) greater than 10,000 pounds.

SOURCE: "Table 37. Large Trucks in Crashes by Vehicle Configuration," in *Large Truck Crash Facts 2001,* Analysis Division, Federal Motor Carrier Safety Administration, Washington, DC, January 2003 [Online] http://ai.volpe.dot.gov/CarrierResearchResults/CarrierResearchResults.asp?file=PDFs/LargeTruckCrashFacts2001.pdf [accessed May 27, 2003]

were involved in the crash, a fault on the part of the truck driver was reported in fewer than one-third (30.2 percent) of cases. The report *Large Truck Crash Facts 2001* stated that 16.7 percent (797) of the truck drivers were not wearing a safety belt. A blood alcohol content of 0.08 or higher (the national standard for impaired driving in most states) was reported for 1.1 percent of the truck drivers, compared with 22.9 percent of drivers of passenger cars involved in fatal crashes.

Preliminary figures for 2002 issued by the NHTSA in April 2003 indicated that car-truck crash fatalities were on the decline. According to the ATA, if the preliminary number of 4,902 fatalities for 2002 remains unchanged, it will represent a 3.5 percent decline over 2001 and will be the first time since 1995 that fatalities have fallen below 5,000.

Driver Fatigue

Table 6.5 shows that driver fatigue was a factor in 65 fatal large-truck crashes in 2001 (1.4 percent). Driver fatigue is difficult to measure and few studies have been done that document its extent. A 1990 National Transportation Safety Board (NTSB) study of 182 heavy-truck accidents in which the driver was killed is considered authoritative because of the thoroughness with which it examined the circumstances surrounding the accidents. The study showed that driver fatigue was a factor in 31 percent of the accidents investigated. The study is cited in the NTSB report *Evaluation of U.S. Department of Transportation Efforts in the 1990s to Address Operator Fatigue* (Safety Report NTSB/SR-99/01, Washington, D.C., 1999). Also cited are 1998 estimates from the Federal Highway Administration that fatigue was a factor in up to 1.3 percent of police-reported large truck crashes, in up to 6.5 percent of all fatal large truck crashes, in up to 29 percent of crashes fatal to the truck occupant only, and in up to 2.8 percent of crashes fatal to nontruck occupants.

Because of concern over driver fatigue as a factor in fatal truck crashes, in 1995 Congress directed the FMCSA to study the issue and come up with ways to increase driver alertness. In April 2003 the FMCSA issued the first major revision of hours-of-service rules for truck drivers since 1939. The new regulations, which take effect on January 4, 2004, allow truck drivers to drive for up to 11 straight hours, a 1-hour increase. Drivers must take off at least 10 hours between shifts, a 2-hour increase.

HELP FOR DROWSY DRIVERS. Some truck drivers turn to coffee, short periods of exercise, naps in the back of their cabs, or even amphetamines (illegal stimulants) to wake themselves up when they start to feel tired. Others do nothing and may finally fall asleep at the wheel. In an effort to remedy this situation, some road agencies have installed shoulder "rumble strips" that warn drivers when they are about to run off the road. The U.S. Department of Transportation and the Carnegie Mellon University Robotics Institute have developed the Copilot, a low-cost, dashboard-mounted, video-based system that measures slow eyelid closure, a sign of drowsiness. The device sets off an alarm reinforced by a visual gauge that encourages the driver to either take actions to increase alertness or to stop and rest.

TABLE 6.5

Characteristics of drivers of large trucks involved in fatal crashes, 2001

	Single-vehicle crashes		Multiple-vehicle crashes		Total	
Driver-related factors	**Number**	**Percent**	**Number**	**Percent**	**Number**	**Percent**
Driving too fast for conditions or in excess of posted speed limit	116	14.4%	253	6.4%	**369**	**7.8%**
Running off road	233	28.9%	64	1.6%	**297**	**6.3%**
Failure to keep in proper lane	78	9.7%	203	5.1%	**281**	**5.9%**
Inattentive (talking, eating, etc.)	69	8.6%	174	4.4%	**243**	**5.1%**
Failure to yield right of way	36	4.5%	179	4.5%	**215**	**4.5%**
Failure to obey traffic signs	34	4.2%	139	3.5%	**173**	**3.6%**
Erratic or reckless driving	57	7.1%	107	2.7%	**164**	**3.5%**
Following improperly	1	0.1%	95	2.4%	**96**	**2.0%**
Other non-moving traffic violation	15	1.9%	58	1.5%	**73**	**1.5%**
Non-traffic violation charged (manslaughter or other homicide offense)	5	0.6%	65	1.6%	**70**	**1.5%**
Drowsy, fatigued	38	4.7%	27	0.7%	**65**	**1.4%**
Making improper turn	25	3.1%	35	0.9 %	**60**	**1.3%**
Vision obscured by weather	4	0.5%	45	1.1%	**49**	**1.0%**
Swerving to avoid vehicle in road	5	0.6%	42	1.1%	**47**	**1.0%**
Overcorrecting	28	3.5%	10	0.3%	**38**	**0.8%**
Operating without required equipment	14	1.7%	21	0.5%	**35**	**0.7%**
Ill, blackout	12	1.5%	6	0.2%	**18**	**0.4%**
Starting/backing improperly	8	1.0%	9	0.2%	**17**	**0.4%**
Vision obscured by obstructing angles on vehicle	4	0.5%	1	*	**5**	**0.1%**
Driver-Related Factor(s) Recorded	547	67.9%	1,191	30.2%	**1,738**	**36.6%**
No Driver-Related Factors Recorded	259	32.1%	2,752	69.8%	**3,011**	**63.4%**
Total	**806**	**100.0%**	**3,943**	**100.0%**	**4,749**	**100.0%**
Violation(s) Recorded	85	10.5%	482	12.2%	**567**	**11.9%**
No Violations Recorded	721	89.5%	3,461	87.8%	**4,182**	**88.1%**
Total	**806**	**100.0%**	**3,943**	**100.0%**	**4,749**	**100.0%**

* Less than 0.05 percent.

Note: A large truck is defined as a truck with a gross vehicle weight rating (GVWR) greater than 10,000 pounds.

SOURCE: "Table 57. Drivers of Large Trucks in Fatal Crashes by Driver-Related Factors and Violations Recorded," in *Large Truck Crash Facts 2001,* Analysis Division, Federal Motor Carrier Safety Administration, Washington, DC, January 2003 [Online] http://ai.volpe.dot.gov/CarrierResearchResults/CarrierResearchResults.asp?file=PDFs/LargeTruckCrashFacts2001.pdf [accessed May 27, 2003]

TRANSPORTATION OF HAZARDOUS MATERIALS

The Laws

The federal government set standards for the transportation of hazardous materials in the Hazardous Materials Transportation Act (PL 93-633) of 1975 and in numerous regulations set down thereafter by the DOT. Hazardous materials are listed in the Code of Federal Regulations (Title 49, Subsection 172.101). The list runs for more than 140 pages and features such obviously dangerous objects as rockets, radioactive materials, and grenades, as well as seed cake and electric wheelchairs.

The Motor Carrier Safety Improvement Act of 1999 (PL 106-159) established the Federal Motor Carrier Safety Administration (FMCSA) within the DOT. The agency's original mission was to help reduce fatalities per 100 million vehicle miles traveled from 2.8 in 1996 to 1.6 in 2008. (The rate was 2.2 in 2000, according to *Large Truck Crash Facts.*)

The September 11, 2001, terrorist attacks exposed apparent deficiencies in federal oversight of hazardous materials. Dozens of people were arrested shortly after the attack and charged with fraudulently obtaining HAZMAT licenses; some were suspected terrorists. In testimony before a Senate committee on October 10, 2001, Joan Claybrook, president of the consumer advocacy group Public Citizen, asserted that under then-existing federal regulations, terrorists could set up a trucking company in the United States or Canada, easily obtain CDLs and an endorsement to haul hazardous materials, and operate for 18 months without any federal or state safety or security check, merely by paying a fee. Claybrook claimed that the FMCSA, the agency responsible for highway safety, had failed to enforce the oversight and reform measures mandated by Congress. Indeed, just a year and a half earlier the DOT had concluded that it did not have comprehensive information on hazardous materials manufacturers, carriers, freight forwarders, and shippers and therefore could not properly manage the program.

TABLE 6.6

Serious hazardous materials incidents, 1993–2002

Mode	1993	1994	1995	1996	1997	1998	1999	2000	2001	2002	Total
Air	8	7	8	6	13	23	17	35	36	15	168
Highway	362	349	353	423	409	356	456	463	487	317	3,975
Railway	57	82	61	74	61	72	70	75	60	68	680
Water	1	1	I	1	1	5	0	2	1	2	15
Total	428	439	423	504	484	456	543	575	584	402	4,838

Note: Starting with reporting on 2002 incidents, RSPA defines serious incidents as incidents that involve:
- a fatality or major injury caused by the release of a hazardous material,
- the evacuation of 25 or more persons as a result of release of a hazardous material or exposure to fire,
- a release or exposure to fire which results in the closure of a major transportation artery,
- the alteration of an aircraft flight plan or operation,
- the release of radioactive materials from Type B packaging,
- the release of over 11.9 gallons or 88.2 pounds of a severe marine pollutant, or
- the release of a bulk quantity (over 119 gallons or 882 pounds) of a hazardous material.

On this report, for comparison purposes, years prior to 2002 are also based on this new definition.

SOURCE: Adapted from "Serious Incidents (New Definition): Incidents by Mode and Incident Year," U.S. Department of Transportation, Research and Special Programs Administration, Washington, DC, 2002 [Online] http://hazmat.dot.gov/files/hazmat/10year/10yearfrm.htm [accessed May 29, 2003]

Furthermore, it was not known who in the department was actually responsible for carrying out the program (*Departmentwide Program Evaluation of the Hazardous Materials Transportation Programs,* U.S. Department of Transportation, Washington, D.C., March 2000).

On November 19, 2001, President George W. Bush signed into law the Aviation and Transportation Security Act (ATSA; PL 107-71), which (among other things) established a new Transportation Security Administration (TSA) within the DOT (on March 1, 2003, the TSA became part of the Department of Homeland Security).

Government Assumes New Responsibilities

According to Kevin Johnson, TSA branch chief for highway transportation, the federal government considers HAZMAT trucks and food haulers a top priority because they are at high risk for terrorist tampering (John D. Schulz, "Reasonable But Strict: TSA Trucking Standards to Emphasize Common Sense, Efficiency, Ground Chief Says," *trafficWORLD*, January 27, 2003). Johnson is working with freight shippers to tighten security measures.

The FMCSA assumed responsibility for reducing the security risks of hazardous materials that could potentially be used to harm the public and environment. Its first act was to dispatch agents to investigate the security of every company that hauls hazardous materials. The FMCSA is also responsible for implementing more frequent highway stops of drivers carrying hazardous materials for "level three checks" of the drivers' credentials, operator licenses, endorsements, shipping paperwork, and destination. These and other new security measures have burdened the transportation system by causing long delays at ports and borders and adding costs and uncertainties to the shipping process.

The Numbers

The Office of Hazardous Materials Safety (OHMS), part of the DOT, estimates that 800,000 hazardous materials shipments occur each day, adding up to more than 3 billion tons of hazardous materials shipped each year (based on a 1998 analysis, the latest data available). About 770,000 of these shipments are on trucks, which make 445,000 daily shipments of chemical and allied products; 313,000 daily shipments of petroleum products; and upwards of 10,000 other shipments of hazardous waste materials, medical wastes and various other hazardous materials. According to the DOT's *Departmentwide Program Evaluation,* in 2000 the nation's HAZMAT fleet of trucks numbered around 195,000 with a potential 6.4 million trucks that could carry hazardous materials from time to time.

Reporting a hazardous materials leak or spill to the DOT is required by federal law. A reported incident is a report of any unintentional release of hazardous material while in transportation (including loading, unloading, and temporary storage). Table 6.6 shows the number of serious hazardous materials incidents by mode of shipment and year. Between 1993 and 2002, 3,975 serious HAZMAT incidents occurred on the nation's highways. The DOT's 2000 *Departmentwide Program Evaluation* concluded that the nation's safety record is "relatively good." The report noted that the cause of most (80 percent) transportation incidents involving the release of hazardous materials is human error. Most hazardous materials fatalities occur on highways and usually involve collisions of passenger vehicles with trucks carrying flammable liquids, frequently due to the failure of the driver of the passenger vehicle to yield.

TABLE 6.7

Air pollutant emissions from mobile sources, selected years 1970–2015

Source	1970	1975	1980	1985	1990	1997	2005	2015
			Total criteria pollutant emissions (1,000 tons/year)					
On-road motor vehicles								
Gasoline	106,392	99,526	92,061	91,161	67,692	59,184	46,356	34,031
Diesel	3,088	3,904	4,567	4,594	4,387	3,919	3,774	6,632
Total emissions*	226,037	205,380	201,339	187,898	161,742	148,894	128,650	116,709
			Nitrogen oxide (NO_x) emissions (1,000 tons/year)					
On-road motor vehicles								
Gasoline	5,714	6,504	6,128	5,666	4,802	5,103	4,177	2,372
Diesel	1,676	2,141	2,493	2,423	2,238	1,932	1,619	682
Total NO_x emissions*	23,876	25,296	26,859	23,488	23,793	23,565	20,359	17,200
			Particulate matter (PM10) emissions (1,000 tons/year)					
On-road motor vehicles								
Gasoline	307	294	189	134	101	105	111	131
Diesel	136	177	208	229	235	163	93	74
Total PM10 emissions*	12,528	7,410	6,613	3,799	3,435	3,104	3,067	3,071

* Note: Total from all sources, including electric utilities; industrial fuel combustion; commercial & institutional fuel combust ion; residential fuel combustion; industrial processes; waste disposal; non-road vehicles & engines; aircraft, locomotives, and marine vessels; and micellaneous.

SOURCE: Adapted from "Table 2: Total criteria pollutant emissions for the United States," "Table 4: Nitrogen oxide (Nox) emissions for the United States," and "Table 7: Particulate matter (PM10) emissions for the United States," in *Progress in Reducing National Air Pollutant Emissions 1970–2015,* Prepared by Tech Environmental, Inc., for Foundation for Clean Air Progress, Washington, DC, June 1999 [Online] http://www.cleanairprogress.org/research/report.pdf [accessed April 14, 2003]

TRUCKS AND THE ENVIRONMENT

The Clean Air Act of 1970 (CAA; PL 91-604) and the Clean Air Act Amendments of 1990 (CAAA; PL 101-549) called for reduction in air pollutants from truck engines. Engine manufacturers have totally redesigned their motors to reduce emissions of the six major pollutants—carbon monoxide, lead, oxides of nitrogen (NO_x), hydrocarbons, particulates, and sulfur dioxide. Table 6.7 shows trends and projections of air pollutant emissions from on-road motor vehicles and the total emissions from all sources. The data are from the Foundation for Clean Air Progress (FCAP), a non-profit organization dedicated to providing public education and information about America's air quality progress. In January 2002 FCAP released its analysis of federal government data on air quality dating back to 1970 and reported that even as Americans have consumed more energy, air quality has improved. The only pollutant that increased during the 30-year period was NO_x, which rose by 22 percent. As shown in Table 6.7, NO_x emissions are targeted for reduction by 2015 and are expected to decline due to new diesel fuel requirements and technological advances.

CHAPTER 7

AIRLINES AND AIR TRAVEL

From ancient times, people have dreamed of flying. Greek mythology tells the story of Icarus, who strapped on primitive wings, attached them with wax, and tried to fly. Soaring through the sky, he flew too close to the sun. His wings melted and he plummeted to his death.

Not until 1783, when two Frenchmen—the Montgolfier brothers—sent a hot-air balloon aloft, did manned flight seem a real possibility. Benjamin Franklin, then U.S. ambassador to France, witnessed the flight and was asked what good it was. Seeing the beginning of a limitless new era of flight, he replied, "What good is a newborn baby?"

The prototype of today's airplanes finally rose into the air on December 17, 1903, when Orville Wright took off from a beach near the town of Kitty Hawk, North Carolina, flew for 59 seconds, and landed half a mile away from the take-off point. Just eleven years after the Wright brothers' first flight, the combatants of World War I enlisted airplanes for military use. In 1918 the first U.S. airmail postal delivery began, with regular service between Washington, D.C., and New York. Air flight was no longer experimental. By 1919 a "flying boat" (an airplane that takes off from and lands on water) was the first plane to cross the Atlantic Ocean, flying from Newfoundland, Canada, to Lisbon, Portugal. In that same year KLM Airlines was founded in the Netherlands, beginning regular, scheduled passenger service from Amsterdam to London in 1920.

In 1925 two airline companies were established in the United States, companies that would later become Trans World Airlines and Northwest Airlines. At about the time Charles Lindbergh made his celebrated solo flight across the Atlantic in 1927, Pan American Airways also started up business. That year, U.S. airlines flew six million miles and carried 37,000 passengers. Commercial airline travel had begun.

The 1930s were years of expansion for the airline industry. The Civil Aeronautics Act of 1938 created the Civil Aeronautics Authority, largely to regulate safety provisions and aid in the modernization of airports. By 1939 U.S. airlines transported passengers all over the globe. Pan American's glamorous Clippers (large flying boats) flew routes across the Atlantic and Pacific and featured passenger cabins, sleeping berths, and full-service dining rooms.

During the years of World War II, the airlines, like all other U.S. industries, were enlisted in the war effort and put few resources into development of their own industry. But after the hostilities ended, new technology developed during the war and a booming economy paved the way for explosive airline growth. In the 1950s jet aircraft joined the air fleets. Planes got bigger and faster and air travel became more common. With increased demand airlines developed more and more routes to cover more destinations. Eventually, they connected even more destinations through use of hub-and-spoke networks. Under this system, passengers boarding at many different locations arrive at one of the nation's 31 large hub airports. (See Figure 7.1.) Connecting flights then transport them through the spokes to their final destinations.

FEDERAL LEGISLATION

Unlike the railroads, the airline industry was heavily regulated almost from its beginning. The rapid growth of airplanes and air services in the early 1920s prompted legislation both to support and to control the growing industry. The transport of mail, initially the province of the federal government, was opened to private operators by the Kelly Air Mail Act of 1925 (45 Stat. 594). The U.S. government used air mail contracts to subsidize commercial airlines. The Air Commerce Act of 1926 (44 Stat. 568) promoted air safety. It authorized the Secretary of Commerce to register aircraft and certify pilots, established air traffic

FIGURE 7.1

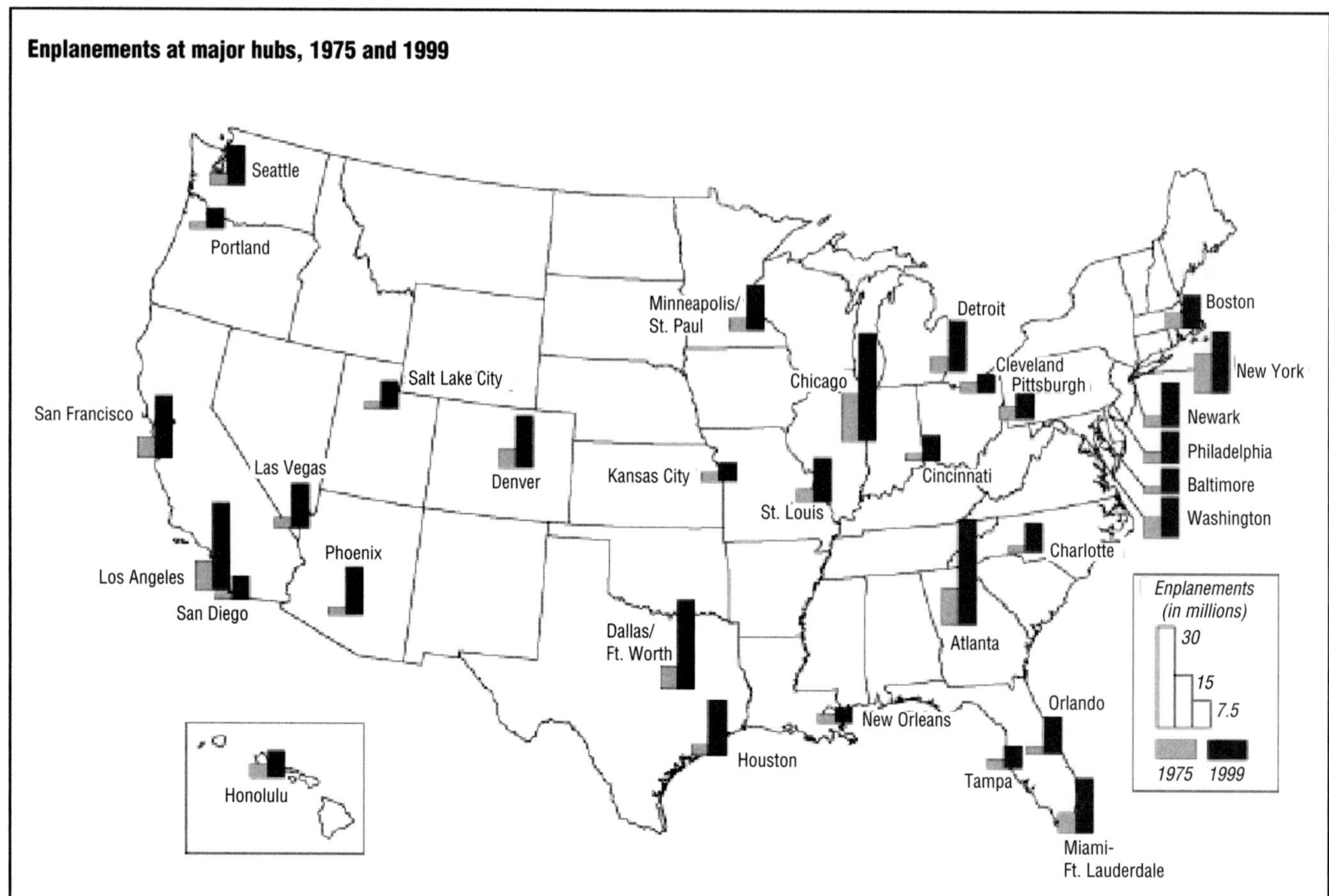

Note: These data include hubs that were classified as large hubs in either 1975 or 1999 or in both years. A large hub is a geographic area that enplanes 1 percent or more of nationally enplaned passengers. A hub may include more than one airport.

SOURCE: "Map: Enplanements at Large Air Traffic Hubs: 1975 and 1999," Bureau of Transportation Statistics, Washington, DC, 2000 [Online] http://www.bts.gov/publications/tsar/2000/chapter4/enplanements_at_major_us_airports_map.html [accessed April 14, 2003]

rules, and required the government to supply and maintain lighted runways.

The Civil Aeronautics Act of 1938 (72 Stat. 731) created the Civil Aeronautics Authority (CAA) to provide economic regulation, investigate accidents, and administer airport construction and maintenance. The CAA would eventually become the Federal Aviation Administration. Economic regulation and safety functions were turned over to the newly formed Civil Aeronautics Board (CAB) in 1939. The Federal Airport Act of 1946 (60 Stat. 170) provided financial assistance for airport development.

The Airways Modernization Board was formed to study a national air navigation and traffic control system. The Federal Aviation Act of 1958 (PL 85-726) brought its work under the jurisdiction of the new Federal Aviation Agency. It became part of the Department of Transportation (DOT) in 1966 when DOT was created, and the agency was given its present-day name, the Federal Aviation Administration (FAA). Air safety functions were taken over by the new National Transportation Safety Board (NTSB).

The Airport and Airway Development Act of 1970 (PL 91-258) provided increased financial support for airport development. Taxes and fees on air travelers and airlines have been accruing in a trust fund. To make federal budget deficits appear smaller, Congress appropriated these dedicated funds far slower than the FAA or the airlines would like, thus delaying the improvement of the air traffic system.

Post-September 11 Legislation

The airline industry was ailing financially when the September 11, 2001, terrorist attacks led to an abrupt decline in air travel. To keep the industry from going bankrupt, President George W. Bush signed the Air Transportation Safety and System Stabilization Act (PL 107-42) on September 22, 2001. The act established the Air Transportation Stabilization Board to administer $10 billion in loan guarantees to qualifying air carriers. The Aviation Security Act (PL 107-71), signed on October 11, 2001, requires that federal government personnel conduct screening of baggage and passengers at all large hub airports. The bill provides funds to reimburse

FIGURE 7.2

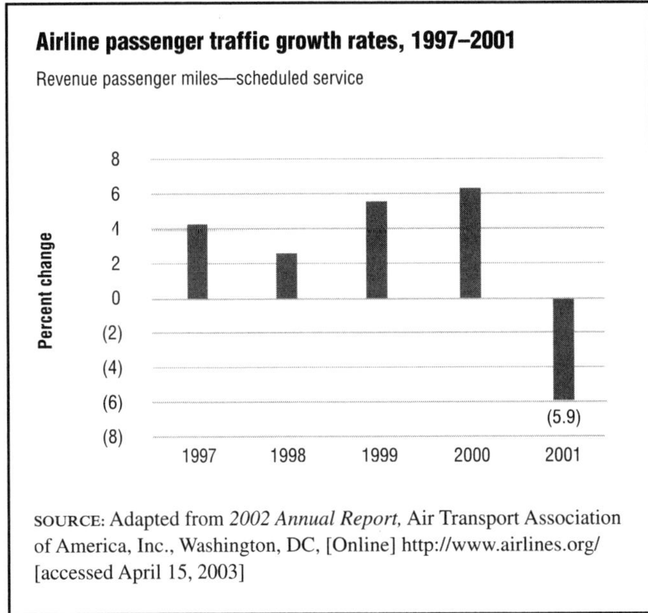

SOURCE: Adapted from *2002 Annual Report,* Air Transport Association of America, Inc., Washington, DC, [Online] http://www.airlines.org/ [accessed April 15, 2003]

TABLE 7.1

Summary of scheduled airlines, 2000–01

In millions, except as noted	2000	2001	Percent change 1999-2000	Percent change 2000-2001
Traffic - scheduled service				
Revenue passengers enplaned	666.2	622.1	4.6	(6.6)
Revenue passenger miles	692,757	651,663	6.2	(5.9)
Available seat miles	956,950	930,486	4.1	(2.8)
Passenger load factor (percent)	72.4	70.0	+1.4	-2.4
Freight & express revenue ton miles	21,443	20,109	9.5	(6.2)
Aircraft departures (in thousands)	9,035	8,789	4.2	(2.7)
Financial				
Passenger revenues	$93,622	$80,936	11.0	(13.5)
Freight & express revenues	12,486	11,892	5.1	(4.8)
Mail revenues	1,970	1,058	13.6	(46.3)
Charter revenues	4,913	4,459	NA	(9.3)
Total operating revenues	130,839	115,425	8.8	(11.8)
Total operating expenses	123,840	125,489	10.6	1.3
Operating profit (loss)	6,999	(10,064)	(15.7)	(243.8)
Net profit (loss)	2,486	(7,710)	(50.7)	(410.1)
Operating profit margin (percent)	5.3	(8.7)	-1.6 pts	-14.1 pts
Net profit margin (percent)	1.9	(6.7)	-2.0 pts	-8.6 pts
Rate of return on investment (percent)	6.4	(6.9)	-4.5 pts	-13.3 pts
Employees				
(Average full-time equivalent)	679,967	670,730	5.1	(1.3)

SOURCE: Adapted from *2001 Annual Report and 2002 Annual Report,* Air Transport Association of America, Inc., Washington, DC [Online] http://www.airlines.org/ [accessed April 15, 2003]

airports for the costs of complying with the new security requirements.

AIRLINE DEREGULATION

Prior to 1978, an airline company needed government approval to enter the market, merge with another company, engage in foreign commerce, establish a new route, abandon an existing route, or set or change fares. While this regulation of airlines ensured service to a great number of cities, it discouraged competition on the basis of low prices. Airlines, instead, vied for market share by attempting to provide the best service.

Many Americans think that government intervention in any industry restricts free competition and is thus detrimental to the public interest. Critics of airline regulation had pointed out during the 1970s that airlines operating entirely within one state, thereby escaping Civil Aeronautics Board (CAB) regulation, charged far lower fares for routes of the same distance than CAB-regulated carriers. In 1978 these critics convinced the federal government to pass the Airline Deregulation Act, which eliminated many government restrictions on airline behavior, allowed competition between airlines, and led to the elimination of the CAB in 1984. The act was intended to increase competition in the domestic airline industry by easing the requirements for new airlines entering the market, reducing 40 years of restrictions on routing and scheduling, and eliminating price controls. Its supporters believed that competition and "free market forces" would benefit both the industry and the public with more choices, lower fares, better service, and increased passenger loads.

The Airline Deregulation Act had far-reaching and surprising effects on the airline industry. While fares did drop, service did not improve. The expected boom in new airlines did not materialize. Advocates of deregulation apparently did not foresee how effectively the largest airlines would use their size advantage to thwart the smaller airlines and the numerous newcomers to the market. They also did not predict that intense fare competition would make it difficult for new entrants to finance their growth, or even for some of the established airlines to maintain their profits. Instead of expanding, the industry concentrated, with only a small number of major carriers able to survive in such a competitive environment. While there were a few successes, most notably the expansion of Southwest Airlines across much of the country, a number of major airlines, including Braniff, Pan American, and Eastern, went out of business after deregulation.

Deregulation produced an air travel system dominated by a relatively small number of carriers. Of the 614.2 million passengers who flew in the United States in 1999, 48 percent flew on Delta, United, and American, and 78 percent flew on the six largest airlines, according to the Air Transport Association of America (ATA; *Air Transport Association 2000*, Washington, D.C., 2000). With most of the industry operating under the hub-and-spoke system, some airports are served by a single airline. Many people complain that this lack of choice means that airlines can get away with high prices and poor service. ATA asserts that while only two-thirds of airline passengers had a choice of two or more carriers in 1978, by 2003, 85 percent of passengers had such a choice. Furthermore, ATA cited 1999 research showing that American travelers had saved more than $20 billion a year since deregulation if lower fares and increased frequency of flights were considered.

TYPES OF CARRIERS

Traffic at an airport falls broadly into three categories: (1) large commercial airlines and cargo haulers, (2) commuter, or regional, airlines and air taxis, and (3) general aviation. In general, commercial airlines are very large operations that fly between the major "hub" cities and have fleets consisting mainly of large jets. Regional, or commuter, airlines provide regularly scheduled service from the hubs to smaller, outlying communities and have fleets predominantly comprised of aircraft with 60 or fewer seats. General aviation refers to airplanes, almost all of them very small aircraft, owned and operated by individuals or companies for their private use.

Due to the dramatic growth of the regional airlines and the scramble to claim a share of the different market segments following deregulation in 1978, these categories are no longer clear-cut. The Federal Aviation Administration (FAA), which regulates airlines, refers to the larger airlines as "commercial air carriers" and to the smaller airlines as "regionals" or "commuters," even though the regionals are, in fact, commercial airlines that operate for profit.

Large commercial airlines are sometimes referred to as scheduled airlines, because they usually fly only on regular, fixed schedules. Again, regional airlines also offer scheduled services. In some cases, the term "scheduled" refers to both types of carriers. In addition, both types of carriers may provide charter, or "unscheduled," services.

THE AIR TRAVEL INDUSTRY TODAY

In the 1960s, only 25 percent of Americans had ever flown commercially. By the late 1980s, 72 percent of Americans had done so, and the percentages continued to rise in the 1990s, according to the FAA. The years 1997 through 2000 continued the steady growth of the airline industry. (See Figure 7.2.) According to the ATA, in 2000, 666.2 million passengers flew on more than 9 million flights on major U.S. airlines. (See Table 7.1.)

The air travel industry was immediately and profoundly affected by the terrorist attacks of September 11, 2001. W. Douglas Parker, Chairman, President, and CEO of America West Airlines, summarized the situation in the ATA *2002 Annual Report*: "The year 2001 was the most difficult in the history of the U.S. airline industry." This is reflected in Figure 7.2, which shows a decline of 5.9 percent in revenue passenger miles (RPMs) in 2001 compared with 2000. (A revenue passenger mile is one fare-paying passenger transported one mile.) In 2001, 622.1 million passengers flew on 8.8 million flights on major U.S. airlines, a flight decline of 2.7 percent. (See Table 7.1.) RPMs were down 8.2 percent in 2002, according to the FAA.

Of all the components of the transportation industry, the airlines were the hardest hit by the recession that began in March 2001 and the events of September 11. By 2002 several airlines were teetering on the edge of bankruptcy. The situation was exacerbated by the 2003 war with Iraq. In March 2003 Jim Corridore, Standard & Poor's equity analyst, expressed the opinion that the U.S. airline industry was facing extremely hard times. He estimated that the top 10 U.S. airlines would lose around $6.5 billion in 2003, possibly even more due to the war in Iraq.

Fear of Flying

When asked in March 2002 by University of Michigan researchers how concerned they were about their safety while performing various activities, 69 percent of those who ordinarily flew on an airplane said they were more concerned about their safety than they had been before September 11, 2001. In the Omnibus Household Survey conducted by the DOT between April and October 2002, an average of about 38 percent of U.S. residents reported having flown on a commercial airline at least once during the year preceding the survey. A majority (an average of about 78 percent) reported that the screening process was adequate and they were confident that screeners could keep air travel safe. However, only 37 percent of residents who had not flown in the previous year had a high level of confidence that screeners could guarantee safe travel ("Airline Passengers Give High Marks to Security Screening Procedures at Nation's Airports," *OmniStats*, vol. 2, issue 3, October 2002).

The Crowded Skies

The privately owned, fixed-wing, general aviation fleet (non-commercial airplanes with wings fastened to the fuselage, as distinguished from helicopters) numbered approximately 175,200 in 1998 (the latest data available), with turbine-powered engines accounting for about 12,000 of that number, split roughly half turboprop, half turbojet. The rest of the fleet had piston engines turning propellers ("No. 1045. Airports, Aircraft, and Airmen: 1980 to 1999," in *Statistical Abstract of the United States: 2002*, U.S. Census Bureau, Washington, D.C., 2002). Individuals or companies privately owned almost all of these aircraft. The 5,335 planes owned by major airlines were powered by jet turbines (*Statistical Abstract*), as were the vast majority of the approximately 2,300 aircraft belonging to regional carriers ("U.S. Regional Airline Fact Sheet," Regional Airline Association, April 12, 2002). Other types of aircraft include helicopters, balloons, gliders, and blimps.

With the economy booming in the 1990s and all of these craft airborne, the skies were indeed crowded. Delays at the nation's busiest airports led to an FAA decision to craft a ten-year plan to increase the capacity of the National Airspace System (details of the "Operational

TABLE 7.2

Top 25 airlines worldwide, by various characteristics, 2001

In revenue passenger kilometers (RPKs)

Rank	Airline	RPKs (000,000)
1	United	187,666
2	American	170,883
3	Delta	163,663
4	Northwest	117,658
5	British Airways	106,270
6	Continental	98,374
7	Air France	94,415
8	Lufthansa	86,695
9	JAL	84,265
10	US Airways	73,930
11	Southwest	71,591
12	Singapore	69,145
13	Qantas	67,894
14	Air Canada	67,016
15	KLM	57,818
16	All Nippon	56,904
17	Cathay Pacific	44,792
18	Thai Int'l	44,039
19	Iberia	41,297
20	Korean	38,453
21	Malaysia	38,313
22	Alitalia	36,524
23	Swissair	32,981
24	TWA	31,848
25	America West	30,690

In operating revenue

Rank	Airline	Op. revenue (000)
1	AMR Corp.	$18,963,000
2	UAL Corp.	16,138,000
3	FedEx	15,166,933
4	Lufthansa Group	14,687,000
5	Delta	13,879,000
6	JAL Group	12,373,846
7	British Airways	12,176,000
8	Air France Group	11,024,640
9	Northwest	9,905,000
10	All Nippon	9,265,000
11	Continental	8,969,000
12	US Airways	8,253,356
13	Air Canada	6,040,514
14	KLM	5,744,000
15	Southwest	5,555,174
16	Singapore Group	5,252,977
17	Qantas	5,202,000
18	SAS Group	4,969,000
19	Alitalia Group	4,698,320
20	Korean	4,284,000
21	Iberia	4,169,658
22	Cathay Pacific	3,895,808
23	Japan Air System	3,300,000
24	Air New Zealand Group	3,231,760
25	Airborne Express	3,211,089

In operating profit

Rank	Airline	Op. profit (000)
1	FedEx	$778,489
2	Southwest	631,122
3	Qantas	561,357
4	Singapore Group	546,770
5	Air France Group	206,800
6	All Nippon	177,000
7	China Southern	169,073
8	Continental	144,000
9	Ryanair	141,752
10	Emirates	133,638
11	Cathay Pacific	106,496
12	China Eastern	105,595
13	UPS	101,099
14	China Airlines	96,232
15	SkyWest	75,256
16	Lufthansa Cargo	57,200
17	EasyJet	56,041
18	LanChile	50,252
19	Atlantic Coast	44,194
20	South African	43,330
21	WestJet	37,333
22	Air Transat	36,765
23	AirTran Holdings	35,709
24	JetBlue	26,800
25	Cargolux	22,347

In net profit

Rank	Airline	Net profit (000)
1	Southwest	$511,147
2	FedEx	452,951
3	Singapore Group	351,225
4	Qantas	216,008
5	Air France Group	134,640
6	Ryanair	130,826
7	Emirates	127,467
8	Cathay Pacific	84,000
9	China Eastern	65,409
10	SkyWest	56,428
11	EasyJet	55,723
12	China Airlines	51,769
13	South African	50,853
14	Iberia	46,762
15	Thai Int'l	44,888
16	Aeroflot	44,300
17	China Southern	41,031
18	JetBlue	38,500
19	Atlantic Coast	24,322
20	WestJet	23,380
21	Go	20,294
22	Vietnam	19,544
23	Luxair Group	18,900
24	Bmi British Midland	18,228
25	Atlantic Southeast	18,117

In passengers

Rank	Airline	Pass. (000)
1	Delta	104,943
2	American	78,178
3	United	75,457
4	Southwest	64,447
5	US Airways	56,114
6	Northwest	54,056
7	All Nippon Group	49,306
8	Continental	44,200
9	British Airways	40,004
10	Lufthansa	39,694
11	Air France	39,067
12	JAL	37,183
13	Iberia	24,928
14	Alitalia	24,926
15	SAS	23,244
16	Air Canada	23,100
17	TWA	22,214
18	Japan Air System	21,760
19	Korean	21,638
20	Qantas	20,193
21	America West	19,576
22	China Southern	19,121
23	Thai Int'l	18,271
24	Malaysia	16,745
25	KLM	15,995

In freight ton-kilometers (FTKs)

Rank	Airline	FTKs (000)
1	FedEx	11,045,328
2	Lufthansa Cargo	7,081,000
3	UPS	5,958,328
4	Singapore	5,884,463
5	Korean	5,571,000
6	Air France	5,117,000
7	KLM	4,464,287
8	JAL	4,190,263
9	British Airways	4,033,000
10	China Airlines	4,030,141
11	Nippon Cargo	3,925,574
12	Cathay Pacific	3,887,087
13	Cargolux	3,768,075
14	EVA	3,279,012
15	United	2,801,563
16	Northwest	2,789,996
17	American	2,561,406
18	Martinair	2,395,169
19	Asiana	2,382,846
20	Delta	2,311,180
21	Malaysia	1,837,426
22	Swissair	1,793,704
23	Thai Int'l	1,670,203
24	Qantas	1,572,069
25	Air Hong Kong	1,550,338

In employees

Rank	Airline	No. of employees
1	AMR Corp.	118,400
2	United	92,900
3	Lufthansa Group	87,975
4	Delta	76,273
5	Air France Group	64,717
6	British Airways	57,227
7	Continental	48,000
8	Northwest	46,364
9	Air Canada	40,000
10	US Airways	35,232
11	Southwest	31,580
12	Qantas	29,217
13	Iberia	28,320
14	KLM	27,573
15	Thai Int'l	25,000
16	Saudi Arabian	24,259
17	Alitalia	24,023
18	SAS	22,656
19	Malaysia	21,072
20	Egyptian	21,000
21	Indian	20,703
22	Pakistan	17,472
23	Air-India	17,200
24	Varig	16,993
25	JAL	16,552

In fleet size

Rank	Airline	No. of aircraft
1	American	881
2	FedEx	644
3	Delta	588
4	United	543
5	Northwest	444
6	Southwest	355
7	Continental	345
8	US Airways	342
9	American Eagle	276
10	British Airways	266
11	Air France	254
12	UPS	252
13	Air Canada	242
14	Lufthansa	236
15	Continental Express	197
16	Iberia	187
17	SAS	150
18	Alitalia	144
19	America West	142
20	All Nippon	141
21	JAL	141
22	Atlantic Southeast	132
23	SkyWest	129
24	Saudi Arabian	128
25	Korean	127

SOURCE: "The World's Top 25 Airlines," ATW Research, Direct airline reports [Online] http://www.atwonline.com/Pdf/tables.pdf [accessed April 15, 2003]. Reprinted with permission.

TABLE 7.3

Airline passenger yields, 1991–2001

Revenue per passenger mile (in cents)	Passenger yield 1991	2000	2001
Domestic	13.24	14.57	13.41
International	11.32	10.59	9.65
Total	12.74	13.51	12.42

SOURCE: "Passenger yield," in *2002 Annual Report,* Air Transport Association of America, Inc., Washington, DC [Online] http://www.airlines.org/ [accessed April 15, 2003]

TABLE 7.4

Airline industry employment, 1991–2001

U.S. scheduled airlines	1991	2000	2001
Pilots & copilots	49,232	72,379	71,266
Other flight personnel	8,033	10,819	9,554
Flight attendants	81,794	112,623	112,866
Mechanics	58,819	72,092	70,017
Aircraft & traffic service	237,292	311,724	303,672
Office employees	44,304	44,028	43,436
All other	54,091	56,303	59,919
Total employment	533,565	679,967	670,730
Average compensation per employee			
Salaries & wages	$40,376	$54,489	$55,846
Benefits & pensions	7,231	10,180	12,089
Payroll taxes	3,038	3,765	3,899
Total compensation	$50,645	$68,434	$71,834

SOURCE: "Employment," in *2002 Annual Report,* Air Transport Association of America, Inc., Washington, DC [Online] http://www.airlines.org/ [accessed April 15, 2003]

Evolution Plan" can be viewed online at http://www2.faa.gov/programs/oep/History.htm). After the September 11, 2001, terrorist attacks, the skies were not so crowded. By 2003 the airlines had excess capacity, expressed in terms of a "parked" fleet of 2,250 aircraft that were not required in a depressed market in which airlines were cutting routes (*Aircraft Technology Engineering & Maintenance*, April/May 2003).

A License to Fly

In 1999, 635,472 people had licenses to fly in the United States (including 37,373 women), up from 618,298 in 1998 (*Statistical Abstract*). Of that number, 97,359 held student licenses and were learning to fly. Approximately 258,000 had private licenses that permitted them to fly small planes. Another 124,261 had commercial licenses that allowed them to fly smaller commercial airplanes owned by the airlines. More than 137,000 pilots held airline transport licenses, which permit them to fly the big jets owned by the airline companies. More than 7,700 had licenses for helicopters and 9,390 for gliders.

THE TOP AIRLINES

As shown in Table 7.2, Delta Airlines led the industry in 2001 in number of passengers carried (nearly 105 million). Second was American (78.1 million), then United (75.4 million). Federal Express carried by far the largest number of freight ton kilometers (FTKs), followed by Lufthansa Cargo (a German company) and United Parcel Service (UPS). American Airlines, Federal Express, Delta, and United had the most operating planes (fleet size).

Yield—or fares per passenger per mile—inched up in the early 1990s. In 1991 airlines received an average yield of 12.74 cents per passenger mile. (See Table 7.3.) By 2000 the yield was 13.51 cents per passenger mile. In 2001 it declined to 12.42 cents per passenger mile.

Employment

The major U.S. airlines employed 670,730 people in 2001, a 1.3 percent decrease from 2000, when airlines employed 679,967 people, but up 26 percent from 1991. (See Table 7.4.) Most of these employees work on the ground, servicing and maintaining aircraft and running the business side of the airlines. Only about 29 percent of airline employees serve on the flights themselves, and fewer than one-third of them are pilots or copilots.

When jet airplanes became part of the air passenger industry in 1958, pilots were largely recruited from the armed forces. These were men (exclusively) with prior military flight training and experience. Although pilots are private employees of the airline for which they fly, they are subject to mandatory FAA-imposed retirement at age 60. The pool of military pilots has shrunk in recent years, and the rising cost of private pilot training has discouraged many would-be students. Many pilots now begin their careers with regional or cargo airlines in order to get enough required flying hours, hoping to move to the major airlines as vacancies appear.

Some pilots have tried to overturn the mandatory retirement age. The ruling, made in 1959, was intended to reduce the danger of an older pilot suffering a heart attack or stroke while flying. Opponents of the ruling cite recent medical advances that greatly reduce this risk. They argue that older pilots have accumulated a vast store of experience during their many years of flying that classroom training cannot duplicate. The FAA, however, has stood by its decision and indicates that it intends to maintain the age limit. The Ninth Circuit Court of Appeals agreed in *Western Air Lines, Inc. v. Criswell et al.* (709 F.2d 544, 1984), when it decided that the airlines could retire pilots at age 60. Legislation introduced in Congress in March 2003 (HR 1063) would direct the FAA to incrementally raise the mandatory retirement age to 65. The retirement age would increase one year, every year, for 5 years after the bill becomes law.

Jumbo Jets

Jumbo jets, the huge, 600-passenger, four-engine aircraft that airlines use for high-volume routes, are giving way to smaller craft. Major international carriers are building hubs in cities that do not generate enough traffic to fill giant planes. Instead, smaller two-engine jumbo planes such as the Boeing 777 are increasingly being used, because their 368+ seats are more easily filled, making them more efficient. While overseas flights, particularly to Asia, still use the larger aircraft, the fragmentation of air routes (dividing long routes into shorter ones) has created demand for smaller planes.

Boeing, long dominant in the commercial aircraft market, faces a challenge from foreign manufacturers, principally Airbus Industries, a European consortium, the only other manufacturer of aircraft seating more than 100 people. Airbus offers several competitor planes, including the A320, which competes with the Boeing 737, and the A330, a competitor to the Boeing 767 ("Boeing's Trailblazer Becomes an Also-Ran," *Europe Intelligence Wire*, January 1, 2003).

The opening of China and the potential for lucrative routes there motivated Boeing and Airbus to propose larger passenger craft. Airbus expects to roll out the 550-seat, environmentally friendly 380 in 2006. Boeing's first 368- to 550-seat 777-300ER is scheduled for delivery in April 2004; the company is also developing for delivery in 2007 the 7E7, a 200- to 250-seat, fuel-efficient plane designed for routes between 7,200 and 8,000 nautical miles.

Boeing's 2003 *Current Market Outlook* estimated that the world fleet of jets would more than double from 15,612 planes in 2002 to 33,999 by 2022. It is expected that Latin America will be the fastest growing market. About 4 percent of the 2022 fleet will be 747 and larger planes, while the majority (58 percent or 19,720 planes) will be single-aisle airplanes.

Yield Management

Deregulation produced a dizzying array of new fare categories. Fares now swing sharply from season to season and sometimes day to day. Even the most sophisticated traveler can become confused by the multitude of ticket prices offered. These prices result from the airlines' efforts to obtain maximum revenue from each planeload.

The increasing power and sophistication of computer systems have allowed the airlines to develop a strategy called "yield management" or "revenue control." The point is to sell the mix of low-, medium-, and high-priced coach tickets that will earn the most money from each flight. Yield management leads the major airlines to introduce many discount fare categories, each with its own set of restrictions.

Business travelers are the airlines' favorite customers, since they must travel and tend to leave for trips on short notice and since companies usually pay full fare. Business travelers, however, usually buy seats at the last minute and there are not enough of them to fill airplanes. According to information posted on the Travel Industry Association of America's Web site in 2003, 21 percent of total U.S. domestic person-trips are made by business travelers. Airlines attempt to fill the remaining seats at lower prices with leisure travelers. The point of yield management is to charge business travelers, who have the least flexibility, the highest fares. Having maximized their profits with these business travelers, the airlines can then discount fares to fill their remaining seats, which would go empty if they insisted on the high prices. This is because serving one more passenger, even at a deep discount, costs little more than the price of a snack, the ticket taxes, and a slight amount of additional fuel.

Discount fares attract vacation travelers. Restrictions that apply to reduced fares, such as advance-purchase requirements and travel extending through Saturdays, inhibit the use of these fares by business travelers and thus serve to maintain profit margin. Fully refundable tickets, standard before deregulation, are now less common. Most tickets include a charge for refund or exchange.

Frequent-Flier Plans—Wooing the Travelers

The intense competition resulting from deregulation caused major changes in airline marketing strategies. One technique, aimed primarily at the higher-paying business traveler, is the so-called frequent-flier (mileage bonus) program. Such plans offer future free tickets as a reward for accumulating trip mileage on a specific airline, encouraging brand loyalty among those who fly often. Frequent-flier plans also offer seasonal discounts and coupons that the passenger can use to upgrade from a coach seat to the more desirable first-class or business-class sections, as well as other promotions. Since the larger carriers, with their extensive number of routes, offer the most attractive destinations for fliers when they cash in their mileage bonus points, this marketing tool gives them a special edge in the era of deregulation.

The first frequent-flier plan was started by American Airlines in 1981 as the American AAdvantage program and was intended to be temporary. The program was a huge marketing success, however. The airline found that passengers were choosing to stay with an air carrier in order to accumulate miles, and soon other airlines started their own plans. *WebFlyer* magazine estimated total frequent-flier membership worldwide at about 84 million in 2002, with 74 million in the United States (Jim

TABLE 7.5

Regionals/commuters aviation demand forecasts and assumptions, fiscal years 2003–2014

Aviation activity	Historical			Forecast			Percent/point[1] average annual growth				
	1995	2001	2002	2003	2004	2014	95-02	01-02	02-03	03-04	02-14
Regional/commuters											
Enplanements (millions)											
Domestic	55.4	80.4	88.0	94.0	103.2	169.0	6.8	9.4	6.9	9.8	5.6
International	2.1	3.1	2.7	3.1	3.4	5.0	4.0	(13.7)	14.4	8.5	5.3
System	57.5	83.6	90.7	97.1	106.6	174.1	6.7	8.5	7.1	9.7	5.6
RPMs (billions)											
Domestic	12.0	24.2	29.8	34.2	38.8	73.2	13.9	23.1	14.6	13.4	7.8
International	0.4	1.0	0.9	1.1	1.2	2.0	12.9	(6.9)	15.5	9.8	6.4
System	12.4	25.2	30.8	35.3	39.9	75.1	13.9	21.9	14.6	13.3	7.7
Fleet (as of December 31)[2]											
Turboprops/Pistons	2,031	1,581	1,489	1,415	1,341	1,144	(4.3)	(5.8)	(5.0)	(5.2)	(2.2)
Jets	78	782	1,032	1,289	1,538	2,890	44.6	32.0	24.9	19.3	9.0
Total	2,109	2,363	2,521	2,704	2,879	4,034	2.6	6.7	7.3	6.5	4.0
Block to block hours[2]	4,659	5,161	5,486	5,899	6,296	9,554	2.4	6.3	7.5	6.7	4.7
Average aircraft size (seats)											
Domestic	31.0	40.4	42.9	44.6	45.4	50.4	1.7	2.5	1.7	0.8	0.6
International	28.4	44.5	41.8	43.3	43.8	48.8	1.9	(2.7)	1.5	0.5	0.6
System	31.0	40.6	42.8	44.6	45.4	50.4	1.7	2.2	1.8	0.8	0.6
Average trip length (miles)											
Domestic	216.0	301.4	339.1	363.5	375.5	432.9	17.6	37.7	24.4	12.0	7.8
International	193.4	319.1	344.2	347.2	351.1	389.5	21.5	25.1	3.0	3.9	3.8
System	215.2	302.1	339.2	363.0	374.7	431.6	17.7	37.1	23.8	11.7	7.7
Average load factor (percent)											
Domestic	49.2	58.6	61.3	60.3	59.8	64.0	1.7	2.7	(1.0)	(0.5)	0.2
International	59.2	59.1	60.8	60.0	60.0	65.0	0.2	1.7	(0.8)	0.0	0.4
System	49.4	58.6	61.3	60.3	59.8	64.0	1.7	2.7	(1.0)	(0.5)	0.2

[1] Enplanements, RPMs, Fleet, and Hours Flown: annual percent change; all other series, annual absolute change.
[2] Historical and forecast data on a calendar year basis.

SOURCE: "Table 1-4: Aviation Demand Forecasts and Assumptions, Regionals/Commuters Fiscal Years 2003–2014," in *FAA Aerospace Forecasts FY 2003–2014,* Federal Aviation Administration, Washington, DC, 2002 [Online] http://api.hq.faa.gov/foreca02/content_5.htm [accessed April 15, 2003]

Steinberg, "Frequent-Flier Miles Safe Despite Airline Turbulence," *Knight Ridder/Tribune Business News*, August 23, 2002). After many planes became too full to make room for frequent fliers, airlines tightened up the rules, raising redemption levels and combining them with expiration deadlines. In July 1999 American Airlines announced that it would do away with expiration deadlines and that AAdvantage program members would have 36 months for their account to show any activity—from booking a flight to simply making a purchase on an AAdvantage credit card—to keep the miles indefinitely. United Airlines made similar changes to its program.

REGIONAL AND COMMUTER AIRLINES

In response to deregulation in the late 1970s, the regional, or commuter, airlines underwent dramatic changes. Previous restrictions to planes with fewer than 12 seats severely hampered growth, and deregulation freed the regional airlines to increase passenger capacity and passenger revenue-miles. As the major airlines converted to larger turbojets suitable for high-capacity, long-haul flights, the regionals moved into the gap left in the low-density, short-haul market.

Since 1969, when the commuter lines received formal industry recognition, more than 600 different carriers have been in operation at one time or another. However, the consolidation that occurred among the major airlines also affected the regionals. In 2000 there were 94 operating U.S. passenger carriers, down from 214 in 1980 ("No. 1044. Commuter/Regional Airline Operations–Summary: 1980 to 2000" in *Statistical Abstract of the United States: 2002*). Passenger enplanements on commuters totaled 88 million in 2002, a gain of 9.4 percent over 2001. (See Table 7.5.)

The regionals and the commuter industry have created niches in the market tailored to the specific needs of their customers. While the fleet once consisted of a variety of small general-aviation aircraft, the planes are increasingly state-of-the-art, including a growing number of small but comfortable jet aircraft, and the airlines now offer services similar to those of the commercial carriers.

FIGURE 7.3

Active private pilot trends and forecasts, 1997–2014

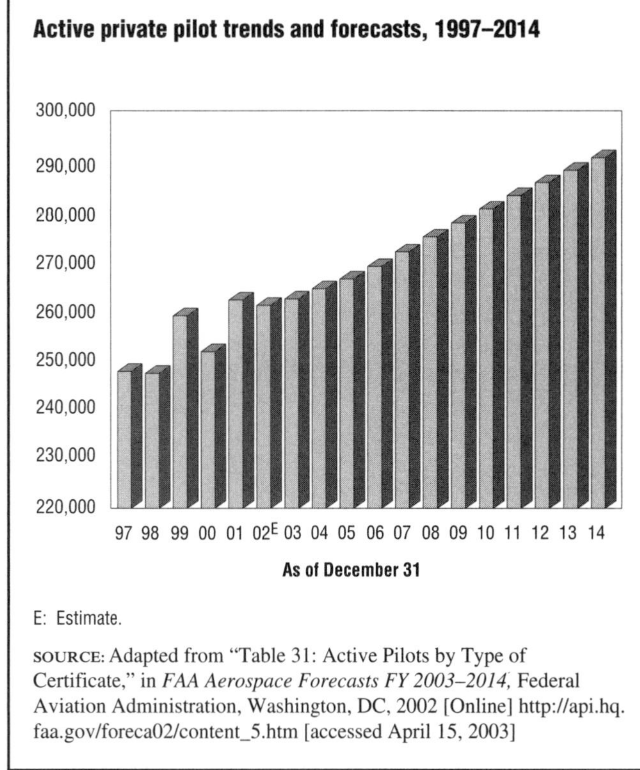

E: Estimate.

SOURCE: Adapted from "Table 31: Active Pilots by Type of Certificate," in *FAA Aerospace Forecasts FY 2003–2014,* Federal Aviation Administration, Washington, DC, 2002 [Online] http://api.hq.faa.gov/foreca02/content_5.htm [accessed April 15, 2003]

TABLE 7.6

U.S. general aviation and air traffic activity, 2000–2001

(Calendar years)

	Estimated active aircraft (thousands)		Estimated hours flown (millions)	
	2001	**2000**	**2001**	**2000**
Total	211.2	217.5	29.1	31.0
By type aircraft				
Piston	163.3	170.5	20.9	22.2
Turbo prop	6.6	5.8	1.9	2.0
Jet	7.8	7.0	2.7	2.8
Rotary wing	6.8	7.2	2.1	2.3
Other	6.5	6.7	0.3	0.4
Experimental	20.4	20.4	1.2	1.3
By type flying				
Corporate	7.8	11.0	2.7	3.8
Business	21.6	25.2	3.4	3.6
Personal	158.3	148.2	12.4	11.7
Instructional	10.5	14.9	4.6	5.4
Aerial application	2.9	4.3	1.0	1.4
Aerial observation	4.6	5.1	1.5	1.6
Aerial other	0.5	1.0	0.2	N/A
External load	0.2	0.2	0.1	0.2
Other work	1.1	1.8	0.3	0.5
Sightseeing	0.5	0.9	0.2	0.2
Air tours	0.3	0.3	0.2	0.2
Air taxi	1.9	3.7	2.2	1.7
Air medical services	1.0	1.0	0.4	0.4

N/A = Not applicable.

SOURCE: "U.S. General Aviation and Air Taxi Activity," in *Administrator's Fact Book,* U.S. Department of Transportation, Federal Aviation Administration, March 2003 [Online] http://www.atctraining.faa.gov/factbook [accessed April 15, 2003]

The regional airlines became an essential element of the hub-and-spoke structure of the major airlines. Many regionals have routes and schedules designed to mesh with major carriers at hub cities. They funnel passengers from smaller cities to flights outbound from the hub and relay arriving passengers to their final destinations. The regional airlines have become an important component in the airline industry, leading some of the majors to buy their connecting regionals to ensure continued operation and cooperation. The regionals also provide a training ground for pilots with backgrounds in military or general aviation who hope to fly for one of the major airlines.

Regional/commuter air carriers are separated into two groups. One group operates commuter aircraft of 60 seats or fewer. The second group operates both large aircraft over 60 seats and smaller commuter aircraft. Both groups experienced growth in 2002. As the major airlines struggled to recover from a post-September 11 decline in air travel, they began transferring a large number of routes to their regional partners. System-wide enplanements showed average annual growth of 8.5 percent in 2001–02. (See Table 7.5.) Revenue passenger miles (RPMs) were up 22 percent and the fleet was 6.7 percent larger. Growth through 2014 is forecast in the regional/commuter industry, as shown in Table 7.5.

GENERAL AVIATION

Since flights by individuals in privately owned airplanes produce no revenue, the state of general aviation is reported in terms of numbers of private pilots, hours flown, fleet composition, and aircraft shipments by the manufacturers of general aviation aircraft. The total number of private pilots decreased from 360,000 in 1980 to 261,927 in 2001. Figure 7.3 shows, however, that the number of private pilots is expected to increase to about 290,550 by 2014. According to *FAA Aerospace Forecast*, such an increase will depend on how successful the general aviation industry is in stimulating new interest in pilot training. Post-September 11 restrictions that were placed on flight schools and student training saw the number of student pilots decline 8.9 percent between 2001 and 2002, from 94,420 to 85,991.

For FAA reporting purposes, the active general aviation fleet consists of those private airplanes that have been flown at least one hour during the previous year. As of 2001, the active fleet numbered 211,200 aircraft (see Table 7.6), down from 217,500 airplanes in 2000.

The total number of shipments of new general aviation aircraft has been declining since 1978, when almost 18,000 general aviation aircraft were shipped. (See Figure 7.4.) In

FIGURE 7.4

Annual new U.S. manufactured general aviation unit shipments/billings, 1973–2000

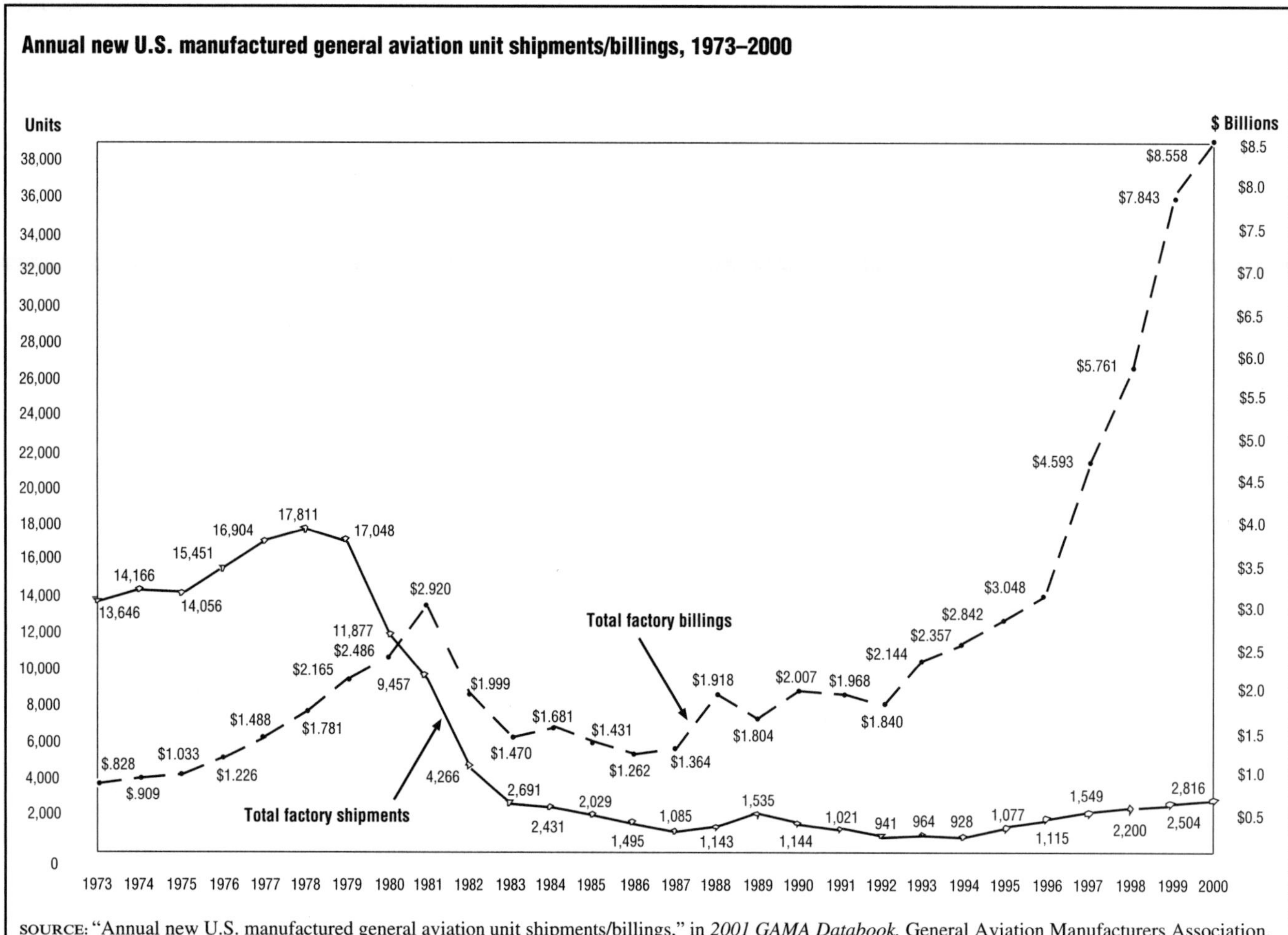

SOURCE: "Annual new U.S. manufactured general aviation unit shipments/billings," in *2001 GAMA Databook,* General Aviation Manufacturers Association, Washington, DC, 2001 [Online] http://www.generalaviation.org/databook/2001/pages4_8.pdf [accessed April 15, 2003]

1994 shipments reached a low of 928. The major cause for the decline was manufacturer liability. Before 1994, any time a general aviation plane crashed, no matter how old or poorly maintained and regardless of the ability of the pilot, the manufacturer was at least partly responsible. It became too financially risky to manufacture aircraft. In 1994, following a virtual shutdown of the general aviation industry, Congress passed the General Aviation Revitalization Act (PL 103-298), limiting the manufacturers' liability and the amount of time during which they could be held legally liable.

The act states that

> no civil action for damages for death or injury to persons or damage to property arising out of an accident involving a general aviation aircraft may be brought against the manufacturer of the aircraft or the manufacturer of any new component, system, subassembly, or other part of the aircraft, in its capacity as a manufacturer

if the accident occurred after an agreed-upon, specified time, which starts on the date of delivery to the original buyer or lessee. Similarly, if the aircraft is delivered to a sales person or company, no civil action for damages may be brought against the manufacturer if the accident occurs beyond an agreed-upon, specified time after that sales person or company receives the aircraft. The same conditions hold true for any new or replacement component, system, subassembly, or other part that was added to or replaced on the aircraft and that is alleged to have caused death, injury or damage.

The passage of the General Aviation Revitalization Act meant that aircraft manufacturers could now buy more reasonably priced insurance. Helped along by the new law and an improving economy, aircraft shipments slowly began to increase. A total of 1,549 planes were shipped in 1997 and 2,816 in 2000. (See Figure 7.4.) Table 7.7 shows the number of purchases of single-engine and multi-engine piston, turboprop, and jet planes between 1963 and 2000.

More recent shipping estimates were reported by the FAA in *FAA Aerospace Forecast Fiscal Years 2003–2014.* Shipments in 2002 were expected to total 2,153, a 17.7 percent decline from 2001. The falling demand for general aviation aircraft may be due in part to a weak economy.

TABLE 7.7

Annual new manufactured general aviation airplane shipments by type of airplane, 1963–2000

Year	Grand total	Single-engine	Multi-engine	Total piston	Turboprop	Jet	Total turbine
1963	7,569	6,248	1,321	7,569	0	0	0
1964	9,336	7,718	1,606	9,324	9	3	12
1965	11,852	9,873	1,780	11,653	87	112	199
1966	15,768	13,250	2,192	15,442	165	161	326
1967	13,577	11,557	1,773	13,330	149	98	247
1968	13,698	11,398	1,959	13,357	248	93	341
1969	12,457	10,054	2,078	12,132	214	111	325
1970	7,292	5,942	1,159	7,101	135	56	191
1971	7,466	6,287	1,043	7,330	89	47	136
1972	9,774	7,913	1,548	9,446	179	134	313
1973	13,646	10,788	2,413	13,193	247	198	445
1974	14,166	11,579	2,135	13,697	250	202	452
1975	14,056	11,441	2,116	13,555	305	194	499
1976	15,451	12,785	2,120	14,905	359	187	546
1977	16,904	14,054	2,195	16,249	428	227	655
1978	17,811	14,398	2,634	17,032	548	231	779
1979	17,048	13,286	2,843	16,129	639	282	921
1980	11,877	8,640	2,116	10,756	778	326	1,104
1981	9,457	6,608	1,542	8,150	918	389	1,307
1982	4,266	2,871	678	3,549	458	259	717
1983	2,691	1,811	417	2,228	321	142	463
1984	2,431	1,620	371	1,991	271	169	440
1985	2,029	1,370	193	1,563	321	145	466
1986	1,495	985	138	1,123	250	122	372
1987	1,085	613	87	700	263	122	385
1988	1,143	628	67	695	291	157	448
1989	1,535	1,023	87	1,110	268	157	425
1990	1,144	608	87	695	281	168	449
1991	1,021	564	49	613	222	186	408
1992	941	552	41	593	177	171	348
1993	964	516	39	555	211	198	409
1994	928	444	55	499	207	222	429
1995	1,077	515	61	576	255	246	501
1996R	1,115	607	42	649	223	233	466
1997	1,549	898	86	984	223	342	565
1998	2,200	1,434	94	1,528	259	413	672
1999	2,504	1,634	114	1,748	239	517	756
2000	2,816	1,810	103	1,913	315	588	903

R=Revised

SOURCE: "Annual new manufactured general aviation airplane shipments by type of airplane," in *2001 GAMA Databook,* General Aviation Manufacturers Association, Washington, DC, 2001 [Online] http://www.generalaviation.org/databook/2001/pages4_8.pdf [accessed April 15, 2003]

Fleet Growth Forecast

As of December 31, 2001, the FAA reported a total of 6,800 active general aviation rotorcraft (helicopters and gyrocopters) and 7,800 jet aircraft in the United States. (See Table 7.6.) Most of these craft are used for sightseeing; agricultural applications; law enforcement; firefighting; personal transportation; emergency medical services; transporting personnel and supplies to offshore oil rigs; traffic reporting; news gathering; corporate or business transportation; and heavy lifting for the oil, utility, and lumber industries. The FAA forecasts an average annual growth rate of 0.7 percent in the active general aviation fleet between 2002 and 2014, spurred mostly by growth in "the more expensive and sophisticated turbine-powered fleet (including rotorcraft)." This sector is expected to grow at an average annual rate of 2.3 percent. The jet fleet alone will grow from 8,000 in 2002 to 12,300 in 2014, assuming that business/corporate travel on the general aviation fleet increases as security restrictions on commercial aircraft become more onerous.

AIRPORTS

Orville Wright's runway was a sand dune; Charles Lindbergh's, an open field. The first airline passengers walked to hangars or fields to board the parked planes. These arrangements soon proved inadequate. Larger planes, heavier loads, and increased traffic required paved

TABLE 7.8

Civil and joint use airports, heliports, stolports, and seaplane bases on record, August 2001

FAA region and state	Total facilities	Total facilities, by ownership		Airports open to the public				Total airports
				Paved airports[1]		Unpaved airports[1]		
		Public	Private	Lighted	Unlighted	Lighted	Unlighted	
Grand total	19,245	5,133	14,122	3,619	268	385	754	5,026
United States—total[2]	19,178	5,098	14,080	3,600	266	385	753	5,004

[1] Includes all airports open to the public, both publicly and privately owned.
[2] Excludes Puerto Rico, Virgin Islands, and South Pacific.

SOURCE: Adapted from "U.S. civil and joint use airports, heliports, stolports, and seaplane bases on record by type of ownership—August, 2001," in *2001 GAMA Databook,* General Aviation Manufacturers Association, Washington, DC, 2001 [Online] http://www.generalaviation.org/databook/2001/pages21_22.pdf [accessed April 15, 2003]

TABLE 7.9

Top 25 airports, 2001

Passengers		(000)	Cargo metric tons		(000)	Operations		(000)
(Arriving and departing)			(Loaded and unloaded)			(Takeoffs and landings)		
1	Atlanta (ATL)	75,849	1	Memphis (MEM)	2,631	1	Chicago O'Hare (ORD)	910
2	Chicago O'Hare (ORD)	66,805	2	Los Angeles (LAX)	2,123	2	Atlanta (ATL)	890
3	Los Angeles (LAX)	61,025	3	Anchorage (ANC)	1,691	3	Dallas/Fort Worth	784
4	Dallas/Fort Worth (DFW)	55,151	4	Miami (MIA)	1,640	4	Los Angeles (LAX)	738
5	Denver (DEN)	36,087	5	New York Kennedy (JFK)[1]	1,500	5	Phoenix (PHX)	561
6	Phoenix (PHX)	35,482	6	Louisville (SDF)	1,469	6	Detroit (DTW)	522
7	Las Vegas (LAS)	35,196	7	Chicago O'Hare (ORD)	1,285	7	Minneapolis/St. Paul (MSP)	500
8	Minneapolis/St. Paul (MSP)	35,171	8	Indianapolis (IND)	1,151	8	Las Vegas (LAS)	494
9	Houston (IAH)	34,795	9	Newark (EWR)[1]	800	9	Denver (DEN)	484
10	San Francisco (SFO)	34,627	10	Dallas/Fort Worth (DFW)	794	10	St. Louis (STL)	474
11	Detroit (DTW)	32,294	11	Atlanta (ATL)	744	11	Miami (MIA)	471
12	Miami (MIA)	31,668	12	San Francisco (SFO)	635	12	Houston (IAH)	471
13	Newark (EWR)[1]	30,500	13	Oakland (OAK)	602	13	Philadelphia (PHL)	467
14	New York Kennedy (JFK)[1]	29,400	14	Dayton (DAY)	551	14	Charlotte (CLT)	461
15	Orlando McCoy (MCO)	28,167	15	Philadelphia (PHL)	536	15	Boston (BOS)	455
16	Seattle (SEA)	27,036	16	Ontario (ONT)	508	16	Pittsburgh (PIT)	452
17	St. Louis (STL)	26,719	17	Honolulu (HNL)	412	17	Newark (EWR)[1]	436
18	Boston (BOS)	24,200	18	Seattle (SEA)	400	18	Seattle (SEA)	399
19	Philadelphia (PHL)	23,927	19	Boston (BOS)	395	19	Orlando Sanford (SFB)	398
20	Charlotte (CLT)	23,166	20	Denver (DEN)	353	20	Cincinnati (CVG)	397
21	New York La Guardia (LGA)[1]	21,900	21	Minneapolis/St. Paul (MSP)	340	21	Washington Dulles (IAD)	397
22	Honolulu (HNL)	21,096	22	Cincinnati (CVG)	338	22	Oakland (OAK)	396
23	Baltimore (BWI)	20,370	23	Houston (IAH)	337	23	Memphis (MEM)	395
24	Pittsburgh (PIT)	19,945	24	Washington Dulles (IAD)	331	24	San Francisco (SFO)	388
25	Salt Lake City (SLC)	18,914	25	Toledo (TOL)	321	25	Orange County (SNA)	379

[1] Estimated.

SOURCE: "Top 25 U.S. Airports—2001," in *2002 Annual Report,* Air Transport Association of America, Inc., Washington, DC, [Online] http://www.airlines.org/ [accessed April 15, 2003]

runways and lighting for night flights and a more orderly system for loading passengers onto planes.

Government interest in airport development lagged behind its support for the industry as a whole. Federal aid was eventually granted under the Federal Airport Act of 1946 (60 Stat. 170), the 1970 Airport and Airway Development Act (PL 91-258) (which, like the Highway Trust Fund after which it was patterned, levied taxes on airline users), and the 1982 Airport and Airway Improvement Act (PL 97-248). Most airports are now owned and operated by the cities or municipalities in which they are located, with funding provided locally and, to a lesser extent, by the federal government.

In 2001 planes could take off and land at 19,178 airports, heliports, and seaplane bases in the United States. (See Table 7.8.) Most of these airports are not big

TABLE 7.10

Top 25 domestic airline markets, 2001[1]

Passengers (thousands)[2]

1	New York	Fort Lauderdale	3,183	14	New York	West Palm Beach	1,495
2	New York	Orlando	2,808	15	Los Angeles	Chicago	1,461
3	New York	Los Angeles	2,652	16	Los Angeles	Oakland	1,436
4	New York	Chicago	2,466	17	New York	San Juan	1,370
5	New York	Atlanta	2,287	18	New York	Miami	1,360
6	Honolulu	Kahului, Maui	2,120	19	Chicago	Las Vegas	1,349
7	New York	Boston	1,192	20	New York	Tampa	1,304
8	Dallas/Fort Worth	Houston	1,789	21	Honolulu	Kona, Hawaii	1,218
9	New York	San Francisco	1,781	22	Chicago	Orlando	1,194
10	New York	Washington, DC	1,725	23	New York	Dallas/Fort Worth	1,183
11	Los Angeles	Las Vegas	1,632	24	Chicago	Atlanta	1,163
12	New York	Las Vegas	1,536	25	Honolulu	Hilo, Hawaii	1,132
13	Honolulu	Lihue, Kauai	1,528				

[1] Includes all commercial airports in a metropolitan area.

[2] Outbound plus inbound; does not include connecting passengers.

SOURCE: "Top 25 domestic airline markets—2001," in *2002 Annual Report,* Air Transport Association of America, Inc., Washington, DC [Online] http://www.airlines.org/ [accessed April 15, 2003]

international airports with towers and multiple runways. Many are privately located in remote rural areas and may be only unlit grass strips. Table 7.9 shows the busiest U.S. airports in 2001. Atlanta, with nearly 76 million passengers, Chicago O'Hare (66.8 million), Los Angeles (61 million), and Dallas/Fort Worth (55 million), served the largest number of passengers in the United States. The U.S. route with the most passengers is from New York to Fort Lauderdale. (See Table 7.10.) Eight of the 10 busiest routes originate or end in New York City.

Local Impact

An airport has an enormous effect on the communities in its vicinity and can be a major benefit to the local economy. Quick, direct access to a city increases business activity. Many companies are attracted to cities with large airport facilities. An airport may employ hundreds and even thousands of people. Local industries, from the food industry to real estate, benefit by serving the needs of both the airport and its employees.

Ideally, an airport is located reasonably close to a community's business district but far from its residential areas. Often this is not the case. Population growth can overtake an airport that was once "out in the country." Smaller airports, built before the advent of jets in 1958, may have been able to coexist with suburban neighbors, but more flights and bigger planes have led to major complaints about noise and concerns about safety in populated areas. The FAA limits the noise that airliners can produce. Some airports impose additional restrictions on noise emissions, operating hours, or flight paths to reduce the discomfort of nearby residents.

The Hub-and-Spoke Network System

The major airlines gradually developed the hub-and-spoke system over the years in order to increase efficiency and thereby maximize their profits. Rather than flying people directly from where they are to where they want to go, in a hub-and-spoke network the airlines fly people from all over the country to one of their major hub airports. Once there, the passengers transfer to flights going to their actual destination. This system enables airlines to send passengers from any airport they service to any other airport they service. Yet it does not require them to schedule flights to and from every airport in the country, a system that would require many more flights and planes to carry the same number of passengers.

Approximately two-thirds of all air travelers go through a hub to reach their destinations. (See Figure 7.1.) Many low-demand routes are no longer served by nonstop flights. On the one hand, travelers benefit, since the hub systems allow them to travel to more destinations and have a wider choice of arrival and departure times. However, the time required for getting a connecting flight at the hub means flight times are longer than for direct flights. By one estimate, the average trip of under 2,000 miles can take twice as long as it did prior to deregulation and the use of the hub system.

The hub-and-spoke system can also cause frequent and long flight delays. Most of the major airlines schedule hub departures and arrivals during the peak time periods—early morning and early evening. When too many jets are scheduled to leave at the same time, the airplanes are forced to line up on the tarmac and wait. Bad weather at a large hub can cause long delays throughout the network.

FIGURE 7.5

Summary of air traffic control over the continental United States and oceans

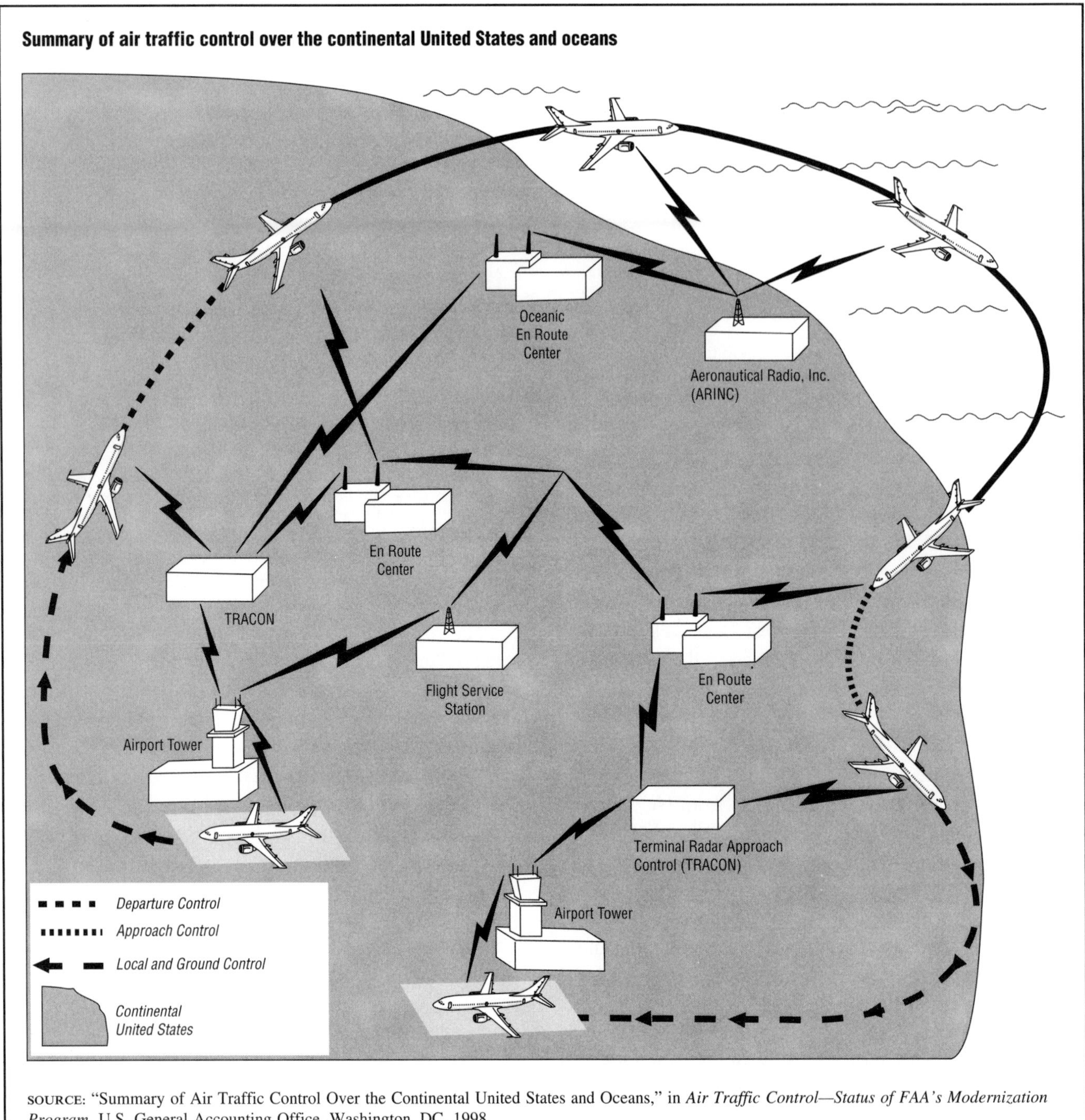

SOURCE: "Summary of Air Traffic Control Over the Continental United States and Oceans," in *Air Traffic Control—Status of FAA's Modernization Program,* U.S. General Accounting Office, Washington, DC, 1998

The problems of congestion and delays at the hubs have displeased many passengers.

For the airlines, the hub system, along with the introduction of sophisticated air traffic control systems and the booming economy of the 1990s, allowed a dramatic increase in passenger load factor. Passenger load factor (the percentage of passengers relative to the number of seats available) increased from 62.4 percent in 1990 to 71 percent in 1999 before declining to 70 percent in 2001. (See Table 7.1.) Relatively speaking, this was a huge increase, which was reflected in the elevated airline profits of the late 1990s. Fuller planes generated consumer complaints, however, as flights became more crowded.

Demand Exceeded Capacity

Before the events of September 11, 2001, lessened the demand for airline services, air traffic reached critical levels as passenger numbers increased. Earlier FAA predictions of 931.1 million passengers by the year 2010—more than the existing system could handle—were scaled back. In 2003 the FAA predicted that passenger enplanements would reach 822.1 million by 2014.

After the airline industry was deregulated in 1978, no major new airports were built in the United States until 1992, when Pittsburgh International Airport opened its new terminal building. The $1.06 billion facility, the nation's most expensive airport at that time, represented a new age of efficiency and convenience. Designed to accommodate the increased traffic of the hub-and-spoke system, it was equipped with innovative security checkpoints, automated baggage handling, and "smart" computer terminals for ticket information, in order to avoid the congestion typical of older airports.

Denver International, which opened in 1995, stirred controversy because of its $4 billion price tag, its two-year delay in completion, its 23-mile distance from the city, and doubts whether traffic volume would justify its cost. Initial difficulties with the baggage-handling system only compounded the problems. Lindbergh Field, San Diego's International Airport, was the most recent hub to have undergone major expansion before September 11; it opened in 1997 and as of June 2003 further expansion was planned. Expansion of Chicago O'Hare, already one of the largest U.S. airports, was proposed in June 2001; by June 2003 the project had not gone forward, due at least in part to by-then financially strapped airlines' objections to contributing to the $6.6 billion cost. Some post-September 11 construction went forward. Detroit's $1.2 billion Midfield Terminal (called the Edward H. McNamara Terminal at the Northwest WorldGateway), opened on February 24, 2002; it offers 97 additional gates, an automated people mover, a parking lot with a capacity of 11,500 automobiles, and an electric generating plant.

With air traffic down, some airport projects were put on hold for a time. However, according to *Business Travel News*, by April 2003 construction was underway at 19 of the nation's 35 largest airports, including 12 new runways ("FAA Gears Up for Further Traffic," April 28, 2003). In June 2003 Houston opened its $225 million terminal, the first phase of a larger expansion. Indianapolis plans to open a $1 billion terminal in 2007.

THE FEDERAL AVIATION ADMINISTRATION AND AIR TRAFFIC SERVICES

Created by Congress in 1938, the Federal Aviation Administration (FAA) oversees airlines operating in the United States. The FAA certifies all pilots and aircraft mechanics. It also tests and certifies all aircraft designs built or flown in the United States and establishes regulations on their required maintenance. Airports are another area of responsibility for the FAA. It manages federal funds for the improvement and construction of airports and sets the official regulations for airport security.

Air Traffic Control

In addition to regulating the air travel industry, the FAA plays a crucial role in its success by providing a nationwide network of air traffic control systems (ATC). It is the ATC that controls the movements of airplanes over and around the United States, allowing safe, orderly, and efficient air travel. (See Figure 7.5.) However, the increase in air traffic in the 1980s and 1990s put a strain on the ATC system. Anticipating this problem, in 1981 the FAA began to modernize its hardware, software, and communications equipment. The multibillion-dollar program has more than 200 separate projects and will be completed by the year 2013. One of the projects, the weather and radar processor (WARP) system, became operational in December 2002. WARP allows air controllers to "see" the same weather conditions that pilots see, allowing controllers to help steer planes clear of storms.

All four aviation system user groups—air carriers, commuter/air taxi, general aviation, and military—use the ATC to maintain the flow and safety of aviation traffic. The ATC is made up of five types of facilities:

- Flight service stations—usually used by private aircraft for flight plan filing and weather report updates
- Air traffic control towers—control aircraft on the ground, before landing and after take-off within five nautical miles of the airport and up to 3,000 feet above the ground
- Terminal radar approach control (TRACON) stations—communicate with pilots to line up and separate aircraft as they approach and leave busy airports, 5 to 50 miles from the airport, up to 10,000 feet above the ground
- En route centers—control aircraft while in flight over the continental United States. The 20 en route centers usually control commercial aircraft above 18,000 feet
- Oakland and New York (oceanic) en route centers—control in the same way as the other 20 en route centers, but also control aircraft over the ocean, using radar for up to 225 miles offshore. For aircraft farther away than that, they use radio contact to learn aircraft location over the ocean.

AIR TRAFFIC CONTROLLERS. Air traffic controllers are FAA employees specially trained to safely manage air traffic. They work at airport control towers and FAA facilities throughout the country. In 1981 a strike by air traffic controllers was broken when President Ronald Reagan fired 11,400 striking controllers, 80 percent of the workforce. The National Air Traffic Controllers Association, a labor union, reported representing more than 15,000 air traffic controllers in 2002, but there is a shortage of experienced

TABLE 7.11

Total system accident data by segment, 1996–2001[P]

Segment	Year	Flight hours	Accidents			Accident rate	
			Total	Fatal	Fatalities	Total	Fatal
Large air carrier	1996	13,746,112	37	5	380	0.27	0.04
	1997	15,838,109	49	4	8	0.31	0.03
	1998	16,813,435	50	1	1	0.30	0.01
	1999	17,555,208	52	2	12	0.30	0.01
	2000	18,295,143	57	3	92	0.31	0.02
	2001[P]	16,730,700	40	6	531	0.24	0.04
Commuter	1996	2,756,755	11	1	14	0.40	0.04
	1997	982,764	16	5	46	1.63	0.51
	1998	353,670	8	0	0	2.26	0.00
	1999	342,731	13	5	12	3.79	1.46
	2000	373,649	12	1	5	3.21	0.27
	2001[P]	330,500	7	2	13	2.12	0.61
Air taxi	1996	3,220,000	90	29	63	2.80	0.90
	1997	3,098,000	82	15	39	2.65	0.48
	1998	3,802,000	77	17	45	2.03	0.45
	1999	3,298,000	73	12	38	2.21	0.36
	2000	3,553,000	81	22	71	2.28	0.62
	2001[P]	3,400,000	72	18	60	2.12	0.53
General aviation	1996	24,881,000	1,908	361	636	7.67	1.45
	1997	25,591,000	1,845	350	631	7.21	1.37
	1998	25,518,000	1,904	364	624	7.46	1.43
	1999	29,713,000	1,906	340	619	6.41	1.14
	2000	29,057,000	1,838	343	594	6.33	1.18
	2001[P]	26,220,000	1,721	321	553	6.56	1.22

Rates are per 100,000 hours flown.
Suicide/Sabotage cases are included in "Accidents" and "Fatalities" but not on "Accident Rates."
P = Preliminary data.
Effective March 20, 1997, aircraft with 10 or more seats must conduct scheduled passenger operations under 14 CFR 121.

SOURCE: "Exhibit 7-2. Total System Accident Data by Segment, 1996 through 2001," in *Aviation Safety Statistical Handbook,* Federal Aviation Administration, Washington, DC, October 2002 [Online] http://www1.faa.gov/ats/ata/publications/Aviation_Safety_Statistical_Handbook.pdf [accessed April 15, 2003]

controllers, especially in busy East Coast airports. With a mandatory retirement age of 56, more than half of the civilian air traffic controller workforce will be eligible to retire by 2010. Training new controllers takes two-and-a-half to three years. Congress sets the controllers' salaries and neither the FAA nor union negotiations can change them.

Being responsible for the safety of several aircraft and their passengers makes an air traffic controller's job very stressful, but relief is on the way. New technological developments are in various stages of planning or testing or have recently been released. They include advanced computer automation, navigation, and landing systems that use the Department of Defense's highly accurate global positioning system satellites, microwave landing systems, and onboard anticollision devices. Whether they can completely solve existing problems remains to be seen.

In the mid-1990s air traffic controllers reported that their equipment (technology and computers) was so outdated it was dangerous. Computers at major hubs such as Chicago's O'Hare International were 30 years old. In July 1995 computers broke down in Chicago, requiring use of the back-up system, which, controllers claimed, was inadequate and a safety risk. The FAA set about replacing aging computer systems in major hubs as part of its program to modernize the National Airspace System infrastructure, but by 2000 the situation showed little improvement. In a report dated January 18, 2001, the DOT's Office of Inspector General complained of recent record levels of runway incursions in 2000 (400) and operational errors (1,154). Runway incursions are incidents on a runway that can lead to a potential collision hazard. Operational errors are errors made when an air traffic controller allows the distance between two aircraft to fall below the FAA's minimum separation standards.

Controllers attribute plane separation errors to increased air traffic, overburdened airports, and stressed and tired controllers. When air travel declined post-September 11, so did controller errors. In the year ending September 30, 2002, operational errors numbered 1,061, down from 1,194 reported in the previous year ("Report: Fewer Flights in US Led to Fewer Mistakes Last Yr," April 7, 2003 [Online] http://news.morningstar.com/news/DJ/M04/D07/1049758861627.html).

FIGURE 7.6

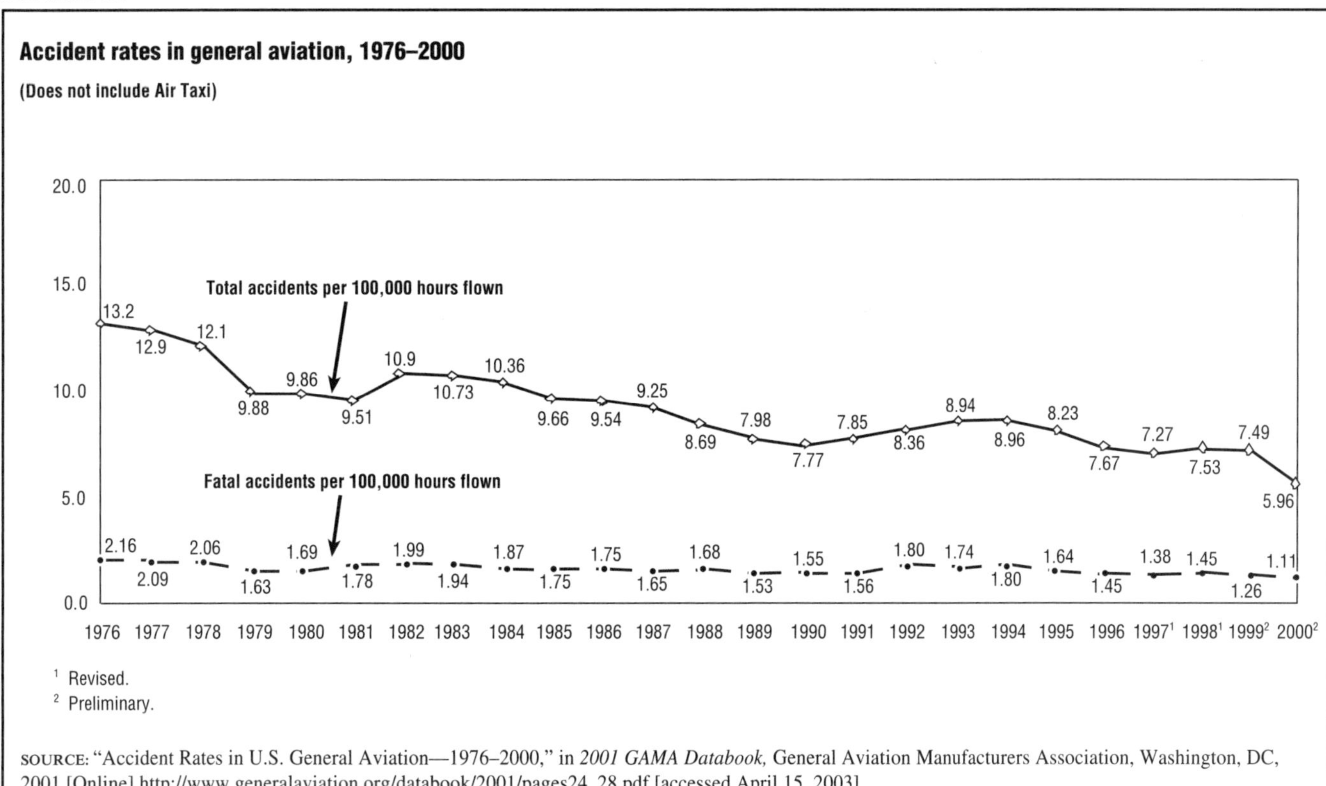

SOURCE: "Accident Rates in U.S. General Aviation—1976–2000," in *2001 GAMA Databook,* General Aviation Manufacturers Association, Washington, DC, 2001 [Online] http://www.generalaviation.org/databook/2001/pages24_28.pdf [accessed April 15, 2003]

Proposals for Free Flight

In response to the crisis in air traffic control, some experts have proposed a method known as "free flight" to replace the existing system. Free flight is exactly what the term implies—pilots take off and land when they want and fly to their destinations by whatever routes they deem optimal. The system is based on the assumption that most aircraft will be equipped with flight management systems that allow them to plot the most efficient routes and to trade navigation data with other planes, thereby enabling them to avoid midair collisions. Advocates of the system believe free flight will yield massive savings for airlines and reduce congestion and delays. The FAA is testing such a system; its Free Flight Program Office regularly submits a *Free Flight Status Report* to Congress.

AIR SAFETY

The crash of a jumbo jet is a major disaster. Hundreds of lives may be lost in a single incident. Although flying on a scheduled air carrier is one of the safest ways to travel and the risk of death or injury is far less than when riding the same distance in a car, events that have occurred since the late 1990s have many Americans convinced that air travel is no longer safe.

Table 7.11 shows the accident and fatality figures for scheduled aircraft from 1996 through 2001. High fatalities in 1996 and 2001 are related to atypical events in those years. In 1996 a ValuJet Airlines DC9-32 crashed in the Florida Everglades, killing all 105 passengers and 5 crew members. On September 11, 2001, an American Airlines 767 was hijacked and flown into a World Trade Center Tower; a United Airlines 767 was hijacked and crashed into the other tower. All 11 crew members, 76 passengers, and 5 hijackers were killed, as were thousands of people on the ground. On that same day, an American Airlines 757 was hijacked and flown into the Pentagon; 6 crew members, 53 passengers, and 5 hijackers were killed. Also on September 11, 2001, a United Airlines 757 was hijacked and crashed outside Pittsburgh; all 7 crew members, 34 passengers, and 4 hijackers were killed. On November 12, 2001, an American Airlines A300-600 on a flight from New York to Santo Domingo, Dominican Republic, crashed into a residential neighborhood just outside JFK airport; all 9 crew members and 251 passengers were killed.

General and Commuter Aviation Accidents

In 1994, after several crashes of small commuter planes known as ATRs, the National Transportation Safety Board called for study of those aircraft and the crashes in order to determine if commuter planes should be held to the same safety requirements as the larger aircraft. It concluded that the commuter airlines' rapid expansion had outpaced regulation. Original regulation of commuter aircraft dated from the 1950s, when small planes were not a major segment of the transportation system.

FIGURE 7.7

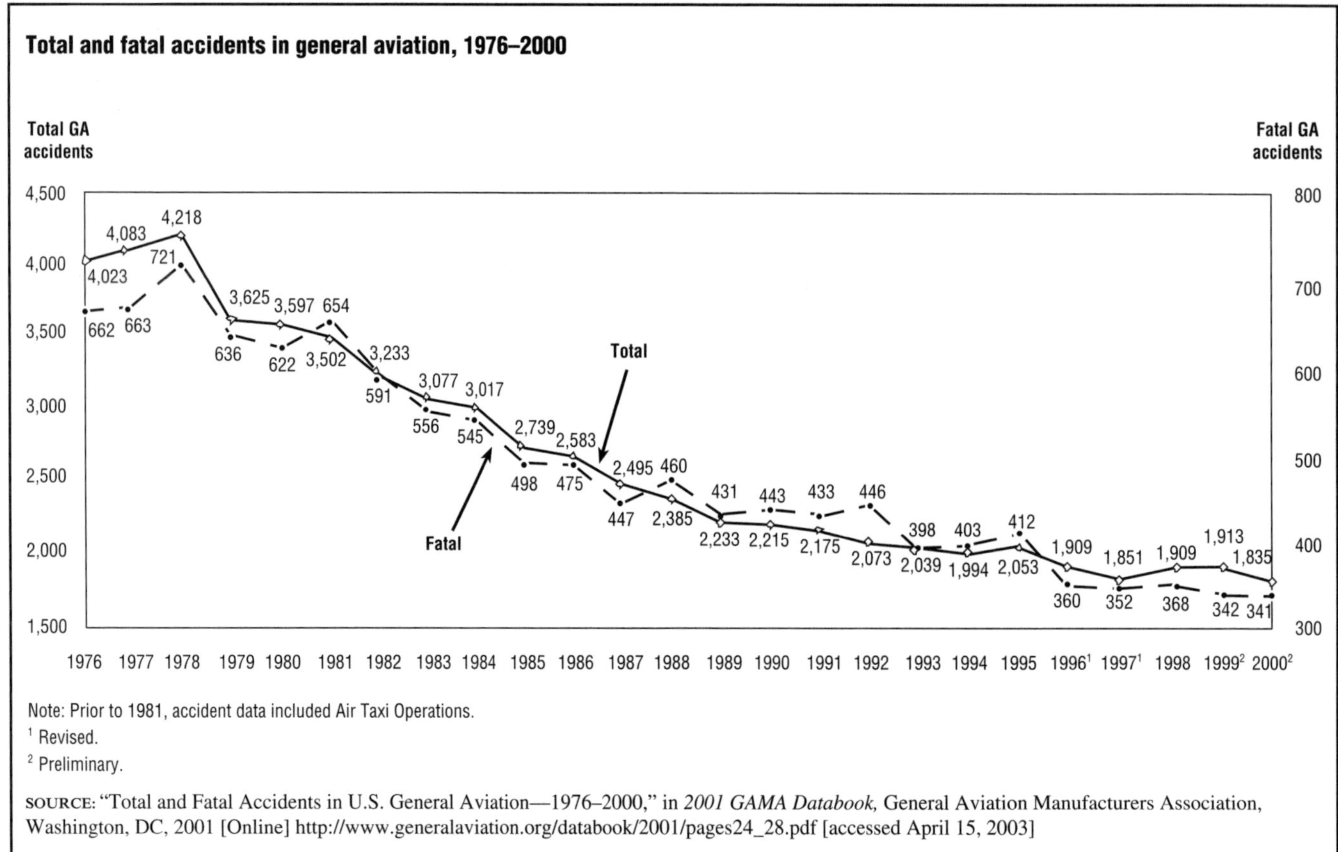

Total and fatal accidents in general aviation, 1976–2000

Note: Prior to 1981, accident data included Air Taxi Operations.
[1] Revised.
[2] Preliminary.

SOURCE: "Total and Fatal Accidents in U.S. General Aviation—1976–2000," in *2001 GAMA Databook,* General Aviation Manufacturers Association, Washington, DC, 2001 [Online] http://www.generalaviation.org/databook/2001/pages24_28.pdf [accessed April 15, 2003]

As Table 7.11 illustrates, the commuter airlines' safety record has swung between one and five fatal accidents per year since 1996, when there was one fatal accident and 14 fatalities. In 1998 there were no fatal commuter aircraft crashes. In 1999 there were five fatal accidents in which 12 people died—a rate of 1.46 fatal accidents per 100,000 hours flown. (In that same year, 12 passengers died in two fatal accidents on large air carriers—a rate of only 0.011 fatal accidents for every 100,000 hours flown.)

The accident and fatality rates of the general aviation fleet are far worse than those of large jets. General aviation aircraft are mostly small, single-engine piston planes, and pilot training and testing are less stringent. As shown in Figure 7.6, the rate of accidents and fatalities in general aviation fell sharply from 1978 to 1979 and then declined much more slowly over the next two decades. Figure 7.7 shows the number of fatal accidents in U.S. general aviation between 1976 and 2000.

Wearing Out

No matter how well designed, properly handled, and carefully maintained, machines eventually wear out, and airplanes are no exception. There is no effective inspection system in place for ensuring the airworthiness of the nation's fleet of aircraft. After the 1996 ValuJet crash, the FAA was severely criticized for its failure to require fire suppression systems and for inadequate oversight of the fast-growing, low-budget airline. In 1998 Congress ordered the FAA to cease promoting the aviation industry and to make safety its sole mission. The newly created Air Transportation Oversight System (ATOS) placed 500 of the FAA's 3,300 aviation safety inspectors in charge of monitoring the nation's 10 largest airlines. By 2001 the FAA was expected to be inspecting all passenger airlines. But in a report released on April 11, 2002, the DOT's inspector general concluded that the ATOS was not fully operational at the 10 original airlines and had yet to be expanded to any of the remaining 129 airlines. Michael Fanfalone, president of the Professional Airways Systems Specialists, a labor union, told *Business Travel News:* "We are concerned that the history of this program—plagued by insufficient staffing, inadequate training, data analysis problems and lack of commitment by FAA management—will thwart the program's laudable goals." (Barbara Cook, "DOT: Air Safety Oversight Program Failing," April 22, 2002).

Meanwhile, financially troubled airlines sometimes refurbish old planes instead of buying new ones. According to the FAA, a new large plane can cost more than $50 million, while it can cost as little as $4 million to refurbish an old plane ("A Message from the Manager of FAA's Aging Aircraft Research Program," *R & D Review*, Fall/Winter 2002). The typical passenger aircraft is designed to last 20 years, but it is not unusual for a plane to be more than

25 years old. Planes that are more than 20 years old are guaranteed to have wiring problems, report Cynthia Furse and Randy Haupt of Utah State University ("Down to the Wire," *IEEE Spectrum Online*, February 2001). In 1999 the average age of the commercial fleet was 18 years and 41 percent of the U.S. fleet of planes belonging to major airlines was at least 20 years old.

However, when air travel declined after September 11, 2001, the nation's largest air carriers retired many of their older, less efficient planes, according to *FAA Aerospace Forecast Fiscal Years 2003–2014.*

Safety Measures Post 9/11

On November 19, 2001, President George W. Bush signed into law the Aviation and Transportation Security Act (ATSA; PL 107-71), which established a new Transportation Security Administration (TSA) within the DOT. Its mission is to ensure a secure air travel and cargo shipment system. The TSA has overseen the spending of billions of dollars on new security measures, including the hiring of more than 60,000 passenger and baggage screeners, training pilots to use handguns, and reinforcing cockpit doors on commercial jets. Under the TSA's "known shipper" initiative, anyone wishing to ship cargo by air must have at least a two-year shipping history or pass a TSA inspection. TSA's budget for Fiscal Year 2004 is $4.82 billion. Under consideration by the TSA in 2003 was an initiative called the Trusted Traveler program. Trusted Travelers provide personal information (credit reports, names of employers, previous addresses, for example) in exchange for a card entitling them to be screened separately and more quickly than other travelers. Some travelers have expressed reservations about the invasion of privacy such a program would entail.

Industry analysts say it will take billions of dollars and many years to make flying safer, at a time when the federal government is facing a deficit and the airlines are in trouble. *Fortune* reported that air carriers lost almost $25 billion between September 2001 and April 2003, representing more money than they had made in the previous five years, according to the authors (Nelson D. Schwartz and Julie Creswell, "Flying Scared: Seven Ways to Make Air Travel Safer," April 28, 2003).

CUSTOMER DISSATISFACTION

The modern, deregulated airlines received mixed reviews from consumers. After an initial period of extremely low fares, ticket prices rose on many routes, especially to areas served by only one or two carriers. Before September 11, 2001, ridership nevertheless increased, suffering only a slight setback in the early 1980s. The airlines point out that airline ticket prices have lagged well behind the Consumer Price Index and are a good buy. In addition, fare wars, ticket sales, Internet promotions, and advance purchase tickets allow passengers with time to plan a trip to get greatly-reduced-price tickets. In fact, it is possible that one passenger, who bought a bargain advance purchase ticket, may be sitting next to a business traveler who paid four times as much for his or her last-minute ticket on the same flight.

After deregulation, customer complaints about flight delays and cancellations, overbookings (flights with more tickets sold than seats actually available), bad airline food, cramped seating conditions, and lost luggage skyrocketed as new carriers entered the market and airlines began to experience cost pressures and cut corners on service. Passengers were flying on more crowded airplanes, waiting in more congested hub airports, facing more delayed takeoffs, and putting up with more stopovers en route to their destinations than ever before. These aggravations contributed to occasional cases of "air rage," when out-of-control passengers fought with flight crews and endangered the lives of everyone on the plane. The Association of Flight Attendants reported in 2001 that there were approximately 4,000 cases of air rage each year, and they complained that although air rage is a felony, few cases were prosecuted. Air rage most often involved passengers who drank alcohol excessively, smoked in lavatories, or continued to use their electronic devices when told to turn them off. More recently, flight attendants have complained about the quality of the air in aircraft cabins, which they say causes health problems. ("What You Should Know About the Air You Breathe at Work," Association of Flight Attendants [Online] http://www.afanet.org/aq_bulletin.asp [accessed June 17, 2003]).

Air passengers have endured long hours strapped into airplane seats on the tarmac, waiting, without being told the reason for the delay. They have arrived at the airport and found their flights cancelled. They have sat for long flights in narrow seats, sometimes with the passenger in front leaning back, inches from their face. They have arrived at their destination, only to find that their luggage was sent elsewhere. With record numbers of airline delays in 2000, and a 16 percent increase in consumer complaints, Congress considered a "Bill of Rights" for airline passengers, which would ensure passengers' rights and regulate how the airlines treat their customers. Such a measure was introduced in the Senate in 1999 and again in 2001.

The problems cannot all be attributed to deregulation. From 1980 to 1998, the number of domestic passenger miles more than doubled from 204.4 billion to an estimated 459.7 billion. Also, the number of aircraft used by certified air carriers more than doubled from 2,818 to 5,961. These were huge increases in a short period of time. While airports expanded, they did not keep up with this rapid growth. Furthermore, the FAA, which controls

FIGURE 7.8

Domestic and international share of passenger enplanements, projected for 2003 and 2014

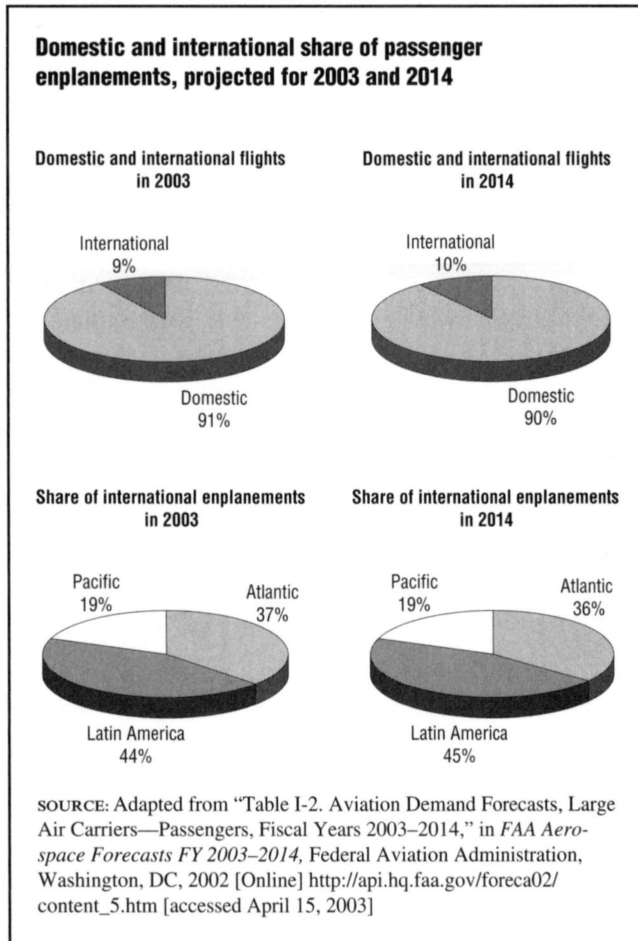

SOURCE: Adapted from "Table I-2. Aviation Demand Forecasts, Large Air Carriers—Passengers, Fiscal Years 2003–2014," in *FAA Aerospace Forecasts FY 2003–2014,* Federal Aviation Administration, Washington, DC, 2002 [Online] http://api.hq.faa.gov/foreca02/content_5.htm [accessed April 15, 2003]

the movement of these aircraft, still works with outdated equipment, some of which is decades old and in the process of being replaced.

Post-September 11, 2001, passenger complaints declined. According to the DOT's *Air Travel Consumer Report* for July 2002, there were 755 complaints in May 2002 compared with 1,149 in May 2001. The majority of the complaints (418) involved flight problems (cancellations, delays, misconnections), customer service, and baggage handling.

GOING GLOBAL—FOREIGN MARKETS

Under the Carter Administration, Congress passed the International Air Transportation Competition Act of 1979 (PL 96-192), intended to create a more competitive international system of airline travel. Despite concern among many foreign governments about the new law, a few governments—mainly those that realized their national airlines had more to gain than to lose—edged toward the U.S. "open skies" objective (the easing of restrictions between the United States and other countries to allow market demand, not governments, to dictate routes, prices, etc.). With the signing of an agreement with France on January 22, 2002, the United States had open skies arrangements with 56 nations. The Air Transport Action Group forecast that by 2010, the economic impact of open skies agreements would approach $2 trillion, accounting for more than 30 million jobs ("Open Skies Agreements Have Resulted in Major Benefits for Consumers," U.S. Department of Transportation, Washington, D.C., December 3, 1999).

The International Market

Since September 11, U.S. air carriers have scaled back their international flights. Earlier FAA forecasts had predicted that international enplanements would grow at a faster rate than domestic enplanements, rising to 11.1 percent by 2010. More recent estimates placed international enplanements at 10 percent by 2014. (See Figure 7.8.) The FAA estimates assumed a strong economic recovery both at home and abroad in 2003 and did not take into account the 2003 war with Iraq and the outbreak of Severe Acute Respiratory Syndrome (SARS). Speaking at the 59th annual general meeting of the International Air Transport Association (IATA) in Washington, D.C., on June 2, 2003, Giovanni Bisignani, IATA Director General and CEO, told the audience: "Crisis is the only way to describe the state of our industry today. . . . The successive impact of September 11, a world economic slowdown, Iraq and SARS has been devastating."

International aviation is important to U.S. airlines. The FAA forecasts that in response to industry crises, U.S. carriers will undergo major international route restructuring in 2003 and 2004, resulting in foreign flag air carriers taking over part of the market. In cases where those foreign carriers have signed agreements with U.S. carriers, the U.S. carriers will be able sell travel to foreign lands without actually operating planes on those routes.

According to the FAA forecast, total international passenger traffic in 2002 was estimated at 122 million. Although this was down 5.2 percent from 2001, it is predicted that international passenger traffic will return to pre-September 11 levels by 2005. International freight (revenue ton miles) carried by all-cargo carriers, although down 0.2 percent in 2002, surpassed domestic shipments, reflecting the increasing importance of international air cargo and foreign trade. Air cargo traffic should increase faster than passenger traffic. Passenger traffic will increase most in Latin American and Pacific markets, growing at an estimated annual rate of 5.0 and 4.9 percent, respectively, between 2003 and 2014.

EUROPE. Europe is the favorite overseas destination of U.S. travelers. According to the DOT, of the 27 million overseas visits made by U.S. residents in 2000, more than 13 million were to points in Europe, a 66 percent increase over the 8 million visits in 1990 (*U.S. International Travel and Transportation Trends*, Bureau of Transportation

Statistics, BTS02-03, 2002). In 2000 the top three European destinations were the United Kingdom, France, and Germany.

Teaming up, or forming alliances, is emerging as one way American and foreign airlines can gain footholds in each other's territories, in spite of continuing governmental controls that hamper foreign competition. Although airlines claim these unions produce smoother, "seamless" travel for passengers, the greatest benefit for the airlines is a financial one—greater access to markets. Under such pacts, two or more airlines operate as one to avoid foreign ownership limitations.

The FAA expects the industry to continue toward globalization through agreements. The number of alliances is growing. Three of the dominant alliances in 2003 were Sky Team (AeroMexico, AirFrance, Delta, and Korean Air), Star Alliance (15 airlines, including United, Lufthansa, SAS, Thai Airlines, Air Canada, and Varig), and OneWorld (American, Aer Lingus, British Airways, and several others). Alliances also offer shared frequent flier benefits to passengers. Critics complain that the alliances are driving smaller carriers out of business and will eventually lead to higher prices for passengers and reduced services as unprofitable routes are eliminated.

Despite the fact that Europe's population is larger than that of the United States, intra-Europe air travel accounts for a very small percentage of the world's scheduled airline traffic compared to travel within North America. Air travel in Europe is complicated by certain structural factors. An outdated air traffic control system limits capacity. Restrictions on over-flights (the right to fly over another country's territory) mean that some flights between countries in Europe use more time and fuel than would otherwise be necessary. Many European airports are at capacity, thus discouraging new service. Most Europeans prefer to travel by train, particularly for shorter distances. Train fares are often much lower than air fares, and seating on European trains is more comfortable than the typical coach seat on any jumbo jet. In addition, trains generally drop the passenger off downtown in their destination city.

CHAPTER 8

BUSES AND MASS TRANSIT

BUSES FROM CITY TO CITY

Buses, also called motorcoaches, have played a significant role in the U.S. transportation system, connecting small towns that do not have railway or airline service with other towns and cities. However, the nation's scheduled intercity (between cities) bus system has been in decline since the end of World War II.

Growing Competition

In the early 1950s, buses saw competition on a number of fronts. After World War II, automobiles began to be more readily available to the public, and America's love affair with the automobile began. The construction of the national highway system, which began in earnest in the 1950s, enabled people to drive long distances. At the same time, airline fares became less expensive, and more travelers could enjoy the convenience, speed, and comfort of air travel. The 1971 creation of Amtrak, the national passenger railroad system, also posed a threat to commercial bus carriers—because the federal government supported the new rail company, it could offer cheaper fares to its riders. In addition, Americans began leaving rural areas—best served by buses—for the cities and suburbs.

By the late 1960s and early 1970s, ridership on intercity buses had dwindled to about 400 million riders annually ("Bus Profile," in *National Transportation Statistics 2002,* Bureau of Transportation Statistics [BTS], Washington, D.C.). In subsequent years, the number of people using intercity buses continued to drop. Between 1987 and 1997, scheduled intercity bus traffic did increase 5.3 percent, from 333 million to 351 million riders, and has increased slightly since. But bus ridership declined in relation to the overall passenger transportation market. Bus passengers represented 30.8 percent of intercity passengers in 1991 and 26.0 percent in 2001. (See Figure 8.1.) Bus ridership rose in 1998 to 358 million and in 1999 to 359 million ("Bus Profile").

FIGURE 8.1

Domestic intercity passengers carried by for-hire modes, 1991 and 2001

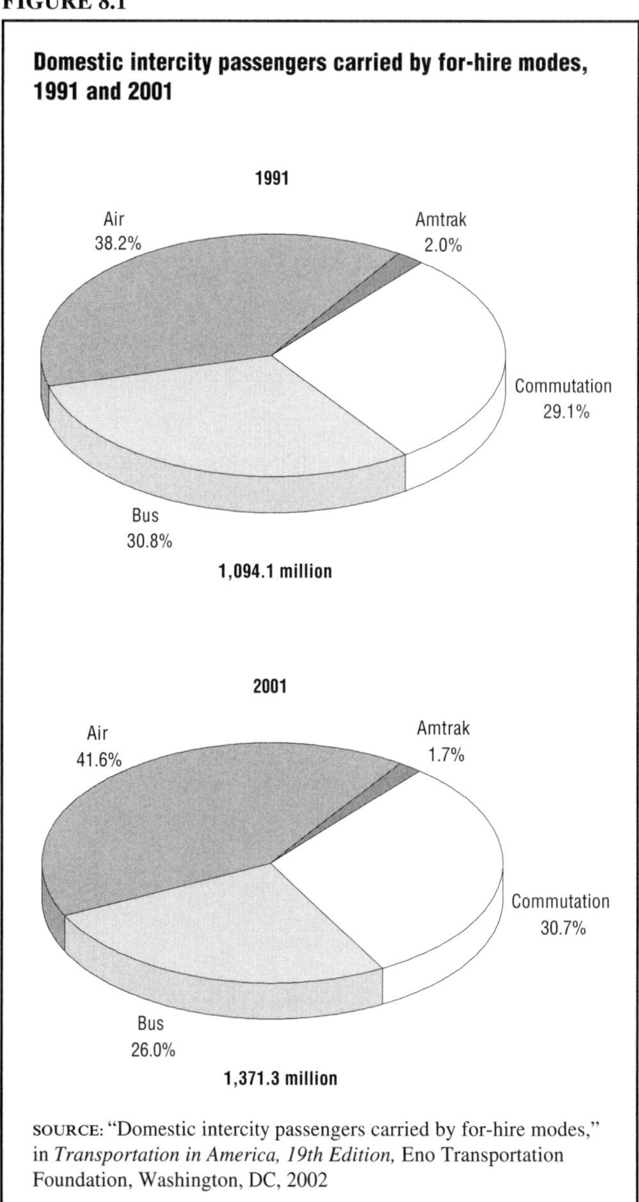

SOURCE: "Domestic intercity passengers carried by for-hire modes," in *Transportation in America, 19th Edition,* Eno Transportation Foundation, Washington, DC, 2002

FIGURE 8.2

Domestic intercity passenger-miles, 1991 and 2001

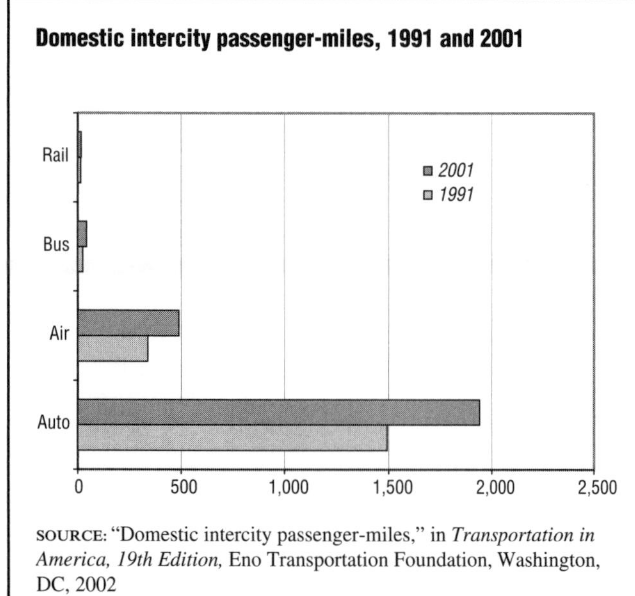

SOURCE: "Domestic intercity passenger-miles," in *Transportation in America, 19th Edition,* Eno Transportation Foundation, Washington, DC, 2002

The number of locales served by intercity buses fell from 11,820 locations in 1982 to fewer than 6,000 in 1991 ("Surface Transportation: Availability of Intercity Bus Service Continues to Decline," U.S. General Accounting Office, GAO/RCED-92-126, June 1992). By 2000 intercity buses served only 5,000 communities (Eileen S. Stommes and Dennis M. Brown, "Transportation in Rural America: Issues for the Twenty-First Century," *Rural America*, vol. 16, issue 4, Winter 2002).

The number of Class I companies operating intercity buses also fell, from 143 companies operating 272,129 intercity buses in 1960 to 15 companies operating 749,548 intercity buses in 2001 ("Bus Profile"). By 2003 there were only 12 Class I companies, defined by the Bureau of Transportation Statistics as those having revenues of at least $10 million annually; there are also hundreds of smaller companies providing intercity bus transportation, according to the Transportation Security Administration. In 1997 intercity buses accounted for 29.6 billion passenger-miles (the cumulative sum of the distances ridden by each passenger), just 1.2 percent of domestic intercity miles traveled. (See Figure 8.2.)

GREYHOUND LINES

Greyhound Lines, Inc., is the largest of the private bus companies and is the only remaining nationwide provider of scheduled, regular-route intercity bus service. Greyhound reported that it carried 25 million passengers in 2001 (more than 60 percent of intercity bus passengers) with service to 2,600 destinations across North America.

Decades of industry decline, along with the pressures of union wage disputes, culminated in Greyhound's filing for bankruptcy protection in 1991. Although it emerged from the bankruptcy intact, Greyhound continued to struggle for survival and underwent major restructuring. In 1998 Greyhound reported net income of $35.2 million, or $0.50 per share—the first full-year profit realized by the company since 1993 (James F. Peltz, "Riding a Turnaround; Once-Sluggish Greyhound Is Expected to Post 1st Annual Profit Since 1993," *Los Angeles Times*, August 7, 1998).

Struggling with years of declining ridership, bankruptcy, and a poor image, Greyhound took measures to attract the public back to bus service. It renovated bus stations and increased security at terminals. In addition, Greyhound instituted airline marketing techniques such as online purchase and mail delivery of tickets and computerized reservations. A smoking ban keeps the air fresher and express routes between big cities decrease travel time.

Greyhound offers casino trips to popular gambling destinations around the country and other specialized travel tours. In 1998 its casino ridership contributed more than $30 million to the company's revenues. Bus-to-air travel service is another option offered by Greyhound. The service was initiated in the mid-1990s at Hartsfield Airport in Atlanta; by 2003 Greyhound served 21 airports around the country. The bus company provides pickup and drop-off service to terminals at selected airports. A similar service is available to various Amtrak stations.

Changes at Greyhound

In 1998 Greyhound formed joint ventures with several Mexican bus carriers to create Autobuses Americanos and Autobuses Amigos. The two new companies, operating under a Greyhound subsidiary, Sistema Internacional Transporte de Autobuses, Inc. (S.I.T.A.), provide cross-border bus service between several states and cities in Mexico. In 2002 Greyhound signed an agreement with Estrella Blanca, the largest bus company in Mexico, which allows the two companies to sell tickets for each other (Suzanne Marta, "Greyhound Turns Attention to Mexico," *Knight Ridder/Tribune Business News*, December 11, 2002). By doing so, Greyhound hopes to increase its market share of passengers bound for Mexico from the 2002 level of 25 percent.

Greyhound ridership increased 60 percent between 1994 and 2000 (Terry Maxon, "Greyhound Finds Its Refocusing Strategy Paying Off With Increased Ridership," *Knight Ridder/Tribune Business News*, July 28, 2002). Like other transportation sectors, the intercity bus industry saw ridership decline after the September 11, 2001, terrorist attacks and the recession that began in 2001. Greyhound's 2001 net profit was $1.98 million.

Greyhound has been in the shipping business since 1930. In 1999 Greyhound expanded its shipping services when it acquired On Time Delivery, a Minnesota-based courier company. In June 1999 the company further expanded shipping in the Midwest with the acquisition of Larson Express, a Chicago-area courier. In 2002 Greyhound expanded its shipping capabilities nationwide by adding United Parcel Service authorized outlets; as of 2003, 38 cities offered the full menu of Greyhound shipping services.

Security at Greyhound

The Transportation Security Administration, established on November 19, 2001, with the signing of the Aviation and Transportation Security Act (PL 107-71), has identified buses as being at high risk for security breaches. When the TSA announced in 2003 that $15 million would be made available for the Intercity Bus Security Grant Program, the agency noted that Greyhound drivers and passengers had been the targets of at least four serious assaults in 2002.

Before the grant money became available and in response to security concerns post-September 11, Greyhound had already replaced its old surveillance cameras with digital cameras and had equipped drivers with cell phones preprogrammed to call local 911 and the Greyhound Operations Center by pressing a button. Drivers were instructed to remove aggressive passengers from buses. Although Greyhound does not screen or profile passengers, its employees began to carry out random checks of passengers and carry-on luggage with a metal-detection wand and conducted more thorough pre- and post-inspection of vehicles ("Transit Agencies Quietly Beef Up Security," *eWeek*, September 10, 2002). Newer security measures made possible by federal grants focus on protecting drivers; they include ticket identification, increased security personnel, giving the driver the right to limit access to the first row of seats, and establishing more sophisticated communications systems.

REGULATORY, FUNDING, AND SAFETY ISSUES

Congress had hoped to reverse the downward trend in the bus industry by enacting the Bus Regulatory Reform Act (PL 97-261) in 1982. This act deregulated the bus industry, diminishing the role of the federal Interstate Commerce Commission (ICC) (since replaced by the Office of Motor Carriers) and state agencies and giving bus firms greater freedom to set rates and determine routes. Despite the act, bus companies continued to face declining profits.

The Intermodal Surface Transportation Act of 1991 (PL 102-240) was an attempt to further improve bus transportation. The law required the states to use 15 percent of certain federal transportation grants to help promote intercity bus traffic. For fiscal years 1992 through 1997, the act set aside about $122 million in federal grant funds for states to use specifically for intercity bus service. A state does not have to use the funds, however, if the governor certifies that the state's bus needs are met by local funding or passenger revenues.

In 1998 Congress passed the Transportation Equity Act for the 21st Century (TEA-21; PL 105-178). It included funding for improved rural (city to city) bus service and for new buses that operate on cleaner fuel, such as natural gas. The Blue Bird Corporation, of Macon, Georgia (a British-owned company) began manufacturing school buses that run on natural gas. Motorcoaches using natural gas engines are in operation in Los Angeles, San Diego, Atlanta, Phoenix, Tampa, Miami, Washington, D.C., New York, and numerous other cities, mainly in city transit systems, and a handful of cities are using electricity or biodiesel (B20, a blend of 20 percent biodiesel and 80 percent petroleum diesel) to fuel their bus fleets. Some city fleets have changed over entirely to natural gas buses. According to the U.S. Department of Energy (DOE), there were 487 alternative-fueled intercity buses in use in 2000, up from 107 in 1998; the DOE also reported that the top five states for intercity bus users were California, New York, Texas, Arizona, and Georgia.

TEA-21 expires on September 30, 2003. If passed by Congress, its replacement, the Safe, Accountable, Flexible and Efficient Transportation Equity Act of 2003 (SAFETEA), will authorize $425 million in grants to fund capital improvements to improve intercity bus access to intermodal facilities (intermodal refers to transportation by more than one means of conveyance). Testifying before Congress in support of this legislation, Greyhound Lines' Craig Lentzsch envisioned a seamless system in which all modes of public transportation are linked from origin to destination ("Testimony of Craig Lentzsch, President and Chief Executive Officer, Greyhound Lines, Inc., Before the Highways and Transit Subcommittee, House Transportation and Infrastructure Committee, On the Role of Intermodalism in TEA-21 Reauthorization," June 18, 2002).

Safety

As of 2003 the Federal Motor Carrier Safety Administration requires that new motor carriers must prove that they are knowledgeable about federal motor carrier safety standards. Applicants must demonstrate such knowledge on their application to operate and must undergo an on-site safety inspection within the first 18 months of operations before they will be granted a permanent license to operate. New operators must also agree to comply with rules covering driver qualifications, hours of service, controlled substance and alcohol testing, vehicle condition, accident monitoring, and hazardous materials transportation.

CHARTER AND TOURIST BUSES

A charter bus is rented for a special reason. If, for example, a student group plans to attend a museum or special event, it may rent—or charter—a bus for a day. If the students are visiting a distant city, they might choose to buy a ticket on a sightseeing bus that will show them city landmarks and sights. A bus used for this purpose is called a tourist bus.

Charter and tourist buses have become an increasingly large part of the bus system as intercity passenger traffic has declined. According to a survey commissioned in 2000 by the American Bus Association, one-half (49.9 percent) of mileage accumulated in 1999 was due to scheduled intercity service, one-third (32.8 percent) was accumulated by charters, and the remaining mileage was divided among tours (6.7 percent), private and contract commuters (5.3 percent), sightseeing (1.3 percent), and other uses ("Motorcoach 2000 Census," conducted by R.L. Banks & Associates, Inc. for the American Bus Association, July 2000). At a time when most intercity passenger carriers are losing money, charter and tourist bus companies are often quite profitable.

BUILDING BUSES

There were eight manufacturers of buses in the United States in 2003 (Motor Coach Industries, Dina, Neoplan, Supreme, Thomas Built, Blue Bird, Nova, and Setra), only one of which (Supreme) is American-owned. The American Bus Association provided 2002 bus sales figures from *National Bus Trader Magazine*: The total number of motorcoaches sold in the United States and Canada was 2,402, which represented a 14.1 percent decline from the previous year. The decline began in 1999, but 2001 sales were higher than in every year from 1985 through 1996, per "Motorcoach Industry Facts."

Buses built today are not necessarily made for commercial bus companies. Many buses are now custom built for private use. These vehicles may be very luxurious, with comfortable chairs and beds for sleeping. Some buses are built to be used as mobile medical clinics for delivering vaccinations, performing health screenings, or taking blood donations. Entertainers and performers who tour from city to city also use customized buses.

In addition, manufacturers build buses as recreational homes for people who want to live in the bus and travel the country. These buses often have many features of a home, such as bathrooms and kitchens, televisions, and compact disk (CD) players. Some very expensive motor-home buses can cost more than a million dollars. Industry sources estimate that there are thousands of these recreational buses traveling the roads of the United States.

Until the mid-1980s, buses were also often seen on the political campaign trail, but fell out of favor when candidates decided they needed faster modes of transportation. Since Bill Clinton revived campaigning by bus in his 1992 quest for the presidency, more candidates for public office have turned to buses in order to visit small cities and towns and appear more accessible to voters. These campaign buses are equipped with multiple telephone lines, faxes, and satellite phones.

Cost

According to the "Motorcoach Census 2000," the average cost of a new 45-foot motorcoach (more than 90 percent of motorcoaches are 40 feet or longer) is more than $350,000. For fuel economy, buses average 5.8 miles per gallon of fuel, but, if they are carrying an average of 30 passengers, that is said to be equivalent to 165 passenger-miles per gallon. In 2001 the operating cost for a motorcoach was figured to be $1.90 per mile, including driver and fuel, according to the American Bus Association. This figure varies with fuel price changes.

Hybrid Buses

Hybrid buses are designed to use less energy and run on cleaner or more efficient fuels than traditional buses. New York City began testing heavy-duty diesel/electric hybrid transit buses in September 1998 and by mid-2000, 10 such buses were in service in the city. Tests sponsored by the DOE found that the hybrid buses were indeed more fuel-efficient and produced lower emissions than traditional diesel-fueled buses (Kevin Chandler et al., *New York City Transit Diesel Hybrid-Electric Buses: Final Results,* July 2002).

In 2002 atmospheric scientists funded by the U.S. Environmental Protection Agency rode behind New York City buses in vans equipped with laser sensors to test the amount and type of pollution the different types of buses emitted. Test results showed that conventional diesel buses were relatively fuel efficient, but they produced nitrogen oxide pollutants and large quantities of fine soot and sulfate particles. It was also found, however, that each type of vehicle tested (conventional diesel buses with pollution controls called soot particle oxidation traps, compressed natural gas (CNG) fueled buses, and hybrid diesel/electric buses) posed a different pollution problem (Goddard Space Flight Center, "Laser Technology Helps Measure Pollution from NYC Buses," December 6, 2002). The study was closely watched by the many other cities that are in the process of deciding what type of transit buses to purchase.

On the other side of the country, the nation's first hybrid unleaded gasoline/electric transit buses were put into service in San Bernardino, California, in late 2002. A California Air Resources Board (CARB) study showed that this type of vehicle emitted significantly lower

TABLE 8.1

Urban mass transit active fleet and infrastructure, 2000

	Urbanized areas over 1 million	Urbanized areas under 1 million	Total
Vehicles			
Buses	45,017	20,418	65,435
Heavy rail	10,260	0	10,260
Light rail	1,273	65	1,338
Self-propelled commuter rail	2,461	5	2,466
Commuter rail trailers	2,712	31	2,743
Commuter rail locomotives	565	11	576
Vans	10,596	5,638	16,234
Other (including ferryboats)	5,361	1,982	7,343
Rural service vehicles [1]	0	19,185	19,185
Special service vehicles [2]	4,300	24,364	28,664
Total active vehicles	**82,545**	**71,699**	**154,244**
Infrastructure			
Track mileage			
Heavy rail	2,178	0	2,178
Commuter rail	7,081	283	7,365
Light rail	949	52	1,001
Other rail	23	6	29
Total track mileage	**10,232**	**341**	**10,572**
Stations			
Heavy rail	1,009	0	1,009
Commuter rail	1,134	17	1,151
Light rail	556	59	615
Other rail	40	10	50
Total transit rail stations	**2,739**	**86**	**2,825**
Maintenance facilities [3]			
Heavy rail	53	0	53
Light rail	62	0	62
Commuter rail	26	4	30
Ferryboat	6	1	7
Buses	272	221	493
Demand response	44	66	110
Other	3	1	4
Rural transit maintenance facilities	0	510	510
Total maintenance facilities	**466**	**803**	**1,269**

[1] Status of Report on Public Transportation in Rural America 2000.
[2] FTA, Fiscal Year Trends Report on the Use of Section 5310 Elderly and Persons with Disabilities Program funds.
[3] Includes owned and leased facilities; directly operated service only.

SOURCE: "Exhibit 2-16. Urban mass transit active fleet and infrastructure, 2000," in "Chapter 2: System and Use Characteristics," in *Status of the Nation's Highways, Bridges, and Transit: 2002 Conditions and Performance Report,* U.S. Department of Transportation, Federal Highway Administration, Washington, DC, [Online] http://www.fhwa.dot.gov/policy/2002cpr/pdf/ch2.pdf [accessed April 17, 2003]

smog-producing emissions than either diesel or comparable alternatively-fueled vehicles (Nicole Ramos, "Omnitrans Introduces First Electric/Gasoline Hybrid Bus in Nation," November 14, 2002).

URBAN MASS TRANSIT

The term "mass transportation" encompasses a wide range of vehicles and systems but generally includes transport by bus, rail, or other conveyance, either publicly or privately owned, that provides service to the public in a particular region on a regular, frequent, and continuing basis. However, mass transportation can also include less formal arrangements known as "ridesharing," the voluntary association of individuals in a variety of conveyances including vanpools, carpools, and shared-ride taxis. It differs from intercity buses, railroads, and other forms of transportation because it is designed to carry people over relatively short distances, such as their commute from home to work.

While the motor bus is the most widely used mass transit vehicle, a variety of fixed-guideway modes (steel wheels or rubber tires on a set path) operate in U.S. cities. These modes include rapid rail, light rail, commuter rail, subway, trolleys, cable cars, ferryboats, and tramways. Table 8.1 shows the array of vehicles and types of infrastructures that make up the U.S. transit system.

A HISTORY OF MASS TRANSIT RIDERSHIP

In 1827 a 12-passenger horse-drawn carriage began carrying passengers along Broadway in New York City, marking the debut of what would become mass transportation. Horses continued to pull most passenger cars for most of the nineteenth century, but in 1887 Frank Sprague built and profitably ran an electric streetcar (trolley) company in Richmond, Virginia. Cars moved through streets with the help of electric current, delivered by overhead trolley lines connected to a central power source.

Sprague's success led to a veritable explosion in electric car lines, and by 1895 approximately 850 electric car lines were running over 10,000 miles of track. In 1897 Boston officials came up with the innovative idea of putting the electric cars underground, creating the country's first subway line. In 1904 New York City inaugurated its subway service.

In such cities as New York, Chicago, and Boston, the electric streetcar and subway offered a major advance in comfort and relatively pollution-free transportation. Previously, these cities had built overhead railroads or "els" (elevated railways). These "els," however, were expensive to construct and blocked out light to the streets underneath. Furthermore, the small steam engines that usually pulled three or four cars proved to be hazardous, because they dropped soot and hot coals on the pedestrians below.

By comparison, electric trains were far cleaner and safer. Many cities introduced cable cars during the latter part of the nineteenth century, but only San Francisco's cable car system remains active today, amusing tourists and transporting residents. In 1905 the first motorized bus company began operating in New York City.

Transit ridership has gone through several major cycles of growth and decline over the past century. For the first three decades (1900 to 1929), mass transit grew steadily in popularity. (See Figure 8.3.) By the late 1920s, more than 1,000 cities and towns had trolley systems operating nearly 63,000 streetcars over about 40,000 miles of track. During the Great Depression (from 1929 through the 1930s), there

FIGURE 8.3

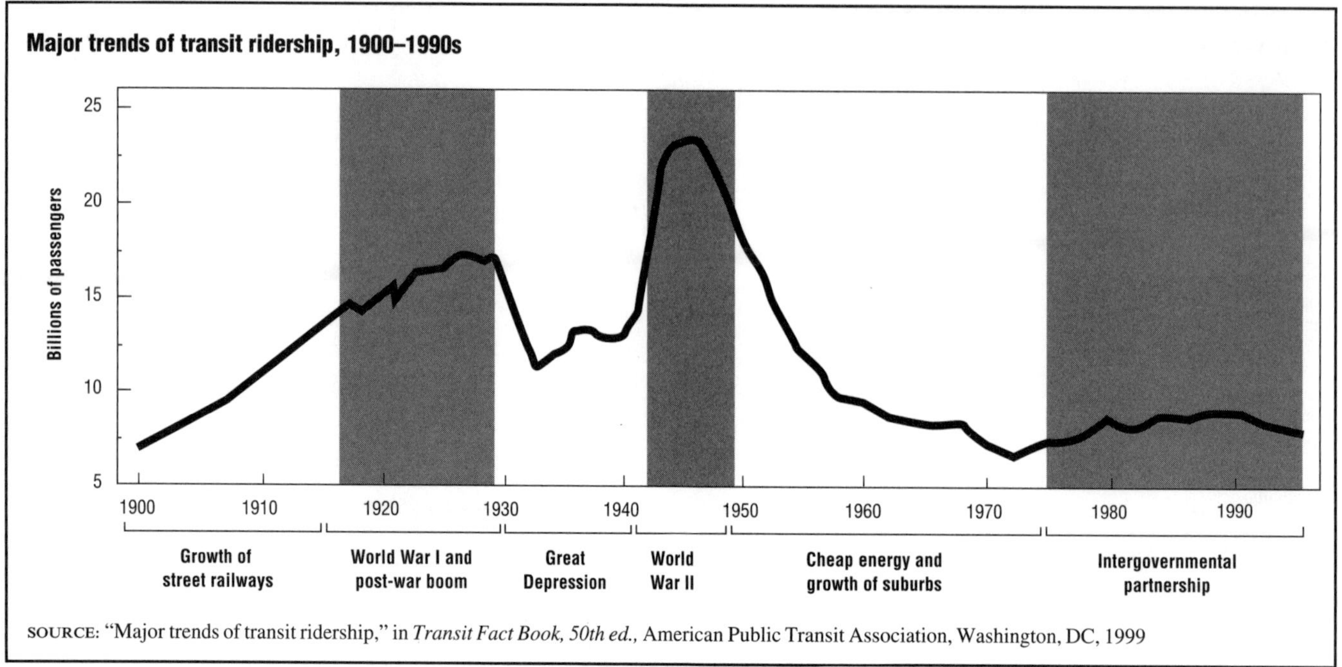

SOURCE: "Major trends of transit ridership," in *Transit Fact Book, 50th ed.,* American Public Transit Association, Washington, DC, 1999

was a steep decline in the number of transit riders. Unemployed people were no longer traveling to work and money was scarce, making pleasure trips infrequent.

Post-War Ridership Decline

World War II (1939–1945) brought about another surge of interest in mass transit, because gasoline and rubber tires were strictly rationed and automobile manufacturers built fewer cars and more military equipment, such as jeeps and tanks. During the war years, employment was high, especially among the growing female labor force, and public ridership shot up 80 percent. The number of transit passengers peaked at an all-time high of more than 23 billion in 1946.

Following the war, a number of factors contributed to the decline in ridership on transit systems. Low-cost, tax-deductible mortgages, a growing number of highways, and inexpensive fuel prices made suburban living and car ownership extremely attractive. Returning soldiers began buying the newly available cars, starting families, and purchasing houses in less congested areas. The rapid growth of suburban living contributed to a decentralization of housing, employment, shopping, and recreation.

The popularity and affordability of the automobile and the increasing development of new highways led many Americans to rely more heavily on their personal cars. Cars promised a wonderful world of speed, freedom, and convenience, taking drivers and passengers in comfort and privacy wherever and whenever they wanted to travel. Americans' love affair with the car has never waned.

Government officials began seeing public transportation as a relic from an earlier time and, consequently, gave it less support. As a result of these changing attitudes, private transit systems were faced with a deadly spiral of increasing costs, deferred maintenance, rising fares, declining ridership, shrinking profits, deteriorating equipment, and decreasing quality of service. Mass transit became an increasingly unappealing alternative to the private automobile. These factors combined to produce a steep decline in the public's interest in using mass transit. In 1973 transit ridership reached an all-time low of 7 billion passengers. (See Figure 8.3.)

A Renewed Interest—The Government Becomes Involved

Not until the 1960s and 1970s did serious interest again develop in mass transit. Urban and suburban growth led to frequent traffic jams. Noise and air pollution became an increasing worry. Rising fuel prices provided further incentive to seek alternatives to cars. In 1961 Congress included a $25 million mass transit pilot demonstration grant in the Housing and Urban Development Act (PL 87-117). Three years later, in 1964, Congress approved the Urban Mass Transportation (UMT) Act (PL 88-365). Passed mainly to help public authorities take over ailing private transit systems, the bill also called for improved mass transit. The UMT Act established federal matching grants (two-thirds federal, one-third local) for repairing, improving, or developing mass transit. A 1966 amendment to the UMT Act directed the Secretary of Transportation to establish a comprehensive research plan.

The Urban Mass Transportation Act of 1970 (PL 91-453) created the Urban Mass Transportation Administration (UMTA, which was renamed the Federal

FIGURE 8.4

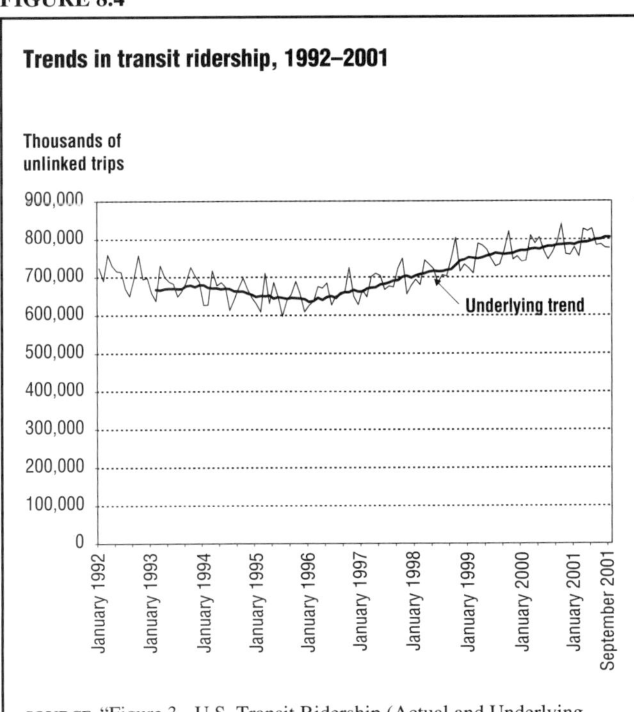

SOURCE: "Figure 3 - U.S. Transit Ridership (Actual and Underlying Trend)," Bureau of Transportation Statistics, December 2002 [Online] http://www.bts.gov/transtu/indicators/Special/html/A_Time_Series_Analysis_of_Transit_Ridership.html [accessed June 24, 2003]

FIGURE 8.5

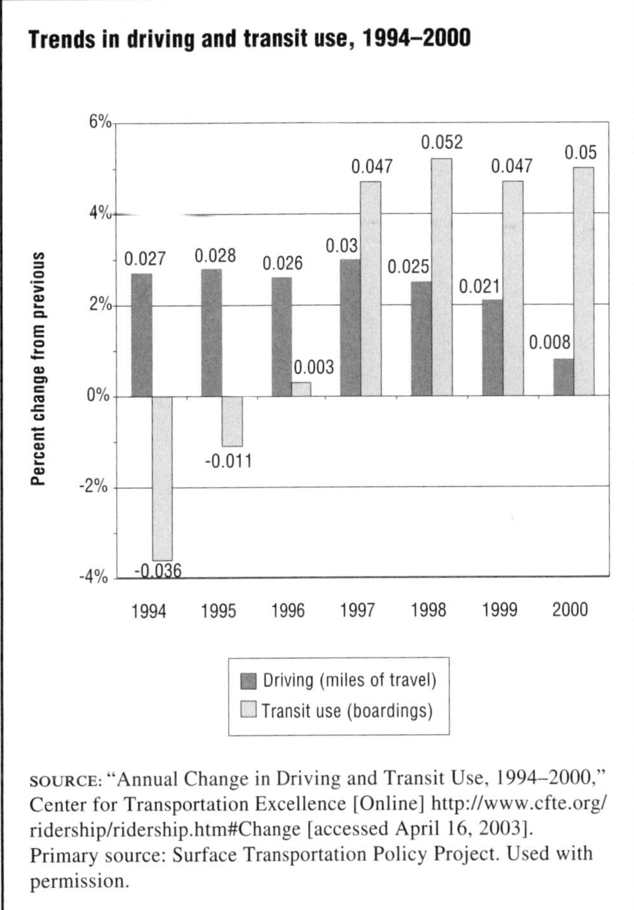

SOURCE: "Annual Change in Driving and Transit Use, 1994–2000," Center for Transportation Excellence [Online] http://www.cfte.org/ridership/ridership.htm#Change [accessed April 16, 2003]. Primary source: Surface Transportation Policy Project. Used with permission.

Transit Administration in June 2003). It also replaced the year-to-year financing for transportation measures with a more reliable 12-year federal funding plan. Other provisions promoted a greater commitment to urban transit construction. The Federal Aid Highway Act of 1973 (PL 93-87) made highway trust monies available for urban mass transit. It increased the matching grant share to 80 percent federal, 20 percent local.

In 1974 transit ridership began to rise again, as price spikes and gasoline shortages caused by the Organization of Petroleum Exporting Countries' (OPEC) oil embargo left many motorists either waiting in long lines at gas stations or with empty gas tanks. This crisis prompted the National Mass Transportation Assistance Act of 1974 (PL 95-503), which allocated federal aid for capital expenses and permitted assistance for operating expenses.

The Federal Public Transportation Act of 1978 (PL 95-599) established a $16.4 billion grant and loan program for public transit capital and operating assistance through 1982, the largest commitment ever. Ridership rose until about 1980 and then leveled off.

The Reagan Administration

The administration of President Ronald Reagan (1981–89) adopted a policy arguing that it was not the responsibility of the federal government to subsidize mass transit. The use of federal funds, the administration claimed, contributed to local inefficiencies, such as underused routes and unrealistically low fares. Consequently, with every budget proposal, the Reagan administration tried to phase out operating subsidies, although the Transportation Assistance Act of 1982 (PL 97-424) authorized continued operating subsidies through 1986. Even though President Reagan attempted to reduce the actual authorizations, mass transit continued to receive subsidies for capital purchases (buses, railway cars, stations) because the legislation mandated that one penny of the nickel-a-gallon gasoline tax increase be used for mass transit.

Mass Transportation in the 1990s

Legislators from urban areas most directly affected by the proposed cuts successfully prevented the Reagan administration from eliminating federal subsidies. Under the George H.W. Bush administration (1989–93), Congress passed the Federal Transit Act Amendments, extending transit assistance through 1997 at higher levels than before, to be used for the modes of transportation best suited to individual areas and states.

In 1996 an upward trend in transit ridership began. (See Figure 8.4.) Figure 8.5 shows that growth in transit use outpaced growth in driving from 1997 through 2000, a trend that continued through 2002 and marked the first

FIGURE 8.6

Comparison of share funding sources by size, 1991 and 2000

UZAs with more than 1 million population

1991

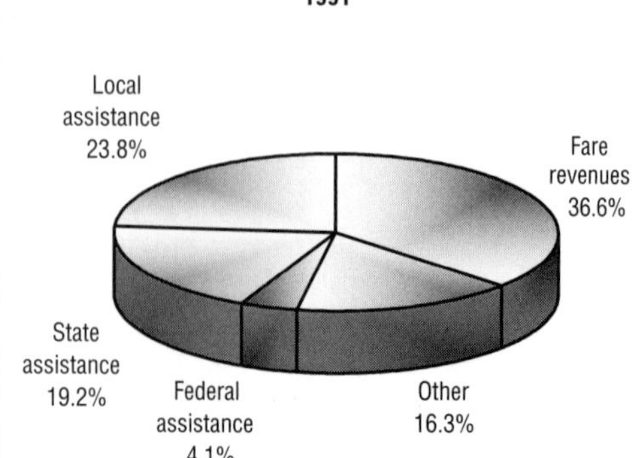

2000

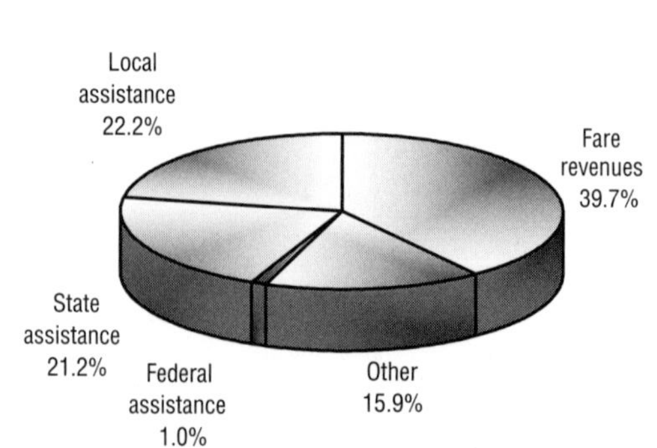

UZAs with more than 200,000 and less than 1 million population

1991

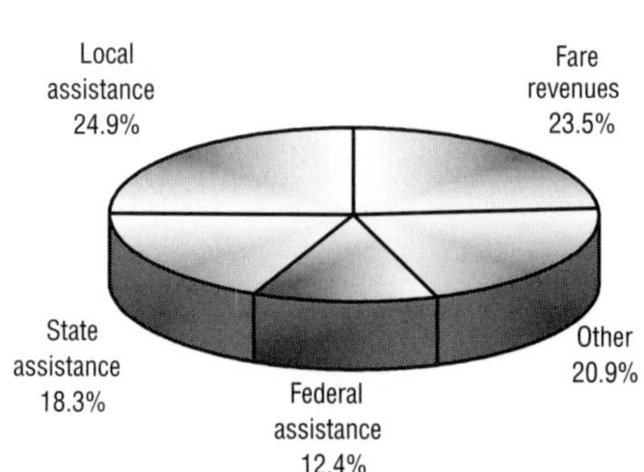

2000

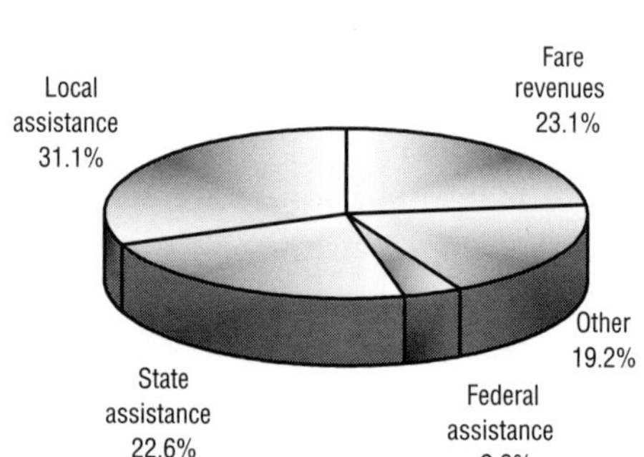

UZAs with less than 200,000 population

1991

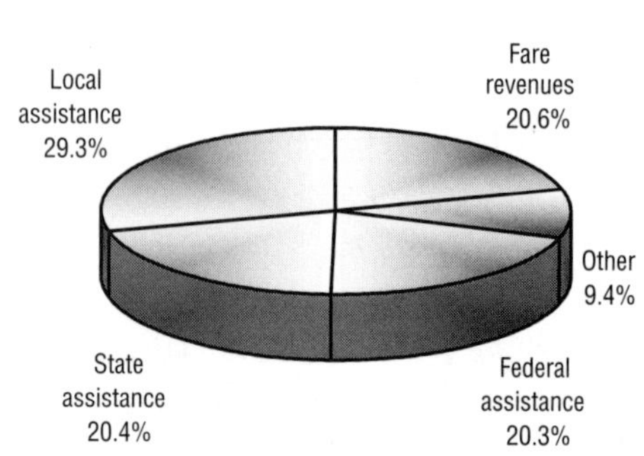

2000

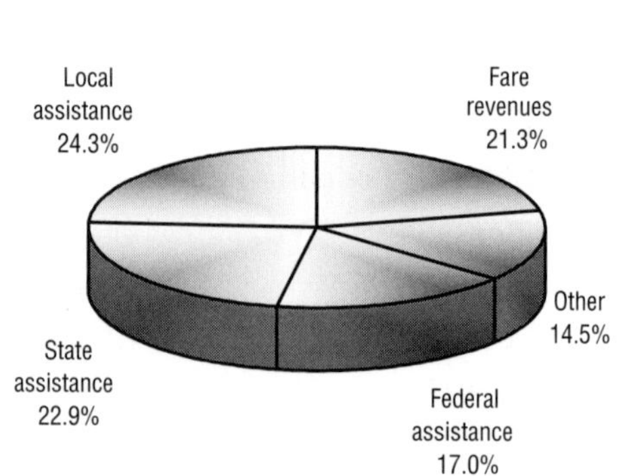

UZA Urbanized Area. For National Transit Database purposes, the National Transit Summaries and Trends groups urbanized areas by 3 size categories:
1. Large urbanized areas: population of more than 1 million (34 urbanized areas, 210 agencies or 35.8 percent of all agencies reporting).
2. Medium urbanized areas: population of more than 200,000 and less than 1 million (122 agencies or 20.8 percent of all agencies reporting).
3. Small urbanized areas: population of less than 200,000 and more than 50,000 (280 urbanized areas, 254 agencies or 43.3 percent of all agencies reporting).

SOURCE: "Comparison of Share Funding Sources," in *2000 National Transit Summaries and Trends,* Federal Transit Administration [Online] http://www.ntdprogram.com/ [accessed April 16, 2003]

TABLE 8.2

Examples of fuel savings to a person commuting to work on public transportation

Length of trip	Miles traveled per year[a]	Annual fuel savings, gallons based on following fuel efficiencies					
		15 miles per gallon	20 miles per gallon	25 miles per gallon	30 miles per gallon	35 miles per gallon	40 miles per gallon
2 miles	944	62.9	47.2	37.8	31.5	27	23.6
5 miles	2,360	157.3	118	94.4	78.7	67.4	59
10 miles	4,720	314.7	236	188.8	157.3	134.9	118
20 miles	9,440	629.3	472	377.6	314.7	269.7	236
30 miles	14,160	944	708	566.4	472	404.6	354
40 miles	18,880	1,258.70	944	755.2	629.3	539.4	472
50 miles	23,600	1,573.30	1,180.00	944	786.7	674.3	590
60 miles	28,320	1,888.00	1,416.00	1,132.80	944	809.1	708

[a] Based on 472 trips per year based on 365 days minus 52 Saturdays minus 52 Sundays minus 7 holidays minus 10 days vacation minus 8 days sick leave times 2 trips per day.

SOURCE: "Table 68. Examples of fuel savings to a person commuting to work on public transportation," in *Public Transportation Fact Book,* American Public Transportation Association, Washington, DC, 2001

time ever that such a phenomenon had occurred five years in a row ("Transit Growing Faster Than Driving: A Historic Shift in Travel Trends," Surface Transportation Policy Project, May 29, 2002).

Funding for Transit

TEA-21 provided funding for public transportation through September 2003. The federal appropriation for 2003 was $7.2 billion and about the same amount was proposed for 2004 by President George W. Bush in his version of the Safe, Accountable, Flexible and Efficient Transportation Equity Act of 2003 (SAFETEA), the act that will replace TEA-21 if passed by Congress.

The U.S. Department of Transportation estimated that $20.6 billion is needed each year in order to do the sorts of maintenance projects necessary to properly maintain and improve the performance of the nation's transit systems (*Status of the Nation's Highways, Bridges, and Transit: 2002 Conditions and Performance Report*). According to the American Public Transportation Association (APTA), $11.4 billion from all sources was dedicated to public transportation in 2001.

In 2000, the latest year for which data were available, passenger fares and other directly generated funds contributed 55.6 percent to transit revenue in the largest urban areas, 42.3 percent in medium-size urban areas, and 35.8 percent in the smallest urban areas. (See Figure 8.6.) Federal government, state funding, and local assistance supplied the remaining funds needed to operate the systems. Mass transit is highly subsidized: state and local funding together (an average of 48.1 percent in the three types of transit systems shown in Figure 8.5) accounted for more revenues than did passenger fares (an average of 28 percent), except in the largest urban areas.

ADVANTAGES OF MASS TRANSIT

Transit and Basic Mobility

Mass transit offers many advantages and may be the only alternative for many people. It gives mobility to those who cannot afford to purchase or maintain an automobile. It offers greater mobility to the handicapped, the young, and older Americans, freeing family and friends from the obligation of providing transportation for these individuals. It also gives the commuter the opportunity to leave the frustrations of driving in heavy traffic to someone else. Inner city residents use public transportation most often.

Mass transit often provides only minimal service to outlying suburbs, where job growth is the greatest. Therefore, this link between central city residents without cars to possible suburban jobs is weak or, sometimes, nonexistent. According to a report entitled "Transportation in Rural America: Issues for the 21st Century" (Eileen S. Stommes and Dennis M. Brown, *Rural America*, Winter 2002), rural public transportation is available in only about half of the rural counties nationwide (a total of about 1,200 systems) and typically exists only in the more populated rural areas. Few transportation systems are found in the most rural, isolated areas

Fuel and Dollar Comparisons

For many commuters, mass transit can be more economical than driving to work alone. Annual transit costs can range from $200 to $2,000, depending on such factors as the number of miles traveled, transfer fees, and peak-hour surcharges, according to the APTA in 2003. The APTA also estimated that the annual cost of commuting to work for a single-occupant driver ranged from $4,800 for a small car to $9,700 for a large vehicle, depending on the number of miles driven. Table 8.2 shows the APTA estimates of the annual number of gallons of gasoline

TABLE 8.3

Means of commuting to work, 25 largest cities, 2000

[In percent, except as indicated (353.1 represents 353,100). As of April 1. For workers 16 years old and over. Based on sample data from the 2000 Census of Population and Housing.]

		Percent of workers who—						
		Commuted by car, truck, or van						
City	Total workers (1,000)	Drove alone	Carpooled	Used public transportation[1]	Walked	Used other means	Worked at home	Mean travel time to work (min.)
Austin, TX	353.1	73.6	13.9	4.5	2.5	2.1	3.4	22.4
Baltimore, MD	249.4	54.7	15.2	19.5	7.1	1.1	2.3	31.1
Boston, MA	278.5	41.5	9.2	32.3	13.0	1.6	2.4	28.8
Chicago, IL	1,192.1	50.1	14.5	26.1	5.7	1.3	2.4	35.2
Columbus, OH	367.4	79.0	10.8	3.9	3.2	0.8	2.3	21.9
Dallas, TX	537.0	70.8	17.8	5.5	1.9	1.2	2.8	26.9
Denver, CO	278.7	68.3	13.5	8.4	4.3	1.8	3.7	24.5
Detroit, MI	319.4	68.6	17.1	8.7	2.8	1.1	1.8	28.4
El Paso, TX	208.1	76.5	15.8	2.3	2.0	1.2	2.2	22.4
Houston, TX	841.7	71.8	15.9	5.9	2.3	1.7	2.3	27.4
Indianapolis, IN[2]	385.2	80.0	12.3	2.4	2.0	0.8	2.5	22.7
Jacksonville, FL	350.5	79.2	13.4	2.1	1.8	1.6	1.9	25.2
Los Angeles, CA	1,494.9	65.7	14.7	10.2	3.6	1.6	4.1	29.6
Memphis, TN	274.9	76.6	15.7	3.0	1.9	1.0	1.7	23.0
Milwaukee, WI	249.9	68.8	13.6	10.3	4.7	0.9	1.7	22.5
Nashville-Davidson, TN[2]	274.0	78.5	13.5	1.8	2.4	0.9	3.0	23.3
New York, NY	3,192.1	24.9	8.0	52.8	10.4	1.0	2.9	40.0
Philadelphia, PA	569.8	49.2	12.8	25.4	9.1	1.6	1.9	32.0
Phoenix, AZ	599.6	71.7	17.4	3.3	2.2	2.2	3.3	26.1
San Antonio, TX	491.4	75.6	15.2	3.8	2.2	1.1	2.2	23.8
San Diego, CA	580.3	74.0	12.2	4.2	3.6	2.0	4.0	23.2
San Francisco, CA	418.6	40.5	10.8	31.1	9.4	3.6	4.6	30.7
San Jose, CA	428.0	76.4	14.1	4.1	1.4	1.5	2.5	27.8
Seattle, WA	316.5	56.5	11.2	17.6	7.4	2.7	4.6	24.8
Washington, DC	260.9	38.4	11.0	33.2	11.8	1.9	3.8	29.7

[1] Includes taxicabs.
[2] Represents the portion of a consolidated city that is not within one or more separately incorporated places.

SOURCE: "No. 1390. Commuting to Work—25 Largest Cities: 2000," in *Statistical Abstract of the United States: 2002,* U.S. Census Bureau, Washington, DC, 2003

saved by a commuter when making a daily trip by public transportation instead of by car.

Congestion and Land Use

Public transportation reduces congestion on the nation's highways, most notably during the already overcrowded "rush hours." Cities dependent on the automobile must set aside more land for streets, highways, and parking lots. Consequently, they tend to become more spread out. For example, streets and highways take up 68 percent of the land in Los Angeles. In downtown Chicago, which grew up before the automobile and has an extensive bus and rail system, roadways account for only 36 percent of land use. Not only do roadways cause the city to spread out, but they can also lower the tax base, since land used by public highways does not generate taxes.

The Bureau of Transportation Statistics reported that people in 75 metropolitan areas spent an average of 27 hours per year delayed in traffic in 2000, up from 19 hours in 1990 ("Table 15: Roadway Hours of Delay and Congestion Cost Per Person in 75 Metropolitan Areas: 1990 and 2000," in *Pocket Guide to Transportation,* U.S. Department of Transportation, Bureau of Transportation Statistics, Washington, D.C., January 2003). The cost per person was $507, up from $267 in 1990.

Usage of mass transit varies widely from city to city. In the metropolitan area of New York City, more than half the people (52.8 percent) used mass transit to get to work in 2000. (See Table 8.3.) About one-third of workers in Washington, D.C. (33.2 percent) and San Francisco (31.1 percent) used mass transit, and about one-fifth in Baltimore (19.5 percent). Only 1.8 percent of workers in the Nashville-Davidson, Tennessee, area used public transportation.

Economic Considerations

Since most downtowns were built before the explosion in automobile ownership and the migration to the suburbs, few can supply enough parking spaces to make shopping convenient. In addition, the growth of the suburbs has

TABLE 8.4

Number of transit agencies by mode, 2003

Mode	Number
Aerial tramway	2
Automated guideway transit	5
Bus	2,264
Cable car	1
Commuter rail	21
Demand response	5,251
Ferryboat (a)	42
Heavy rail	14
Inclined plane	5
Light rail	26
Monorail	2
Trolleybus	5
Vanpool	67
Total (b)	6,000

(a) Excludes international, rural, rural interstate, island, and urban park ferries.
(b) Total is not sum of all modes since many agencies operate more than one mode.

SOURCE: "Table 2. Number of Transit Agencies by Mode," in *Public Transportation Fact Book,* American Public Transportation Association, Washington, DC, 2003 [Online] http://www.apta.com/research/stats/overview/agencies.cfm [accessed June 25, 2003]

meant that downtown shopping districts are miles away from potential suburban shoppers. As a result, downtown stores have lost significant amounts of business to suburban shopping centers and malls. In fact, the so-called "Main Streets" of the 1950s have been replaced in most suburbs by malls. Teenagers, mothers of young children, workers, and the elderly go the local malls to shop, eat, and see movies.

Effective public transport has helped to support some downtown business or, as in the case of BART (Bay Area Rapid Transit) in San Francisco, to revitalize it, but this is the exception, not the rule. Many systems have not met their original projections for ridership. Those who support mass transit claim that to simply add up direct financial costs and compare them with revenues does not give the full picture. A simple profit and loss statement does not take into account benefits to society, such as increased mobility for those without automobiles, increased employment opportunities, less congestion, better land use, increased downtown economic growth, and less pollution and energy use. These factors not only benefit society generally, but also have a real financial value that can justify considerable public support through financial subsidies.

Environmental Pollution

Nearly half (43 percent) of all air pollution comes from transportation sources, most from automobiles, according to the APTA. In the report *Conserving Energy and Preserving the Environment: The Role of Public Transportation* (Robert J. Shapiro et al., APTA, Washington, D.C., July 2002), the authors concluded that public transportation generates 95 percent less carbon monoxide (CO), 92 percent less volatile organic compounds (VOCs), and about half as much carbon dioxide (CO_2) and nitrogen oxide (NO_x) per passenger mile than do private vehicles.

Energy Use

If more people used mass transit, the nation would use less energy, according to Shapiro et al. Most of the energy used for transportation is consumed by cars and light trucks. The Shapiro study showed that public transportation saves more than 855 million gallons of gasoline or 45 million barrels of oil a year. The report asserted that "increased use of transit offers the most effective strategy available for reducing energy consumption and improving the environment without imposing new taxes, government mandates, or regulations on the economy or consumers."

TRANSIT SYSTEMS—A VARIETY OF TYPES

In 2001, 6,000 transit agencies were transporting passengers in the United States, up from 5,975 in 1997. (See Table 8.4.) The following is a list of the most common modes of transport in service today.

- Transit Bus—a generic term for a rubber-tired vehicle with front and center doors and a rear-mounted diesel engine, usually designed for frequent-stop service. It is not equipped with luggage storage or restroom facilities. Many newer buses are fueled by gasoline or alternative fuels, which significantly reduces emissions.
- Heavy Rail—an electric transit railway with the capacity for a heavy volume of traffic and characterized by multi-car trains, high speed, rapid acceleration, and exclusive rights-of-way. Heavy rail systems are also known as subways, elevated railways, rapid rail or rapid transit, or metropolitan railways (metros).
- Light Rail—a type of electric transit railway with a light volume of traffic compared to heavy rail. Generally, light rail includes streetcars (trolley cars) and tramways.
- Commuter Railroad—a "main line" railroad (not electric) that involves passenger train service between a central city and adjacent suburbs. Commuter railroad service typically is characterized by multi-trip tickets, specific station-to-station fares, and normally only one or two main stations in the central business district. It is also known as a suburban railroad.
- Demand Response Service—a type of non-fixed-route bus or van service that typically picks up and drops off passengers at any location within the transit provider's service area. The vehicles provide services at times requested by the passengers. Demand response is also known as paratransit or dial-a-ride.
- Ridesharing—an informal and voluntary association of individuals in a variety of vehicles, including vanpools, carpools, and shared-ride taxis.

FIGURE 8.7

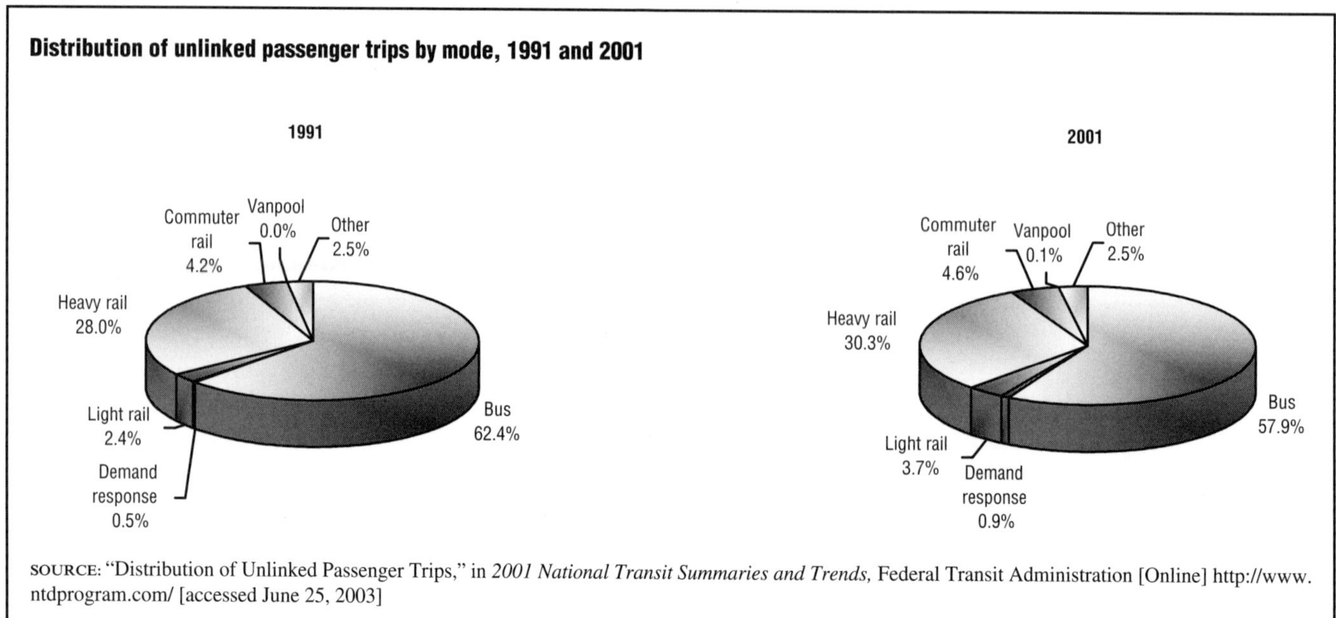

SOURCE: "Distribution of Unlinked Passenger Trips," in *2001 National Transit Summaries and Trends,* Federal Transit Administration [Online] http://www.ntdprogram.com/ [accessed June 25, 2003]

About 9.7 billion trips were made by way of public transportation in 2001, a 3 percent increase over 2000, according to the APTA "Public Transportation Overview." The largest number of mass transit riders took the bus (57.9 percent); 30.3 percent traveled by heavy rail; 4.6 percent by commuter rail; 3.7 percent by light rail; and approximately 1 percent by demand response. (See Figure 8.7). (The APTA defines Unlinked Passenger Trips as "the number of passengers who board public transportation vehicles. Passengers are counted each time they board vehicles no matter how many vehicles they use to travel from their origin to their destination.") According to the APTA, 54 percent of trips in 2001 were for work, 15 percent for school, 9 percent for shopping, 9 percent for social visits, and 5 percent for medical reasons.

Mass transit passengers traveled more than 49 billion miles in 2001. (See Table 8.5.) Nearly half (44.9 percent) traveled by bus; 28.9 percent by heavy rail; 19.5 percent, commuter rail; 2.9 percent, light rail; and the rest by demand response and trolley bus.

Americans With Disabilities Act of 1990 (ADA)

The ADA (PL 101-336) requires that transit agencies provide service accessible to persons with disabilities. As of October 2002 all motorcoach operators must fulfill a request for a wheelchair-accessible coach on 48-hours' notice. Any new buses must be accessible if more than 25 percent of a company's fleet is involved in fixed-route service.

According to the APTA, in 2003, 93 percent of all buses were wheelchair accessible, as were 94.1 percent of demand response vehicles. More than two-thirds (68.4 percent) of commuter rail cars could accommodate wheelchairs, as could 98.7 percent of heavy rail cars and 82.2 percent of light rail cars.

A LOOK AT TRANSIT RIDERS

The Federal Transit Administration conducted surveys between 1996 and 1998 on car ownership, frequency of transit use, and transit purpose; the results are summarized in *Status of the Nation's Highways, Bridges, and Transit: 2002 Conditions and Performance Report* (U.S. Department of Transportation, Federal Highway Adminstration, Washington, D.C., 2002). The surveys provided a wealth of data about users of public transportation. A majority (68 percent) did not have access to a car at the time their trip was made. A little over 70 percent of trips were made by passengers who used public transportation at least five days a week. About 70 percent of users began their trip on foot, suggesting that public transportation is used primarily by those who live within walking distance of a transit line. Half (50 percent) of transit users were on their way to or from work; 12 percent were on their way to or from school; 4 percent were on their way to or from medical appointments; 13 percent were shopping; and 14 percent used transit for social, religious, or other personal reasons. Women (55 percent) made more trips than men (45 percent) by public transportation. A majority (59 percent) of bus users and rail users (52 percent) were women.

The surveys showed the importance of public transportation to people with limited incomes. (See Figure 8.8.) Half of the users of public transportation in the survey had household incomes of $20,000 or less. Among that group, 54 percent rode buses and 38 percent took rail trips. At the other end of the income scale, 5 percent of those with household incomes of $80,000 or greater used pub-

TABLE 8.5

Passenger miles by mode of travel, 1984–2001
(Millions)

Year	Bus	Commuter rail	Demand response	Heavy rail	Light rail	Trolley bus	Other	Total
1984	21,595	6,207	349	10,111	416	364	382	39,424
1985	21,161	6,534	364	10,427	350	306	439	39,581
1986	21,395	6,723	402	10,649	361	305	369	40,204
1987	20,970	6,818	374	11,198	405	223	360	40,348
1988	20,753	6,964	441	11,300	477	211	434	40,580
1989	20,768	7,211	428	12,030	509	199	458	41,603
1990	20,981	7,082	431	11,475	571	193	410	41,143
1991	21,090	7,344	454	10,528	662	195	430	40,703
1992	20,336	7,320	495	10,737	701	199	453	40,241
1993	20,247	6,940	562	10,231	705	188	511	39,384
1994	18,832	7,996	577	10,668	833	187	492	39,585
1995	18,818	8,244	607	10,559	860	187	533	39,808
1996	19,096	8,351	656	11,530	957	184	604	41,378
1997	19,604	8,038	754	12,056	1,035	189	663	42,339
1998	20,360	8,704	735	12,284	1,128	182	735	44,128
1999	21,205	8,766	813	12,902	1,206	186	779	45,857
2000	21,241	9,402	839	13,844	1,356	192	792	47,666
2001 P	22,022	9,548	855	14,178	1,437	187	843	49,070
2001 % of total	44.9%	19.5%	1.7%	28.9%	2.9%	0.4%	1.7%	100.0%

P = Preliminary

SOURCE: "Table 30. Passenger Miles by Mode, millions," in *Public Transportation Fact Book,* American Public Transportation Association, Washington, DC, 2001, and "Table 6: Passenger Miles by Mode, millions" [Online] http://www.apta.com/research/stats/ridership/passmile.cfm [accessed June 16, 2003]

lic transportation; of those, 3 percent took bus trips and 8 percent took rail trips.

In an effort to lure commuters to mass transit, cities have experimented with a variety of innovations—unusual design including futuristic architecture, use of artwork, and decoration with color murals and lighting—color, fantasy, and whimsy that planners hope will draw commuters. Some cities that have experienced loss of riders on subways and buses have discussed restructuring fare schedules to allow riders to transfer from subway to bus and better connecting routes for such transfers. Another frequently mentioned suggestion to attract transit riders: make public transportation free.

SUBURBAN COMMUTING

As families headed to the outlying areas in the 1950s and 1960s, many businesses followed. Between 1960 and 1980 alone, the growing suburbs doubled in size and received approximately two-thirds of all job growth. Public transportation did not always move with the jobs. Reconciling the needs of the segment of the population that does not have adequate access to public transportation with the explosion and shifting of growth must be a major factor in transportation planning.

Many workers have to commute many miles from one suburb to another in large metropolitan areas. In fact, the most common commuter pattern now is the trip from one suburb to another. Suburb-to-suburb trips have dominated work trip growth since the 1970s and by 1995 made up one-third of metropolitan commuting. In some communities, suburb-to-suburb commutes constituted a far higher percentage of commuting (48 percent in Chicago, for example) (Katherine S. Hooper, "Innovative Suburb-to-Suburb Transit Practices," Transit Cooperative Research Program sponsored by the Federal Transit Administration, TCRP Synthesis 14, National Academy Press, Washington, D.C., 1995).

Commuting to and from suburbs heavily favors the use of the private automobile. (Auto commuting refers not only to cars, but also to light trucks, vans, and sport utility vehicles.) The number of cars per household has risen steeply since 1960, and the number of available vehicles per person has almost doubled. In fact, the majority of households of every size have more vehicles than workers. The Federal Highway Administration (FHWA) reported that in 1995 (the latest year for which data are available), 40 percent of American households owned two vehicles, while those households owning three or more vehicles totaled nearly 20 percent. (See Figure 8.9.) The doubling of the number of cars available for travel meant that car commuting increased at the same time that mass transit use declined. As discussed earlier, that pattern started to change in 1996 (see Figure 8.5).

In contrast, according to the Volpe Center, a federal agency, the number of households with no access to private transportation shrank to 8.1 percent in 1995. (See Figure 8.9.) Two-thirds of the households without vehicles also had no workers, and another 28 percent had only one worker. Zero-vehicle households are usually very small

FIGURE 8.8

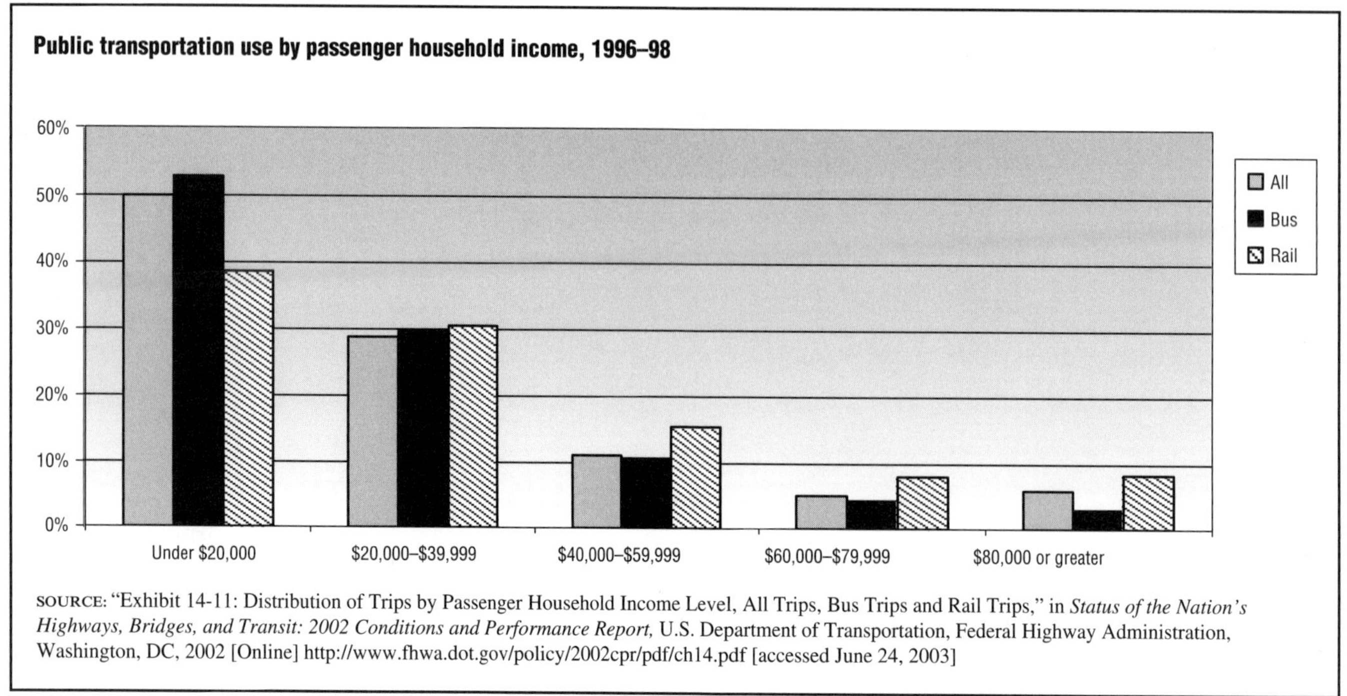

SOURCE: "Exhibit 14-11: Distribution of Trips by Passenger Household Income Level, All Trips, Bus Trips and Rail Trips," in *Status of the Nation's Highways, Bridges, and Transit: 2002 Conditions and Performance Report,* U.S. Department of Transportation, Federal Highway Administration, Washington, DC, 2002 [Online] http://www.fhwa.dot.gov/policy/2002cpr/pdf/ch14.pdf [accessed June 24, 2003]

FIGURE 8.9

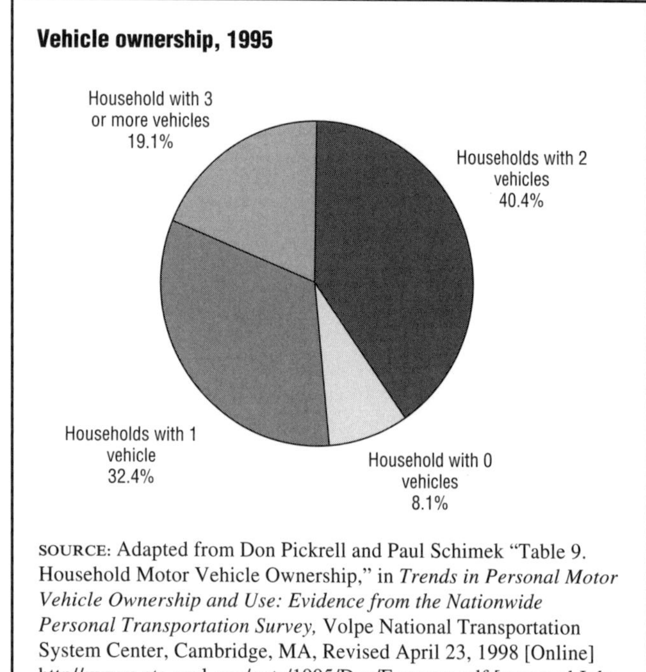

SOURCE: Adapted from Don Pickrell and Paul Schimek "Table 9. Household Motor Vehicle Ownership," in *Trends in Personal Motor Vehicle Ownership and Use: Evidence from the Nationwide Personal Transportation Survey,* Volpe National Transportation System Center, Cambridge, MA, Revised April 23, 1998 [Online] http//:www-cta.ornl.gov/npts/1995/Doc/Envecon.pdf [accessed July 25, 2003]

and are located in large central cities. The New York City area led the list, with 20 percent of its households having no personal vehicle.

GOVERNMENTAL ATTEMPTS TO CHANGE COMMUTER BEHAVIOR

Urban traffic congestion imposes large costs on society. Time spent in traffic results in lower productivity, excess fuel consumption, and increased pollution. The federal government, under mandate of the Clean Air Act Amendments of 1990 (PL 101-549), the Intermodal Surface Transportation Efficiency Act (ISTEA; PL 102-240) of 1991, the Transportation Equity Act for the 21st Century, which reauthorized ISTEA (TEA-21; PL 105-178), and other state and local regulations, has attempted to discourage drive-alone commuting.

Carpooling

Despite energy issues, pollution, and traffic congestion, most motorists shun carpooling. Campaigns to persuade people to carpool or vanpool have generally failed. Among the reasons motorists prefer to drive alone are the ability to come and go at will, freedom to run errands with their own autos, fear of liability in case of an accident, and the ability to depart immediately in the case of family emergencies. Also cited are the choice of radio stations, privacy, and, most importantly, an unfettered, go-as-you-please American individualism.

When Congress passed the Clean Air Act Amendments of 1990 (PL 101-549), it intended to address some of these issues. In certain polluted regions, such as New York, New Jersey, Southern California, and the Chicago area, companies employing more than 100 people at a single site must develop plans to increase the number of employees using mass transit or carpooling. The amendments include fines against companies that have not drawn up such plans.

According to Civic Strategies, a strategic planning firm that devises policy solutions for cities and regions, a successful strategy implemented by New Jersey Transit

FIGURE 8.10

Growth in light rail system mileage, 1985–2000

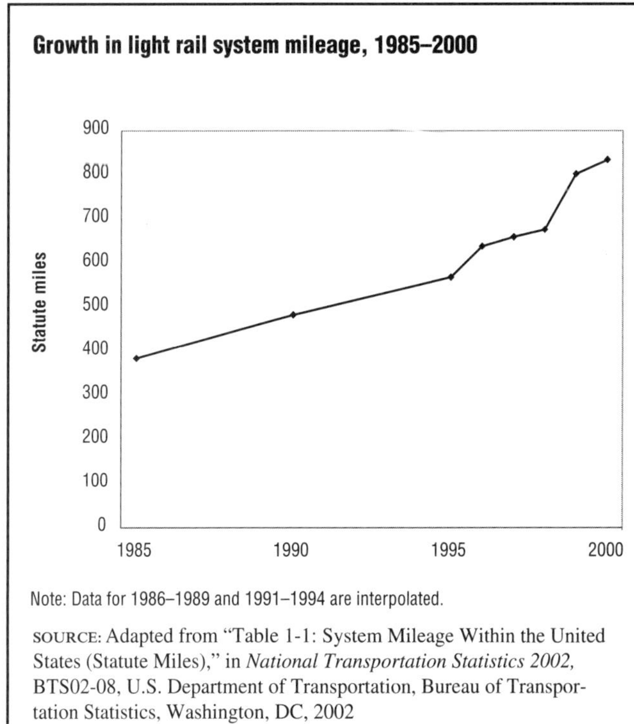

Note: Data for 1986–1989 and 1991–1994 are interpolated.

SOURCE: Adapted from "Table 1-1: System Mileage Within the United States (Statute Miles)," in *National Transportation Statistics 2002,* BTS02-08, U.S. Department of Transportation, Bureau of Transportation Statistics, Washington, DC, 2002

involves employer distribution of "Ozonepasses" to employees on the day preceding a bad ozone day when alerted by the transit authority. The pass costs the employer about half the usual fare.

Following the September 11, 2001, terrorist attacks, New York City adopted an emergency carpool rule banning single occupant vehicles from driving into lower Manhattan from 6 A.M. to 10 A.M. According to Environmental Defense, far fewer cars entering the city daily resulted in "markedly improved" air quality ("The Tide May Be Turning in New York City's Traffic Wars" [Online] http://www.environmentaldefense.org/article.cfm?contentid=2022 [accessed June 25, 2003]).

Funding Special Projects

The ISTEA (through September 1997) and TEA-21 (from 1998 through September 30, 2003) authorized special funding for projects likely to reduce vehicle miles traveled, decrease fuel consumption, or otherwise reduce congestion and improve air quality. TEA-21 retained the basic structure of the federal transit programs authorized under ISTEA. TEA-21 provided $41 billion in transit funds between 1998 and 2003. The money was to be spent in both rural and urban areas. New transportation systems were to be built and existing ones improved and modernized. The Rail Modernization Program increased the proportion of new funds for newer fixed-guideway (steel wheel or rubber tires on a set path) systems.

Another benefit of TEA-21 was a $100 per month tax-exempt employee allowance that was made available for workers who used public transit, effective December 31, 2001. Prior to TEA-21, the maximum benefit was $65 per month. Two new programs were also created under TEA-21. The Clean Fuels Formula Grant program provided funds for adoption of clean fuel technologies, including purchase or lease of clean fuel buses and facilities. The Job Access and Reverse Commute Program funded projects designed to help welfare and low-income families and others who did not own cars get to and from higher-paying jobs in suburbs without bus service, or to travel to and from off-hour jobs when other forms of public transportation had stopped running.

TEA-21 expires on September 30, 2003. SAFETEA, the replacement legislation proposed by the Bush administration, called for a total of $45.7 billion over six years for transit. This version of SAFETEA would permit special funding for bus rapid transit non-fixed guideway and other new, lower-cost non-fixed guideway projects. The American Public Transportation Association, on behalf of the public transportation industry, expressed disappointment that the proposed legislation did not provide adequate funds for transit improvement ("Growing Transit Investment Needs Not Addressed by 'SAFETEA' Proposal," June 25, 2003).

TRANSIT SAFETY

The U.S. Department of Transportation monitors mass transit workers for drug and alcohol use. Congress mandated the testing program in 1991 in response to a series of accidents involving alcohol. Among them were the *Exxon Valdez* oil spill in 1989, which was partly attributed to the captain's drinking, and the derailment of a subway train that killed five people in New York City in 1991, in which the motorman's drinking was blamed. The regulations apply to truck drivers, school bus drivers, railroad employees, pilots and air traffic controllers, merchant mariners, and others involved in "safety sensitive" jobs. New employees are tested and random tests of those already employed are conducted.

The transportation industry had long held that testing was an invasion of privacy, but federal courts, in *Skinner, Secretary of Transportation et al. v. Railway Labor Executives' Association et al.* (839 F.2d 575, Ninth Circuit, 1989), decided that safety considerations can override privacy concerns, as in the decision to require drug testing of transportation employees.

Drug and alcohol abuses are not the only causes of accidents. Sometimes, trains are not equipped with the latest safety features. Following a 1996 accident that took three lives in New Jersey when a transit train ran a red light and collided with another train, New Jersey Transit decided to install Positive Train Stop, an automatic braking system that stops trains that fail to obey signals and was designed

FIGURE 8.11

Deployment of intelligent transportation systems (ITS) in 75 metropolitan areas, 1997, 1999, and 2000

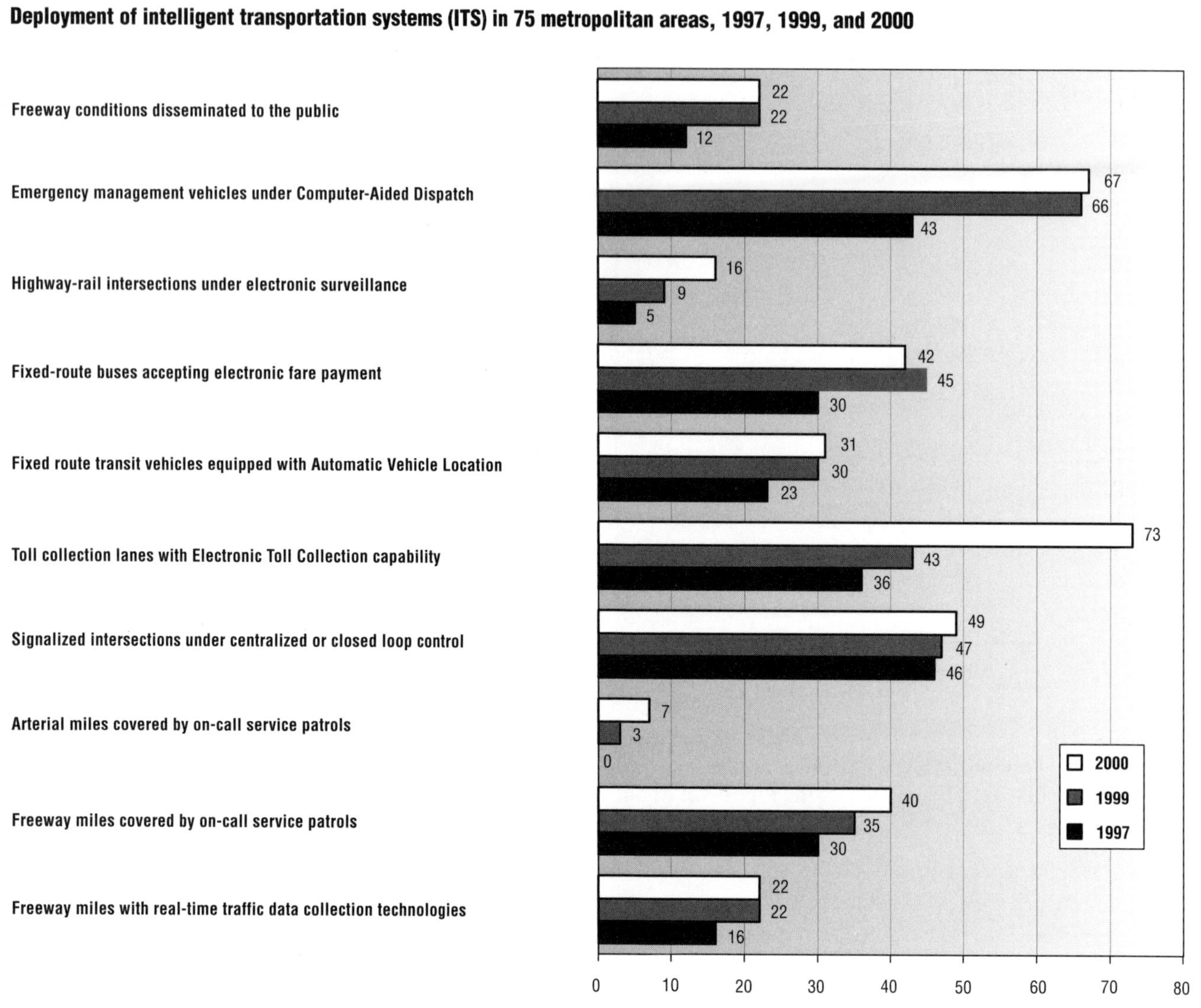

SOURCE: "Exhibit 2-12: Deployment of Intelligent Transportation Systems (ITS) in 75 Metropolitan Areas, 1997, 1999, and 2000," in "Chapter 2: System and Use Characteristics," in *Status of the Nation's Highways, Bridges, and Transit: 2002 Conditions and Performance Report,* U.S. Department of Transportation, Federal Highway Administration, Washington, DC [Online] http://www.fhwa.dot.gov/policy/2002cpr/pdf/ch2.pdf [accessed April 17, 2003]

to prevent the type of human error that was blamed for the crash in 1996. Such systems are expensive; New Jersey Transit earmarked $150 million to install automatic braking systems on every line (P.L. Wyckoff, "NJ Transit's New Stopping System Succeeds Where Engineers May Fail," *The Star-Ledger,* April 2, 1999).

Overly long work shifts are often responsible for contributing to fatigue and human error. Split shifts—extended work periods of up to fourteen and one-half hours with only a four-hour break in the middle—have been blamed for several accidents. One such case involved a shift that began at 6 p.m. and finished at 8:30 a.m. the following day, with a four-hour break during the night. In this accident, three people were killed and more than 160 were injured.

Security Concerns Post-September 11

After terrorists hijacked airplanes and destroyed New York's World Trade Center in 2001, transit security became an urgent issue. The Federal Transit Administration, part of the U.S. Department of Transportation, ordered vulnerability checks and in January 2003 identified 20 items it considers the most important elements transit agencies should incorporate into their System Security Program Plans. These include maintaining and updating written security and emergency management plans, sharing sensitive intelligence information, conducting background checks on employees, security training and drills, and controlled access to security systems and documents.

THE FUTURE OF MASS TRANSPORTATION

In a 2003 poll conducted by Wirthlin Worldwide, four out of five Americans (81 percent of 1,003 resident adults aged 18 and over) expressed the opinion that public funds should be invested to improve public transportation because such an investment would be good for the economy, would reduce traffic congestion and air pollution, and would save energy ("Most Americans Link Increasing Investment in Public Transportation to Solving Congestion and a Better Quality of Life," *US Newswire*, March 12, 2003). More urbanites (85 percent) than suburbanites (76 percent) agreed that public investment in public transportation would have these beneficial effects.

Light Rail Systems

Many U.S. cities have introduced light-rail lines and ridership has been higher than expected. (See Figure 8.10 and Table 8.5.) Such systems are expensive to build and to operate and most do not make a profit. In 2001 an ambitious plan to build a $100 million light-rail system at the Grand Canyon, the first to service a national park and designed to reduce congestion and pollution, was shelved in favor of a less expensive alternative involving a bus-based system. In 2002 ballot initiatives, voters across the country resoundingly rejected tax increases for light rail projects, according to the Light Rail Now! organization.

Intelligent Transit

Many analysts believe the future of mass transit lies not in light rail but in the less expensive alternative of bus rapid transit. Passengers complain that buses lack the amenities of rail transit; are too slow; take long, circuitous routes; and are plagued far more frequently with safety problems. The FTA's Bus Rapid Transit Initiative seeks to address some of these problems through Intelligent Transportation Systems (ITS) technologies. Figure 8.11 shows the percentage of metropolitan areas that deployed elements of ITS in 1997, 1999, and 2000. Electronic tolling was the favorite element in 2000, with 73 percent of the 75 metropolitan areas using this device. The use of electronic means to pay for bus fares actually declined from 45 percent in 1999 to 42 percent in 2000. Automatic Vehicle Location was a feature in 31 percent of fixed route transit vehicles in 2000. Also of benefit to bus service was the use of signalized intersections in 49 percent of the metropolitan areas surveyed. According to the Federal Transit Administration, in the future, upgraded bus service may also include exclusive right-of-ways, on-board passenger information systems, and more efficient routing, among other features ("Bus Rapid Transit," Washington, D.C. [Online] http://www.fta.dot.gov/research/fleet/brt/brt.htm [accessed June 26, 2003]).

IMPORTANT NAMES AND ADDRESSES

Air Traffic Control Association, Inc.
2300 Clarendon Blvd., #711
Arlington, VA 22201-3367
(703) 522-5717
FAX: (703) 527-7251
URL: http://www.atca.org
E-mail: info@atca.org

Air Transport Association of America
1301 Pennsylvania Ave. NW, #1100
Washington, DC 20004-1707
(202) 626-4000
FAX: (202) 626-4166
URL: http://www.air-transport.org
E-mail: ata@airlines.org

American Automobile Association
1000 AAA Drive
P.O. Box 28
Heathrow, FL 32746-5063
(407) 444-4240
FAX: (407) 444-4246
URL: http://www.aaa.com

American Bus Association
1100 New York Ave. NW, #1050
Washington, DC 20005-3934
(202) 842-1645
FAX: (202) 842-0850
URL: http://www.buses.org
E-mail: abainfo@buses.org

American Public Transportation Association
1666 K Street NW
Washington, DC 20006
(202) 496-4800
FAX: (202) 496-4321
URL: http://www.apta.com

American Trucking Associations
2200 Mill Rd.
Alexandria, VA 22314-4677
(703) 838-1700
URL: http://www.truckline.com

Association of American Railroads
50 F St., NW
Washington, DC 20001-1564
(202) 639-2100
URL: http://www.aar.org

Bureau of Transportation Statistics
400 7th St. SW, Rm. 3103
Washington, DC 20590
(800) 853-1351
URL: http://www.bts.gov
E-mail: answers@bts.gov

Eno Transportation Foundation, Inc.
1634 I Street NW, #500
Washington, DC 20006
(202) 879-4700
FAX: (202) 879-4719
URL: http://www.enotrans.com

Federal Aviation Administration
800 Independence Ave., SW
Washington, DC 20591
URL: http://www1.faa.gov/

Federal Highway Administration
400 7th St., SW
Washington, DC 20590
(202) 366-0660
URL: http://www.fhwa.dot.gov

Federal Transit Administration
400 7th St., SW
Washington, DC 20590
URL: http://www.fta.dot.gov

General Aviation Manufacturers Association
1400 K St. NW, #801
Washington, DC 20005
(202) 393-1500
FAX: (202) 842-4063
URL: http://www.gama.aero/home.php

Highway Loss Data Institute
1005 N. Glebe Road, #800
Arlington, VA 22201
(703) 247-1600
URL: http://www.highwaysafety.org

Motorcycle Safety Foundation
2 Jenner St., #150
Irvine, CA 92618
(949) 727-3227
FAX: (949) 623-1143
URL: http://www.msf-usa.org
E-mail: vday@msf-usa.org

National Automobile Dealers Association
8400 Westpark Drive
McLean, VA 22102
(703) 821-7000
(800) 252-6232
URL: http://www.nada.org/
E-mail: nadainfo@nada.org

National Bicycle Dealers Association
777 W. 19th St., Suite O
Costa Mesa, CA 92627
(949) 722-6909
FAX: (949) 722-1747
URL: http://www.nbda.com
E-mail: info@nbda.com

National Center for Bicycling and Walking
1506 21st St. NW, #200
Washington, DC 20036
(202) 463-6622
FAX: (202) 463-6625
URL: http://www.bikefed.org
E-mail: info@bikewalk.org

National Highway Traffic Safety Administration
400 7th St. SW, #5232
Washington, DC 20590
(888) 327-4236
URL: http://www.nhtsa.dot.gov

National Railroad Passenger Corporation (Amtrak)
60 Massachusetts Ave., NE
Washington, DC 20002
(202) 906-3860
(800) USA-RAIL
URL: http://www.amtrak.com

National Safety Council
1121 Spring Lake Dr.
Itasca, IL 60143-3201
(630) 285-1121
FAX: (630) 285-1315
URL: http://www.nsc.org
E-mail: info@nsc.org

National Transportation Safety Board
490 L'Enfant Plaza SW
Washington, DC 20594
(202) 314-6551
(800) 877-6799
URL: http://www.ntsb.gov

Recreational Vehicle Industry Association
1896 Preston White Dr.
P.O. Box 2999
Reston, VA 20195-0999
URL: http://www.rvia.org

Regional Airline Association
2025 M Street, NW
Washington, DC 20036
(202) 367-1170
E-mail: raa@dc.sba.com
URL: http://www.raa.org/

U.S. Army Corps of Engineers
441 G Street, NW
Washington, DC 20314
(202) 761-0008
FAX: (202) 761-1683
URL: http://www.usace.army.mil/

U.S. Department of Homeland Security
Washington, DC 20528
URL: http://www.dhs.gov/dhspublic/index.jsp

U.S. Department of Transportation
400 7th St., SW
Washington, DC 20590
(202) 366-4000
URL: http://www.dot.gov
E-mail: dot.comments@ost.dot.gov

RESOURCES

The U.S. Department of Transportation (DOT) is an excellent source of information about all types of transportation. The DOT prepared *The Changing Face of Transportation* (2000), a comprehensive history of transportation in America and a vision of transportation in the twenty-first century. The Bureau of Transportation Statistics, a DOT agency, publishes several excellent annual compendia, including *Transportation Statistics Annual Report* (2000) and *National Transportation Statistics* (2002), as well as the 2003 *Pocket Guide to Transportation.*

The Federal Highway Administration (FHWA), also part of the DOT, publishes data on the state of the nation's highways and bridges, including *Status of the Nation's Highways, Bridges, and Transit: 2002 Conditions and Performance Report* (2002). The Federal Motor Carrier Safety Administration, a DOT department, published *Large Truck Crash Facts 2001* (2003). The National Highway Traffic Safety Administration, a department of DOT, prepared *Traffic Safety Facts 2001* and many other pamphlets. The Maritime Administration of the DOT provides a wealth of online information about the nation's marine transportation system (http://www.marad.dot.gov). The Federal Transit Administration, another DOT agency, maintains the National Transit Database (NTD; http://www.ntdprogram.com/NTD/ntdhome.nsf?Open Database) containing data from more than 600 of the nation's transportation providers. The data are summarized in an easy-to-read format and layout (*National Transit Summaries and Trends*).

The Federal Aviation Administration (FAA), another DOT agency, in its *FAA Aviation Forecasts—Fiscal Years 2003–2014* (2003), provides valuable information on the nation's aviation system, including present conditions and future forecasts. The FAA also publishes *The Aviation Safety Statistical Handbook* (2002), which reports on accident data, and *Free Flight Status Report* (2002).

The U.S. Department of Energy publishes comprehensive statistics on transportation activity, including the *Transportation Energy Data Book: Edition 22,* (September 2002).

The Air Transport Association's *2002 Annual Report* is a very useful source for statistics on many facets of the air travel industry; historical statistics are available free of charge on the agency's Web site (http://www.airtransport.org). The General Aviation Manufacturers Association granted permission to reproduce data from its *Statistical Databook* (2000). *Air Transport World* magazine's annual "The World Airline Report" is an invaluable survey of the international airline industry.

The Association of American Railroads, an industry trade group, furnishes data on the nation's freight trains in its annual *Railroad Facts* (2002). The U.S. General Accounting Office, an investigative agency of the U.S. government, published several reports on the rail industry, including *Intercity Passenger Rail: Congress Faces Critical Decisions in Developing a National Policy* (2002) and *Intercity Passenger Rail: Potential Financial Issues in the Event That Amtrak Undergoes Liquidation* (2002). The GAO also published *Transportation Security: Post-September 11th Initiatives and Long-Term Challenges* (2003).

Waterborne Commerce of the United States (2001), prepared by the Department of the Army Corps of Engineers, reports on the commercial shipping of both foreign and domestic cargo and the condition of the nation's waterways and harbors.

The American Public Transportation Association provides a wealth of online information on mass transit (http://www.apta.com). *Motorcoach 2000 Census* (2000) and other data from the American Bus Association are available on its Web site (http://www.buses.org).

The American Trucking Associations' *American Trucking Trends, 2003 Edition* gives the current status of the trucking industry. Also useful are the websites of the National Automobile Dealers Association, the National Bicycle Dealers Association, and the Recreation Vehicle Industry Association. Ward's Communications publishes *Ward's Automotive Yearbook 2003,* which furnishes complete information on the production and sales of the nation's cars and trucks.

The National Safety Council prepares the annual *Injury Facts*, and the Insurance Institute for Highway Safety researches and reports on a wide variety of highway safety issues. The Eno Foundation for Transportation, Inc., a nonprofit organization founded in 1921 dedicated to improving all modes of transportation, published *Transportation in America* (1998), an excellent resource for the entire field of transportation.

INDEX

Page references with the letter t *following them indicate the presence of a table. The letter* f *indicates a figure. If more than one table or figure appears on a particular page, the exact item number for the table or figure being referenced is provided.*

C

D

E

F

G

M

N

O